SCHOOLING

IN THE SOUTH ATLANTIC ISLANDS

1661-1992

ABOUT THE AUTHOR

Born in Kent, Dorothy Evans was a child of the Second World War,
spending her schooldays in Worcester after being bombed out of
London. She gained her teaching qualification at Homerton College,
Cambridge, BA Hons with the Open University and, in 1989, MPhil
by research with Bristol University. After several years of teaching
mathematics and physical education, she became a teacher trainer at
the Lady Spencer Churchill College, Oxford, and Oxford Polytechnic.
As Vice Principal of the College of St Paul and St Mary, Cheltenham,
she became the Chairman of the St Helena Link Committee, working
with many St Helenian teachers both in the UK and on the Island
during extended visits. Her additional personal contacts with teachers,
education officers and other Islanders from Ascension, Tristan da
Cunha and the Falkland Islands are reflected in the pages of this book.
In 1988 she received the MBE for her educational services to St Helena.
She now enjoys the opportunities which retirement gives for reading,
writing, travelling – and maintaining links with the islands.

Schooling in the South Atlantic Islands 1661-1992

'Friends To Their Children'

Dorothy Evans

Dorothy Evans

ANTHONY NELSON

First published in 1994 by Anthony Nelson
PO Box 9, Oswestry, Shropshire SY11 1BY, England

ISBN 0 904614 51 4

Typeset in Linotype Baskerville
by Nene Phototypesetters Ltd, Northampton
and printed by The Bath Press, Avon, England

ERRATUM: p 204. The picture on this page has been reversed in printing.

Acknowledgements

The author is indebted to the Education Department of St Helena for financing publication of this book. She also wishes to thank the very many people who have contributed to its contents – in correspondence, consultation and conversation. In particular she acknowledges with deep gratitude the major personal involvement, interest and support of each of the people mentioned or grouped below:

Foreword
HRH Prince Andrew.

St Helena
HE The Governor, Alan Hoole; Chief Secretary, Michael Hone; Attorney General, David Jeremiah.

Education: Education Committee, Ruth Pridham (Chairman) and Members; Chief Education Officer, Basil George, whose unfailing support has enabled the book to be written; Education Officers, Lily Crowie and Edith Timm; Assistant Education Officers, Patsy Flagg, Eric M. George, Betty Joshua; Head Teachers, Heather George, Stedson George, Joyce Harris, Muriel Leo, Rita Nicholls, Joan Thomas, Maisie Thomas, Muriel Williams and Elizabeth Young; Teachers in all schools; Education Office and Teacher Education Centre Staff, Pat Duncan, Peter Johnson and colleagues.

Many former Education Officers, Head Teachers and Teachers, including: Penny Porter, Norman Kerr, Charles Dixon, Tony Cross, Alan Johns, Cliff Huxtable, Arnold Flagg, Martha George, Cissie Stevens, Iva Henry, Evelyn Bagley, Elvina Mercury, John Birchall, Terry Ward, and many others who have willingly contributed their part to the story.

Historians: Trevor Hearl, whose contributions and advice have been invaluable; Percy Teale.

Archives and Museum: Island Custodian of Records, Cecil Maggott; Archives Assistant, Maureen Stevens; Museum Curator, Mabel George.

Church: Bishop John Ruston; the Late Bishop Edward Cannan; present and former Anglican, Baptist and Roman Catholic Ministers.

Librarians: Prince Andrew School, Gwen Yon; Jamestown Library Staff; Agriculture and Forestry Dept and Library Staff; Rhodes House, Alan Bell; Bodleian Library Map Room; FCO, Kathy Chapple; India House Librarian; Public Record Offices, Kew and London; Commonwealth Society, Miss Barringer; Rewley House, Oxford.

Government Departments: St Helena Chief of Police; Inspector John Clifford; present and former Information Office Staff, Alicia Thomas and Marian Jeremiah; Development Office, Graham Rogers and Sheila Dance.
Youth Groups: Scout Commissioner, Eric W. George; Guide Commissioner, Daphne Francis.
St Helenians: Very many islanders who have recalled childhood and teaching experiences.
Other contributors, including John Beadon, George Moss, Joyce Thorpe and Nick Thorpe.

Ascension Island
Administrator, Brian Connelly.
Education: Head Teacher, Bryan Grey; School Secretary, Coral Moyce.
Several former Education Officers and Head Teachers, Kenneth Simmons, Margot Hutchinson, Alun Thomas, Keith Sedgwick.
Several former pupils and teachers on Ascension Island.
Major Departments: AIS, Graham Avis; Chief of Police, Lawson Henry.
Other contributors: Wing Commander Ken Pickup.

Tristan da Cunha
Education: Several Former Education Officers and Headteachers, including: Mrs Handley, Jim Flint, Kenneth Schurch, Nigel Humphries, Jim Kerr.
Other contributors: Father Brendan Sullivan, whose personal research on Tristan has been of great value; Lady Elizabeth Elliott; Allan Crawford; Michael Swales; John Bailey.

The Falkland Islands
Director of Education, Phyllis Rendell, whose contributions and support have been of great importance; Travelling teacher, John Leonard; Archivist, Jane Cameron; islanders, Joan Bound, Owen and Marjorie McPhee.

Overall support and encouragement
Publisher, Tony Nelson, and script reader, Penny David.
St Helena Link Committee, Jack Shepherd and members.
ODA, Andrew Kirk.
Proof reading and comments: Barbara George, Betty Martin, Marlene Swain, Sue Ward.
Illustrations: David Bentham, Johnny Drummond, Brian Frederick, and others who have contributed photographs.
Daily Information, Oxford, for computer assistance.
Many other friends, for interest and support.

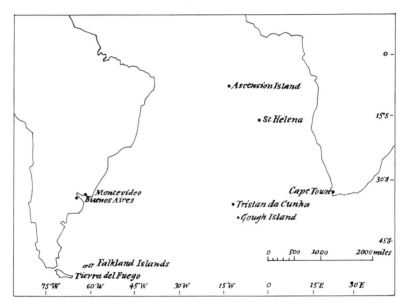

The South Atlantic Islands

Contents

Foreword

BUCKINGHAM PALACE

Anywhere in the world the story of schooling is important because it reflects the very nature of that particular society and the ways in which it prepares future generations to fulfil their potential. Children can rightfully claim to be the future of that society and, indeed, to be its ambassadors to the rest of the world.

For each of the South Atlantic Islands of St Helena, Ascension, Tristan da Cunha and the Falklands the history of schooling and the history of the Islands themselves have helped to determine each other. Since the times when settlers occupied these small, remote, isolated communities, the challenges and tasks faced by those who sought to educate their children often appeared to be insuperable but this book, based on extensive research and enquiry, reveals how nevertheless the indomitable spirit of the Islanders prevailed.

This is an important story to tell, not only because it captures the past and helps to preserve the heritage of these unique islands, but also because it is a human story of courage, endeavour and achievement, and of promise for the future.

List of Illustrations

Introduction

Yes, we are the future of our island
Prince Andrew School Song, St Helena, 1988[1]

This book tells the story of education on each of the four British islands in the South Atlantic Ocean – St Helena, Ascension Island, Tristan da Cunha and the Falkland Islands. In each case the story has reflected that of the island itself and education has both helped to mould and been moulded by the society and needs of the community it has served. The geographical location, the people of the island and their place in British history have all helped to shape the development of each island's unique educational progress.

ST HELENA (15°55S, 5°41W) is a tiny volcanic island of 47 square miles in the mid-South Atlantic Ocean lying approximately 5,000 miles almost due south of Britain. The 5,000 people are British and originate from various cultures, including African, British, Chinese, Huguenot, Indian and Malagasy, together with individuals from many other parts of the world. The remoteness and isolation of the island have had a profound effect in determining its history and, within this, the development of the education system. Discovered in 1502, it was not until 1659 that St Helena became an important British trading post for the East India Company. Systems for the government and welfare of Company employees and settlers were developed and the first school was established in 1673. As the story of education has developed systems have come and gone. Fluctuating periods of hardship and prosperity, and strategic happenings on the island, have fundamentally affected the very lifeline of its people and, accordingly, the nature and organization of schooling. Such events include the presence of Napoleon which brought a big increase in population and temporary prosperity; the abolition of slavery on the island; the transition of government from the Company to the Crown; the decline of the trade routes via St Helena and the Cape and the corresponding emptiness of the vast ocean around St Helena; the presence of as many Boer Prisoners as there were islanders and all the 'busy-ness' which they generated among St Helenians; and the rise and decline of the once-flourishing flax industry.

Throughout these happenings, education has sought to equip the younger generation with the skills to cope with both the present and the future. School systems have begun and ended, or perhaps evolved into others, masterminded by indomitable educationalists on whose shoulders others have been able to stand in order to try to see the way forward – stalwarts in the form of island teachers; island craftsmen; visiting advisers; UK and St Helenian government officers and generous benefactors such as the Church, the Benevolent Society and the Rebecca Hussey Charity.

The present ten schools on St Helena are structured on a three-tier system of education, including one centrally sited comprehensive high school, three middle and six first schools geographically placed over the island. Introducing this system in 1988, Basil George, the first St Helenian to hold the post of Chief Education Officer, recognized that another important new beginning was being made. Echoing T. S. Eliot – 'To make an end is to make a beginning'[2] – Mr George stated: 'The new system is however only a new beginning. We have not arrived in education, we have just made a fresh start. But it is a start that lays the foundation for the future.'[3]

ASCENSION ISLAND (8°oS, 14°15W) forms part of the Colony of St Helena, lying approximately 780 miles to the north west. It is roughly 35 square miles in size. The people on this volcanic island have a proud history of education of their own, their schools based upon the English system, but developed within island circumstances and needs. Records have been traced back to the first 'beginning' when in 1815 Captain Bate claimed the island for the British Empire and it became strategically significant, first to prevent attempts to release Napoleon from St Helena between 1815 and 1821, but in recent years as an important communication centre both for the UK and the USA.

The first school began in 1830 in Georgetown. Since that time the story of schooling has experienced many changes, depending on the transitory population. Educational progress has mirrored the involvement of major groups of workers from, for example, the Marines, the Navy, the Eastern Telegraph Company, Cable and Wireless, the British Broadcasting Corporation, and British and American Air Force

Bases. Sometimes no schooling has been needed, there being no children of school age on Ascension. Since 1921 there has been a resident population comprising mainly St Helenian people, caring for the needs of the long-term and short-term visiting personnel. The story of how schooling was provided for the diverse needs of such a population is one of challenges, characterized by beginnings and endings.

TRISTAN DA CUNHA (37°6S, 12°20W), also in the Colony of St Helena, is known as the smallest and remotest populated island in the world. It is described as a symmetical cone, 18,000 feet from the bed of the South Atlantic and 6,700 feet above sea level, with surrounding ridges rising to a central peak. Around the island is a rim of more level land, and the community of approximately 300 people is clustered in one part of the rim which has been named Edinburgh. Their ancestors originated mainly from Britain, Italy, America and St Helena. The one school has developed along British lines, although local circumstances have determined how best to prepare its people for life on the island or, for some, elsewhere. The beginning of Tristan's story of education goes back to 1816 when Scottish Corporal William Glass chose, with his family, to stay on Tristan. Since then generations of children have been taught by visiting priests, visiting teachers and islanders, and the island has experienced many beginnings and endings of the work of dedicated people. In the eyes of the world, the people of Tristan experienced an ending to beat all endings in 1961 when a volcanic eruption caused an immediate total evacuation to Britain. However, the islanders knew better and two years later were making a fresh beginning on Tristan. A proud educational history has evolved amid the rigours of extreme isolation, and the island boasts a lively school and now, for the first time, an island-born Education Officer.

THE FALKLAND ISLANDS (between 51° and 53°S, 57° and 62°W) lie some 8,000 miles from Britain. The territory comprises two large islands – East Falkland and West Falkland – some 200 smaller islands, with a total land area of approximately 4,700 square miles. Many of the widely scattered British population have in the past received schooling in their isolated homes from peripatetic teachers arriving on horseback. The Falkland Islands have an education system unique to the environment. In spite of the inherent difficulties arising from the location and circumstances, many visiting and local teachers have ensured over the years that the children have had opportunity to equip themselves for their future. These islands, whose recent turbulent history has put them even more firmly on the world map, have experienced many beginnings and endings, ranging from the first school established in the Army Barracks in 1846, the development of small settlement schools and the introduction of itinerant teachers, to an 'ending' which came at the time of the Argentine invasion. But to the intrepid Falkland Islanders, this gave opportunity for a new beginning, bringing with it a greater opportunity than ever to determine their own educational future. They now have their own first island-born Director of Education, and are proud of their new Community School which was opened in Stanley in 1992.

These are the thoughts that provide the basis of the sometimes incredible, sometimes heart-warming, sometimes frustrating, yet always courageous stories of education which are unfolded in the pages to follow. They are important stories because the young people on any one of these South Atlantic Islands can echo the words of the Prince Andrew School Song – 'Yes, we are the future of our island'.

Part I

Island of St Helena

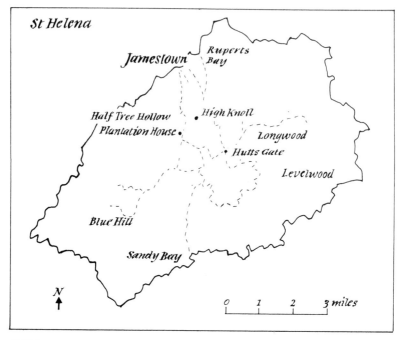

St Helena

1
Schooling under the Honourable East India Company 1661-1810

... That they would lay aside all unnecessary and frivolous excuses and be so much Friends to thier Children as to send them to the said Schoole, and keep them there as constantly as possibly they may.
Company Advertisement, 1678[1]

1661-1714: The Beginning of the Story

Under a Charter granted in 1661 to the East India Company, systems were established for the welfare of people on the island. Within this provision, during the early days of the Company's control, schooling became the responsibility of the chaplain appointed by the Company.

The population was unique in that it originated from the people recruited to serve the Company on the island, a number of whom were illiterate. They included both military and civilian personnel from Britain and elsewhere, and also Huguenots. Some settlers were refugees from the Great Fire of London. In addition, there were people brought from their Malagasy and Asian homelands to supply labour, together with a number of people of other cultures, including Indian, who were employees of the Company.

As the population grew, both in number and variety, other teachers became involved – soldiers, visitors with some special interest or expertise, and local people eager to spread the opportunity of education to the diverging and increasingly segregated sections of the community. The Company realized the need to concern itself with black and white, bond and free, employee and settler, fortunate and less-fortunate.

The first chaplain, the Reverend Noakes, arrived in March 1671. However, it was not until late 1673, after the recapture of the island from the Dutch, that Company records refer to the appointment of a chaplain whose role specifically included the task of schoolmaster. This was the Reverend William Swindle (or Swindel) appointed, according to the *Company Minute Book* on 3 December 1673: 'A satisfactory character having been received of William Swindel, he is elected chaplain of St Helena and schoolmaster at the salary and gratuity agreed for that post, to preach once and to catechise every Lord's Day and to teach or direct the teaching of children as their Schoolmaster, and also as many of the Negro children as are capable of learning. His allowance £50 a year as Minister, £25 as Schoolmaster and £25 gratuity, to have his dyett at the Governor's table and also at Plantation.'

This is the first record of a school on St Helena. Poor Swindle died in July 1674, but 'in the short time permitted him he had done what he could to remedy the neglect of the months preceeding his appointment when the island had no chaplain. He had instituted divine worship, taught the faith, gathered the children together for instruction, distributed the Bibles and Catechisms he had brought with him'.[2]

His successor, the Reverend John Wynne, did not arrive until July 1676. His instructions were clear: 'The Minister we have entertained and is now residing on our Said Island is not onely to preach every Lord's day, but to Catechise the Youngest Sort of people and Negroes Children at convenient times for which he is to receive the Annuity of 50 pounds per Annum and Twenty five poundes per Annum for teaching School, and five and Twenty poundes more per Annum for a gratuity if he shall be found painfull and deserving.'[3] The new minister/teacher found that 'all Swindel's good, if brief, work went to pieces' and that he, Mr Wynne, 'had much to put up with in the ignorance and indifference of many people neglecting to send their children to school'.[4]

Orders for books to assist in the work were sent to London. An invoice of 1677[5] lists the following:

4 Dozen of Primmers at 2:6 per doz.	10s
4 Dozen of Horne Bookes at 1:0	4s
4 Dozen of Psalters at 1:0 per book	£2 8s
4 Dozen of Bibles at 4:0 per par	£9 12s
4 Dozen of Testaments at 1:6 per par	£3 12s
2 Dozen of Pieties at 1:6 –	£1 16s
	£18 2s

These numbers are likely to have reflected the number of pupils at the time. However, to impress upon the inhabitants the value of education, an advertisement was publicly read in church and also pinned to the church door, exhorting the parents to send their children to school:

Whereas it hath pleased the Honourable East India Company to have so much regard and respect unto the good and welfare of thier Island, and all the Inhabitants thereof, That they have ordered and appointed a publick School to be kept at thier own Charge to teach the Children of the said Inhabitants to Read and to Instruct them in the Principals and Fundamentalls of the Christian Religion, As well the Blacks as the English.

John Wynne, the Minister, had appointed John Baxter 'to teach and instruct the Children in the English Tongue', under his supervision. The advertisement concluded:

These are to Advertise all the Inhabitants of the Island And earnestly to invite, and desire everyone that hath children capable of learning, and that can possibly spare them, That they would lay aside all unnecessary and frivolous excuses and be so much Friends to thier Children as to send them to the said Schoole, and keep them there as constantly as possibly they may. That they would not be so great Enemies to thier Children, and to Learning, as to detain them at Home about small and trifling matters, or send them soe seldome, and so uncertainty to the said School, and Catechising as that they should recieve but little or no profit or benefit thereby; And so the Gratious Intendment of the Said Honourable Company be slighted, the Designe of this Advertizement frustrated, the Minister and Schoolmaster discouraged, and the poor Childrens welfare Neglected.[6]

Mr Wynne quickly tired of the work, however, and asked for leave to return to England. There followed a six month period in which John Cramond, the chaplain from the ship *President* held the reins until March 1679 when Joseph Church was appointed Chaplain 'who is not only to discharge the office of Minister among you, but to catechise the Youngest sort of people and to teach the Children of the Inhabitants to read English'.[7]

Meanwhile, in 1680 people in the interior of the island petitioned the Council to have a school of their own, in view of the distance to Jamestown. On 16 February, the Council considered an appeal from several inhabitants in the Eastern Division 'to build a place for publick worshipp and wherein to keep a Schoole for thier children'. They were granted permission to 'build such a house or place of whatever dimensions they think fitt, and where they or the major part of them shall judge will bee most commodious and advantageious for themselves and ffamilys'.

A similar request was made from the western district a few months later: 'Att a Councill held on Monday ye 25th of 8ber. 1680 at Fort James', a petition was presented for a Country School. Accordingly, 'they desire liberty to erect and build, att theire owne personal cost and charges, a house, in some fitt place, nott yett allotted to any freeman; and that some part of ye sallary which ye Hon'ble Company hath allowed for ye teaching of Children, may be allowed towards the maintenance of an approved schoolemaster as they shall pitch upon'. The Council agreed, subject to the petitioners conferring with Mr Church about the allowance for this out of the budget. The Council at this time was chaired by Governor Blackmore, and it comprised three military people and three civilians, Robert Swallow, John Greentree and John Colesone, the latter signing with a cross.

In the late 1670s the Company also employed a soldier, William Melling, as a schoolmaster. This followed their practice, established in Madras in 1662, of employing non-churchmen in this capacity, and it is likely that his intended role was to teach the children of the garrison sited in Jamestown. However, he quickly caused trouble with one of his pupils, the child of an early settler on the island, and in 1679 'was dismissed for incivility to Mary Wrangham a scholar'. His further penalty was to ask pardon on his knees from her. He did not seem to learn from his experience as the following year he was charged with incivility to Mrs Orlando Bagley 'and saying there were noe spirits and none need fear to die'. His penalty this time was to ride the wooden horse for two hours with a bag of shot at each heel.[8] Presumably he was reinstated as schoolteacher, because we read that in 1683 he was allowed to keep school in the church on condition that 'Scholars do not goe into the reading pew or pulpitt or spoile the seats'.[9]

Obviously with an eye to using any available expertise, it was reported in the Company records of 16 January 1682 that Mr Scudder, a Quaker, was 'said to have some skill in the Mathematics the art of Navigation and other Sciences and may teach and instruct the youth of the Island in those things therefore allowed the privileges of a free planter'. However, Mr Scudder, too, soon fell foul of the government and the following March was 'deprived of land and [obliged] to leave the Island for uncivil words and actions to the Government'.[10]

Soon the Reverend Church was experiencing difficulties with his tasks as chaplain and schoolmaster. In February 1683 the Court of Directors informed the Council that 'he should have the same privilidges that Mr Wynn enjoyed not to be obliged to teach any children butt such as can already reade, and this wee beleive may dispose him to continue his paines among you ... We hope he will not so fare disappoint you as to leave the island'.[11] In the event, the Reverend Church died three months later, in May 1683.

In addition to making regulations concerning the schooling of children, the Company also found it necessary to oversee the conditions for orphans, establishing an Orphan Court to ensure compliance. For example, the Council ruled that John Orchard, aged 11, was to be looked after by Mr J. Knipe who promised 'to teach him a trade of a Tannor and also to read and wright English'. Mr Knipe was to give him 'two complete sets of Apparoll, one for Holly days and ye other for working days'.[12]

Clearly problems arose when the role of schoolmaster was held by the chaplain. There were frequent changes of chaplain and it was proving to be very difficult to provide suitable chaplains who could be responsible for both the spiritual and the educational welfare of the people on St Helena on a regular basis. In fact, until 1699 most of the chaplains were non-resident ones from passing ships. When available, the Company employed other people to be schoolteacher under the general supervision of the chaplain if there was one. For instance, in 1692, teaching at the Company School in Jamestown had been taken over by William Clifton, a soldier and schoolmaster, who also undertook the role of registrar of christenings and marriages; but for the next few years, specific references to schooling are sparse. Certainly on 18 June 1695 a Reverend Bartholomew agreed with the Council to stay on the island for a salary of £50 per annum and a £25 gratuity, but he stayed only until February 1696, after which there was again no settled minister until 1699, when the Reverend John Humphreys appeared – for a brief period. However, some schooling must have been taking place, because on 3 April 1700 Philip Leggett, School Master, was granted 'For writing and cyphering 10s per quarter; For writing only 8s ditto; For Reading 4s ditto'.[13]

As the number of settlers grew, including those soldiers and the white and free black settlers who became the first St Helenians, schooling was established in the Plantation area as well as Jamestown, and the church found it necessary to levy fees to carry out their building and teaching programmes and to establish firmer rules and regulations for their pupils and teachers.

Education was not necessarily confined to the schools and to the younger generation but included adults too. For instance, on 26 August 1707, Instructor John Clavering made a formal complaint in Council against a certain Walter Belvard 'for Denying to pay him Five Dollars according to Agreement to Learn Arithmetics, he the said Clavering being now ready to perform his part in Instructing him to cypher as farr as the Rule of Three. Belvard says he made such a contract to learn so farr, but having no minde to be Instructed any farther than he has already learnt, which is only some part of Addition'. Wise judgement prevailed and it was ordered "That the said Belvard pay the said Clavering the sum of Three Dollars, and pay Council Charges'.[14]

On 24 August 1707, a Mr Samuel Brome, 'souldier, presented his petition this day, desired to be admitted as a schoolmaster to teach children in Reading, Writeing &c, at the Countrey Church'. The Company decided: 'that the said Bromes request be granted for the time of three months to try and see what progress he will make in the matter, but left to the approbation of the Governor'.[15] It is a matter of speculation whether the earlier request in 1680 of the people of the western division to build and establish their own school had materialized, or had survived the intervening years. Certainly the Company was treating Samuel Brome's application as somewhat of an experiment. Sadly, we do not learn the outcome of Mr Brome's probationary period.

A population census of 1714 gave figures as follows:

Whites	Men	77 (+125 soldiers, not included in total)	
	Women	81	
	Boys	113	
	Girls	134	Total 405
Blacks	Men	144	
	Women	55	
	Boys	57	
	Girls	46	Total 302[16]

Apart from the soldiers, these numbers included settlers and civil servants of the Company. Some of the white children were allowed to go to England to school. These were mainly the children of employees of the Company who were likely to return to England for later schooling. Gabriel and Thomas, the respective sons of Gabriel Powel (Powell) and Chaplain Goodwin were included.[17] Others, including the children of settlers, attended the available schools, either in Jamestown or at Plantation, subject to their parents' attaching greater importance to education than to the children's usefulness at home helping with the difficult task of eking out a living from the land.

1715-95: Who will come to be taught?

By 1715 the number of whites had risen to 545, the major increase being among the men, whose number rose to 195. Richard Beale, a native of the island, was appointed schoolmaster in 1720 and was obviously a well-respected person. T. H. Brooke, in *History of St Helena*, describes Mr Beale as 'a very respectable and intelligent inhabitant' who fulfilled the duties of schoolmaster there for many years, with credit to himself and great advantage to the community. In 1725 the Governor received a petition from Mr Beale, which stated: 'There are abundance of children upon the island whose parents being in very poor circumstances are not able to put them to school to be instructed to the great grief of themselves and loss to their children'. He continued 'that he is willing in the consideration of the usual allowance of salary from the Honourable Company to teach any poor people gratis. There being several instances of this nature and being very sensible that there is abundance of young children as well as a great want of a fitt person to teach them'. The Council ordered 'that the said Beale be allowed to teach school and to have the usual allowance for his future encouragement'.[18] Mr Beale resigned his post as schoolmaster in 1769 after 'long and devoted service'.[19]

Few black children were able to attend school at this time. Most were slaves, although there were some 'free blacks' for whom access to schooling depended upon the attitude of their proprietors – whether they preferred their labour rather than their learning. The Court of Directors in 1726 confirmed that 'The most adult of the boys are employed in looking after cattle, sheep, goats and hoggs and the rest put to such little service of which they are capable – as weeding in the garden'. Indeed, although schools were made available for the diverse population, the opportunity was denied to many, both black and white. Chaplains continued to be employed by the Company and to have responsibility for ministering to their flock and helping those inclined to be able to read sufficiently to follow their Catechism. Company records barely mention the subject of schooling, but short items related to schools, as raised at vestry meetings, were recorded in the St James' Church Books. In deliberations following Richard Beale's resignation from his teaching post in Jamestown, £450 was set aside for accommodation for a schoolmaster, and schooling for each child was to be '20 shillings a quarter for reading and 10 shillings more for writing and learning to cast accounts'. Eight poor children were to be taught free. By May 1770 a Mr Congreve had been appointed. In January 1772 it was 'agreed between the Inhabitants and Mr Congreve – will for a year Educate, Board and Victual such Children as shall be offered him during that time, not exceeding the number of twelve at the rate of £13-10-0 pa'. By 1779 it had become necessary to lay down firm regulations and restrictions for the Schoolmaster including the use of the buildings and grounds – 'The sole use of the schoolyard is for the Children to recreate and amuse themselves in. It is not to be converted into a Garden or Plantation'. And further – that the eight poor children to be taught were to be chosen by the Churchwardens and that 'they are not to be expelled from the said School without their consent'.[20]

The *St Helena Diocesan Magazine* of January 1927 speculated about the whereabouts of this building. One opinion was that it was the property which later became the Ragged School (in Market Street) which, said the report, 'was allowed to fall into complete ruin'. Another possibility was mentioned: 'Failing the Ragged School, perhaps the Boys' School (in Upper Jamestown) was the original School house'. Unfortunately there appears to be no evidence to substantiate either of these locations.

1788-1810: Strong Personalities among the Schoolmasters

For the remainder of the century, education remained in the hands of people appointed by the Company, including ministers of the church and members from the military sector and the civilian population. The prime purpose of the major school in Jamestown was to teach the children of the Company and it was largely based on its British counterparts, both in curriculum and teaching methods.

From 1795 the island population included a number of Malay people. They had been captured by the Dutch, but when the Dutch vessels themselves were captured off the coast of St Helena, the Malays were released and strenuous efforts made to repatriate them, although some chose to remain in the island community.[21]

School and education frequently became the subject of the island Council's deliberations, which were fully recorded in the St Helena Records. The Reverend J.F.Wilkinson had been appointed to be the Island Chaplain in 1788. In the absence of a schoolmaster, he took on teaching duties at the Company's School in Jamestown, a task which he fulfilled for the next 18 years. However, this came to an end in December 1805 with the unexpected arrival on the island of an eminent naturalist, William Burchell. The Governor and Council, being convinced of the desirability of keeping the work of chaplain and teacher distinct from each other, had sought the Court of Directors in London to send a qualified teacher to the island. When no such person arrived, and recognizing the academic abilities of the unorthodox visitor, Governor Robert Patton laid a Minute before the Board, first indicating that he had had expectations that a schoolmaster might arrive on the next store ship 'failing of which it was my intention to propose the appointment of a competent person to fill that office, which had been so long vacant, until the pleasure of the Court of Directors should be known'. He continued: 'The person whom I meant is Mr Burchell, whose attainments, I have been assured from good authority, are very superior, being not only qualified to teach the Ancient and Modern Languages, but the Science of Mathematics in its various branches, and the Art of Drawing, which would prove an essential advantage to the young men of the Island, who are to bear Military Commissions in the Honorable Company's Service. I am told that he is proficient in Natural History, and an expert Botanist, with a competent knowledge of Chemistry; and I am assured that his moral conduct is correct, and his manners are mild and unassuming.'[22]

The hapless Reverend Wilkinson was defenceless in the face of this paragon and his lengthy correspondence with the Governor and Council, protesting against his deposition as schoolteacher was reported in the St Helena Records. On 17 June 1806 he claimed: 'The house I've occupied for 18 years belongs to the Inhabitants of the Island; and being unacquainted they wish me to quit it, with the important charge of their children's Education, I must wait their further Decision, or the arrival of the person you expect on the store ship.' A week later, he wrote again concerning his 'uneasiness of mind at the idea of soon being deprived of a situation which I have held above 18 years to the satisfaction of my Honorable employers. The parents at present signify their entire approbation of my conduct of education and attentions towards them, with thankfulness. Some of those parents, with many young gentlemen of the Island I have solely instructed in several branches of Literature, now do a credit to their different professions, as well as a great assemblage of young ladies, who are an ornament to society'. Notwithstanding these arguments, the Governor and Council pressed forward with their plans and offered the post of schoolteacher to William Burchell, who replied promptly that he had 'a great satisfaction in accepting the situation' but that the state of his health prevented him from starting immediately. To Mr Wilkinson, on 30 June 1806, they wrote that they were as a loss to understand his letter and that clearly he was trying to obtain two salaries: 'Desiring both salaries indicates a want of both moderation and modesty which are qualities highly becoming the clerical character'.

By early August 1806, Mr Burchell was fit enough to take up the role of Company schoolmaster. In spite of his acceptance letter, his diary indicates that he was extremely reluctant to take over the role of schoolmaster, but did so for fear of incurring the displeasure of the

The Head School, Jamestown, from an etching by William Burchell 1810. Royal Botanic Society, London

Governor who had invited him to do so, and who could have chosen to deport him as an unexpected entrant. He would have preferred to continue his researches into the plants on the island, as he was no mean naturalist, artist and writer; he has since become better known in history for his crossing of the Camdeboo in 1813 than for his teaching on St Helena. Nevertheless, two of his diaries for the period 1806 to 1809 (the *Burchell Journal*, to be found in the Castle Archives on St Helena) throw extremely interesting sidelights on his work there as a teacher.

One relates to Mr Wilkinson's school, which was becoming a rival to Burchell's school. Clearly the intrepid Mr Wilkinson had not relinquished his teaching, in spite of his altercation with the Governor and Council. While writing to the Council in May 1807 to request an Assistant Chaplain, the Reverend Wilkinson added: 'I also request to intimate a circumstance, which your Honorable Board cannot be altogether strangers to that from earnest solicitations of Parents and Guardians on the Island, I have found it incumbent upon me to devote all my leisure time to the Education of their numerous families in my own private rooms, which are not well calculated for air and health.' Apropos of Wilkinson's 'school', Burchell recorded the following incident on 28 November 1806:

At noon after school, Kennedy, one of the scholars, came up to me and said Mrs Hodgson desired him to ask me for my bill as she meant to send him to Wilkinson's. The poor boy cried at leaving me … and said he knew Mr Wilkinson would not take such pains with him.

Neither the Reverend Wilkinson nor Mr Burchell was happy with his lot. The former continued to be unpopular with both the authorities and other citizens, and in yet another letter to the Council in July 1808 he protested strongly against accusations made against him: 'I have from present motives of Humanity and Friendship educated many children gratis who have been left destitute of paternal or maternal care and protection,' and that he had been 'deeply afflicted by the recent calumny and malevolent aspersions, after a period of above twenty years of conscientious services with unremitting assiduity in my professions on this island'. He requested leave, which he was granted. He took two islanders with him as servants.

Meanwhile Mr Burchell received another letter from the Governor on 5 September 1806 requesting him to 'give the young gentlemen who are candidates for the appointment of Cadets and who shall attend a course of Education under you, the degree of proficiency required in Mathematics and in the Art as well as the Science of Drawing'. The Governor wished to extend the qualification of the Infantry as well as the Artillery, 'as it is my desire that the whole Military Establishment of the Island should be practical Artillerists'. Some time after this, records of a testimonial written by Burchell on Cadet George den Taaffe certified that the young man had 'prosecuted his studies under me with a degree of assiduity that claims my particular praise', and he was recommended for promotion. But this was not in order, since the cadet was only 13 years old. However, even with this added interest of working with the Military, Burchell did not find his work fulfilling. In fact in his *Journal* on 24 December 1807 he described teaching as 'one the most opposite to my inclinations' and 'a troublesome confinement to a dull regular duty'. Nevertheless, during his time as schoolmaster, he also pursued his scientific interests, including biology and astronomy.

Eventually, after three years, he was relieved of his duties as a teacher and appointed as Botanist, the St Helena Records of 14 September 1808 affirming that the latter role 'accords with the more general nature of his enquiries: his occupations in this capacity appear also better suited to his inclination than those duties of schoolmaster, which the Board understand he is desirous to resign'. He was to continue as schoolmaster until a replacement was found. His school-

master's duties eventually came to an end and his Journal entry for
10 June 1809 concluded:

What a delightful state I feel in, to be now released from the disagreeable duty I
have too long had to perform. I quite disagree with Locke that it is a delightful
task to rear the tender mind. I may lay claim to the title of Philosopher in
having borne it so long.

In 1810 William Burchell made a painting of the school, but the
building depicted cannot be identified now. Almost certainly it was on
the site of the later, newly built Head School, which itself later became
the Infants School, and is now the Community Centre.

Another characterful personality came to the island as the Company's chaplain in 1808. This was the Reverend Samuel Jones, and
thus began another period of lengthy interchanges between the chaplain and the island authorities. When William Burchell relinquished
his post as schoolmaster, the Reverend Jones informed the Council on
12 June 1809 that he accepted the role 'until the arrival of a person
regularly appointed as schoolmaster'. He was to be paid £80 per
annum, while Mr Burchell's salary rose to £300 per annum as Botanist.

David Kay, Junior, one of the sons of the island's Colonial Surgeon,
became Mr Burchell's successor in 1810. He obviously enjoyed success
and popularity with both pupils and parents, who quickly rallied to his
support when he made a request to the Council after four months of
teaching for an increase in pay. A letter in his support was signed by
twelve parents, including significant names such as Saul Solomon and
Gabriel Doveton. They were 'highly gratified by the improvement they
[the children] have made and thankful to you for the care and kind
attention you have shown them'.

After some time as schoolteacher, the Reverend Jones realized that
there was a serious lack of suitable schooling for the poorer children on
the island. To a certain extent, this need may have been met by the
classes offered by his predecessor, the Reverend Wilkinson, until his
departure from the island. From a later document written in 1813, we
learn that the Reverend Jones, with the backing of the Company, set up
the school on 15 July 1809 for the benefit of the poorer children of the
island and it became known as the Under School.[23] This school quickly
gained popularity as it offered a curriculum which was far more
appropriate to the islanders than at the Head School, which mainly
sought to prepare the young gentlemen sons of the Company's
employees to return to the UK for further schooling, university or some

designated profession. Mr Jones took charge of the school and reports made over the next few years paid tribute to his work in the light of his pupils' progress.

2

Expansion of Schooling for the Islanders by the Company and the Benevolent Society 1811-34

We have another edifying spectacle before us. The children of what complexion soever are assembled together and engaged in the same labour.
Governor Walker, 1824[1]

1811-16: Greater interest in island-wide education

Increasingly the need for more schooling for the islanders, as well as for the children of the Company personnel, was apparent and during this time the second Company school in Jamestown was becoming firmly established, mainly for this purpose.

The names of three more characterful churchmen occur in educational matters throughout the final two decades of the Company's control of the island. The Reverend Richard Boys, Mr John S. Firmin and the Reverend James Bowater Vernon between them held the roles of Senior and Junior Chaplains, Superintendent of Schools (including both the Head School and the recently established Under School) and Master or Assistant Master in the Head School. The Senior Chaplain had overall responsibility for all schools in addition to his church responsibilities, while the Junior Chaplain assumed particular responsibility for the Head School.

In 1811, the Reverend Boys, one of the most colourful personalities in the history of schools on the island, was appointed to be Junior Chaplain under the Reverend Jones. Described by Chaplin as 'an honest, but rigid and uncompromising divine',[2] Mr Boys also held the post of Master of the Company's School in Jamestown. By now this was known variously as the Head School, the Grammar School or the Upper School. Throughout his ensuing career of 19 years on the island, Boys made both friends and enemies, not fearing to be outspoken whether in the presence of the Governor, colleagues in the church, educationalists, people of the island – or even Napoleon himself. One of his first tasks was to deal with the need for teachers and he recommended that Cadet John Worral Torbett was well qualified to assist

The Reverend Richard Boys

him in the Company's Upper School. This request was granted until another assistant arrived from England.

Meanwhile, the Under School was led now by Mr J. McDaniel, under the general supervision of the Reverend Jones. The pupils were clearly making good progress, and the efforts to expand educational opportunities for the poorer islanders were rewarding to those involved, but Governor Alex Beatson was keen to expand them even further. In a

Minute to the Board in 1813, he reported: 'The Reverend Samuel Jones has reported that the children in the Company's Under School have made great proficiency in Reading, Writing and Arithmetic, and the number of Boys and Girls thus educated by Mr McDaniel is 58 – that amongst them are some whose parents cannot afford to pay for their tuition and that these Mr McDaniel has kindly instructed gratis; and Mr Jones is of the opinion that many children would yet be sent to school if their parents had the means of defraying the charge of their education'. After stressing that 'this laudable institution' was deserving of the most serious attention because it would help to further religious and moral instruction, the Governor continued: 'Mr Jones has also informed me that if encouragement were held out there might be above one hundred pupils in the Company's Under School. Supposing this to be the case, and that fifty additional children were added to the institution, what a humane and charitable act would this be to rescue from total ignorance and from idle and perhaps vicious habits, this number of poor children and to train them up to be useful to themselves and to the island in general.'

To support his Minute, the Governor had devised a plan. First the Arrack Cellar in Jamestown would be converted into a schoolroom and fitted with forms and desks for 100 children. If more came the adjoining room would be used to make space for 150 scholars. The Head Master's house would be built on the south side of the new market place. Fifty children whose parents could not afford fees would be paid for by the Company, at half the normal rate. Furthermore, Mrs Gregg – 'a respectable young woman, who I am told is in every respect qualified' – should be appointed as assistant at £30 per annum. The schoolroom was to be partitioned – boys at one end with Mr McDaniel (or whoever was in charge of the whole school), and girls at the other with Mrs Gregg, who would teach them to read and write and to do needlework. She would receive half of the fees paid by parents. Demonstrating that the whole plan would cost less than £200, the Governor concluded: 'I conceive that this sum would be a mere trifle compared with the benevolent object and the permanent advantages that would result from the adoption of the plan I now propose.'[3]

The Board approved the plan unanimously, pending the pleasure of the Honourable Court of Directors in London and decided how it would be implemented. First the Governor's minute was to go to churchwardens, who would be asked to furnish an exact list of the families of the lower classes – names, ages of children, male or female, their previous instruction in reading and writing, and the occupation of parents. Then a public notice was to be published to invite parents to apply to the churchwardens for free education. Thereafter, the Reverend Jones was to share out the money received from individuals or the Company between Mr McDaniel and his assistant. Accordingly, on 24 May 1813, a Public Notice was issued, beginning 'All the parents of the poorer class of people are hereby invited to send their children to school' ...

During 1813 two young men, Messrs Firmin and Hobman, were recruited from England to teach on the island using the Bell's Madras System. This system of teaching had been invented in India in 1790 by Dr Andrew Bell, an Anglican clergyman, to counteract the shortage of both money and teachers at the very time when there was need for an expansion in elementary education. Dr Bell explained his system in *An Experiment in Education made at the Male Asylum at Egremont, near Madras* (1797). It was first adopted in London in 1798. Coincidentally, Joseph Lancaster, a Quaker, devised the similar 'Monitorial System' intended to produce a cheap, efficient and disciplined means of mass instruction. 'The central idea was to enable a single schoolmaster to cope with a very large number of children by the employment of monitors i.e. making use of the older and abler pupils to teach the others. Lancaster boasted that the system made it possible for one master to teach a thousand pupils'.[4] Bell's system was adopted by the Church of England because not only was it cheap to run, but it also claimed to encourage initiative and confidence in both pupils and monitors.

An insight into views about personal status is provided by correspondence which Governor Beatson put before the Board on 21 August 1813. A letter from the Reverend Jones extolled the virtues of Mr McDaniel. 'I have at least one source of heartfelt satisfaction – that of being the honoured instrument in the hand of God on introducing Mr McDaniel into this Island.' But a second letter, from the Reverend Boys, was not so complimentary to Mr McDaniel. The Reverend Boys had been put in charge of the two new teachers from England and was concerned 'that measures should be taken to uphold their respectability in Society and effectually to prevent the possibility of their falling into such company as might either corrupt their morals or diminish that respectability of character and that rank in society upon which their usefulness here must depend'. Mr Boys continued: 'I differ entirely with Mr Jones in thinking Mr McDaniel a fit person to take charge of either of them, for although Mr McDaniel is a most worthy and useful man, and the Island are highly indebted to him for his indefatigable labours in the Under School, yet his entire want of rank in society ... is

so far below what I conceive would be proper for these young men …'
He offered to have the two young men himself – for a suitable fee of
course, and also asking for financial assistance towards their laundry.
Mr McDaniel's 'want of rank' may refer to his inferior training
compared with the other clergy and schoolmasters, but clearly he
achieved respectability by 1829 when he held the position of President
of the St Helena Auxiliary Missionary Society, with Captain O'Connor
as his Treasurer and Secretary.

The Reverend Boys put forward a further suggestion that if it were
considered sufficient for only one of the two newcomers to teach at the
Under School, the other could be employed as an assistant at the Head
School – for which he was responsible – subject to undertaking further
study so that he could teach 'much higher branches than Dr Bell's
system embraces'. The Reverend Boys had offered them his leisure
time for this additional study and, in fact, they had already started.
This had given him a higher opinion of the junior one, Mr Hobman,
who 'writes a much better hand and is rather more ready in Arithmetic', whom he felt should be the one to assist at the Head School. He
assured the Board, of course, that as general superintendent for the
island, he was anxious to promote and accomplish 'an object so noble
and so humane as the instruction of the Island, whether amongst the
higher or the lower orders'.

As part of their education policy, the Company encouraged the
education of their civilian and military personnel and, in this respect,
Governor Wilks established a Public Library in 1813. There are
records of the existence of an island library as early as 1781 when the
Reverend Mr Robartes Carr offered to sell a large collection of books to
Governor Skottowe and his Council. Mr Carr, the brother-in-law of the
Governor, assured the Board that the books 'were in good order and
none of them are in the present library'. The Board agreed to buy all of
the 217 volumes, at a cost of £66 8s 6d. They included Raleigh's *History
of the World*, Camden's *Britannia*, Holwell's *India Tracts*, Bellamy's *Family
Preacher*, *Modern History* in 42 volumes, St John's Sermons, Broome's
Poems, and many others.[5] Such erudite literature had only a limited
appeal, particularly because as yet a high proportion of the islanders
was still unable to read. A further mention of an island library occurs in
1803 when the Reverend Wilkinson wrote to Governor Patton asking
'that a regular inventory be taken of the Library'.[6] No doubt, Governor
Wilks hoped that the re-establishment of the Library in 1813 would
help to further his aim to spread education to more people.

However, in 1815 other matters preoccupied the people of St Helena who found themselves in the centre of attention on the world map. 'And then came the *Northumberland*, bringing Napoleon Bonaparte, and all these quiet, unimportant people were to find themselves living in the most famous, the most discussed and most written about spot in the whole universe'.[7] Sir Hudson Lowe became Governor, with the specific task of guarding Napoleon, who arrived in 1815. The increase in the size of the Garrison due to the presence of Napoleon also increased the flock for which Mr Boys felt responsibility. At the same time, the arguments between the Reverend Jones and his Junior Chaplain, Mr Boys, developed into a bitter controversy. It eventually came to a head in 1815 when the Reverend Jones was suspended from duties and caused to retire on 5/- per day. Mr Boys continued, however, to hold the post of Master of the Head School until 1816, when he was appointed in place of the departed Reverend Jones as the Senior Chaplain on the island. Accordingly, he was relieved of his duties at the Head School and Mr McDaniel was put in charge, with Mr Firmin as his Assistant. The Reverend Bowater James Vernon became the Junior Chaplain, and was careful to avoid becoming involved in the squabbles roused by his fiery Senior Chaplain. Clearly, over the next few years Mr Boys felt the pressures of his extra responsibilities, because in May 1823 he asked the Board for an additional allowance for him due to the extra work.[8] Two weeks later he asked for a further increase to enable him to send his three daughters to school in England.

Another significant event in the history of education on St Helena was the founding on the island of a Committee of the Benevolent Society in 1814. Governor Wilks, who had succeeded Governor Beatson the previous year, had been instrumental in introducing this. Several years later, he reported that the major purpose of the Society was 'to rescue from the trammels of ignorance and vice, the children of slaves, free blacks and the poorer classes of the community' and to provide 'the means of education to numbers among the lower orders'.[9] The Benevolent Society's efforts were further advanced by the law passed on the island in 1818 under which, from Christmas Day 1818, all children born of slave women were to be free, 'but to be considered as apprentices to the proprietors of the mothers if males, until the age of eighteen years, and if females, until sixteen; and that the masters and mistresses were to enforce the attendance of free-born children at Church and the Sunday schools'.[10]

Any schools which the Society established were under the patronage and control of the East India Company's Government. Initially the Government Schools and those of the Society were united, the Government contributing money to provide free schooling for those in need.

1816-24: 'White, Slave and Free' in School

The memories of a child born on the island in November 1816 throw an interesting personal light on some of the events happening at the time. In his autobiography, *Reminiscences of George Brooks Bennett, 1816-1886*, the son of Captain James Bennett of the St Helena Foot Regiment (and brother of the future wife of Governor Sir Patrick Ross) said that his recollections of childhood on St Helena were scanty but 'consist mainly of my journeys to school upon a little pony, Black Prince, accompanied by my nurse'. He wrote of the 'ever memorable 9th May 1821, when the mortal remains of the once "Great" Napoleon were committed to the tomb and seeing, as a child of five, the long procession from Longwood filing around the edge of the Devil's Punch Bowl and then descending into Sane's Valley'. Many years later, in 1840, he also witnessed the exhumation of Napoleon.

It was clear that his schooling on St Helena stood him in good stead. In England he attended Mr Sauley's school, and later wrote: 'I can recall to mind my beginning lessons. Mr Sauley's son Theophilus was just my age and we worked together. I fancy it was not a fair start, and that I got ahead of him because with me the a-b-c part had all been mastered in Mrs Weston's School in St Helena'. There are later records of a Government school attended entirely by black children at Plantation in the charge of a Mr and Mrs Weston, and it is likely that George Bennett's teacher was the same Mrs Weston, running her own private establishment.

In theory all schools on the island were available to any children or adults, whether black, white, slave or free. In practice, however, the school population was substantially segregated, due to a number of causes and circumstances. Statistics supplied by the Reverend Vernon in November 1818[11] at the request of the Governor are significant:

	Children and Adults:			
	White	Slave	Free	Total
Honble Co Head School	40	–	–	40
Honble Co Under School	36	2	44	82
Plantation House School	–	37	26	63
Plantation Sunday School	–	47	24	71
Sunday School in Town	–	27	2	29
Evening School in Town	–	104	30	134
Clara's School in Town	–	4	81	85
				504

At the Head School, both the grammar-school type teaching methods and the classically based curriculum were geared mainly to equip the children and employees of the Company to continue their education abroad, should this be their intention. This type of work was not appropriate for those children – and adults – whose destiny was likely to be on the island. It is noticeable that the entire population of the Head School was white.

At the Under School, however, there was a mixed population, roughly balanced between whites and free blacks with, interestingly, two slaves. The owners of the latter appear to have been sufficiently enlightened and generous to allow them to attend school during the day, with the other 80 people. The curriculum at this school was geared mainly to the basic skills of reading, writing and arithmetic, with religious instruction, and did not include an emphasis on classical learning as in the Head School.

All of the other schools were populated by slaves and free blacks and it is significant that two were Sunday Schools, a comparatively new phenomenon. In the Plantation House area a school was established in premises in the lower field below Plantation House, which met on weekdays and on Sundays, with some overlap of pupils. The Sunday School enabled children and adults who had to work during the week to benefit from some teaching on Sundays. One of the teachers in the Plantation House School is named as J. Thompson. Was he perhaps a member of the Thompson family who played a significant part in teaching on the island through the greater part of the nineteenth century – including Thomas Thompson, first Assistant at the Second School under Mr McDaniel, and his son W. P. Thompson?

A later report, submitted on 21 January 1819 to the Council by the Reverend Vernon, requested some resources for the Plantation House School, saying that it was 'very scantily provided. It receives no allowance from Government, the Committee of the Benevolent Society alone granting £3 per annum, two-thirds of the children attending this school being slaves to the Honble Company, I trust that His Excellency and the Council will have the goodness to authorise the Masters drawing a stated supply at the rate of half the allowance given to Mr McDaniel [at the Head School]'. Accordingly the school received 600 quills, 3½ reams of demy paper, and 1 dozen papers of ink powder.

Similarly, the Sunday and Evening Schools in Jamestown were attended mainly by slave people who were not freed by their owners to go to the day school, together with some pupils who were also attending the Under School in the daytime during the week.

The final entry in the table above refers to the school of a remarkable woman named Mrs Clara George, who herself was making educational history on the island. As Miss Rich, a slave, she married a free slave, Charles George, in 1814, and herself became free. She began by teaching her own children, then in 1816 she included her neighbours' children too, and this enterprise developed into a school in Jamestown. Clara's School was clearly flourishing in 1818 with 85 pupils, mainly from the freed slave population. Many of her pupils were young children who were being taught to read and write and also girls who were learning skills with their hands such as needlework and lacemaking. This attracted the attention of the Benevolent Society. The Council reported to their Headquarters in London on 12 January 1824 that 'for some years a poor woman of the name of Clara George has kept a large and flourishing school in the Town, mostly very young, which the Committee have agreed henceforth to take under their auspices, and to admit 15 at the Society's expense. This is from a desire to assist a poor woman of no ordinary merit, who has had to struggle through almost insurmountable difficulties, for a period of 7 or 8 years both in obtaining proper books for the children, and in raising sufficient money to pay the rent of her schoolroom. She charges 9 shillings per child per quarter but nearly half of the number, which consists of about 80, she instructs gratuitously. The school was exhibited at the annual examination (at only a day or two notice) and it afforded the most unequivocal testimony of the constant attention paid to the children'.

As the total number of people attending school in 1818 – 504 – includes some overlap and also some adults, the actual child population in schools was a mere fraction of those living on the island. But there was much opportunity for children to obtain work instead of going to school in view of the largely increased population. By 1820 the 7,998 people on St Helena were listed as 3,534 whites, 1,156 slaves, 481 Chinese, 613 free blacks, 33 Lascars, 1,483 Troops and 698 Honourable East India Company Troops. The teaching establishment managed to maintain some stability for these few years, the 1820 listing in the East-India Register and Directory being: The Reverend Boys, Senior Chaplain, having overall supervision of all schools; the Reverend Vernon, Junior Chaplin, being Master at the Head School with John Firmin and Henry Kay as his Assistants; and Mr McDaniel back again at the Under School as Master, following Dr Bell's system there. Mr Kay was one of the 14 children of David Kay Senior, who had come to St Helena in 1775 to be the Superintendent of the Medical Establishment. Four of his children were recorded as being born of a black woman, including Henry who, like his siblings, had the advantage of some schooling.

In addition to accepting the major responsibility for schools, the Company also continued to make provision for adults by maintaining the St Helena Library and bringing supplies of books from England. This library was almost certainly based at the Castle. One such Requisition List of books bought from Black, Kingsbury, Parbury and Allen, Booksellers and Stationers, Leadenhall Street, London in 1820 included a total of 160 titles, in 564 volumes, at a total cost of £500 16s 5d. Examples of titles included in the requisition were the Duke of Marlborough's *Blenheim Papers*, Beauchamp's *Invasion of France, 1814*, Wordsworth's *Ecclesiastical Biography*, Parkhurst's *Greek Lexicon*, the works of Molière, Defoe's *Robinson Crusoe*, and Bunyan's *Pilgrim's Progress.*[12] Clearly, as yet this list was catering for the tastes and capabilities of the minority of the population.

Governor Walker, in office from 1823 until 1828, was keen to support all branches of education and to ensure that the inhabitants of the island appreciated its value. With his active interest and support and the endeavours of the worthy clergymen of the time, education was enjoying a high profile.

Attempts were again being made to establish a school at Longwood. Some 150 years earlier, the request of the church people in the eastern country to build a school had been allowed by the Company Court of Directors. No further record about schooling in this area occurs until 22 May 1823 when there was speculation in the Council about a suitable future for the new house at Longwood built for Napoleon, but never occupied by him. 'To what purpose this handsome edifice could or should be applied, has been a subject for conjecture ... as a seminary of education it would be well adapted, and to this desirable use it is not unlikely it may be applied.' No doubt with this in mind, the Reverend Vernon had written to the Council of the Company saying that all efforts to secure a governess from England to teach the girls of European residents – possibly in a boarding school – had come to naught and that, as a result, there were no alternatives but to send daughters to England, or to keep them on the island for education up to a 10-year-old standard. Mr Vernon was prepared to receive girl boarders into his own home, but where could this be? He sought approval to use the new house at Longwood for the purpose. As an added inducement, he offered to teach the children of the Indian employees – including oriental languages – who at present either had to remain in India or go to the UK. Mr Vernon further asked to secure the services of a friend from India, and he assured the Council that none of this would interfere with his Jamestown Day School responsibilities. The Council gave their blessing but, sadly for all concerned, the school did not succeed. A letter from Mr Vernon six months later on 11 December 1823 requested permission to go back to his own home, instead of the comparative isolation of Longwood, in view of 'the plan, having failed, and the residence of my family in that remote quarter of the island being attended with much serious inconvenience and expense'. He offered to continue the church services in Longwood, however.

Although there had been military personnel on St Helena from the earliest days of the East India Company's control, the story of formally organized army education appears to start from 1823 when there were many military personnel, including the Artillery, based at Ladder Hill, and the Infantry based in the garrison in Jamestown. Regarding the Infantry, on 16 October 1823 the Governor declared in a Minute: 'I derive the utmost satisfaction in laying before the Board an address from 20 Sergeants, 15 Corporals and 42 Privates including drummers of the St Helena Regiment, announcing their intention, if permitted of subscribing to defray the expence of a school for their own instruction. They have agreed to subscribe for this purpose as follows: Staff Sergeants each 2s 6d, Sergeants 1s 6d, Corporals 10d, drummers and privates 6d per month, because being as they observe illiterate men, they feel it their duty for the better discharge of their several duties and for their information to form a school. In their zeal to promote this object they have found a teacher. The objects to which they propose to direct their attention are reading, Arithmetic and writing. Though no pecuniary aid is solicited, I have reason to think that some little assistance in fitting up the school would be acceptable. A schoolroom will be provided without expence within the Barracks, but it must require some furniture of seats and tables.' After explaining that there were already elementary books on the island, the Governor asked for some moral or religious books to be sent from England.

Regarding the Artillery at Ladder Hill, Governor Walker was responsible for the founding of the Military Institution. This fell in line with the policy of the Board of the Company that, following an edict requiring the compulsory training for the cadets of the St Helena Artillery at the Company's Seminary at Addiscombe, it was considered to be necessary for the cadets and other officers of the St Helena Artillery to undertake further study. The curriculum was to include 'the knowledge of celestial bodies' and the intention was to establish an observatory on a small scale at Ladder Hill which would 'not only enable the young officers to become practical Astronomers, but would enable ships to correct their chronometers'. Meanwhile 'the young Gentlemen are acquiring practice and proficiency with what instruments are available'. Philosophically he concluded his report of October 1823: 'Observations of this kind tho' chiefly important on account of their practical utility, are likewise sources of delight to the inquisitive and active, and lead to an accuracy in our ideas concerning the phenomena of nature which are not obtained but by observation and study'.

An Inspector of Schools, Mr Vernon reported to Governor Walker expressing satisfaction at the general progress in the Head School. However, at the February 1824 Distribution of Books and Medals, the parents were reminded that: 'Education is a labour in which the Parent must co-operate with the Teacher. They must be confined entirely to his government and direction. The Teacher is the best judge of that which the Pupil should learn and any undue interference on the part of Parents must in general prove hurtful.'[13]

By 1823 the records of the Benevolent Society show that 35 of the children attending the Head School were partially supported by the Society, in pursuit of their purpose to enable any members of the community to benefit from the education offered.[14]

In the general atmosphere of encouraging education, Mr Vernon submitted some draft regulations for the Head School to the Court of Directors on 2 February 1824. Establishing first his overall control of the immediate direction and management of the School with the assistance of Messrs Firmin and Kay, he affirmed: 'Although this school is more particularly intended for the Education of the Children belonging to the Honorable Company's Civil and Military servants, nevertheless it is open to those of the respectable Inhabitants.' The draft regulations fixed the fees – 'three guineas per quarter and five shillings per quarter for pens, ink etc to such as learn to write'. While the Master was subject only to the Governor and Council concerning what to include in the curriculum, Arithmetic and Mathematics were to be particularly cultivated, alongside 'an acquaintance with the classical writers', Latin and Greek, French and Religious Instruction – the latter to be taught from 3 to 5 p.m. on Sundays. A Register of Proficiency was to be presented quarterly to the Council, and an Annual Public Examination held 'at which every schooler must attend'.

On 12 February 1824, a few days after the authorization of Mr

Vernon's draft regulations as being 'perfectly proper', the Governor submitted a long report to his Council on the state of the schools. He praised the clergymen responsible for 'the gradual and extensive progress which education has made under their fostering care and patronage'. To the Reverend Vernon, the Master of the Head School, the Governor said: 'The evidence this day afforded by the Young Ladies and Gentlemen of their progress and advancement in learning is highly satisfactory, and while it reflects great honor on you, it does credit to their own diligence: for it is the application of the Scholar, that can only give due effect to the Instructions of the Teacher.' He extolled the virtues of a classical education: 'There is a notion among some people that the dead languages are not necessarily for those who are to be engaged in Business: but this is an error. There is no knowledge perhaps more useful in fitting men for the active pursuits of life. After commenting on the work in French, writing, pronunciation, arithmetic, mathematics, cyphering, geography, elocution – and on the achieve-ments of individual scholars – he turned his attention to exhorting the parents to send their children to school regularly: 'They are not to be withdrawn either for the sake of their own indulgence or parental gratification. They must be induced to love their lessons and to respect their teachers. It is this alone that can render the duty of the Teacher pleasant and successful.'

To the Reverend Boys, responsible for superintending the work of the other schools on the island, Governor Walker was equally expan-sive and congratulatory in his February report: 'The blessings of Education diffused through a large portion of our population, are in great measure, I might say principally, owing to your persevering exertions.' Referring to the Under School in Jamestown and the Under School in the Plantation area, he continued: 'It is on every hand acknowledged that there is a great moral and religious improvement among that class of Society, to whom the labours of these Schools are chiefly devoted.' He noted the fact that 400 boys and girls were being educated, of whom 269 were present for the occasion of the examina-tion, including those from Mrs George's preparatory school, and the remainder belonged to the Evening and Sunday Schools.

He was very pleased to record that 'We have another edifying spectacle before us. The children of what complexion soever are assembled together and engaged in the same labour. They are assimi-lated by the same tasks and are only distinguished from one another by their different degrees of application and industry. This indiscriminate association must remove many of those prejudices which have frequently no other foundation than in the colour of the skins.' Stating that 'St Helena has a fair prospect of acquiring in some years, a virtuous and industrious free peasantry, in lieu of a race of slaves', he was keen to see employment after school using local natural resources, particularly for women and the less active men.

There was, however, one dissatisfied member of the Head School. John Firmin, the First Assistant, sent a ten-point letter, dated 26 February 1824, to the Governor relating to his dashed hopes of being appointed Master of the Head School. He pointed out that he had been appointed in 1813 to introduce the new 'Madras System' of education, and that since then he had received 'flattering testimony of his superiors'. He had been Acting Head of the Head School from 1818 to 1820 during the leave of the Reverend Boys. He asked to be transferred to another post, outside teaching – but nevertheless he remained in teaching for at least twenty more years.

1824-25: Governor Walker: Champion of Education

Governor Walker demonstrated his interest in education by involving himself personally, insisting on seeing the situation for himself, and presenting his own reports and recommendations. He held very strong views about the importance of school leavers' retaining the skills and attitudes they had acquired at school. His long report of February 1824 addressed this concern:

It appears to me, that all the benefits of Education cannot be ensured to the rising generation and, of course, to this community, unless some attention is paid to the conduct and disposal of the children after they shall leave School ... It is an imperious duty to watch their progress and to give a direction to their course in life. They should be made to depend as much as possible on the Mechanic Trades to which the natives of this Island have not yet sufficiently directed their attention, and which therefore open a wide field for their exertion.

In 1824 Governor Walker laid the foundation stone of the new building for the Head School in Jamestown, thus giving the school an important vote of confidence for the future. The fact that the entire labour had been executed by the 'free men of colour' was welcomed warmly by the Governor in September 1825 with the words: 'This work may be called their first fruits and pledge that the native population will be adequate for all the labours of the island.' In *St Helena: A History of the Development of the Island*, P.C. Teale refers to this school as the Colonial Grammar School. The building still exists in Jamestown, having been used variously as the Head School, an Infants School and a Community Centre. The commemorative stone over the door is inscribed:

LONGO POST TEMPORE DILAPIDATUM JAM
TANDEM CONDITUM EST AEDIFICIUM

GUBERNANTE   ALEXANDRO WALKER
CONSULENTIBUS   T H BROOKE
                                                  G BLENKINS

D Kinnard   AD   B I Vernon
Op Inspect   1824   Ludimagist

This inscription, bearing the names of the Governor, two Consultant Councillors, the Works Inspector and the Headteacher, carries the message liberally translated as 'After a long period in disrepair, this new building is at last completed'. The stonecutter was a Corporal Galway who was commissioned to construct the West window of the School and also to carve the Company's Arms over the doors of the School and the Military Offices.

The Lower School at this time was housed on the site of what is now the Jamestown Market. It is marked in the Royal Engineers' plan of the town, made sometime between 1825 and 1843. In his Minute before the

The Honourable Company's Head School, Jamestown (built 1824)

Board on 23 December 1824, Governor Walker was pleased that 'many of the Pupils have made very good advances in the different branches of Education'. Taking each school in turn he demonstrated his personal interest in their progress. He wrote of the highly meritorious and satisfactory work at the Head School and the progressive improvement at the Town Day School. He gave the highest commendation to the Country Day School and, of the 120 children at Mrs George's Preparatory School, he wrote: 'The progress made by these children, most of whom are very young, in reading and writing has been considerable.' Good progress in reading, writing and ciphering had been made at the Evening School and he was pleased that at the Valley Sunday School a total of about 213 people who did not have opportunity to attend during the week were receiving instruction in the morning and the afternoon. At the Plantation Sunday School all the scholars were 'in a state of rapid improvement'. The Sandy Bay Sunday School had been established the previous September and already had 45 people attending, and similarly the Hutts Gate Sunday School established some two weeks prior to Sandy Bay promised to do well with 40 on its list.

Governor Walker's major concern related to the fact that there were only 36 pupils at the Head School, 'which is not equal to the Class of Society whose children ought to be sent to this School'. He added: 'Some it is true have sent them to be educated in England and many Parents who live in the Country cannot afford to send their children to Town, but the evil will in some degree be corrected and the expense much lessened by the plan which the Reverend Mr Vernon has formed of taking Boarders on very moderate terms.' Unfortunately this plan did not materialize.

Summing up his December 1824 report in his now well-known philosophical style he remarked: 'The real benefit of these Schools does not so much consist, especially in very young children, in any rapid progress in learning to read, as in training them from early infancy to discipline, order, and subjection to authority, and in sowing the seeds of moral and Religious principles, and conduct, which cannot be judged till the fruits appear in after life.'

On 30 December 1824 two more educational documents were produced, one on school leavers and one on the regimental schools. They were Public Letters from the Governor to the Auditor's Office about his continuing concern to follow up the progress of young people after leaving school. The first stated: 'The superintending eye of Government must not cease with the termination of the School instruction of their Children; their welfare and that of the Society at large must in a great degree depend upon their first steps in embarking in life; and to give a proper direction to those first steps is becoming an important duty on our part. An ample field is open for those who have a disposition to follow mechanical trades … and such as have no turn for mechanical pursuits are not likely to want employment so long as the lands are cultivated, fish consumed and household servants are required.'

The second document, dated 23 December 1824, was a Military Letter relating to the progress of the two Regimental Schools. The Governor expressed his gratification at the success of both of them. Of the Infantry Regimental School in Jamestown, he stated that 'many of the men are regular in their attendance and have made a respectable progress in Reading, Writing and Arithmetic. This disposition of the Soldiers to employ themselves in their own instruction must deserve our best encouragement.' For the work to be encouraged and advanced, the Governor sought resources and support to establish two libraries, one for each Corps, just as the Company had established libraries in their India Settlements. The Company had a system of sending a complete collection of books to places where their employees were settled. The Governor's request for libraries on St Helena bore fruit, the Consultations of August 1827 indicating that the Librarian was to be allowed 6d per day, 'having books of the East India Company to a considerable value under his charge'.

In his Public Letter of June 1825, reported in the *St Helena Records*, the Governor, who continued to be a man of many words, was optimistic that the spread of religious teaching to more people must be having beneficial effects – 'As not less than 500 children of the lower classes are now imbibing a religious education, there is every reason to expect an increased difference of moral sentiment in proportion as the present generation shall be supplanted by a race enjoying blessings to which their progenitors were unfortunately strangers.'

T. H. Brooke records that in 1823 Governor Walker, pursuing his philanthropic measures, was also responsible for founding the Agricultural and Horticultural Society, and 'for promoting agricultural fairs, ploughing matches and other means for encouraging inhabitants to rely more on the produce of the soil'.[15]

1824-34: The end of an era for the East India Company and the island

This period of time was to include a number of important events which had a significant effect upon the life on the island, including on the schools and teachers. It saw the end of the period of office of two key figures in Education – Governor Walker and the Reverend Boys – and it also heralded the end of the control of the island by the East India Company.

Several of Governor Walker's efforts were bearing fruit, and most schools over the island were benefiting from the high profile being given to education. Annual public school examinations were held, as in England, which could be attended by any interested persons in addition to the civic dignitaries, this giving both motivation to the pupils and teachers and also opportunity for others to assess the system. This practice was still in existence more than fifty years later. After attending the examinations in December 1825, Governor Walker produced his traditionally long report for the Council on 6 February 1826. His overall satisfaction with the island's schools was overshadowed by his concern that 'the number of Scholars at the Head School is only 22 and ought to be at least 60'. What were the causes for this, asked the Governor – negligence of parents? Children sent to England? Inability to pay the fees? Distance from the town? Fewer Foundation Scholarships?

Another educational enterprise which was still flourishing after several years in existence, and which received the warm support of Governor Walker in January 1826, was the now 125-strong Preparatory School conducted by the intrepid Mrs Clara George, where her assistants, Mrs Rich (perhaps a sister-in-law?) and Mrs Phillips promoted the skills of lacemaking, knitting and needlework 'instructing a class of 14 in these useful arts'.

Governor Walker was also concerned to stimulate the minds of the adult members of the community. It was under his patronage that in 1826 a group of men set up a Literary and Reading Society. It was formally instituted on 5 June 1826, and in the list of founder members in the *Prospectus of the Literary Society* there were several names well-known for their part in the educational system of St Helena. These included, for instance, the Reverend J.B.Vernon, the Reverend R.Boys, Mr J.N.Firmin and Mr Henry Kay, in addition to other now well known names such as T.H.Brooke, G.W.Melliss, G.W.Janisch, H.Doveton, T.B.Knipe, W.Carrol and S.Solomon. The purposes of the group were to discuss 'literary or scientific subjects of popular interest, and for reading the most useful books'.

The records of the Literary Society cover the period from 12 June 1826 to 10 August 1829 and the various subjects discussed covered a wide range of interests. An early discussion was on 'Female Education', led on 26 June 1826 by Dr James Arnott, the President, assisted by four other members including the Reverend Vernon. Unfortunately, the records do not indicate the nature of the discussion or the conclusions drawn. Nor, sadly, is a later discussion on 31 July 1826 on 'Practical Observations on the Education of the People' described.

After three months, the Reverend Vernon took over the presidency of the Society, and a decision was made to apply to the Governor and Council for authority and resources to accommodate 'such natural curiosities as shall hereafter be procured for the intended Museum' – certainly a forerunner of the present Museum in Jamestown. A topic selected for discussion a week or two later was entitled 'Vulgar Error', in which one item discussed was 'That the education of the lower classes is an evil, making them proud and dissatisfied and unhappy', but, again, no report of the discussion is available – without doubt Governor Walker would not have agreed with the sentiment, having spent much time promoting education for all islanders. Soon after this, the attendance dropped and membership dwindled to only six members, these including the stalwarts William Janisch, the Reverend Boys and John Firmin.

Later, on 24 December 1828, Governor Walker presented another comprehensive minute to the Council giving a report of the progress of the schools on the island, and this marked the end of an era – the impending retirement of the Reverend Boys. After giving a highly satisfactory report about the Day, Evening and Sunday schools, the Governor took the opportunity to affirm that 'we are in a very considerable degree indebted to the exertion of the General Superintendent of Schools, the Reverend Mr Boys'.

Throughout his career on the island the Reverend Boys had been outspoken on what he believed to be right about any aspect of island life. He had not confined his criticism to the general public. As the Senior Chaplain, he was reported as being 'constantly in conflict with authority, Sir Hudson Lowe in particular; and among others, he had occasion to rebuke a certain Admiral who was living in an improper manner at the Briars'.[16]

Nevertheless, his contribution to education was significant. T. H. Brooke wrote: 'With regard to the present Clergymen, the indefatigable labours of the Reverend Richard Boys, in superintending the education and religious instruction of the blacks and lower orders, are producing incalculable benefits to the community; and the preaching and practice of the junior chaplain, the Reverend B.J. Vernon, are such as are every way benefiting his sacred calling.'[17] Praise for the Reverend Boys' work came from another source also. T. Robson, a contemporary of Boys, wrote in his *St Helena Memoirs*: 'the work of the Lord is flourishing abundantly, particularly among the slaves … and the schools have greatly increased in numbers, so that the rising generation, in this once abandoned and profligate island, is now brought up strictly in the nurture and admonition of the Lord.'[18]

Richard Boys retired from the service of the Company in 1829 at the age of 45, amid praise for his 'faithful and energetic appeals from the pulpit – for his diligent and earnest ministrations to his flock – and for his active and increasing endeavours for the prosperity of St Helena'. He died many years later aged 82 in Kent. His obituary in the *St Helena Guardian* of 11 April 1866 recalled his indefatigable exertions and the incalculable benefits his work had given to the island, concluding with: 'Well done, good and faithful servant'.

Governor Walker's term of office came to an end in 1828. He had certainly left an educational legacy on the island which helped to set a programme for much of the rest of the nineteenth century, and which, within a few years, helped education to weather the difficult transition period during which the government of the island transferred from the East India Company to the Crown.

The days of the Honourable Company on the island were by now fast running out. As recorded by E. L. Jackson, quoting from Melliss, the East India Company was to receive some unwelcome news: 'The island was a flourishing and peaceful colony when a heavy blow fell on them, a blow from which the island has never recovered. In 1833, the islanders received the news that, by Act of Parliament dated August 20, 1833, the East India Company's rule would end on the following April 22, 1834.'[19] This was to have both immediate and far-reaching effects. On the transfer, clearly the existing form of government changed; the garrison was disbanded, many members being pensioned off with very low pensions from the Company; many of the islanders who had worked for the Company no longer had employment, because the new government had a policy of employing their own people first before taking on new employees. So for some years, the island experienced a turbulent period. What of the schools, the children and their teachers during this time? Suffice it to say that, as a result of the change of control in 1834, most of the schools were themselves destined for considerable change.

3
The Island Under Crown Control
1834-67

Slavery shall be, and is hereby utterly and for ever abolished, and declared unlawful within this colony.

Crown Ordinance, 1839[1]

1834-38: An Uncertain Period of Transition

The *Reminiscences of George Brooks Bennett 1816-1886* recall the difficult times experienced during the prolonged transition period when the control of the island was handed over from the Company to the Crown. Mr Bennett wrote about the state of indecision felt by the islanders from 1834 to 1836 – 'they actually did not know who their Masters were'. At the request of the British Government, the Company was still managing the island while the permanent arrangements for the future were being made, so during the two years of waiting the Company's structures, including the schools, had continued.

A Minute Book of the Committee of the Benevolent Society, preserved at Bishopsholme on St Helena, records their deliberations for several years and is entitled *Schools 1835-1852*. During the period of uncertain control during the transition the Society decided that the time had come to establish its own Infants School in Jamestown. It had clearly been helping to support a school for infants in Jamestown run by W. P. Thompson. Accordingly a Public Notice was issued by J. N. Firmin, Secretary of the Committee:

INFANT SCHOOL

TO PARENTS

The Committee of the Benevolent Society have resolved to open a School for the Instruction of children of both sexes, from two to seven years of age under the patronage of the Honorable the Governor and Council.

The design of this Institution is to afford protection, and supply the want of parental care to the offspring of those who are engaged during the day, in providing by their honest labors, for the support of their families, at that early age when children are neither capable of being usefully employed, nor admissable to other schools.

Love and kindness are the means by which it is proposed to inculcate lessons of wisdom and virtue, adapted by their simplicity to the tender capacities of Infants ...

The Infant School will open on Monday 15th instant ...[2]

In view of its responsibility for this new school, the members of the Committee of the Benevolent Society decided to reduce their support for the existing Preparatory School, still known as 'Mrs George's School', though now being run by Leah Rich. The Society had been paying 9d per day, plus £18 per annum, for the use of the house for the school premises, but Mrs Rich was informed on 1 June 1835 by the Reverend Firmin, the Secretary of the Society, that her allowance was to be changed to just one shilling per day instead, 'this being half of that yearly rental allowed you for the use of the school. The school room and the adjoining room are to be immediately filled up for the accommodation of the Infant School which will be open for the reception of Scholars on Monday 15th inst.' Miss Jane Preston was to be the 'Matron' of the Infant School, for £1 per month. The other Infants School in Jamestown, led by W. P. Thompson, was not to receive any more money from the Society. He was evidently intending to relinquish his post, much to the displeasure of the late Government and the Society who had 'been at considerable expense establishing this school, and enabling Mr Thompson's son to qualify himself to conduct it'.[3] Details of the nature of this qualification and how it had been achieved are not apparent, but the expense could have been incurred by sending Mr Thompson to England.

Since its establishment the Society had also developed another significant new venture for St Helena – a School of Industry. In 1835 a new mistress, Mrs Brown, was taking over – 'a very competent person and one who was educated at Mrs George's School under the auspices of the Benevolent Society'.[4]

A significant decision affecting every aspect of the island including education, was made by the outgoing Governor and Council in 1836, with directions from the Court of Directors of the East India Company. It declared that 'all persons then being Slaves on the island of St Helena became emancipated and free'. All children born of slaves had been free since 1818 and from that time many had been able to participate in schooling, as recorded in the previous chapter. In 1839 slavery was finally laid to rest by the *Crown Ordinance No 24* and this gave added impetus to the work of the Benevolent Society whose special concern was for the poorer classes of the population.

Eventually the period of indecision ended with the arrival in 1836 of the Crown's Officer A.C.G. Knowles, this event being – 'the very first step in the resolving of this doubt, and you may judge how great was the interest excited'. However, the problems of the islanders were by no means over and historian E.L. Jackson records the hardship subsequently felt by those who were not suitably pensioned by the Company for whom they had worked and could not get work under the Crown's policy of employing their own people first.[5]

Soon after the Crown had taken over, there was a major reorganization of schools throughout the island. *The 1838 Blue Book* listed the nine schools which had previously been in operation under the Company. These lists gave the number of pupils, which totalled 401, including 224 males and 177 females, their teachers and, for some, the mode of instruction. (Bell's System, also known as the Monitorial or Madras System, is described in Chapter 2.)

Colonial Grammar School, Jamestown	28 (24m/4f)
English, Classical and Mathematics	
Lower School, Jamestown	79 (79m/0f)
Madras System	
Country Day School	60 (44m/16f)
Sunday School, Plantation	13 (11m/2f)
Sunday School, Sandy Bay	21 (8m/13f)
Girls School, Plantation	50 (0m/50f)
Infant School, Jamestown	81 (43m/38f)
2nd Infant School, Jamestown	54 (15m/39f)
School of Industry, Jamestown	15 (0m/15f)

By the time of the production of the *1839 Blue Book*, the list had been somewhat refined to read:

A Public School in Jamestown	26 (26m/0f)
Bell's System	
A Second School in Jamestown	124 (66m/58g)
Bell's System	
An Infant School in Jamestown	73 (18m/55f)
Infant system, writing etc	
Central Free School near Plantation Church	102 (67m/35f)
Bell's System	
Sandy Bay School	36 (16m/20f)
Partially Bell's System	
Hutts Gate School	44 (20m/24f)
Partially Bell's System	

This list gives a total of 405 pupils, 213 male and 192 female. The differences between the two lists point to a significant reorganization of the schools across the island as described below.

THE PUBLIC SCHOOL: The former Colonial Grammar School, which itself had previously been called the Head School, was now being called the Public School and admitted boys only, free, from the ages of eight to 12 years. Its Master was Henry Kay (£150 p.a.), son of the Colonial Surgeon on the island and previously for 18 years in the employment of the Company and Assistant Master (£150 p.a.) at the Grammar School under the Mastership of Mr Firmin (£100 p.a.). Mr Kay was given authority to augment his income by taking up to six private pupils at £6 each per annum. His Assistant was to be W. P. Thompson (£50 p.a.), and the school was to be granted £4 for stationery. All finances were from government money.

THE SECOND SCHOOL AND THE INFANTS SCHOOL: The pupils from the former Lower School in Jamestown and the two Infant Schools in Jamestown were now divided between two schools – one called the Second School, free, under the united control of Mr and Mrs F. Jones (who were to have £120 p.a. 'and a very indifferent house'), and the other called the Infants School, free, except for 21 private pupils at a rate of 8d per month, under the leadership of Jane Preston (£24 p.a. and £10 in lieu of a house). The Second School was reported to be housed 'in an old Brewery, the School House or room being in a dilapidated state' and it was to be funded entirely from government money. The new Infants School was funded by the Benevolent Society, plus the fees from the private pupils. The Second School took boys under 8 years of age and girls under 12, while the Infants School took boys and girls under 8. Mr and Mrs Jones and Miss Preston had all been teachers in schools under the Company.

THE CENTRAL FREE SCHOOL: The Country Day School and the Plantation Sunday School were merged into the Central Free School near Plantation Church, catering for boys and girls under 12 years of age. The Master of this school was to be H. Weston (sometimes recorded as Western) who had previously been Master of both the Country Day School and the Plantation Sunday School under the Company. With his wife, their joint salary was to be £120 p.a. plus a house, compared with their previous total emoluments of £112. According to the Society Committee Minutes, the third school in that area, the Plantation Girls' School, had been closed by the Benevolent Society on 6 August 1839 because 'Miss M. Den Taaffe had expressed her inability to continue the superintendence'. The new school had 102 pupils, 67 male and 35 female, while the previous three had catered for 123 pupils, 55 male and 68 female.

SANDY BAY SCHOOL: Some of the loss of numbers at the Central Free School could have been accounted for by an increase in numbers at Sandy Bay School, which in 1839 was now listed as a free, day school taking in 16 boys and 20 girls under 12 years of age, still under the headship of Mrs Isaake (variably spelt Isaacke or Isaac), now to receive £24 p.a. plus a £4 stationery allowance, instead of her previous £12 p.a. This school was entirely funded by the Benevolent Society.

HUTTS GATE SCHOOL: This school appears on the later list – free for boys and girls under 12 years of age, of whom there were 44. This school had been planned in 1838 by the Benevolent Society, to operate in the premises previously known as Griffon's House, and adapted and repaired at the cost of £25 for the purpose of a school. On 26 July 1839, the Benevolent Society unanimously appointed Flavilia Burnham as schoolmistress. Miss Burnham was to receive £24 p.a. plus £4 for stationery and £12 for house rent.

THE INDUSTRIAL SCHOOL: The Industrial School listed in 1838 had been closed, at least temporarily, by the Benevolent Society in view of the fact that Mrs Brown, the Mistress of the School, had resigned after being called to task in May 1838 for admitting 14 under-age children to her school; for not teaching the seven children above age to work; and for not disclosing how the fees had been expended. Support for the school was withdrawn in August and it was ruled that the twelve children still attending should go to Miss Preston's School, the Infants School in Jamestown, until some new arrangements respecting the School of Industry could be made.[6]

On the whole, the teachers seem to have fared well during the transition period although, as we shall see, there were winners and losers.

1839-50: Winners and Losers in the New System
It was inevitable that there would be some casualties of the reorganization, one being school teacher Thomas Ford Thompson whose complaints were recorded by the Benevolent Society on 13 January 1839

'respecting his nonemployment by the Society as a Master of the Town School and also that of his son (W. P. Thompson) as Master of the Infants School'. The Committee of the Society assured Mr Thompson, Senior, of their high regard for the work of both men and that each would receive a gratuity of six months' salary, and be well placed to be employed by the Society in future. Clearly his pupils at the Town School appreciated his work as, several years later, they subscribed to a commemorative plaque which is now on the altar rail of St James' Church. The inscription reads: 'Schoolmaster in this Island and Clerk in this Church upwards of XX years, a worthy and kind tutor'. He had been appointed by the Benevolent Society as Assistant Teacher at the school in 1827 and in charge of it since 1833.

Similarly, Mr Weston (Western) appealed concerning his loss of the post of Master of the Country Day School, and he too was granted a gratuity of six months' salary. Mr Jones' appeal of a similar nature regarding the loss of his Assistant Master post at the Jamestown Lower School was rejected.

W. P. Thompson was subsequently appointed on 29 November 1839 to be Master of the Under School, a post he was to hold until well into the 1870s. The *Blue Book* lists of the following year, 1840, show that Thomas Thompson was running a flourishing evening school in Jamestown for 43 boys and 23 girls, using Bell's System, and being paid £30 by the Benevolent Society. A member of the Thompson family was also running a Private School in Jamestown with 102 pupils (62 boys and 40 girls), partially under Bell's System, and not under any patronage. It appears that several people on the island were still apprehensive about the success of the educational reorganization under the Crown and were 'going private'.

Leah Rich also felt disadvantaged by the transition, because the arrangement which had been made a short while before for the use of her house for the new Infants School had come to an end. Mrs Rich had now become a debtor to the Government for £69 2s 4d, and so appealed in July/August 1839 to the Board, through the Colonial Secretary, for help in view of the fact that 'the Government of the EIC had engaged to hire her house, as a School House, at a rent of £36 a year'.[7]

Another person who felt himself to be a casualty of the new arrangements was Mr Firmin, a teacher of long-standing service on the island since 1813, who during his career had risen to be in charge of the Head School in Jamestown. He repeated his action of 15 years previously, writing a letter of complaint to the Colonial Secretary. In his letter dated 19 February 1839, he objected to losing his status, Mr

Kay having been declared Master of the Public School. Mr Firmin applied for the post of Clerk to the Peace 'in view of the peculiar circumstances in which I have been placed by the recent arrangements in the School Department'. He was successful in his application and became both the Clerk to the Peace and Master of the Upper School. However, some nine months later he sought the Governor's permission to resign the Mastership of the School as his duties as Clerk of the Peace and Acting Queen's Advocate 'leave but a very inconsiderable portion of either time or attention to the due discharge of the duties required of me at the Upper School'. In his letter of 30 November 1839 he hoped that the Colonial Secretary would consider his reasons 'sufficient to justify my wishing to retire from the arduous and responsible charge of an Institution in connection with which I have labored for a period of nearly 27 years'. The records are unclear about the outcome of this correspondence but it is likely that Mr Kay continued to run the Head School while Mr Firmin held the overall control. Mr Kay eventually retired from the Head School in 1849 at the age of 53.

A further private school which demands mention from this period was the Lemon Valley School. This was run by a Mrs Homans who, according to the *Benevolent Society Minutes* of 14 January 1841, had applied to the Society 'to allow her £5 as a Gratuity for her past services in keeping a school in Lemon Valley for the last five years'.

The working relationship at this time, and in fact until 1873, between the Government and the Benevolent Society was that the schools were kept distinct but the Governor continued to be *ex officio* a Patron of the Society. Membership of the Committee was held voluntarily by islanders, including clergy and military and government personnel. With voluntary financial contributions, the Society ran its own schools and also continued to support a number of the poorer children, enabling them to attend the Town School in Jamestown and the Plantation House Day and Sunday Schools. It also gave some financial backing to other schools which were admitting Free Black and Slave children and adults.

For several years the structure of the school system on the island remained substantially the same. Methods of instruction changed, and the *1841 Blue Book* recorded that the Jamestown Second School operated the National Society's System, which used pupil teachers, the Infants School adopted the Wilderspin System, and 'other schools taught in classes'. The Wilderspin System had been devised in the 1830s by a Londoner, Samuel Wilderspin, who ran the Infant School

Society from Cheltenham. The system aimed to educate the whole being and to cultivate all human powers. 'He trained the body through games and exercises; moral feeling through precept and example; ear and voice through music; the senses and intellect through object and picture lessons and oral narrative.'[8]

School rules came under scrutiny and in 1842 the *Colonial Secretary's In-Letters* of 30 May included a request for 600 copies of the rules – 'some inconvenience having arisen from the absence of an authorised code of rules for the Government Schools in this Colony'.

One significant development at this time is marked by the fact that Jamestown Public (Head) School, the Evening School and Sandy Bay School were each described as 'promiscuous', meaning that they were open to all people in the community. While in the past it had been possible for both freed slaves and slaves to attend school, there was little encouragement for them to do so, particularly in those schools with a curriculum specifically designed for the children of employees of the Company. Now there were attempts to improve the opportunities of African boys from the Liberated African Depot, also called the Station. A directive was given in *Ordinance No 10, 1842* that 'All such liberated Africans above the age of ten, and under the age of sixteen years, may be apprenticed by their fathers, mothers or guardians, to any trade, in the practice of which any peculiar art or skill is requisite, the term of such apprenticeship not to exceed five years'. The *1842 Blue Book* indicated that of the 67 attending the Evening School, 12 were African boys. The numbers of pupils altogether at schools on the island in 1843 was 592, 346 male and 246 female.

The Benevolent Society was still concerned, though, at the want of regular instruction for the liberated Africans and in 1843 it asked for representations to be made on their behalf. Over a year later the Committee members decided that, having allocated £15 p.a. of their funds, with more available according to numbers, they would advertise for 'any person who might be disposed to further this object by opening a Sunday School in the Country, chiefly for the above class'.[9] One application was received, from Stephen Young. He was appointed and the Barrack Room on the Outer Parade at High Knoll was made available for the purpose. The Governor indicated that he had 'no objection to a part of the building being used, with a clear understanding that no expense for repairs be made to the Ordnance Department', and that the building, when required, should be given back in the same state of repair.[10] The Clerk was to obtain three stools for the school.

A certain continuity of personnel existed in the schools through the latter half of the 1840s. Henry Kay and W. P. Thompson were giving some stability to the Head School and the Under School; Reverend Frey, a German national, was appointed to be head of the Country School, referred to as the Plantation School, with a few complaints that the pupils found it difficult to understand his pronunciation; Thomas Thompson was still running the Evening School in Jamestown, using the monitorial system, with 83 pupils (59 male and 24 female); and Mr Young at the High Knoll School for Liberated Africans flourished with 48 male students. Altogether there were over 560 pupils attending schools.

The state of the Under School building in 1844 was giving cause for concern. Governor Hamelin Trelawney, who declared that he was 'deeply interested in the welfare of the rising generation', sent a Despatch to the Secretary of State which included a report from the Superintendent of Schools 'that the room occupied as the Under School is, in its present state, unfit for the reception of 126 children, with a due regard to their health, and suggesting that the whole building be thrown into one room by removing the upper floor.'[11] He explained that originally the lower floor had been a bakery for the Garrison and the upper floor a Silk Worm Establishment. The latter had become the school, and the lower floor had now been abandoned by the Garrison. Hence his scheme was feasible. Unfortunately the site of this building cannot be confirmed, but the Silk Worm Establishment was thought, at one stage, to be at Briars.

Concern that women teachers were less reliable than men is reflected in various incidents. It was the policy of the Benevolent Society to decrease the salaries of those teachers who were in schools supported by the Society if the numbers attending went down. At this time the teacher at Sandy Bay School, Louisa Isaake, was leaving her post. The Society's Committee (composed of seven gentlemen, including Solomon and Melliss) minuted on 2 April 1849 that they considered it of importance 'to recommend an increase of stipend viz £10 in order to ensure greater permanency and efficiency by advertising for a Master instead of a Mistress'! Accordingly the application went out, for a Master – or Mistress – at £40 p.a. Meanwhile, dissatisfied with the work of Flavilia Burnham at Hutts Gate because the school 'was conducted with great irregularity, and reduced to the lowest ebb in points of numbers', the Society sent her notice on 23 August 1849 that her job would be terminated on 1 October. Her successor, selected from seven applicants, was a woman, Miss Fanny Dickson, 'with the understanding that she reside on the premises'.

Across the schools, the work of the pupils and their teachers was subject to public examination, a typical announcement of the time being made on 5 February 1849: 'A General Examination of the Evening and Infant Schools of the Benevolent Society will take place at the Head School at 1 o'clock on Thursday 15th inst. HE The Governor will be presiding. Friends of the Society and the Scholars are invited to attend'.

Two schools which do not feature in the main island lists, but which are mentioned in the Society minutes, are a small private school at Longwood for which Mrs Hillman was awarded a gratuity of £1 for keeping the school creditably for five months, and High Peak School, for which £12 8s 0d remained available in November 1849 towards its erection. The latter does not appear to have survived, as several months later it was recorded that no provision was to be made for a teacher there.

1850-60: A decade of mixed fortunes in schools

Several efforts were made at this time to try to improve standards within the school system, including closing schools which did not rise to expectations. In June 1850 the Laws and Regulations of the Society were revised. The Minutes recorded that it was to be named 'St Helena Benevolent Society' and under the revised management the General Superintendent of Government Schools should be a permanent member of their Committee. Within twelve months poor reports were coming in about two schools under their auspices – the Jamestown Infants School and the High Knoll School. Letters were sent to the two respective head teachers, Mrs Rich and Mr Young, saying that their services were being terminated, and tenders were put out for replacements. Eight tenders were received but the Society decided to open only one school, this to be in Jamestown 'for Infants and Elder Girls', the teacher in charge to be Miss Caroline Grant.

A further move to raise standards involved the introduction of new regulations for schools. In 1850 Governor Ross wrote a letter to the Secretary of State in the UK, the Rt Hon Earl Grey, giving some new regulations for the better management of the schools, pointing out the 'want of a proper and efficient Head Master, capable of training teachers in the colony'. He continued: 'The present regulations as your Lordship will observe afford an opportunity to the poorest lad in the Colony, by proficiency to ascend to the very head of the Grammar School free of expense.'[12]

Consequently, to oversee these measures, a new Inspector of Schools, the Reverend J.Chambers, arrived in 1851. He was to be in charge of the Upper Division of the Head School, with William Brown in charge of the Lower Division. This news was welcomed by the editor of the first private and non-governmental newspaper to be produced on the island, which began to appear in 1851. The editorial in *The Advocate* (also called *The St Helena Weekly News*) of 16 October 1851 expressed the hope 'that before long a more useful and practical system will be adopted, the present in our opinion being far too restricted and limited only to one or two subjects of study. With the two new Masters now at the head of Scholastic Affairs, we have reason to hope that new life and vigour will be infused into the youngsters entrusted to their charge.' W.P.Thompson had been transferred to be the Master of the Under School. The newspaper also had 'pleasure in announcing that a Board or Committee is at present sitting to enquire into the present position of St Helena schools ... selected without reference to sect or party'. This appears to have been a St Helena Government initiative. The editor hoped that 'ultimately a Board of Education will always be in existence on the island to watch over the schools'.

Later, on 18 November 1852, *The Advocate* published an article under the heading 'The New School', in which the editor congratulated the readers 'upon the establishment of a School for Young Ladies', but he entreated the young lady in charge not to discriminate but 'freely to receive all whose conduct may not render them objectionable'. This referred to Miss Caroline Grant at the Jamestown School for Infants and Elder Girls.

To facilitate the introduction of the new measures to improve standards, the Government increased the resources made available to schools. In his report of 1852, the Reverend Chambers made reference to these and confirmed that the new rules and regulations had caused a marked improvement in the schools by extending the former routine of instruction, and establishing a library in each of the government schools. But the Reverend Chambers was dissatisfied with general attitudes towards education. He made an appeal to the Governor: 'There are but too many persons in St Helena who are incapable of appreciating the benefits of good education, but it appears to me to be the more necessary on that account to place the means of obtaining it within reach, in the hope of creating a desire for, and proving the advantage of it. Viewing the case in this light, I should wish for a member of one of the universities, who understands the art of teaching on the very improved principles lately introduced.'[13]

The opportunities for Africans to receive education were increased by the efforts of two former slaves to establish a school for them. Two particular teachers received special tribute at this time in island records – Jacob Faithful, in charge of the African School in Jamestown, and his fellow teacher, Jack March. Referring in 1853 to the Examination of the Benevolent Society schools, a correspondent 'Observer' to the *St Helena Herald*, another island newspaper, wrote: 'There were also present a number of Africans, male and female, from a school of 25, under the auspices of the Rural Dean, who were taught by Jacob Faithful and Jack March, now Christian Teachers, who, a few years ago, were captured slaves.' The correspondent commented on 'their praiseworthy desire for instruction, after their daily labour was over'. He regretted that so few of the parents and inhabitants attended the occasion – 'Can it be that the parents feel no interest in the matter so vitally affecting the future welfare, fortune and eternity of their offspring?'

While there was no day school for the children of Levelwood yet, certainly a Sunday School was in operation as recorded in the *1853 Blue Book*.

Meanwhile, in the Head School the rapidity with which the masters in charge changed was probably the major reason for its fluctuating success. In an attempt to revive its fortunes and to persuade the Reverend Chambers to stay, in spite of his doubts about attitudes, the Freemasons gave funds to the school, but the death of Mr Chambers in 1854 opened up speculation as to how to get a suitable successor. William Brown, the Reverend Chambers' Assistant in charge of the Lower Division of the Head School, became Acting Inspector of Schools and Master of the Head School, and he reported 'great deficiency in schools, particularly in the Head School'. 1855 saw the island still looking for a clergyman/schoolteacher, and the Bishop of Cape Town reported that 'St Helena is in a sad state'. Another member of the Janisch family is listed in the *Blue Book* of 1854 as Acting Assistant Teacher at the Lower Division of the Head School, this being Voteur Lambe Machado Janisch, several years the junior of his brother, Hudson.

The Reverend Bennett appeared in 1855 and, after some initial misunderstanding about his salary, took over the job, but within two years had applied for a year's leave of absence, during which time the Reverend Lambert took the role. On his return, Mr Bennett was awarded a salary of £200 per annum to have the joint post of Master of the Head School and Inspector of Schools, but he incurred the wrath of some correspondents in the *St Helena Guardian*, who had noted his absence from the Treat Day celebrations. This is one of the first references to this important occasion in the island's calendar, usually celebrating an official event such as a royal birthday.

Certainly, apart from the Head School, this period from 1855 to 1858 was one in which the schooling system was comparatively stable. In addition to the Reverend G. Bennett and William Brown (sometimes recorded Browne) at the Head School, the teaching establishment included the now well-known names of W. P. Thompson and Mrs C. Miller at the Lower School, the Reverend and Mrs Frey at the Plantation Country School, and Jacob Faithful at the Jamestown Evening School for Africans. There were, however, still many young people who were not yet involved in regular schooling. These included a number of unfortunate children who were the subject of a letter from 'Hope' to the *Herald* on 26 January 1854: 'I trust to see at no distant day a Ragged or Industrial School established under the management of a Master or Mistress.' 'Hope' continued to describe the institution in mind – it was to provide for board and lodging for the fatherless, motherless and friendless children, who should receive an education that would fit them for a middling class of society; the products of their work should be sold, the proceeds going to the funds of the school, and the children were to be discharged only when provided for.

Three weeks later 'Quisquis' took up the correspondence, applauding the initiative that 'Hope' had made and listing in detail the necessary qualities of a master for such a school – good, industrious, ingenious, educated, able to turn his hand to anything, capable of teaching the boys to read and write and to work at some manual labours – 'a man of such a stamp as to be able to control and govern boys and girls who are not wont easily to submit to authority'. The mistress was to be a similar paragon, in order to perform her share of the duties faithfully. 'Now let your correspondents search the Island and see if they could find two such in the whole of it', 'Quisquis' challenged.

The search clearly succeeded because, included in the Civil Engineer's Letters of June 1858-July 1860, an undated instruction 'By Command of His Excellency' was given to the civil engineer: 'Required at the Ragged School, Rhubarb Hall, Four forms 14 feet in length (each). The room to be colored and cleaned. Steps required at the entrance.' Rhubarb Hall was in Market Street, on the site now occupied by the home of Mrs Cissie Stevens (the original building was burned down).

Shortly afterwards, on 23 August 1860, the *St Helena Record* called for a Penitentiary for offenders in order to 'save these objects of degradation and disease from their present and pitiful condition', adding that 'Nearly allied to this subject is the Ragged School. We were most agreeably surprised to find a knot of between 70 and 80 of these neglected ones who in time to come are to represent the present generation, collected around a teacher, learning the first rudiments of education, the most of whom for the first time in their lives yielded to the discipline of a School ... We only observed a few benches or stools with a chair and a table in the room; and yet this is the nucleus of what may, with care and sympathy, become one of the most useful institutions for drying up the sources of that corruption which is the bane of our moral pretentions.'

After making the usual report on the school establishment in the *1858 Blue Book* to the Colonial Office, giving a total of 888 students in the island schools, the statement was made that a separate school for girls was in contemplation by the Government.

1860-65: Expansion of the School Population and Provision

Through the late 1850s and early 1860s, the numbers of people enrolled at the schools gradually increased, rising from 656 in 1855 to 1,000 in 1862, the latter at a time when the child population of six- to 12-year-olds was 1,204. Some reorganization of schools was being considered. Records of 1858 include a Garrison School and also an indication that, concerning the Head School, the Government was contemplating a separate school for girls. The *1860 Blue Book* accordingly listed the schools as reorganized:

Head School, Jamestown	46 m/o f (Grammar School)	Reverend Bennett
		Asst Reverend Lambert
Lower School, Jamestown	150 m/o f (National Sch)	W. P. Thompson
Girls School, Jamestown	o m/92 f (National Sch)	Eliza Denton
Plantation School	30 m/34 f	Reverend Frey
Evening School, Jamestown	10 m/o f	Edward Dowding
Evening School, Jamestown	56 m/33 f	W. P. Thompson
Day and Infant School, Jamestown	44 m/37 f	T. Goodwin
Sandy Bay School (Baptist Sunday)	18 m/27 f	J. Edmonds
Hutts Gate School	9 m/8 f	F. Dickson
Half Tree Hollow School	20 m/12 f	– Davids
Evening School, Redhill	21 m/o f	W. F. Buxton
Free School	41 m/51 f	Miss Rich

Baptist Day School, Jamestown	30 m/35 f	Mrs Pierce
Sandy Bay School	10 m/10 f	Ellice Pompey
Garrison Schools:		
Jamestown	33 m/34 f	Sergeant Robins
Ladder Hill	15 m/12 f	Sergeant Carson
Total	533 m + 385 f = 918	

Additionally it was estimated that about 50 pupils were being educated in other private schools on St Helena.

It will be noted that this list includes two Baptist schools. The Baptists had come to the island in 1845 led by the Reverend Mr Bertram and found a place to meet in the Janisch home. Hudson was one of their first converts and he was later described in a letter to Mr Bertram as 'the Rev Mr Janisch with his brilliant intellect, discriminating mind and elevated tone of piety'.[14] The Baptists at first introduced Sunday teaching within their church and later started the day schools in Jamestown and Sandy Bay as listed above. The list also includes some new names of schools and people, notable ones being the Girls' School in Jamestown, the day school at Half Tree Hollow, the Free School in Jamestown and two Garrison schools. The Girls' School experienced some difficulty finding where to meet and for some time was housed in two areas in the Castle, premises they were destined to use for a number of years. Regarding Half Tree Hollow, this appears to be the first mention of a day school there. The Free School in Jamestown, led by Miss Rich, was the Ragged School in all but name. The Garrison Schools in Jamestown and at Ladder Hill were well subscribed with both girls and boys, there being an expectation that children of the Garrison would attend. In 1861 a schoolmaster from one of the Garrison Schools, Mr Lowman, became known for his magic lantern lectures given to the non-commissioned officers and men of the St Helena Regiment, on such subjects as astronomy, and for his 'laughter-provoking experiments in that amusing science, yclept Electro-Biology, or Mesmerism'.[15]

The annual prizegivings were important events. At the Head School in December 1860, the ceremony was attended by a large number of island dignitaries, and the prizes ranged from *Robinson Crusoe, Theophilus Anglicanus, Ancient Cities, The Seven Wonders of the World* (awarded to Saul Solomon) and Wood's *Natural History*, to items such as a case of mathematical instruments, a box of colours, a silver pencil case and a set of chessmen. These were all presented by the wife of the Governor, Mrs Drummond-Hay.[16]

A population census taken in 1861 gave the number of children between the ages of 6 and 12 on the island to be 1,204, of whom 1,000 were on the school rolls, giving an enrolment of 83%. In addition, it was estimated that only 30 children were now attending two private schools. It is difficult, however, to reconcile these statistics with those quoted in the following newspaper article. The *Record*'s successor, the *St Helena Guardian*, established in 1861, frequently became a mouthpiece for education, the editor being prepared to enter into discussion and correspondence about the concerns of the day, including such aspects as industrial education, the controversial state of the Head School, and the curriculum. The edition of 26 December 1861 took stock of the present educational system. 'We propose to glance briefly at the state and prospect of Education in this Colony. And we are glad at the out-set to feel assured that in these we can find abundant matter for satisfaction.' On attendance, the record was that one in seven of the children of school age were registered, whereas in England it was only one in eight. And the actual attendance of those of school-leaving age was three out of four. The editor recommended that the Government Girls' School should be enlarged from 100 to 150 scholars, and that the Government should extend its schools into Longwood and the scattered district around High Peak, so supporting the efforts of the Benevolent Society.

The *Guardian* proceeded to give warm 'encomiums' to the Benevolent Society School under Mr Goodwin, to Miss Denton at the Girls' School, and to the Head School, the Town Lower School and the Plantation School. It continued to praise the work of Mr W. P. Thompson at his Evening School, and the Benevolent Society for supporting the school, reporting that 'Upwards of 60 grown up boys and girls, some apprentices, some servants, are receiving an education which they failed to obtain when younger, or are regaining a knowledge of useful things once possessed but now forgotten, or adding to it.'

The Free School, by 1863 called the Ragged School again, continued to operate with large numbers of children. A letter of 12 November 1863 to the Colonial Secretary from Mr Eden Baker, a local shipping agent and merchant who was also Schools Visitor, sought the authority of the Governor to move to better buildings. Mr Baker detailed the conditions under which this transfer would be made, including the financial implications. The 'improved school room and Master's Residence' was to be the large cellar under the Benevolent Society's School, and the old building adjoining this was to be converted into having two floors 'besides the cellar and the lower floor, to be fitted as a residence with three rooms'. Governor Elliot agreed to these proposals. From 1864, the official name, Ragged School, Jamestown, was listed in the annual *Blue Book* Reports to the Secretary of State, with Miss Rich still in charge. The age range was described as infants, and the number of pupils given as only 40, all girls. The improved buildings and the move appear to have changed the nature and original intention of the school. Conjecture causes one to note the name of the teacher, Miss Rich. Was the 1864 Ragged School yet another metamorphosis of Mrs Clara George's Preparatory School?

Provision and regulations concerning Juvenile Offenders were clarified when the *1865 Ordinance No 2* became law on the island. After determining a daily routine for the offenders in the place where they were housed, starting at 5.00 a.m. in summer and 5.15 a.m. in winter – with a penalty of no breakfast or a whipping if they were late – provision was made for two hours during each of three days for washing, mending and school instruction 'and for the purposes of school instruction lights will be allowed until 8.30 p.m.'. Some junior officers were to help with the teaching, while the minister was to give religious instruction and the warden to keep Sunday School.

Similarly there were clearly some homeless children on St Helena because the *1865 Ordinance No 3* provided a reformatory and 'industrial training' for Vagrant Children.

The year 1865 saw troubles continuing to accumulate for the Head School, and in consequence, for St Helena. The Reverend Grey was now in charge of the school and his period of leadership was turbulent. But it was now the turn of the Assistant Master, Mr Griffiths, to get into hot water. Not only was he accused of being intoxicated at a theatre performance at the Garrison, but also he was involved in the circumstances which led to the expulsion of a pupil, John Marshall, son of the late Parish Surgeon, who – unable to do a sum to the satisfaction of Mr Griffiths – had been beaten 'in an unjustifiable and cruel manner'. Mr Griffiths was convicted and fined, but the pupil was nevertheless expelled by the Master, the Reverend Grey. However, the mother appealed to the Governor who rescinded the expulsion, writing a note to the mother to the effect that the boy 'can return to the Institution whenever she sees fit to send him there'.[17]

Concerned that the teachers under his charge were not rising to his expectations, the Reverend Grey determined to control the curriculum too. For instance, after instructing W. P. Thompson at the Under School to teach the boys of the first class for two lessons a week on the geography of Great Britain, he warned that he would be coming to examine the pupils on the subject. However, his problems did not rest there as he had occasion to send a firm ultimatum to Mr Thompson 'that the keeping of fowls, ducks, rabbits and the like in the yard leading into the school is not conducive either to the cleanliness of the schoolroom or the health of the boys. If any such be allowed there, the practice may be discontinued'. The Governor became involved – and the menagerie was now said to contain a monkey and a pig! The wisdom of Solomon was used and the Governor directed Mr Thompson to take care that his poultry did not find their way into the schoolroom.[18]

At the Head School the sword of Damocles was already hanging over the head of the Master, the Reverend Grey, who had incurred the displeasure of Governor Charles Elliot over several matters. On 12 May 1865, the Governor informed the Secretary of State that 'serious injury having been occasioned in this Community during the past few years by the interruption in the Head School for considerable intervals of time ... I propose with your sanction to inform that Gentleman that we will not require his services beyond 12 months from the date at which such notice is communicated to him'.[19] The objections were that Mr Grey had been seeking permanent employment in other directions without previous notice; during his time at the school the numbers of pupils had fallen from 45 to 16; there appeared to be some discrepancy over fees; there was the pupil's expulsion – and now there was the dispute over Mr Thompson's chickens! Although Mr Grey threatened to take the matter as far as the Secretary of State and, if necessary, to Parliament, the subsequent official report stated that he was dismissed because 'he was careless in his duties and otherwise an ineligible person for the instruction and guidance of the youth of the better classes', and also due to the fact that the school had declined in reputation 'from want of confidence in his diligence and steadiness'.[20]

With the subject of education so much to the fore on St Helena, the *Guardian* frequently suggested what purposes it should serve. The paper's 'Own Correspondent' wrote: 'The real object of Education should be to give children resources that will endure as long as their existence, and habits that will ameliorate that existence by inducing principles of the true law of liberty, which will develop the whole of man and complete the divine intention of creation and redemption.'[21]

1866-67: The Rise and Fall of Island Schools
Meanwhile, once again, the saga of trying to find a new head for the Head School began and during this process the school was closed.

Various individuals and groups had views on what should happen now. A leading article in the *St Helena Guardian* in April 1866, based on the current Benevolent Society Report, commented: 'There is an interesting class which has not been provided for since the establishment of the Government Head School. We require a school to give a finish to the education of the children in the respectable labouring and the inferior grades of our artisan classes to meet the requirements of the position they will probably be placed in in after life. The Government School under the tuition of Mr Thompson [the Under School] in some degree answers this purpose, but many pupils leave and are sadly deficient in education for practical business purposes. The distance between the Government Head School and the preparatory schools is too great; neither does the meeting of the higher and lower classes of society at the Head School work well.'

The Benevolent Society realized that they had a part to play in this difficult period, and that this would be a good time to call upon the public for funds to help to improve their own provision. Accordingly they appealed in the *Guardian* on 14 November 1866 for specific help towards their school building in Jamestown. 'The noble effort that is now being made to make permanent her institutions and to secure the health and comfort of the children placed under her charge for education, as well as for the health and comfort of those who conduct the school, in the purchase of the new schoolroom in Napoleon Street, should be liberally supported.' At this stage the Benevolent Society also became responsible for the Sandy Bay School buildings and resources.

In his *Despatches* of August 1866 the Governor himself listed the attributes and job description of a suitable Head Master of the Head School. He was to be a layman, but a member of the Church of England. His task was to prepare the youth for the active business of life, such as Commerce, Civil Engineering, a seafaring life, the Merchant Service, Navy or Army. He was not to include classical instruction, 'as this is quite useless to them in those pursuits in which they must seek livelihood', and exceptional boys who needed such classes were to be sent to England. He was to teach the elements of chemistry, physics, physical geography, practical surveying, sketching and plan drawing, and to ground the boys well in one or two modern languages.

The person would be on two years' probation, on both sides, to receive £200 per year, rising by increments of £25 to £300; with a house allowance of £50, and the potential to earn another £100 from fees. Since there were only twelve pupils, the post of Assistant Master would be abolished; a committee of Official Visitors would report on the school regularly, three times a week. Concluding with the fact that some of the most intelligent merchants and the most able and trusty among the Government Officers had been brought up entirely at the Head School under the control of the East India Company, he called for 'a return to that useful and sound system of Education, with modern improvements and extensions'.[22] Six months later the post of Head was still vacant.

However, St Helena had meanwhile received a long-term benefit on another front. In 1865 Rebecca Hussey bequeathed a half-share of £22,000 for the benefit of liberated slaves on St Helena, the other half-share going for the same purpose to Lagos, Nigeria. Rebecca Hussey is reputed to have lived in Liverpool and to have had specific yearning to help liberated slaves. A local Board of Trustees, set up to administer the money, decided to establish schools to achieve their purposes. On 9 September 1865 they issued general rules for the government of any Hussey Charity Schools established on St Helena, for Africans.

Teachers were precluded from accepting any other emolument without the sanction of the Board; they would have discretion to select the branches of knowledge to be taught, but must submit these for approval to the Board; regular returns on scholars were to be submitted to the Board; and on Sundays they were to give instruction to the children in the afternoon. Regulations concerning the scholars included that the school was to be open to persons of African birth or descent, without respect of creed; application for admission to any of the schools was to be made direct to the Masters, who were to give immediate notice to the Board if they rejected or dismissed any scholar. The school year was mapped out, allowing holidays every Saturday and on Her Majesty's Birthday, with one week at Easter, two at midsummer and three at Christmas.[23]

By 23 April 1866 the Trustees had decided to set up a school based in Jamestown for the benefit of Liberated Africans, and also a model industrial farm for those resident in the country. For the latter they applied for the 99-year lease of Friar's Lodge. An invitation to prospective scholars of the School for Africans was published in the *St Helena Spectator* on 27 October 1866, the Master to be Mr Hoskin. Presumably to awaken the conscience of the Government in this matter, the leading article in the paper the following week posed the question: 'Is it desirable in the interest of a community that the members thereof should be liberally educated?' Stressing that it was the

Government's responsibility to take action in the matter of education, the article continued: 'The education of the people is a common good, and the cost thereof ought in all fairness to be borne by all.' Nevertheless, like the Benevolent Society, the Hussey Charity was to bring much good to education on the island over several decades to come.

The *1866 Blue Book* listed a record number of 20 schools on St Helena. Besides schools previously listed, there was first mention of a Baptist Mission School in Ruperts Valley; two Hussey Charity Schools, one a free weekday school in Napoleon Street, and the other a Night School in the same premises – they were run by Mr and Mrs Hocking and had already attracted a total of 88 scholars, 51 in the day, and 37 at night; and a Baptist Sunday School at Knollcombes, run by Mr Short, with 20 scholars.

Increasingly, the need arose for greater provision of schooling in the Longwood area, where the population had steadily increased, and where requests for a truly local school had been made for several decades. Matters were brought to a head when, in 1866, consternation was caused in Longwood by the closure of a private school run by Mr Deason. The Reverend Bodily, the vicar of the parish, was concerned that 16 children would lose their instruction, this being a particularly serious situation since the present day school 'had at no time been efficient'. He called for a Government grant to establish a good day school in Longwood for 60 to 80 children, in view of the 'non-attendance on the part of some children, and attempts to avail themselves of distant schools on the part of others'. This was a reference to the school at Hutts Gate which had been established in 1839 in premises acquired from Colonel Griffon and led by its first school teacher, Miss Flavilia Burnham. Hutts Gate was the destination for many Longwood children for several decades because the school requested at the time did not materialize.

Meanwhile school life was certainly not all work and no play. As far back as 1855, records had referred to the existence of a Treat Day but no details of the activities organized on such days have come to light until a description of the 1866 event appeared in the *St Helena Guardian* of 21 February 1866: 'We think the prettiest sight ever witnessed in St Helena was that of Friday last, when upwards of 1,000 schoolchildren were collected together on Francis Plain for the purpose of making merry.' Altogether we should say there were upwards of 2000 adults present besides about 600 children in addition to the schoolchildren – and these out of a population of 6000.' A full programme was arranged. After approaching Francis Plain carrying their own banners, the schools were settled in groups and played 'various games' and then were seated in rows near to the Militia Drill Shed and were 'soon employed in eating bread and meat, cake, fruit etc, moistened with wholesome but unintoxicating drinks', all furnished by Mr Scott of the Imperial Hotel. Further games such as racing competitions followed during the afternoon, all to the accompaniment of the Volunteer St Helena Band playing quadrilles, polkas and waltzes. The afternoon proceedings were ended by the schools marching off cheering each other and 'the Longwood School stopping several times to give one more cheer'. As an afterthought, the article added: 'Conspicuous by its absence is the Head School.'

But the Head School had problems of its own. It had reached its lowest ebb. Mr Eden Baker, one of the Official Visitors for the Government Schools, wrote to the Colonial Secretary on 18 December 1866 on 'The Decline of the Head School'. He attributed the start of the decline to the period when the Head of the School had also been the Inspector of Schools, so that no real inspection of the school had been made by independent assessors. The *St Helena Guardian* of 9 January 1867 bemoaned 'the irreparable loss sustained by the rising generation from this pervertion of the most interesting and useful institution under the Government'. Recommending that in time a young active Assistant Teacher should be appointed, the editorial continued: 'We say, break up the present system which has so signally failed and make [create] the institution which it should be for the purpose of giving our youths a complete education necessary to qualify them to fill the position designed in after life.' Furthermore, the writer recommended that payments by results should be introduced. This would involve regular inspection of schools, as had been introduced into the UK.

The Governor, Admiral Sir Charles Elliott, had had enough of the saga. The *Star* newspaper reported on 26 January 1867: 'HE the Governor has taken the Head School in hand, and we are right glad of it. There is no gainsaying the fact, that for a number of years the school has been in a state of decadence ... all the time it was under lay mastership it thrived; and (we think we might safely write) all the time it was under clerical authority it decayed.' The Head School was closed pending more satisfactory arrangements regarding its leadership.

Meanwhile, forward progress continued in the other schools on the island. Mr Eden Baker summarized his view of the island's schools: 'On the whole the large number of schools and of scholars in proportion to the population shows clearly that there is neither want of the means of instruction nor of disposition to take advantage of them on the part of the people of St Helena.' However, after pointing out that much of the instruction was elementary, many of the pupils were infants, and the attendance at school was irregular, he continued: 'The chief deficiency is in means of education for children who have advanced beyond the rudiments of the school course. For the above reason, the very high numbers shown in the return do not fairly represent a corresponding high ratio of sound education at St Helena.'[25]

On 24 December 1867 one of the regular public examinations of the three Benevolent Society Schools took place in the New School Room in Napoleon Street in Jamestown, in the presence of the Governor, the Bishop, the Chief Justice, the Rector, parents and 120 scholars. The programme comprised examination both orally and in written form of the work achieved in Scripture, History, Reading, Dictation, Exhibition Writing, Arithmetic, Geography and Needlework. Interspersed with the subject examinations were the singing of hymns and songs, and the event ended with the National Anthem.

The *1867 Blue Book* omitted mention of the Head School, but otherwise its list showed a healthy attendance at other schools in Jamestown and Ruperts Bay, St Paul's area, Sandy Bay and High Peak, and at Hutts Gate, for the Longwood area. Regarding High Peak, a map of the time shows the position of a School House at High Peak, although further information about this school cannot be found, nor the site positively identified. Altogether at the island's schools there were 1,053 scholars, 593 boys and 460 girls. While the Head School building was not being used, the Benevolent Society was permitted to use it to set up a private school under the care of the Reverend Bennett.

4
Education for All:
Progress and Setbacks
1868-1903

Their fresh country faces had looks of intelligence, and the children had a great capacity for receiving instruction
Hutts Gate School, 1874[1]

1868-74: Continued Ups and Downs in Island Schools

At last, in September 1868, a gentleman by the name of Newenham Travers, an Oxford University graduate, was found to take up the post of Master of the Head School. The school buildings were received back from the Benevolent Society, new rules and regulations were created, and Mr Travers launched into the task of giving the school a new look. He even ordered some gymnastics equipment, and also started giving a series of public lectures on erudite subjects, such as 'The Wars of the Roses'. For a short while the fortunes of the school seemed to turn, possibly due in part to the calibre of the pupils of the time, who included two sons of Hudson Janisch – Noel, who came first in all subjects and later became a teacher at the Head School, and George, who later became a doctor but died at the age of 32. There were also brothers, John and Robert Pooley, two of the three sons of the Clerk at Solomon, Moss, Gideon and Co. Robert later became the US Consul on St Helena. Members of this family were related to the present, long-established Gunnell family whose records precede 1792.

It will be noted that the 'new look' given to the Head School by Mr Travers was modelled on the latest practices in the UK, so reflecting an obvious desire to copy the UK whether it was relevant in St Helena or not. Undoubtedly, this contributed to the eventual failure of the school some years later.

The *1868 Blue Book* list continued to reflect the same pattern of schools, although it is interesting to note that the Ragged School was included only in pencil, as an afterthought, in spite of the fact that it had 78 children, 34 boys and 44 girls. It was still in the charge of a member of the Rich family, Emma. Another addition from the previous year was that of the regimental schools, one at Ladder Hill with 30 pupils taught by NCO R. Arty, and one at the Town Barracks School with 20 pupils taught by an NCO from the 9th Regiment.

In 1869 another school was established in Jamestown, this time by the Church through the initiative of the Bishop. A bazaar raised £70 towards a school building, and it was named St John's School. The building still stands at the foot of Ladder Hill and its plans are displayed in the Jamestown Museum. Describing the bazaar, the *Guardian* on 8 April 1869 reported: 'That Miss Bell, the Mistress of the little School, was able to supply a stall with the needlework of her pupils is a pleasing and promising feature of the Bishop's scheme.' The article continued with an appeal for a further £35 'to all who desire the good of the poor and unfortunate people of Chinatown, to aid in carrying out the experiment of a School in connection with the English Church and completely under the control of its Clergy.'

After two years in office, Eden Baker reported again on the schools of the island. After praising the work of W. P. Thompson at the Under School, Mr Baker complimented Miss Welch at the Girls' School which had been established in 1860 – 'one of the most judicious measures ever adopted by the St Helena Government'. Ninety girls, previously not catered for, were receiving appropriate education. The only difficulty was the need for a convenient and suitable schoolroom. 'The premises at the Castle now allotted to this purpose are highly inconvenient.' There were complaints about the lack of space, the separation into two parts of the building – and the heat. His further concern was that many children were still not involved in schooling. His report continued: 'There is need for liberal support of education for the rapidly increasing coloured population, who are in extreme poverty, and have improvident habits. Children are allowed to grow up without any schooling instruction whatever, producing another generation totally reckless, vicious and uncivilised.'[2]

These were not happy times for St Helena, due to matters beyond the island's control. The opening of the Suez Canal in 1869 reduced its trade drastically. Within the space of a few months, the garrison had been reduced by 300 men, the squadron of the Royal Navy was withdrawn, the establishment for liberated Africans was abolished, and there was a significant decrease in Imperial expenditure from £67,000 to £20,000. These events had a depressing effect upon the people and their livelihood although the islanders carried on their daily lives as best they could.

A stimulus came in 1870 when, for a short while, island-born

Hudson Ralph Janisch became Acting-Governor. In 1873 he resumed the role, then became Governor from 1875 until his death in 1884. He was the first of 13 children of George William Janisch, who came to St Helena as Secretary to Sir Hudson Lowe. The Janisch family played an important part in the history of the island, not least within the education system. Two of H. R. Janisch's sons were pupils and later teachers at the Head School.

During this time the number of people participating in schooling was increasing. An additional entry appears on the *Blue Book* list of 1870 schools, this being a government-supported Sunday School at Farm Lodge. The school was led by H. Timm, had 30 pupils, 13 male and 17 female, and its purpose was to teach Elementary Religion. By 1872 it had moved premises to Crack Plain, still under the same leadership, but now supported by voluntary contributions. Its membership had risen to 48, 18 male and 30 female.

Once again, in August 1870, the Head School hit the headlines. Mr Travers, who had come to the island with such promise in 1868, resigned. The Reverend George Bennett was appointed in his place, but within a short time he too returned to the UK on sick leave. Nevertheless, the annual school examination of the pupils at the Head School which took place in the Council Chamber at the Castle in the presence of the Governor, members of Council, representatives of the parents and other interested persons, received a favourable report from the two examiners, the Lord Bishop and the Hon H. R. Janisch. They praised the appearance of the boys and the rendering of the passage selected from Xenophon. They added: 'The readiness with which solutions of equations and problems in Euclid were given proved clearly that neither the Master nor his scholars had been idle during the past year.'[3]

Then began the Pooley incident which was recorded fully in the *Governor's Despatches*.[4] On 15 August 1871 Mr Pooley, Senior, had complained to the Governor that his three sons were being deprived of schooling, since there was no teacher at the Head School. The Governor had assumed that the Deputy was taking charge at the School, but he too had left. Mr Pooley was surprised when the Governor responded immediately by asking whether his son, John, a lad of 15, who was senior boy in the school 'could not act as a monitor for that purpose for a short time until I could make some other provision?' Mr Pooley was concerned that his son might 'be unable to command the boys, but he would allow him to make the attempt if the Colonial Secretary would be good enough to be present at the school on the following morning and request the boys to be obedient'. So the 15-year-old held the fort. However, two days later the Governor received another communication from Mr Pooley objecting 'in the strongest manner' that the Governor had supplanted his son by another lad of 15 who was no further advanced than John.

Meanwhile the Hussey Charity School in Jamestown was progressing satisfactorily under the direction of Mr Marriott. This school met in the building adjacent to the Benevolent Society School. In the Report of the annual examinations in December 1871, it was claimed that the school could bear comparison with any of the other schools on the island. Tribute was paid to the fact that 'the girls and boys were neatly clad in clothes of their own making'. The fact that the singing was not very good pleased the reporter because it meant that time had not been wasted on such activity! 'No doubt it is much more agreeable to teach a clever class part singing than to go on always with the eternal grind of ABC and three times four makes twelve. But there is danger of this being carried too far and we would rather see the prizes given to little brats of five and six years old who can spell easy words than to big boys and girls who sing so sweetly and work such hard problems on their slates, but who will soon have to drive donkeys and stand over wash-tubs. In the opinion of all present, the examination of Mr Marriott's School shewed a great improvement and very careful teaching.'[5]

The *1872 St Helena Almanac and Annual Register* contained the following entry concerning the Government School Establishment:

High School	Headmaster:	—
Upper School	Master:	W. P. Thompson
	Asst Master:	J. A. Storer
Girls' School	Mistress:	Miss Elizabeth Welch
Country School	Master:	Mr W. Mitchell
	Mistress:	Mrs Mitchell

So, who now was to be Acting Head of the Head School during the absence of Mr Bennett? Various people were in line: James Storer? – no, he had offended the Governor by his rudeness; Mr Baker, the previous Assistant to Mr Bennett? – no, he had gone to South Africa; the Reverend Whitehead (Superintendent of the Benevolent Society Schools)? – no; Noel Janisch (son of the future Governor)? – yes, he was the only other qualified person whose services could be obtained. He was efficient and had previously assisted Mr Travers, who had been very pleased with him. Eventually Noel Janisch was appointed at a salary of £60, plus fees, but only seven boys attended the school, according to the *Blue Book of 1872*. Nevertheless he succeeded in giving the ill-fated Head School a little stability as Master for the seven years from 1871 to 1878 when he resigned.

Meanwhile, in the nearby Government Under School under the redoubtable W. P. Thompson, there were 154 boys. Numbers were also increasing in the Benevolent Society's Jamestown School where, by 1873, 60 boys and 20 girls were being taught by Mr and Mrs Brady, and even more in the St Paul's Country School where Mr and Mrs Storer taught 86 boys and 89 girls.

Two years of comparative stability followed in the schools on the island. The Head School, albeit with very small numbers, had an opportunity to re-establish itself under the leadership of its St Helenian Head Teacher; the close proximity of the Benevolent Society and the Hussey Charity Schools in Jamestown worked favourably for both institutions, creditable results being recorded. In 1873 the Hussey Charity School used a novel way of selecting prizewinners – in the absence of their Instructor in Tailoring and Carpentry, the class members were told to stand up and say the names of the best carpenter and the best tailor. If there was agreement the named individuals were presented with the prizes by the Governor. 'Who shall say that this is not as good a way of giving prizes as the usual one?' queried the *Guardian* reporter.[6]

The Public Library in Jamestown was also continuing satisfactorily. The Committee overseeing its progress comprised the Bishop of St Helena as chairman, with H. R. Janisch, the Reverend Bennett and Eden Baker as members; and Miss S. Scott as Librarian. Members of the public paid a subscription of £1 10s per year, and Naval Officers were allowed to use the Reading Room for a year or for a month for a donation of 7s 6d or 5s. The Public Library was a long-standing institution having been officially established in 1813 during the time of Governor Wilks – although a Public Library had existed as far back as 1783.

Two husband and wife teams, working in the same school as each other, featured in the official lists of school teachers in 1873. Mr and Mrs Storer at the Government Country School at St Pauls were receiving £100 and £20 respectively per annum, and Mr and Mrs Brady at the Jamestown Benevolent School were receiving £60 and £10 respectively. This over the years had been an often used system, and without doubt it was an economical one for the paymasters as only one house had to be provided, and usually the wife received only a bare

allowance to supplement the salary of her husband. Long-serving
W. P. Thompson still appeared in the lists as Master at both the
Government Under School on weekdays and Sundays, and also at the
Benevolent Society School in Jamestown on weekdays and Sundays!
Altogether, the school system was catering for 1,026 students, 538 girls
and 488 boys.

The arrival of a trained Army Schoolmaster in 1873 heralded the
revival of the Regimental School. The *Guardian* of 26 June reported: 'It
is some time since a regimental school was open for children. At present
there is a great deal of work for the Schoolmaster; a number of men are
unable to pass the 4th class; large numbers have passed the 4th and 3rd
classes and been promoted to Corporal; a small number have 2nd class
and been promoted to Sergeant; only two in the Garrison have 1st class
and been promoted to Staff Sergeant.' The teacher was Mr Lowry who,
with his wife, taught the 25 students, 9 male and 16 female, at Ladder
Hill.

Another of the Hussey Charity Schools, Hutts Gate, received mixed
praise from the *Guardian* reporter at its annual examination on 18 June
1874. At the 'pretty little school house', under the Mastership of the
Reverend J. C. Hands, there were 50 children, mostly girls, the majority
under 10 years old. 'Their fresh country faces had looks of intelligence,
and the children had a great capacity for receiving instruction.
However, there had been great irregularity of attendance, especially by
the boys whose parents were at fault for keeping them away to earn
money.'

1874-85: Compulsory Schooling on St Helena

The first steps towards compulsory schooling in England in 1870 no
doubt encouraged the Government of St Helena to tackle the problem
of irregular attendance. First a draft and then a final version of
Education Ordinance No 4 introduced compulsory education to St Helena.
There had for some time been considerable concern that some parents
were keeping their children, boys particularly, away from school to
earn money, and also because they could not afford the fees. The
number of children receiving schooling fluctuated from year to year,
dropping to only 1,026 in 1873. However, compulsory schooling caused
the numbers to reach a peak of 1,203 in 1874, but they fell away to
1,147 by 1877.

The introduction of compulsory education caused much discussion
on St Helena, echoing the controversy in England between compulsion
and 'the voluntary principle'. Under the terms of the Ordinance,

signed by Hudson R. Janisch, there was to be compulsory elementary education in Reading, Writing and Arithmetic for all 9- to 12-year-olds. For children over 10, there could be partial exemption from attendance on a maximum of two days in the week. The times of attendance were laid down; religious instruction was not to be compulsory; and, in the case of poverty, there was to be provision of fees. A Board of Education was to be formed (its members nominated by the Governor), and could appoint an officer to help to implement the ordinance. The schedule of schools to which the ordinance was to apply included all Government Day Schools, the Benevolent Society Day School, the Hussey Charity Day School, St John's Day School and the Baptist Mission Day Schools. An examination was to be conducted in the three Rs.

An irate parent wrote to the *Guardian*: 'Is it reasonable to suppose that the inhabitants would calmly allow the Government to take out of their hands the management and regulation of those schools which are supported totally independent of Government aid?' Objecting further to the fact that the Board members were to be nominated by the Governor with no reference to any qualification, the parent concluded: 'The objects of the Draft are excellent, but the scheme for carrying it out is bad.'[7]

A leading article in the *Guardian* took up the subject of Compulsory Education: 'Voluntary is best, and by sending their children to school the people of St Helena have filled all the Schools in Schedule A, and several others to overcrowding the buildings, and to overworking the masters and mistresses. Our schools are full. If more must be instructed, more school buildings, more schoolmasters and school-mistresses, school books, and school materials must be provided. Our present Government is so poor ... the whole thing has the air of a sham.'[8]

During this controversy, the Garrison schools on St Helena were not experiencing the same level of problems with regard to attendance. Considerable importance was put upon educating the troops during their period of service, wherever they were stationed. In 1874 an average on St Helena of 22 out of the 27 adult students were attending regularly, there was no absenteeism among the nine grown children, 12 of the 13 infants over four years of age were attending regularly and, at the Sewing School, an average attendance of 16 out of the 19 grown girls and infants over four years of age was being achieved. The numbers of students at the Garrison schools clearly fluctuated over the years, according to the size of the companies stationed on the island. Each year the number of volumes kept in the Garrison Library was maintained at around 800 books, while more than 4,000 volumes were issued annually to the troops on St Helena.[9]

Regarding school buildings, a map dated 1880 shows that a house at the back of the lower Jamestown gardens, known as the Garden House, later to become a museum and now occupied by Mr Fred Ward, was a school at that time, but records cannot be traced as to which school it was. It can be speculated that the Jamestown Girls' School, established in 1860 and accommodated at the Castle, may have been the occupants. The same map also substantiates that the Head School, the Hussey Charity Town School and the Benevolent Society Town School were all in Napoleon Street, and a further school, possibly the Government Under School, was now occupying the former St John's School building at the foot of Ladder Hill.[10]

Exhaustive but generally abortive attempts were made by the Board of Education to enforce compulsory education. Briefly there was better news of the Head School from 1871 to 1878 during the Mastership of Noel Janisch, but its decline was inevitable as it was not catering for the needs of the island. There was some stability within the ranks of the

Jamestown, 1890. From the Graphic, *15 November 1890. The Old Boys' School is seen in the foreground beyond St John's Church. St John's School occupied the small building behind the church*

island's teachers, but what was going to happen to the Head School? The *Education Ordinance of 1874* was destined to provide a real challenge to those responsible for implementing its regulations, and there followed a period of three years in which strenuous efforts were made by the hard-working Board of Education to do so. The Board included the Chief Justice in the chair, with James Homagee occasionally substituting for him. As a start, at their first meeting in July 1875, they appointed an Attendance Officer, Sergeant Harrison, who was also the Chief of Police. Within two weeks he brought 20 children and their parents to the meeting of the Board, saying that the children all wished to be able to go to school to learn to read and write. They were told that as soon as the schools were ready to receive the children, the parents would be informed. Then the trouble began. Noel Janisch, Master of the Head School, was informed that he would be receiving 20/30 scholars from the Under School. W. P. Thompson from the Under School was instructed to send the 20/30 of his pupils to the Head School and to be ready to receive new children in their place, in accordance with the ordinance. At the same time, the three Mistresses in charge of the Government Girls School, the Ragged School and the Baptist Mission School were asked to receive extra pupils. As these 'suggestions' were strongly resisted, James Homagee as Acting Chairman approached the Benevolent Society and the Hussey Charity Schools to ask if they would receive additional pupils. However, all these efforts were fruitless so an emergency meeting of the Board of Education in December 1875 directed Sergeant Harrison to send the children to the Government schools. Lists of the names of children sent to the schools were presented to the Board, who instructed that no coercive proceedings were at present to be instituted!

But a note from Miss Welch, the Mistress of the Government Girls School, written to the Board and minuted on 9 March 1876, stated that: 'Elizabeth Stevens is dirty, and because the home and character of her parents are not reputable, she refused her admittance into school among her other scholars accordingly. The other children named in the notes were likewise said to be filthy and they were refused admittance.' Using another approach, the Board prosecuted two parents for failing to send their children to school. The plea was that at the time the children had no clothes to wear to school.

As small comfort, one school at least seemed to have no major problems. The school at Half Tree Hollow was flourishing under Edward Short. A report for the Board of Education on 4 September 1876 commended the school, recently established under the auspices of the Hussey Charity Foundation, for meeting 'a long-felt want'; already it had 52 pupils.

Ironically, while the Board of Education was unsuccessful in enforcing compulsory education, there was an increasing demand for education – but it was for evening school provision for those who had to work through the day or who lived in the remoter parts of the island. In 1877 such a demand was presented to the Governor by the Education Committee on behalf of the Longwood area. A later report in the *Guardian* of 14 October 1886 referred to the 'recently-opened' Night School in Longwood, which was appreciated by the labourers and families of that district 'for whose special benefit it was opened'. Whether this school was a continuation of the earlier evening school or a new establishment is not certain, but either way some education was being made available in Longwood at last. An attempt by the Hussey Charity to establish a day school at Longwood under the leadership of Canon Hands in the late 1870s failed, the Trustees deciding on 23 January 1880 that his services would be dispensed with as 'the school was unhappily a failure in his hands'. So there was still no day school in this area and those children who were keen enough were destined for many years to continue to walk to the all-age school at Hutts Gate.

Meanwhile a further series of incidents militated against the desperate efforts of the Board to achieve compulsory education for all in the years following the Ordinance. The Benevolent Society and the Hussey Charity both resisted taking on extra pupils because they were not being paid for by the Government. To add to the problems, the Baptist Mission Day School closed and became a Sunday School only. The Ragged School building became unsafe and the schoolmistress informed Sergeant Harrison that she had 80 scholars, 'which was quite as many as the room should contain'.[11]

Assessing his achievements to date on 6 September 1877, a weary Sergeant Harrison reported that since the Board had been established an extra 56 children had attended school, 13 were now over age and two had left the island. Had it not been for his continued reminding, they would be running wild. Pointing out that 'the whole matter costs much time and trouble', he asked the Board to allow him some remuneration: he had been unpaid up to then. But his subsequent report of 7 March 1878 said that attendance at schools was anything but satisfactory, 29 pupils being regular, 7 irregular and 6 absent, while 16 had left. £12 was awarded to Sergeant Harrison.

In desperation, three months later, George Moss, the Chairman of the Board, signed the following: 'Resolved that this Committee after reviewing the last three years' labor considers the result is unsatisfactory and by this Resolution may be brought to the notice of His Excellency The Governor in order that he may devote some better plan or a discontinuance of the meeting of the Committee for the future.'[12]

The Head School had experienced a little more stability during the seven years of leadership of Noel Janisch, and there were 31 boys on the roll in 1877. It had a change of Master in 1878 when Mr Janisch resigned and the Reverend Joseph Lambert took over, and the numbers rose to 37 boys in 1879. Many years before, in 1861, Mr Lambert had been Under Master at the School, but since then had been away from St Helena teaching in India.

However, then began a drastic decline in the numbers in the Head School. By 1884 it had only 11 pupils. The rumour was going round that 'there will soon be certain changes in the Public Schools in Town'.[13] Other people also voiced their opinions about what schools on St Helena should be doing, including the brother of Benjamin Grant, the Printer, who had returned to the USA after a visit to St Helena. Signing himself F.E.G., he wrote a letter to the *Guardian* expressing the view that 'It seems to me that the boys might learn something about gardening at the Hussey School and might get considerable practice growing cuttings, and raising trees from seed to transplant on the naked hillsides. I am sure it would be useful both physically and morally to the boys, besides doing a too long neglected act of justice to the naked hills'. He also suggested that barbed wire should be used 'to keep boys and goats from doing mischief'.[14]

The Government at last decided that the Head School was no longer fulfilling its purpose. The Reverend Lambert was given a pension of £60. Throughout its comparatively short lifespan of eight decades, the Head School had been dogged by problems – particularly related to frequently changing leadership and to the inappropriateness of its offerings to the people of St Helena. On 31 December 1884 it closed its doors for the last time.

In spite of the traumas experienced in trying to implement the ordinance, there was a continuity of teachers in the schools over the ensuing years. Names such as Storer, Lambert, Thompson, Welch, Brady, Barker, Marriott, Sefton, Scott, Harris and Torbett persist from year to year through the early 1880s. Coincidentally with the closure of the Head School in 1884 came, at last, the retirement of W. P. Thompson, the Master of the Government Under School. He had given 50 years of service to the schools, from the early days when, with his school-teacher father, he weathered the storm of the reorganization of schools in the transition from Company to Crown control in 1834. Predictably, on the closure of the Head School, the schooling system needed some reorganization. For the time being the Under School retained its name and the 118 pupils (all boys) had a new Master, A. S. Brady. The Government Girls' School continued under the leadership of Miss Elizabeth Welch, with over 100 pupils and Miss Georgina Burchell took over Mr Brady's role at the Jamestown Benevolent Weekday and Sunday School. Miss Burchell was almost certainly one of the daughters of George Davenport Burchill (variably spelt Burchell).

1885-1900: Efforts Towards Equal Opportunity

The list of schools from 1884 to 1886, as recorded in the *Blue Books*, remained the same. However by 1887 the Under School and the Infants' and Girls' School were no longer mentioned and instead the names of the Government Boys' School and the Government Girls' School were included for the first time. Mr Brady retained his headship, now of the Boys' School, while Miss Welch retired and Miss Emily L. Warren was appointed to the headship of the Girls' School. Both of her parents were school teachers and she was well acquainted with children, being the fourth child of a family of 14. She had been recruited in the UK under a three year contract to the Colonial Government. She played a full part in the life of the island including organizing many concerts and entertainments, in aid of local charities. While in England for several months, she learned lacemaking and on her return to St Helena encouraged the girls to take up lacemaking and the boys to make bobbins for them – so reviving a skill which had been taught in Mrs Clara George's Preparatory School in Jamestown in the 1820s, and leading to the establishment of a flourishing Lace School a few years later. After the end of her contract she married Thomas Jackson, a chemist and a widower from Jamestown and, as E. L. Jackson, she became the author of the book *St Helena: The Historic Island*.[15]

The mainstream of education of the island continued without any major upheavals for the next decade. Accordingly, when the Governor was required to send his *1887 Blue Book* returns to the Colonial Office, they looked like this:

School	Source of Finance	No of Pupils	Fees	Expend
Town Boys' School	Govt £100	93 boys	£13	£108
Town Girls' School	Govt £92	66girls	£8 10 5	£100
Country School	Govt £120	61b/47g	£12 19 9	£152
Benevolent Society Town School	Vol £50	22b/46g	—	£50
Benevolent Society Country School	Vol £50	26b/42g	—	£50
Jamestown Infants School	Govt £27	26b/25g	—	£27
Hussey Charity Town School	Vol £102	38b/29g	—	£102
Hussey Charity Night School	Vol £30	32b/11b	—	£30
Hussey Charity Longwood	Vol £50	16b/31g	—	£50
Hussey Charity Half Tree Hollow	Vol £60	38b/53g	—	£60
Baptist		40b/60g	—	
Military, Ladder Hill		8m/10w (Adults only)		

Altogether there were 820 students in the eleven schools listed above, excluding the Military School, the Hussey Charity Night School and also any private schools.

Annual Treat Days had become a tradition. In 1887, after describing the great enjoyment of 70 Sandy Bay children in the various games and amusements, a correspondent to the *Guardian* reported 'how quickly baskets of plum cake and the quantity of tea disappeared, trays of bread and butter, jam and honey, and other sweets' – thanks to the generosity of Mr Morrice, an island benefactor.[16]

The Report in the *1888 Blue Book* gave a highly satisfactory report on each of the Government Schools, except for the Infants School 'which had fallen to a low ebb during the control of Miss Welch (now pensioned) and to a still lower ebb during the interregnum which occurred before the arrival of Miss Warren from England'. However, high praise was now given to the Town Girls' School in which the progress was most marked. 'The present educational standards would not compare unfavourably with English elementary schools.' During 1888 Miss Warren sought permission to depart from the terms of her agreement but this was not granted and her resignation was accepted.

On 23 October 1889 Miss Eleanor Short from the UK was appointed to the vacancy. This began a long teaching career on St Helena during which the school for which she was Head Teacher in Jamestown changed in 1905 from being the Girls' School to the Junior Town Mixed School. In 1910 she became Mistress of the Government Mixed

School, while A. S. Brady was Master, both under the Superintendent of Education, Mr Leslie Tucker. When Mr Tucker enlisted during the First World War she also held the position of Acting Superintendent, holding this post until her retirement in 1921. Periodically international events made their mark on the island, such as the arrival in February 1890 of the 18-year-old Zulu Prince Dinizulu and his two uncles, Undabuko and Tshingane. We read that, while on the island, Dinizulu was 'instructed willingly'; his teacher was the Reverend F. H. Baker, the Inspector of Schools.[17] The island was once again put on the map, just as with Napoleon, and in some way this had the effect of revitalizing the people and making them more aware of their place in the world.

Over the years education was growing more important in the minds of the islanders and topics of educational interest attracted people's attention. On 13 March 1890 the Editor of the *Guardian* mused: 'What class of men know the most? So vast has the sum of knowledge now become, that it is perfectly safe to say no single intellect, however brilliant, could possibly grasp more than relative little of the whole.' Taking a sideways sling at the relevance of the school curriculum, he continued: 'Perhaps of mere elementary knowledge, schoolmasters and mistresses have a wider retention than any other class, because it often happens that, outside them, much of the materials which formed the groundwork of education is wholly forgotten in later and profounder years.'

The St Helena Census of 1890 gave the total population of the island as 5,059, 2,573 male and 2,486 female. Of these there were 819 scholars in the island's schools as follows:

	Male	Female	Total
Government Schools	173	155	328
Benevolent Society Schools	70	59	129
Baptist Mission School	44	64	108
Others	150	104	254
Totals	437	382	819

But many of the people, including teachers, had other things on their minds. On the whole, the 1890s were sad years for the island, and a number of its people began to look elsewhere for a better life. The island was no longer the prosperous place it used to be, where ships called in regularly for provisions. In 1891 the *Annual Report on Education* from the Governor reported: 'The results of the examinations were, on the whole, hardly up to those of previous year, but in some of the schools many of the senior pupils had gone out into the world, leaving the upper standards in a somewhat skeleton condition.' The school population was only 819, out of a total population of 3,877, which itself had decreased by 634 since 1881. 'This decrease is due entirely to emigration.' The general malaise seemed to influence most aspects of the island's life, including education. Nevertheless, Governor Grey-Wilson had praise for the work of the two Inspectors of Schools, the Reverend F.H.Baker, son of the former Visitor of Schools, Eden Baker, and the Reverend S.J.Ellis, although he was concerned that different methods should be used by teachers and urged: 'How best to diminish the quantity of parrot-lore and develope (*sic*) that of deduced and applied knowledge is a question I cannot too earnestly press upon the attention of school teachers.'[18] This was another example of a contemporary educational theme in the UK being followed on the island. Similarly St Helena echoed the increased interest at the turn of the century in improving children's health, diet and nutrition, and the *Guardian* urged that 'in one of the many empty houses in Jamestown', a St Helena Cooking School should be established which would be 'of practical and professional domestic value'.[19] No further news of this venture appeared.

The writer of an article in the journal *Greater Britain* of September 1892 captured some of the desolation of the island: 'Greater Britain is so vast, widespread and comprehensive that it is little to be wondered at that those Imperial Officials who look after the outlying possessions of Her Majesty should occasionally, and temporarily, overlook the very existence of an island or two. Nothing is more galling to the loyal Colonist, proud of his British Citizenship, than this. To be flouted, yet borne in mind, would be almost flattery. To be forgotten is grievous.'

R.A.Sterndale, Acting Governor in 1895 and Governor in 1901, produced a document entitled: *Sancta Helena: An Island in Extremis: By one who knew her in her prosperity.* After describing the devastating effect on the island of the opening of the Suez Canal in 1869, causing St Helena to be 'the key of the world' as a port of call for ships, Mr Sterndale said: 'The question now is, what is to be done? ... whilst we are thinking and talking, the pressure of poverty is driving out all the young and able-bodied men to seek their fortunes in other lands. The population is dwindling ...'[20] In his subsequent report to both Houses of Parliament in 1898, after listing the schools – four Government, four charitable, one military, and a Baptist Sunday School – he wrote: 'In none of the schools can more than a good plain English education be imparted, and a good high class school is much wanted. There are no technical schools as yet. In the four schools of the Hussey Charity there is a carpenters' class, and the gardener at Government House Plantation has a class of boys learning horticulture.'

Those responsible for education were keen to effect some changes in the system, it being well over 20 years since the Education Ordinance of 1874 had been introduced. An early Draft of a new Ordinance was produced in July 1896, a major thrust of which was for education to be free on the island, since it was difficult to enforce compulsory attendance at school if parents had to pay. At the same time, indicating that school would only be valued if it were offering its customers a suitable programme, Charles Grant, the Editor of the *St Helena Guardian*, said in his leading article: 'A good plain education is necessary for all our children; not such an education as would unfit them for the state of life to what they are probably called to fulfil – talent always comes to the surface and finds its value.'[21]

A draft form of the Education Ordinance was submitted in the *Governor's Despatches* to the Secretary of State for the Colonies on 15 March 1897, putting forward the proposal that 'The contemplated increase of the Garrison and the consequent large increase of the revenue should render it possible at an early date to extend to St Helena the benefits of free education'.[22] It also requested payment for the Inspectors of Schools of £24 each, as previously they had received no payment.

When no reply had been received over two years later, the Secretary of State was approached again through the Governor's Despatches on 4 September 1899. An answer was urgently required from him: 'Since the increase of the Garrison has rendered labour more difficult to obtain, children of tender age are often employed when they should be receiving tuition in the Schools. Section 7 of this Ordinance is one which is needed to check this practice.'[23]

The turn of the century came – and still the island awaited the reply from the Secretary of State concerning the Draft Ordinance. Perhaps he was too busy on other matters and overlooking the existence of an island or two?

1900-2: Schooling for Islanders – and Boer Prisoners
The new century opened with 746 pupils attending the eleven schools on the official lists. These included four government schools and seven private schools, the latter sponsored by the Benevolent Society, Hussey

Charity or the Church. Although the 1874 Education Ordinance made schooling compulsory, the authorities were still experiencing seemingly insuperable problems in achieving full attendance. Fees were charged at the rate of one penny each week which provided some with an excuse. Some parents considered that their children were more usefully employed at home, so, in spite of all the coercion from the attendance officer the situation remained unsatisfactory. The editor of the *St Helena Parish Magazine* tried encouragement: 'Let those who have the guardianship of the children not grudge them the time that should be devoted to learning. May they forbear to defraud their children by keeping them from school.'[24] But even this did not carry much weight.

The Benevolent Society decided to tackle the problems, and to launch the new century with a set of new rules for their schools. In a comprehensive document, agreed at their Committee meeting on 1 May 1900, they tightened up regulations concerning punctuality and attendance for the five- to 15-year-old children, charging one penny per week per child, and extra for those parents who, according to the poor lists, were receiving more than £200 per year. The subjects to be taught were Divinity, Reading, Writing, Dictation, Arithmetic, Mental Arithmetic, History, Geography, Singing, Grammar, Composition, Recitation and, for the girls, Needlework and Knitting, and for the boys Craftwork. The work to be achieved and examined at Standards I, II and III was clearly written down. Religious Instruction was to be included for all children, except for those whose parents who made a special case for exemption to the Committee; each day was to begin and end with prayers, and every child was required to attend for an hour each Sunday afternoon. After detailing rules on expulsion and punishment, the regulations reminded the teachers that the school was to be used only for educational purposes and that there would be regular inspections.

The authorities were hampered in their work because they still awaited the elusive response from the Secretary of State, to approve the Draft Ordinance which had been first sent to him in 1897. The major features of the Draft, namely the introducing of regulations concerning the employment of young people of school age and the employment of a paid attendance officer, would no doubt help to improve the poor school attendance.

In general, however, morale on the island had lifted, as a result of the presence of the Boer prisoners. At least the island was being noticed and needed, and the existence of the prisoners created employment for many of the local people. The official Census of 1901 recorded the number of prisoners as 4,655, and by the next year it was well over 5,500, virtually doubling the island's population. In his annual report sent with the *1900 Blue Book* to Joseph Chamberlain, the Secretary of State for the Colonies, Governor Sterndale stated: 'The year has been an exceptional one in the history of the island since the days of Napoleon.' The Customs Revenue had reached a new high, due to the large consumption of dutiable imports, these having almost doubled within the year to a record £168,282. The major adverse effect of the boom in employment was that the number of children in school decreased from 793 to 742 'owing to the great demand for labour and the comparatively high wages given to mere children'. While on the island the prisoners created for themselves various support systems, including schools. They were given encouragement in work of all kinds, including being allowed to have aloe poles and fir tree cuttings 'for the construction of recreation and school houses'.

The Boer schools, together with other activities organized by the prisoners, are described in *De Krijgsgevangene*, the newspaper which they produced. On 3 August 1901 the following article appeared:

Kampeschoole: This school was opened on 28 July 1900 by two gentlemen, Maartens and Te Boekhorst. Together they form the School Commission. 400 persons of all ages came to the School wanting all kinds of learning. There was no other equipment than 30 slates and about 100 slate pencils. Now, though, because of the good care of Cape Town people, and especially from Dutch friends, there is plenty of everything, and I am still receiving things. The education at this moment ranges from Standard I to Standard VI in all main subjects, as indicated in the Z.A.R. (South African Republic) and the rules in the school guidelines. (Translated, with permission of the St Helena Chief of Police, by a Dutchman held in St Helena Prison in 1991.)

By July 1901 there were 137 new students coming to the school and four new classes were being created because the existing classes were already full:

Each week they receive three periods of schooling, each of 2 hours duration, others 4 hours. The school buildings are three in number, one tent from the British Authorities and two houses built from funds given by the gentleman, De Witt Hamer. The teachers at present are Messrs Te Boekhorst, Kat, Naude, Scholkmeyer, Webb, Bosman, Vermooten, De Villiers, Bester, Fourie and Swanepoel. Except for De Villiers, they are all from the O.V.S. (Orange Free State). Qualified teachers are from the Z.A.R.[25]

Each half-year an inspection took place, at the beginning of January and the end of June. An Industrial School was also set up by and for the prisoners. In June 1901 it was reported:

For some time, the plan has existed to fund the start of an industrial school – a handicraft school ... The gentleman, S Hite, has been made supervisor, and 12 young men can be taken as students. The plan exists to make the school self-supporting and then the number of students can be increased. The choice of students will be – first poor people in need of money, and then those who wish to learn the craft of wood carving.[26]

Canon Alfred Porter arrived in 1900. Throughout his subsequent 21 years on St Helena, he maintained a strong interest in the schools and their needs and achievements and became a good friend to education. He was an active member of the Benevolent Society Committee and the Hussey Charity Trustees and, in this capacity, carried out periodic inspections of schools and maintained an influential voice on the subject of education. In a supplement to his *St Helena Parish Magazine* of March 1901, he reported the annual prizegiving event for 1900. He regretted that, in spite of the abundance of elementary schools on the island there were still many boys and girls who lived in complete ignorance, unable to read or write, and whose parents kept them from daily attendance – 'robbing them of this precious time and defrauding them of the benefit'. At the other end of the scale, he put forward the idea of a more advanced school or class for those who needed it. The prizewinners included several who were destined to become the future teachers:

Government Town School (Boys):	Class V: W. Corker
Government Town School (Girls):	Class I: Eliza Smith
	Class V: Eva Fagan
Country School:	Class IV: Vida Evans

Another prize winner in Sandy Bay, Class I, proudly held the name of Julia Caesar.

The *1901 Blue Book* reported that there was a total of 614 pupils attending the nine island schools, including the four government schools – the Town Boys, Town Girls, and the Infant and Country Mixed; the three Hussey Charity schools – the Town Mixed, Half Tree Hollow, and Hutts Gate; and two Benevolent Society schools – the Town Mixed and Sandy Bay. In addition there were 105 pupils attending the Baptist Mission Sunday School.

In an article in July 1901 entitled: 'Wanted: Compulsory Education', the editor of the *St Helena Parish Magazine* commented that it was lamentable that of those people who came to sign the Marriage Register, only half could spell their names, and only two-thirds could write them. 'It is time that the law should step in and enforce the English system of compulsory attendance.'

Nevertheless there continued to be successes at the island schools and the list of prizewinners reported in the *St Helena Parish Magazine* of December 1901 included some more future teachers:

Government Boys' School: Class V: J.LeBreton
  Prize: *Fifth Form at St Dominics*
Government Girls' School: Infants: Mildred Smith
  Prize: *Red Riding Hood*
Hussey Charity School, Half Tree Hollow: Class III:
  E Constantine, Prize: *The Pedlar and His Dog*
Benevolent Society School: Class IV: Maurice Young
  Prize: *Own Story Book*

The Hussey Charity School at Hutts Gate experienced difficulties in 1902. Miss Broadway, the Head Teacher, indicated her intention to leave. In June 1902 the *St Helena Parish Magazine* sympathized with her: 'Situated in the teeth of the southern blasts, the School in the winter season is no desirable place to work in. It is, however, the worry of the work, combined with the loneliness of the teacher in an isolated spot that adds to the difficulty of it. Teaching itself is not unpleasant work. It is when there is no sympathy with the teacher and parents taking sides with their children that work becomes drudgery and feels all lost labour.' A little later, the *Guardian* paid tribute to 'the late much respected lady-teacher who had so faithfully discharged her duties during twelve years'.[27] In the subsequent absence of a teacher the school had to close temporarily and in fact was not re-opened until 1904, when it acquired 70 children, 33 boys and 37 girls.

In the same article the *Guardian* editor congratulated the Hussey Charity Trustees on securing 'the invaluable services of a college-trained and conscientious clerical gentleman as Master of the [Hussey Charity] Town Day School' – Mr Gibbons, who was already on the island. 'We wish the energetic and talented young minister every possible success – we know he will try to deserve it.' Frequently outspoken, the editor continued, 'As a rule the public schools in St Helena are of prehistoric order as regards methods, and sadly need more active supervision and up-to-date technique.'

Throughout 1902 there was still no response from the Secretary of State about the Draft Ordinance, in spite of all the efforts of the island to elicit one and the many reports that something needed to be done urgently to enforce the attendance laws. In his *Despatches* submitted to the Secretary of State on 29 April 1902, the Governor wrote: 'How much could be accomplished if the draft Education Ordinance now before you were sanctioned.' He reminded the Secretary that it was first sent on 15 May 1897, a reminder was sent on 4 September 1899, a further reminder on 8 February 1900, and yet another on 16 December 1901, adding that 'here is another copy lest the first one has been mislaid'. He reported further: 'There is not a competent Schoolmaster in the island, the idea seems to have been that anyone was capable of teaching the young and some of those employed can hardly write an ordinary letter.'[28]

1902-3: Island Action

In June 1902, in his capacity as Inspector of Government Schools, Canon Porter submitted a comprehensive *Education Report* to the Government. He clarified the position of the three Hussey Charity schools in Jamestown, Half Tree Hollow and Longwood. They were entirely supported by the Charity 'for the education of natives – those born on the island, of any nationality except European'. The latter could attend the schools if there was room. However, at all the schools the same curriculum was followed, including reading, writing, dictation, geography, English history and plain needlework for the girls, gardening for the country boys. He expressed concern that 'the poorer population consists mainly of coloured people who are scarcely, as yet, sufficiently appreciative of the benefits of education, and therefore there is a somewhat serious irregularity of attendance'. He felt this difficulty was gradually being overcome, although the two attendance officers had a difficult task because of the widely scattered population. Of the teachers, he reported that 'they are necessarily untrained as they are drawn from the inhabitants. His Excellency is desirous, should a suitable vacancy occur, of procuring a trained teacher from England, part of whose duty it shall be to instruct the teachers who need help in the art and science of teaching.' He regretted that there was still no provision for secondary or higher education, and he reported that a school was provided by the Military Authorities for the children of the Garrison.

Regarding the elusive Education Ordinance, the island Council took action into its own hands on 17 January 1903. The members approved for themselves an Education Ordinance in order to meet the present requirements that had not existed when the 1874 Ordinance came into force. They decided that an Attendance Officer was to be appointed at a salary of £24 p.a., in order 'to secure the services of a capable and efficient officer as the nature of the Country over which he will have to travel is difficult and the area extensive'. The new Governor, Lieut Col H. L. Gallwey, an enthusiast on education, stressed that it would be necessary to introduce regulations which would prevent the employment of children under 14, such as assisting with unloading at the wharf when a ship came into port.[29]

A hard-hitting *Report on the State of Education* to the former Governor of St Helena, now in the UK, from the Bishop of St Helena lent weight to argument for urgent action. The Bishop had formerly been a member of the London School Board and had also been connected with education in South Africa. Governor Gallwey, referring to it in his *Despatches* of 27 February 1903, wrote: 'The Report speaks for itself and it behoves the Government to grant greater facilities than it does at present towards educating the children in this Colony. The question of education is a primary one and is of vital interest to the Islanders. I have already inspected some of the schools and was most disappointed at what I saw – not only in the qualifications of the Masters and Mistresses and their methods of teaching, but also in the dilapidated state of the school buildings, and in the want of classrooms. Something must be done to remedy the present state of affairs.' He estimated that an additional £381 needed to be expended yearly on education. He was contemplating levying an annual school rate of 3d in the £; he asked for £25 for the passage of a trained teacher from England; and he requested to be allowed to start the new organization from 1 July 1903.[30]

In addition Governor Gallwey was concerned about the inefficiency of the education system: 'A large number of St Helenians wished to emigrate to South Africa, but most of them were unable to do so, since they could neither read nor write, two essential qualifications for immigration to Cape Colony.'[31]

A major difficulty for the Governor was how to pay for the suggested improvements. He decided to call together a mass meeting of ratepayers to discuss the idea of an education rate being levied. The purpose of this was described by the editor of the *St Helena Guardian* on 10 September 1903 with a measure of scepticism:

We understand it is the intention of the Government to secure the service of a man who can give the youth of St Helena a higher class of education than the present simple elementary one received in the schools: and in order to help the Colony to meet the expense, 3d in the £ annually will be levied on all rateable property. The need of a higher school in St Helena has often been commented on by us, for since the departure of the Reverend Lambert, Master of the Head School, from the island there have been no public and very few private opportunities for having young men and women taught the higher branches of education. The idea of the Government, we understand, is to have a man who will periodically examine the scholars in the under schools, and admit such as are fit to a higher school of which he will be Master, where they will receive an education that will the better enable them to compete with those who in other countries are more favoured in this respect. But – will the ratepayers take kindly to this?

The meeting was called and reported fully in the *Guardian*. Governor Gallwey explained the need for more money to help to implement the anticipated Education Ordinance, the annual cost of education rising from the previous £559 to £980. He reminded them that parents had previously been paying 4s 6d per child per year for schooling, and he appealed to everyone to put the needs of the community first. His scheme, which had already been discussed by the Education Board, was to appoint an experienced head teacher from England to take charge of the Government Boys' School and to train teachers for the other schools. He would reopen Hutts Gate School; take over the one Benevolent Society School; raise teachers' pay; and bring in better equipment, including books and materials. A fee of 1d per week would still be charged per child, as this brought in £42, and the proposed 3d rate would raise a further £115 10s 0d.

The scheme was then discussed in Council and the public were given a month to comment. But the idea did not receive a warm welcome, as the *St Helena Guardian* reported on 24 September 1903: 'The scheme as set forth by His Excellency the Governor in his letter to the Ratepayers is somewhat different to what we understood it was, and though an excellent one in its way, does not appear to meet with the sympathies of the Ratepaying Community ... the new scheme seems to have alarmed them lest a new man be got at the expense of one or more of their fellow inhabitants.' This was an understandable yet common reaction to people employed from overseas, not least because of islanders' mixed experiences of UK personnel.

However, a compromise was agreed, the meeting accepting an alternative proposal made by the Chairman, W.A.Thorpe, which would 'greatly reduce the additional expenditure as suggested in the Governor's Scheme'. A schoolmaster was to be sent for to resuscitate the Head School which had been closed since 1884; he was also to be Inspector of Schools, and trainer of teachers; the Head School should take pupils who wished to stay for an additional two years for continuing instruction; and the fees for children at the Head School would be 5/- per month; no grants were to be given to the Benevolent Society or Hussey Charity Schools; and no additional pay to present holders of office in the Education Department.

Accordingly, in October, still in the absence of a reply concerning the

Draft Ordinance, Governor Gallwey issued a firm statement in his *Despatches* to the Secretary of State that he wished to bring the Ordinance into operation on 1 January 1904, and that he required an experienced head teacher to be sent out to the Colony to take charge of the Government Town School and to train teachers for the other schools.

This time – at last – his voice was heard. On 1 January 1904, the *1903 Elementary Education Ordinance No 11* came into effect. It embraced the earlier Ordinance of 1903 and its terms included 'It shall be the duty of every parent to provide Elementary Education in Reading, Writing and Arithmetic for his children; and for that purpose the parent of every child not being less than 6 or more than 14 years of age shall cause such child to attend School unless there shall be a reasonable excuse for non-attendance'. These excuses could be for illness, for alternative efficient instruction, or if there was no school open within two miles which the child could attend. Parents could withdraw their children from Religious Instruction or observance. Attendance was required every weekday, but not on Sundays or prescribed holidays. Employment of children under 13 was forbidden. Employment of children from 13 to 14 could be authorized under certain conditions. A Board of Education was to be set up, nominated and appointed by the Governor, to superintend the execution of the Ordinance, and the Board in turn could appoint officers to enforce it. The Board would prescribe fees; and also the duties of officers, including those of a Superintendent of Education, but the latter would be appointed by the Governor. The Ordinance was to apply to all schools – whether maintained by Government, the Benevolent Society or the Hussey Charity.

At last, it appeared that education would be established on a firm footing for all children on the island.

5
Into the Twentieth Century
1904-41

We venture to say that some children in our schools will compete with others in far distant countries.
St Helena Guardian, 1907[1]

1904-07: Island Education Enters a New Era

With the implementation of the long-awaited *Education Ordinance 1903*, education was moving into the twentieth century on a sound basis. A number of key figures who were to play an important part in the work of the schools now came on to the scene. For some people on the island, these educationalists are within living memory, and some valuable personal recollections are available.

James Robert Sim was born in 1879 and became headmaster of the Half Tree Hollow School in 1903 'when the girls were as big as he was'. Recalling her schooldays, former Matron of Jamestown Hospital, Grace Sim, talked about being a pupil of her headmaster father. 'I and my sister and four brothers owe everything to my father. In school he was our teacher, and after school he would talk with us and tell us about other countries and people.' Grace now lives in the house which was the original Half Tree Hollow School. The house had not been built as a school and, in fact, was originally a brewery. It holds a commanding position, immediately above the 'new' school which is now the Half Tree Hollow First School. A school in Half Tree Hollow had been mentioned in records since the 1860s.

The old schoolrooms in Halfway House are still in existence, the largest room being where the main lessons took place, one small front room being where the older girls would teach the Standard 3 girls for needlework and other similar skills, and one small back room for the infants. James Sim was the only teacher and so controlled all three rooms.

Ancestors of James Sim had come to the island after the Plague and the Great Fire of London, together with members of the Bagley,

Half Tree Hollow School: the original building for the school

Greentree and Knipe families. Describing her father, Grace said: 'My father was dark-skinned, a St Helenian with some Scottish blood. He was never bad-tempered and had the patience of Job with us. At playtime he had fun with us.' As a pupil himself, he had been at the Government Boys' School under the headship of Mr Brady. When James entered the teaching profession he had had no training. As a teacher he was very strict; he did not give any extra favours to his own family in the classroom and they suffered the same punishments as anyone else. Even when dealing with as many as 120 children he had particular empathy with children with a physical disability, and Grace recalls his anger when other children teased a girl with deformed feet by calling her 'twisty feet'.

The pupils were grouped into Infants, and Standards 1 to 6. The top two standards both included senior and junior children, according to ability. Senior pupils who were capable of doing so were expected to assist with the teaching, and at the age of 13-plus Grace found herself teaching too. Her father did not tell her what to teach, so she modelled her teaching on how her father had taught her. The advice she remembers was 'make what you teach your own'. Subsequently, three of his sons, James, Walter and Douglas, entered teaching, but transferred later to other posts. However, five of their descendants also became teachers.

James Sim had several interests and was active as Bishop's Warden and in the Church Lads' Brigade. He was a member of the Rifle Club and also played cricket and football. He became a member of the island's Council.[2] After his retirement in 1943, he continued his service to education as the representative of the local Trustees of the Benevolent Society on the Board of Education.[3] He died in May 1958, and the epitaph on his grave was: 'A Life dedicated to the Welfare of the People of his Island Home'.

A contemporary of James Sim was Edward Constantine, Head Teacher of Sandy Bay School. His predecessor was Miss Barker who retired in January 1904 having been Mistress for 30 years. While seeking a successor, the Benevolent Society closed the school for several months and then, temporarily, Mrs Painter and her daughter ran the school while Canon Porter sought a permanent appointment. Eventually, in March 1905, he recommended Edward Constantine for the post and the appointment was backdated to 1 November 1904, with a salary of £3 per month.[4]

So, at the tender age of 18, Edward Constantine officially became the head teacher of the school. His training for teaching was mainly on the job and he was destined to hold the post for the next 56 years until 31 December 1960, when he retired at the age of 75.

Edward Constantine is remembered clearly by many people on the island. In 1991, 95 year-old Henry Benjamin recalled Mr Constantine, who had taught him some 85 years previously. He said of his teacher: 'He was interested in us and we in him. His conversation was interesting. He was a remarkable man. He taught us so much and had great concern for his pupils. He gave special teaching as needed, to the advanced pupils and to the weaker ones.' At lunchtime he would play cricket with the pupils and he taught Henry to be both a batsman and a bowler. Henry recalled that Mr Constantine had his lessons planned for each day, teaching all the basic subjects. 'In geography, he took us round the world. I can still remember where on the map to find places when I hear them mentioned on the world news.' He had great concern for his pupils. Before school each day, Henry had to work for his parents, which involved walking – or more often running – to Longwood with fruit, waiting for the money, and then getting to school on time. If on rare occasions, Henry was late for school, Mr Constantine understood the situation and would say 'Don't worry, Henry. Get your breakfast first and then join the class.' Henry's older sister or brother would have brought the breakfast to school for him.[5]

Many other people on the island remember Mr Constantine with affection and respect. Harold Isaac attended Sandy Bay School in the 1940s and '50s. He marvelled at Mr Constantine's wide knowledge across a broad range of subjects which he taught to senior pupils in the all–age school at that time – and to this day remembers studying books like *The Last of the Mohicans* and *Children of the New Forest*. Harold recalls being taught in the old school buildings, which were also St Peter's Church – where they had to pull over the backs of the pews to form the tops of their desks during the week, and then restore them for services for each Sunday. Some of these desk-pews are still in existence today in St Peter's Church.[6]

Mr Constantine's children recall their father's teaching. In school he was the stern but kind teacher, sharing his wide knowledge with them – 'he would spend his last penny on books', said his daughter Phyllis John – and at home he became the caring father. When she was 15, Phyllis assisted her father with teaching the little children. In addition to ensuring that his pupils were proficient in reading and writing, he was also keen to teach them geography and history. 'I knew a lot about England before I ever went there, thanks to my father,' declared his son, Ollie. His great-granddaughter, Mrs Delphia Stevens, a teacher at Jamestown First School (1992), remembers him as a person who was devoted to his job.[7]

He was known as the island historian and was often called upon to

The original Sandy Bay School in St Peter's Church, where backs of Sunday pews swung over to become tops of desks for the rest of the week

give information about it. A hand-written book containing facts which he had collected and written about island life and history demonstrates for itself his thirst for knowledge and his keenness to use it in his teaching. He even records that his 56 years of teaching were 'a record for the island'.[8] In St Peter's Church a memorial has been inscribed by his nephew, Randy Constantine, which speaks for itself:

In Affectionate Memory of
EDWARD FREDERICK CONSTANTINE MBE
Born 7 December 1885   Died 31 July 1967

He served this Parish
As Churchwarden, Lay Reader, Sub Deacon
Chorister and Sunday School Teacher
Also he supervised the building of the Chancel
and Extension of this Church of St Peter
Head Teacher of Sandy Bay School 1904-1960

'Lord now lettest thou thy servant depart in peace'

In October 1958, shortly before he retired, Edward Constantine wrote in an article for *St Helena Wirebird* entitled 'What my life as a School Teacher has taught me':

A parent of one of my pupils recently asked whether I would choose School Teaching as a career if the opportunity to choose was given me once again. I am sure I would have no hesitation in making the same choice. Teaching is creative, it also deals with living and growing material, and this material is so plastic and tractable that the thought of having it to mould at will, and perhaps through ignorance to mar it, is to the earnest teacher a very solemn one. The true teacher moreover does not grow old, and you can tell him anywhere by his irrepressible boyishness and gaiety of heart.[9]

Another person who made an important contribution to education in the early 1900s was Leslie Tucker. An experienced teacher from England, Mr Tucker arrived on the island in 1904 to take up duties as Head Teacher of the Government Boys' School and to train teachers for the other schools. His contribution at this crucial time of the implementation of the Ordinance was significant. Immediately on arrival he threw himself into the work, gaining the admiration and gratitude of all who had the education of island children at heart. Joan Thomas, now in 1992 a long-serving head teacher on the island, chose Leslie Tucker to be one of the subjects described in her unpublished book, *Two Great Educationalists in St Helena in the Early 1900s*. In this she writes of Mr Tucker's insistence on high standards from pupils, pupil teachers and teachers alike, and of the help which he gave them through his own example in teaching and through the special courses which he ran to improve the general level of teaching on the island.[10] Charles George, who received all his schooling on the island, remembers being taught by Mr Tucker, whom he described as 'friendly, a very good teacher, a really strict man'.[11]

At the end of 1904 in a reorganization of the schools in Jamestown, the Senior Town School and the Junior Town School replaced the separate Town Boys' School and the Town Girls' School. Mr Tucker was Head of the Senior School while Eleanor Short was Head of the Junior School. Miss Short had come from the UK in 1889 to be Head Teacher at the Government Town Girls' School and, after the 1904 reorganization, at the Government Junior School. According to a picture of that time, Eleanor Short's School was in Napoleon Street in the house now occupied by Cyril Gunnell, opposite the present Community Centre.[12] There were 132 pupils (56 boys and 76 girls), and Miss Short had three assistant teachers, Ruby Smith, Queenie Gunnell and Mildred Francis. Across the road was the Government Senior School, with 91 pupils (42 boys and 49 girls), where Leslie Tucker was headteacher, assisted by Basil Broadway, Eva Fagan and Eliza Smith.

In the *1905 Blue Book* Governor Gallwey was able to report: 'The great object arrived at in this division was to economise the teaching power of the staff and also to bring the senior boys and girls under the instruction of Mr Tucker, a trained teacher , who arrived in the Colony in 1904.' He continued to surmise that perhaps 'The Senior Town School may in the future advance beyond the elementary stage to secondary or higher education'. In addition he was pleased that classes for pupil teachers, under Mr Tucker, had been started during the last quarter of the year – 'an excellent innovation ... a decided advance in education was made during the year'.

Governor Gallwey further approved a set of Regulations which were published by the Board of Education in July 1906 to supplement the provisions of the recent Ordinance and to ensure uniformity of practice through all the schools. These reflected the new spirit of determination to improve the education provided by the schools, and in no small measure also reflected the influence of Mr Tucker. The regulations tightened up procedures in all schools for the admission and departure of children; for holidays, the collection of fees, the absence of teachers, the inspection of schools, the examination of work, corporal punishment and the subjects to be included in the curriculum. Requiring that a copy of these regulations be hung in every schoolroom, the Board concluded: 'It should be borne in mind that one of the main objects of education should be to stimulate the intelligence of the scholars by careful teaching, making the several subjects as interesting as possible. The ancient method of endeavouring to crowd a child's mind with a mass of facts, very often of a statistical nature, is to be avoided, being quite contrary to the spirit of true education.'

No doubt with this in mind, and also mindful of the need for a school in the Blue Hill region of the island, the Hussey Charity Trustees decided at this time that they would take action. Accordingly, as described in their Minute Book on 1 October 1906 they hired 'in perpetuity' from the Government the land registered as property No 343K, 2 acres, 0 rods and 26 perches, known as 'The School Ground', for one shilling per year, the first payment to be made on 30 September 1907. Blue Hill School was opened in January 1907 under the headship of Caleb John and 12 months later at the annual island prizegiving received high praise from the editor of the *St Helena Diocesan Magazine* of January 1908: 'A good beginning has been made by this school. Started last January, it is the first school in the island that has been run on modern lines and modern teaching methods from the commencement. Thanks to the Master in charge of it, Mr C. John, the School is in good working order, and has thoroughly justified the pains taken in its inauguration. May it ever continue to be, as it is now, a boon to the dwellers in the far west. The School, composed of less than 40 scholars, is an easy handful to manage. There they are, in an open country, as happy as can be. They have the best school playground in the island, and cricket goes on at every opportunity, the boys at one pitch and the girls at another.' Earlier in his career, Caleb John had taught at Half Tree Hollow School and the Country School. Several islanders recall him well, including Mrs Ruth Pridham, who started her schooldays with Mr John at Blue Hill at the age of five. She describes him as being a very capable teacher who was a mine of information. He was the only teacher at the time, with 50 children between the ages of five and 14. He read a lot and was well-educated; 'no child left not being able to read and write'.[13] After many years of teaching at Blue Hill, which had been renamed the Bishop Holbech Memorial School in 1930, he retired in 1941 at the time of the amalgamation of Church and State schools. He subsequently continued his service to education by becoming a member of the Board of Education. He died in 1952 and was buried at the Church of St Helena and the Cross, near to where he had served for most of his life.

1907-10: Advances in Education led by Leslie Tucker
The island's prosperity was at a low ebb again. The departure of the
Boer prisoners in 1902 and the Garrison in 1906 had caused a serious
economic slump, although the flax industry was subsidized to try to
relieve the situation. However, there were other matters which raised
the spirits of the people. In August 1907 the Board of Education
recorded its keenest appreciation of the high achievement of Eva
Fagan, a 13-year-old pupil at the Senior Government School, who,
against world–wide competition, won the Lord Meath Empire Day
Challenge Cup for her essay on 'The History of British India'. Eva
Fagan was born on 28 July 1894, the daughter of George and Emma
Fagan (née George). Her paternal grandfather, William, had come to
St Helena with the St Helena Regiment in 1842 and married Martha
Russell in 1847. She was now being taught by Leslie Tucker.

The *St Helena Guardian* of 24 October 1907 printed the whole of Eva's
1,100-word, award-winning essay. Reporting her success, the editor
reminded the readers that they could be justifiably proud of other
islanders from the past who had achieved overseas success – Noel and
George Janisch; members of the Fowler, Alexander and Pooley families; and the son of Canon Hands – 'We are apt to be looked upon
abroad as poor and ignorant but we venture to say that some children
in our schools will compete with others in far distant countries.'[14]

Eva distinguished herself again the following year by winning the
Senior School essay competition inaugurated by the Governor with her
essay on 'Kindness to Animals'. Maurice Young, later to become a long
serving teacher on the island, won the Benevolent Town School prize.
Shortly after this success, Eva Fagan left school at the age of 14 and on
13 July 1908 became a pupil teacher, being paid at the rate of 5s per
month. But sadly the *Board of Education Minutes* record receiving her
resignation two years later. It appears that she subsequently left the
island to go to South Africa.

The *Board of Education Minutes* of 6 May 1907 reported that Canon
Porter and Mr Tucker were asked to lay down a course of study for
pupil teachers' studies, and a week later Mr Tucker was preparing a
scheme for the 'harmonizing of the methods of teaching in all the
schools'. A letter to this effect was sent to the Benevolent Society to seek
their co-operation. The Society replied that they did not see their way
to converting their town school into a school for infants only, as the
mistress in charge wished to teach beyond Standard IV and also had
success with older children. However, the Society soon realized it did
need to improve the standards at the school. The Benevolent Society

Committee Minutes of 23 April 1909 recorded the decision to let it merge with the Hussey Charity School and be taken under their management. The head teacher, Miss Mary Burchill, would be given retirement. (Mary, the oldest daughter of George Davenport Burchill, had taken over the headship in 1887 from Georgina Burchill, probably a younger sister, who had held it since 1884.) At this time, Sandy Bay School was also taken over by the Hussey Charity.

Mr Tucker was a strong disciplinarian and did not spare the rod, reportedly causing boys to be put through the window and held there in position while they were caned. A former pupil at the Old Boys' School, Cecil Ellick, in a recorded talk made in 1981, remembered Mr Tucker for his ability to teach well across a wide range of subjects. Another former pupil of the school, Charles George, recalling Leslie Tucker's strictness, said that he was a very good and friendly teacher, and that he was sorry that Mr Tucker was called away to serve in the Great War. Each Friday, Mr Tucker visited the school and he taught the teachers, while most of the children went home.

Mrs Joan Thomas wrote in *Two Great Educationalists in St Helena in the Early 1900s* that Mr Tucker would not tolerate slovenliness and was strict about the way in which the trainee teachers spoke. She described the Friday afternoon sessions when the trainees went to the Old Boys' School for the 'Criticism Class', this being a lesson given to the top class by one of themselves. Mr Tucker insisted that the lesson was well planned and delivered with good grammar and pronunciation. The trainees recall feeling extremely nervous under the observation of both Mr Tucker and their fellows, while they were aiming to maintain good discipline and to give the children a good grasp of the lesson. For the more experienced teachers, Mr Tucker ran classes in the vacations. The curriculum he covered included Scripture, the three Rs, Geography, History, 'Object teaching', Hygiene and Physical Education. He is remembered for including a lot of Shakespeare, and his pupils had to remember their parts. He also 'taught beautiful handwriting'.[15]

By 1 January 1910 Mr Tucker had obviously won the confidence of the Board of Education, because Governor Gallwey reported to the Secretary of State that Mr Tucker had been appointed Supervisor of Government Schools and to oversee the Government Senior Town School. He replaced Canon Porter, who was resigning as School Supervisor. At this time a scheme for the reorganization of schools was submitted to the Secretary of State for his approval, while Mr Tucker was again busy on the island devising new curricula for the schools. Both received approval and took effect early in 1910. Mr Tucker

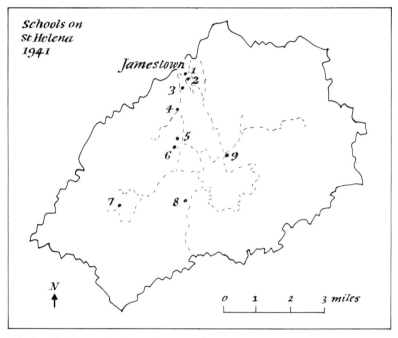

Schools on St Helena after the Amalgamation Ordinance, 1941

1 The Infants School, Jamestown
2 The Junior School, Jamestown
3 Pilling Central School
4 Half Tree Hollow School
  (Junior/Infants)
5 Gosse Central School

6 The Cathedral School
  (Junior/Infants)
7 Blue Hill School (Junior/Infants)
8 Sandy Bay School (Junior/Infants)
9 Hutts Gate School (All-age)

supervised the subsequent redistribution of the teaching staffs of the Government schools, a major aim being to rationalize the use of teachers. At the same time there was a redistribution of the teaching staff in the Government Schools. The schedule of schools in the report, combined with data from the *1910 Blue Book* lists of the Civil Establishment, was:

Senior Town School (52b + 52g) Leslie Tucker, with Eleanor Short teacher i/c, assisted by Eliza Smith
Country School (41b + 41g) Vida Evans i/c
Junior Town School (58b + 72g) Ruby Smith i/c, assisted by Queenie Gunnell and Mildred Smith

Hussey Charity Upper Town School (23b + 12g)
Hussey Charity Lower Town School (54b + 32g)
Hussey Charity – Half Tree Hollow School (42b + 37g)
Hussey Charity – Hutts Gate School (38b + 34g)
Hussey Charity – Blue Hill School (14b + 16g)
Benevolent Society – Sandy Bay School (23b + 21g)
Baptist Sunday School (29b + 49g)

The three teachers named Eliza, Ruby and Mildred Smith were daughters of St Helenian Johnny Smith and, from their early childhood, records show their prize-winning successes. From 1906 they began long teaching careers in the island's schools.

1911-20: Island Education in the Decade of the First World War
An important development which had been growing in strength for many years on St Helena had been the increasing popularity of lacemaking. As far back as 1818 lacemaking had been taught as a skill at Mrs George's Preparatory School, but the major impetus came through Emily Warren who, as recorded earlier, had come to St Helena as a contract teacher in 1886 to become head of the Government Girls' School. She married chemist Thomas Jackson in 1889 and the headship of the school was taken over by Miss Eleanor Short. Mrs Jackson continued with her teaching of lacemaking and in 1907 displayed some island lace from the Government Junior School at an exhibition organized by the Lace Makers' Association in England. Miss Penderel Moody, an instructor to the association, went to the island in 1907 for the purpose of further encouraging the skill, and she was succeeded by Miss Girdwood in July 1908. Miss Girdwood established a flourishing Lace School in Jamestown, at the same time keeping in touch with Mrs Ord Marshall, the Secretary of the League of the Empire, concerning the sale of lace items produced by the school. Over the next few years the numbers of students at the school, including adults, rose continuously until it reached a peak in December 1911 with 203 people listed. Several techniques of lacemaking were taught, developed both on the island and abroad. Tribute was paid in the *Guardian* of 14 May 1914: 'Under the energetic manageress, Miss Girdwood, the School has made rapid strides, and the prospects before them are good, having reached self-support. We congratulate both the manageress and members, and trust that the Lace School will continue to flourish on a firm and ever-increasing successful footing.'

Meanwhile Hutts Gate School, which had been experiencing difficulties over recent years and giving concern to the Hussey Charity

The Lace Depot in Jamestown (now the site of the Main Post Office)

Trustees, had recovered. In fact, just prior to the major redistribution of teachers in 1909, the February edition of the *St Helena Diocesan Magazine* had given Hutts Gate 'honorable mention' reporting that it 'is now a credit to the efforts lately made here in the matter of education, and is in a fair way to excellence'. This was attributed to the work of pupil teacher Mr L. Francis and the paper called for the payment of a fair salary to him. The school continued to increase in reputation and size and by 1912 had 81 children, 46 boys and 35 girls. But the story of the school through these few years was not without incident. At one stage, the young master was accused of cruelty in punishing a child, but the enquiry found in his favour. On another occasion, the Board of Education asked him to report on why an illiterate mother was choosing to teach her child at home, rather than sending her to school.

Governor Gallwey left the island in 1911. His period of office since 1903 had coincided with a crucial time in the development of education on the island and the Board of Education paid tribute to the great part he had played: 'The Board records its appreciation not only of Governor Gallwey's services to Education, but also of the great interest he always took of the welfare and happiness of the Island children. His words and influence cannot fail to have left a great and lasting impression for good upon the rising generation.'

The new Governor, Major Harry Cordeaux, began his term of office in 1912, and his reports to the Secretary of State emphasized the need for some technical training to be established on the island. The Board of Education reported in its Minutes of 9 December 1912 that some initiatives were attempted such as giving schoolboys some technical training in Government shops, supplementary to their general elementary instruction. The Governor hoped to start some carpentry classes for schoolboys, this possibly leading to the future establishment of a Trade School, but this did not succeed as the tenders from the carpenters were 'so exorbitant'.

In May 1912 the Hussey Charity Trustees allowed Mr Tucker payment for his work with the pupil teachers in their schools, and by October of that year he was listed among the Trustees themselves.

Illness on the island has always had a serious effect upon the schools, frequently closing them altogether for a short period of time. A scarlet fever epidemic in 1912 was no exception, and this time the schools closed for three months.

Another person whose contribution was significant to the life and to the education story of St Helena was the Reverend Lawrence Chase Walcott, later to become Canon Walcott. In fact, the *St Helena Diocesan Magazine* of April 1914 marvelled at 'the manifold activities that he has kept going in town, some of which are his own creation, encouraged by a band of faithful workers'. Mr Walcott had succeeded the Reverend F. M. Lane as Vicar of Jamestown on 25 April 1909 and this was the start of his long career on the island. Of both West Indian and British ancestry, the Reverend Walcott had trained for the ministry at St Augustine's College, Canterbury, being ordained in 1906. He had served in Britain and in Cape Town before taking up his work in St Helena. He immediately entered fully into the life of the island, in spite of a doubtful reception by some of the St Helenians who were concerned about his mixed-race background. Within a fortnight of his arrival in Jamestown, however, he declared that he had faith in house-to-house visiting and that he already knew the greater number of people in the town. Typical of his keenness to be involved, he was to be found at the Empire Day Sports in June 1909 acting as starter. He became Chaplain for the Church Lads' Brigade, which had been restarted on 1901 by Canon Porter. The Reverend Walcott also started scouting on the island with the first Jamestown Scout Group in 1915. The island group received official recognition in 1917 and has flourished ever since. More of the story of scouting is included later (Chapter 9).

With Leslie Tucker and Edward Constantine, he helped to mastermind concerts such as the one in December 1913 in aid of the Cement Cricket Pitch Fund, in which Mr Constantine sang two songs – 'The Dandy' and 'Anywhere in Maryland' – and Mr Tucker sang a 'Selection of Songs'. With a group of men like this, who had energy and initiative, the schools, young people and the island benefited greatly.

Meanwhile, beyond the shores of St Helena, the world was approaching war and, as in all parts of the British Empire, the people followed its progress closely and sent some of its men to serve. Leslie Tucker was one who felt the call of duty and he was given leave from his island duties. The schools included teaching about the war in their lessons. The Governor's report in the *1914 Blue Book* said: 'The usual elementary subjects have been taught and no changes in ordinary curriculum have been considered necessary. Lessons on the causes and progress of the War have been given periodically to all standards and the children have taken a keen and intelligent interest in the work.' Phyllis John, the daughter of Edward Constantine, was only two years old when the First World War started in 1914, but she later became aware of the effect the war had on the island. Volunteers from her area, including two of her brothers, were trained in Sandy Bay School, and they had night-time skirmishes and cliff-climbing exercises at Sandy Bay beach. The Royal Marines were stationed in the Baptist Chapel nearby.[16]

In 1915 Maurice Young, another islander who was to spend much of his working life as a teacher, first joined the staff at Half Tree Hollow School at a salary of £2 per month. Together with pupil teacher Emily Thomas, he started to work under the headship of James Sim. Mr Young's daughter, Muriel, reminiscing in 1991 about her father, recalled that he climbed to Half Tree Hollow each day from Jamestown, by way of the Ladder. He had gone directly into teaching from being a pupil and never regretted his choice of career, explaining that, like nursing, 'teaching is one of the best professions to have in life. You are not only paid for it, but you are putting your talent to good use.'[17] Her father had been an all-rounder – a keen reader; secretary of the Ancient Order of Foresters for 38 years; and a member of the choir at St James' Church. A member of a family with 17 children, all musical, he taught himself to play several instruments and became the Bandmaster of the St Helena Band. He was keen to teach music to others and gathered together a group of young boys whom he taught to play instruments. From Half Tree Hollow School he transferred to Hutts Gate School, where he became the head teacher in 1917, and again at first he walked there each morning, but eventually decided to acquire a donkey which carried him from Jamestown each day. In 1933 he was proud to become the first person on the island to own a motor cycle. For some years he came out of teaching, working as a foreman with the Union Cargo Boats, but then returned to the profession again, this time at Pilling School under the headship of John (Jack) Le Breton. It was not long before he transferred again to Hutts Gate as head teacher, where he stayed until the time came for the new Harford School to open in Longwood under his leadership and for Hutts Gate to close. He remained at Harford until he retired in 1965, when Mrs Elvina Mercury took over the headship. He had been very happy in his work with Longwood people: 'My father was very fond of Longwood people. He devoted his life to Longwood,' says his daughter Muriel.

In the absence at the war of Mr Tucker, Canon Porter carried out the inspection of the Half Tree Hollow School on behalf of the Hussey Charity Trustees who were supporting it. Apparently some measure of concern was being felt about attendance records at the school, but Canon Porter's report was favourable.

Non-attendance at school was still causing concern and the Board of Education decided in 1917 that, while Mr Tucker was away at the war, his travel allowance would be given to an Attendance Officer and the Sergeant of Police invited to undertake this role. The striking success of his work was recorded some six months later.

Another major item which required the attention of the Board of Education in 1917 and was recorded in the Minutes referred to the building occupied by the Country School, the former St Paul's Vicarage. Owing to the ravages of white ants, it became unsafe in 1917 for occupation, and the school was transferred to Luffkins Tower, 'a residence which is the property of the Government and well-adapted for the purpose'. Some of the children who attended the Country School while it was at Luffkins recall their experiences clearly. Mrs Cavell Duncan, whose whole school life was spent there from the age of six to 14, did not fully realize at the time that the school was in temporary accommodation. To her it was school. Her head teacher was Vida Evans, whom she remembers as being tall and thin and very strict, carrying a cane ready for use! Miss Evans rode to school on a donkey, but woe betide any child who tried to approach it. Other teachers at the school were Algernon Broadway, Louis Timm and, with the infants, Miss Perthinia 'Teeny' Constantine. Mrs Duncan remembers having needlework and knitting lessons on the upper floor, and other lessons like grammar, dictation, composition, algebra, drawing, history, geography, scripture and general knowledge on the lower floor. Canon Walcott visited the school regularly to test how the children were progressing. She received several prizes, including *The Great Book for Girls* for darning.[18] Another pupil, Mrs Maisie Benjamin, who later became a schoolteacher herself, started at Luffkins at the age of eight, having had two years of private tuition before this. She remembers having lessons in the large double rooms, under the ever vigilant 'strict, but nice' Miss Evans, by whom children were caned on the hand if they had more than six spelling mistakes.[19]

The school used Luffkins Tower for a much longer time than expected due to the extent of the repairs to St Paul's Vicarage. In fact, it was 17 years before the school was able to return, in 1934.

However, the Governor was able to report some more positive news in the *1917 Blue Book*: 'The long want of technical instruction was met in the month of August by arrangements made with the Officer Commanding Troops. Since then, 18 young men and boys have received continuous instruction from skilled men of the garrison in carpentry, telephone work, plumbing and fitting, blacksmithing and shoemaking.'

During Mr Tucker's continued absence in 1919, still on military service, Miss Eleanor Short became Acting Supervisor of Schools. This is believed to be the first time this position had been held by a woman, and she was also the Acting Head of the Government School in Jamestown.

Shortly afterwards, in 1919, Miss Eliza Smith became the Assistant Teacher in charge of the Senior School, there now being 88 pupils, 32 boys and 56 girls. Her sister, Ruby, remained the teacher in charge of the Junior Town School, where there were now 135 pupils, 66 boys and 69 girls; and Mildred had become a pupil teacher at the Junior School. The five Hussey Charity Schools were still flourishing, the largest being the Half Tree Hollow School with as many as 122 pupils, 62 boys and 60 girls. When Mr Tucker eventually returned to the island, the 1920 records list him as the Coroner, with no mention of any involvement in education. Be that as it may, there is no doubt that his contribution to education on the island over the years had been a very important one.

1921-34: Canon Walcott resumes his Service to the Island

The Reverend Walcott returned to the island in 1921 after taking leave in the UK and was appointed to be Superintendent of Schools. Tributes were paid to Eleanor Short, who had been Acting Superintendent and was retiring due to illness. 'For many years Miss Short has done a noble and self-denying work in Jamestown.' Readers were asked to remember her by supporting the charity which she inaugurated, 'The Children's Luncheon Fund to provide food for the poorer children who often have to go breakfastless to school'.[20] Some years later in 1926 she became the first lady member of the Education Board.

During the Reverend Walcott's absence one of the major educational topics for discussion had been the possible introduction of free education. The leading article in the *St Helena Diocesan Magazine* of March 1920 affirmed: 'At a recent School meeting, a resolution was actually passed in favour of it. So that, as far as we can see, the Church Schools are committed to free education. We do not entirely agree with this movement. There are a good many rich people in St Helena.'

Mr Walcott tackled his new role vigorously and immediately set about reorganizing the schools on the island. The major change which he instituted was the separation again of the boys and girls in the Senior Town Government Schools, returning to the pre-1905 set-up. The 1921 Population Census listed a total of 612 pupils on the school rolls, 236 in the three Government Schools, 315 in the four Hussey Charity Schools and 61 in the one Benevolent Society School. The population as a whole was 3,747, including a small contingent of 49 at the Garrison, and 32 prisoners. When compared with the 1911 Census, with the exception of the inclusion of the garrison, the numbers were similar to those of a decade before, indicating that the population of the island had remained relatively stable through the war years.

Mr William Corker was appointed to be Master of the Boys' School from 1 January 1922, assisted by his wife Lilian, and Eliza Smith became Mistress of the Girls' School only, with her sister, Mildred in charge of the infants. The Boys' School occupied the building in Upper Jamestown on the site of the present flats near St John's Church, while the Girls' School and Infants' School continued to meet in the buildings in Napoleon Street. Pupils in the Boys' School remember it as having one long, main room, with a double storey at the far end. Several people still recall, in 1992, being taught by the rather severe Eliza, and her gentler but equally respected younger sisters. Martha George (née Young), herself to become a well-respected head teacher, was a young teacher of Standard 1 in Miss Eliza Smith's school and described her as 'a frank, outspoken person who worked hard for the community as Captain of Guides, organist at St James' Church, and organiser of various activities in the school such as whist drives'. In the Government Girls' School there were four classes of 25/30 pupils in the main building (now the Community Centre), with a class of infants in a room at the back. In Martha's time, Mildred Smith was an Assistant teacher and the infant class was taught by Queenie Gunnell, great-aunt of future Chief Education Officer, Basil George. Mrs Heather Abel, a later pupil, remembers Miss Smith as headteacher of the Junior Section of the school after the amalgamation in 1941 when the schools became co-educational again. It was then called Pilling Junior School and met in the military quarters in Market Street, while Mr William Corker led the Senior Section of the school in the same building. Miss Smith always took her job seriously and she rarely smiled, but 'she was a good teacher' and, with a staff of three other teachers, taught maths and English in the upper rooms, and music and needlework in the lower rooms. Another former pupil, Mr Arnold Flagg, later to become a headmaster and then an Education Officer on the island, remembers his early schooldays taught by Mildred in the Infants School in Napoleon Street, and by Eliza in his junior years remembering her as 'a real taskmaster'.[21]

As in his previous period on St Helena, the Reverend Walcott entered fully into the life of the community, particularly in any activity which added to the education of the young islanders. He assumed the title of Canon Walcott in 1931. Many people at present on the island pay tribute to his work with the Scouting Movement, including Arnold Flagg who enjoyed being a member of the Cub Scouts. Bill Drabble, now an elected member of the Legislative Council, remembers the annual two-week camps in Thompson's Wood as a highlight in his life and in the lives of many other boys. But they had a price to pay! 'If you joined the Cubs you had to go to church parade once a month and to church between whiles. Canon Walcott didn't miss much. To be a scout you had to be confirmed, and all scouts were in the choir.'[22]

He also organized activities for the ladies. Evelyn Bagley, now a keen needlewoman, remembers the Sewing Guild he established at Blue Hill, which is still in existence. The original intention was to make garments for the poor, but now the articles are sold in aid of the church. In addition, he did a considerable amount of teaching to groups at his home, Palm Villa. These included religious studies classes, and also training classes for pupil teachers. Albert Quinn, returning to the island 47 years later, in 1992, recalled with gratitude that, after leaving the Boys' School, he was able to spend two evenings each week receiving extra teaching from Canon Walcott.[23]

In the *1921 Blue Book* Acting Governor Brooke drew the attention of the Colonial Office to the important change during the year of the separation of the boys and girls in the two town schools. 'It is early yet to report results. Much however is expected in the way of improved discipline, attendance and moral benefit, and so far these expectations have been entirely fulfilled.' Perhaps confidence in the new single-sex system received a boost by the results of a competition launched in December 1924 by Governor Peel who offered a prize at the Government Girls' School for the best essay on 'The Change in the Schools', referring of course to 1921. Two prizes were awarded, the senior division being won by Elsie O'Neil and the junior by Sheila Magallen. The *St Helena Diocesan Magazine* commented: 'It is interesting to note that almost without exception the girls rejoiced in having a school to themselves where they can do their own work, and play their own games apart from the presence of the boys.'[24]

One of the major causes of some of the difficulties in the schools had been lack of continuity of teachers, but now we find a number of people who were to feature in educational circles for many years to come, bringing a stability and a respect to the profession, including James Sim of Half Tree Hollow, Edward Constantine of Sandy Bay and Maurice Young, Assistant at Half Tree Hollow and Head of Hutts Gate. Another teacher was William Corker who served education on the island for the whole of his working life and who is well remembered by his former pupils. He was first appointed as a teacher in 1913 at the age of 15, very soon was put in charge of the Hussey Charity School in Jamestown, and by 1922 was head teacher of the Government Boys' School after the reorganization into separate boys and girls schools, receiving an annual salary of £145. At the major amalgamation of government and church schools in 1941, he transferred to become the head teacher of the Government Senior School, while Eliza Smith became head of the Junior Section, each school again reverting to receiving both boys and girls. Mr Corker died in 1950.

Acknowledging the fact that St Helenians were increasingly taking leading, responsible positions on the island, including four headships, Canon Porter commented in the *St Helena Diocesan Magazine* of November 1921: 'To our mind, one of their great merits is they are island-born. The island has produced several eminent men – including a governor, a priest, a doctor, and various others – we see no reason why it should not produce its own head teachers.' A little later, in 1923, the Reverend Walcott succeeded Canon Porter as editor of the *St Helena Diocesan Magazine*. Like his predecessor, he found it gave him a useful platform on which to express his views, particularly about education.

The magazine of April 1925 reported some notable successes in the

South African external examination in Religious Knowledge. While 'a bevy of small girls in Half Tree Hollow came close after the prize winners' in the elementary level exam, including Esther Augustus, Grace Sim, Marion Constantine and Irene George, four islanders were awarded prizes in the more advanced exam, these being Iris Bagley (later Clingham) of Blue Hill, Phyllis Constantine (John) of Sandy Bay, Matthew Crowie of Hutts Gate, and Noreen Duncan (Evans) of Hutts Gate.

In 1925 *Elementary Education Ordinance No 1* made some amendments to the *Education Ordinance* of 1903, although its terms remained substantially the same. It tightened up the employment regulations concerning children, now making it law that no child under the age of 13 was to be employed and those over 13 who were employed must attend school for at least three days each week. School continued to be compulsory for children from 6 to 14 years of age, with some 'reasonable excuses' allowed. The Governor was to appoint a Board of Education who, in turn, were to appoint a Superintendent of Education. School fees were to be waived in certain cases of poverty.

The story of the decade after the end of the war was one of steady movement forward. Out of school activities were picking up again, particularly in sports such as cricket, for which a Schools' League was formed. The Church Lads Brigade, Scouts and Guides were flourishing. The system of giving prizes – abandoned during the war – was resumed, and satisfactory reports were received of progress in the schools. Treat Days were an established part of the school year, for instance on the King's Birthday. Pupils of the day, including Phyllis John, recall the sports organized on Francis Plain, remembering with extra pleasure the buns and treacle, the ginger beer and cake, interspersed with tugs-of-war, 'boat' races and four-legged races for three people.[25]

The profession lost one of its faithful members at the end of 1926, when Mary Burchill died suddenly on the island. Her obituary in the *St Helena Diocesan Magazine* of January 1927 said: 'For many years a teacher in the Benevolent School, recently she has been doing useful work in giving private instruction to small children of the Garrison.' At the same time the profession was welcoming a number of promising pupil teachers such as Edward Benjamin, Vida Evans and Martha Young (later George) who were already giving good service to teaching under the watchful eye of the Reverend Walcott.

The co-operation between the Benevolent Society and the Hussey Charity continued, and a decision was made in the late 1920s to join their two schools in Jamestown by making an interlinking door between them. This was probably a major step towards the eventual merger of these two educational supporting bodies some six years later. The Reverend Walcott, seeking to raise morale during a difficult economic depression, and also being a prolific producer of poetry, published 'In praise of St Helena' which started with the verse:

Of all the Islands in the world
– or coral grown or lava hurled
– Give me the joy of life unfurled
In sun-kissed St Helena.[26]

Continuing to speak through his newspaper, the Reverend Walcott aired his educational views and proposals. For instance, in July 1930 he proposed that the name Blue Hill School should be changed to the Bishop Holbech Memorial School to commemorate the special regard which the Bishop had for this church-established school. Later on, as Canon Walcott, he repeated his hope that St Helenians would increasingly take the leading roles on their island and he called for 'a more advanced education than our primary schools can give, so that in time we might be able to fill the bench and higher government offices with St Helenian born men'.[27] In September 1933 he changed the name of his publication to *St Helena Magazine*, as this gave him greater freedom to express views, although included in the magazine were the 'Diocesan Notes'.

1934-41: Public Debate on the Future of Education

Unfortunately, the comparatively steady life on the island was to be seriously affected by the decline and closure of the flax industry in the early 1930s, when St Helena was once again thrown into a period of serious unemployment. The Hussey Charity Trustees began discussion with the Government about a possible reorganization of schools. Their Town School was needing extensive repair and, unless Government help was forthcoming, faced closure. Similarly, their Hutts Gate buildings were dilapidated, and pressure to open a school at Levelwood was becoming stronger. For several generations the children from Levelwood had walked to school at Hutts Gate, which itself had been established in 1839. Prior to that it seems likely that the Levelwood people had no school at all unless they travelled into Jamestown. Serious calls for a school at Levelwood date back to 1933, in order that the pressure on Hutts Gate could be relieved. Many of the children arrived late because they had to complete some family chores before setting off for school. This situation led the head teacher to be slack at opening the school, so the Trustees of Hutts Gate changed the time of the school day, to start at 10 am and finish at 3 pm, with two short breaks within the day, insisting that these rules should be strictly adhered to.

Nevertheless, in the *1934 Blue Book* the Governor, Sir Spencer Davis, was able to report fairly positively about progress during 1934 and 1935. Money had been granted by the Hussey Charity Committee to repair and improve the Hutts Gate and Sandy Bay Schools. Thirty-six modern dual desks had been provided, giving accommodation for 72 children. Hutts Gate was also to have a new verandah, to help cope with the high numbers of pupils. About the children's work, the Governor added: 'The children are also showing much interest in freehand drawing and painting. Music is not neglected and the singing is of good quality.'

The former buildings used by the Country School at St Paul's Vicarage had been repaired, extended and improved by a new verandah and a well-built outside classroom, so in 1934 the school was able to transfer back from Luffkins Tower which had been its 'temporary' home for the past 17 years.

In 1934 a Joint Board for the Benevolent Society and the Hussey Charity was formed under the chairmanship of the Venerable Archdeacon Warner, other members being Canon L.C. Walcott, the Reverend F. Hall, F. Deason, F. R. Thorpe, W. Corker (Secretary of the Benevolent Society), the Hon H. Solomon OBE, and G. Moss.

Canon Walcott continued to hold an influential place in education on St Helena, not only in his roles as Superintendent of Schools and member of the Joint Board, but also as continuing editor of the island newspaper. His message to the people was unwavering, as included in the *St Helena Magazine* of November 1936: 'Duty to God is the basis of all loyalty and good citizenship. The same principle applies to Christian schools. Every teacher should have a full appreciation of the religious and moral aim underlying the whole process and principles of education, expressed by example as well as by precept.'

Time was running out for the independent existence and control of the schools under the Benevolent Society and the Hussey Charity. The Report issued by J. B. Sidebotham CMG, who made an official governmental visit to the island in 1939, gave the opinion that education in St Helena had declined to a low level. The school buildings were in a dilapidated condition, the teaching methods and textbooks were out of date, and the teaching staff were generally inadequate in both numbers and quality. This report referred to the ten schools, three Government, three Hussey Charity, three Benevolent Society and one Diocesan Church School. He said that one cause of the trouble was that old teachers could not be pensioned off from the Society and Charity schools, which could not afford the pensions. Mr Sidebotham recommended that all schools should be put under Government control as soon as possible. His view was endorsed by both the Bishop and the Archbishop of Capetown, and accepted by the St Helena Government. What was now needed was the drafting and introduction of a new Education Ordinance to bring this about.

For this task of planning and implementing a major reorganization of schools, George Davies Watkins from England was appointed in 1939 to be Superintendent of Education, at a salary of £500 plus £40 travel allowance. The arrival of Mr Watkins brought to an end Canon Walcott's post as Superintendent of Schools and he returned to his work in the parish of St James, though this did not stop him from speaking out on frequent occasions. Over the years Canon Walcott had gained the respect of many people on the island for his energetic interest and outspoken views.

Canon Walcott's high standing did not help the new Superintendent of Education on his arrival. Mr Watkins needed to prove that he was the right man for the major job of reorganization. But Canon Walcott was extremely doubtful about the wisdom of placing all schools on the island under the control of the Government. Accordingly he reported in the *St Helena Magazine* of August 1939 that he was growing 'more and more dubious about the wisdom of the proposed handing over of our Church schools to the State ... rocks are beginning to show their heads ... what might be done in apparent good faith now may in the end prove to be the betrayal of a trust'. Nevertheless, the island held high hopes of Mr Watkins on several aspects of education. And Canon Walcott, himself, challenged: 'We hope to see a real advance made in the establishment of a secondary school for our brighter scholars, development on the technical side in woodwork, handicraft and domestic science and the like.'[28]

Over the next few years the island was to be well served by its new – and first – Education Officer, Mr Watkins. Almost reminiscent of that earlier 'expat' – Leslie Tucker at the beginning of the century – Mr Watkins threw himself immediately into his wide-ranging tasks, and soon after his arrival he was ready to submit a report entitled *Education in St Helena: A Preliminary Survey made in June and July 1939*. He did not mince his words: 'What passes for intelligence in so many of the writings of the people of the island is really a defence mechanism manifesting itself in various self protective and self regarding ways, as the islander can well exploit any circumstances to his own advantage. The Government is wise in not providing much in the way of higher education. However the average level of intelligence in the children justifies a thorough and extensive system of elementary education with a definite vocational bias in a number of directions. A sound broad system of education on these lines, with possible extensions into adult education of a popular nature, is one of the great needs of the island.' He was extremely critical of the schools controlled by the Hussey Charity: 'All the schools controlled by this body in St Helena are housed disgracefully and this is symptomatic of the careless and slipshod methods the Trustees appear to have employed in their management. It is doubtful whether the Trustees in London would continue to subsidize education on these lines if the conditions in St Helena were known to them.' His summary of the island situation included: 'There is no school on the island at present in any way suitable for the proper training of our Senior boys and girls i.e. those of 11 years of age and more.'

Mr Watkins quickly gained the respect of the people of the island, the Council and the Governor. He was seemingly tireless. As Education Officer, he became known as a very strict, punctual leader. He not only started teachers' classes in his house at Francis Plain to help them to prepare for their altered roles, as well as classes for pupil teachers, but he also saw to it that everything was ready in terms of the buildings, the new image and the new identity of the schools, and in the necessary reorganization of the teaching staff. He introduced the system of school dinners. In addition he started recreational sessions of activities such as country dancing and rope making. In spite of, or perhaps because of, his outspoken criticism of their schools, the Hussey Charity Trustees welcomed him in 1939 as a member of their Board.[29]

Over the succeeding months there was much debate about the best way forward for the island's education system, much of it in public in the St Helena Magazine. Canon Walcott continued to be apprehensive that the changes envisaged were not for the best, particularly concerning the church's previous influence and responsibility. In June 1940 he wrote: 'It is, however, too soon to estimate what the present changes, which are still in a state of flux, will effect in contrast with past efforts. It will be soon enough in two years' time when the new education officer has completed his term of office.' And being basically critical of his successor in charge of schools, Walcott remained on the defensive about previous achievements. In his editorial he continued: 'We have no hesitation in saying that the old methods, which are indeed very little different to the new, have little they need be ashamed of. Indeed it could hardly be otherwise when it is remembered that island education for many years had the benefit of such men of culture and educational experience as Bishop Holbech, Canon Porter, Leslie Tucker and others.'

Both Mr Davies Watkins and Canon Walcott continued to air strong views in public, for instance over whether the senior pupils were in fact receiving secondary education in the true sense of the word, or whether it was really only elementary education; and also over what was the right form of education for them. On this Watkins had stated in October 1941: 'True education is training to live and on St Helena that life is rural,' to which Canon Walcott retorted: 'So our children are to be trained to be hewers of wood and drawers of water only.'

Suffice it to say here that the *Sidebotham Report* of 1939, together with the work of Mr Watkins and his teachers, and with co-operation between the Government, the Church, the Benevolent Society and the Hussey Charity, all led to one of the most significant milestones so far in the history of schools on St Helena. This was to be the amalgamation of all schools on the island under one management and direction. To facilitate this an Agreement was signed on 7 July 1941 by the Acting Government Secretary, Frederick Jarrett, on behalf of the Government of St Helena, and the Bishop of the Diocese of St Helena, Gilbert Price Lloyd Turner, who was also signing on behalf of the Benevolent Society and the Hussey Charity. This Agreement had accepted that it was 'necessary and just that in any contemplated scheme of unification of Government and Church Schools (*ie* all the Society, Charity and Church Schools) on this island under one management and direction that the identity and special religious character should in no wise be imperilled or lost'. The supporters of the former Church Schools would retain a right to object to a head teacher appointment and to have entry and undertake religious teaching as prescribed by the Board of Education; the Chairman of the Hussey Charity would remain a member of the Board for the time being; the Charity and the Society had the right to nominate one member each to the Board; pupils were to be encouraged to continue to attend church services; Sunday schools were to be continued in Sandy Bay and Blue Hill Schools, and clergy retained the right to enter other schools. In return, the Society and the Charity agreed that all funds should be submitted to the Education Fund which was to be established; and that the school lands should be leased to the Government for a 'peppercorn rent'.[30]

The pathway for the Schools Amalgamation Ordinance was now clear.

6
Reorganization, Renewal and Revival under Government Control 1941-60

What we know today and in great part the sort of person we are, depends mainly on the ability of the teachers we had.
Charles Dixon, 1957[1]

1941-45: Implementation and Effects of the Schools Amalgamation Ordinance

Signed by Governor Bain-Grey and approved by the Secretary of State. the 1941 *Schools Amalgamation Ordinance No 9* was deemed to have effect from 22 July 1941, bringing together all schools under the control of the Government. The Ordinance specified the schools previously held by the Church, the Benevolent Society or the Hussey Charity, as Hutts Gate School and the nearby Burnham's Field; Half Tree Hollow School and its grounds; Hussey Charity Town School; Benevolent Society Town School and its yard; Sandy Bay School with two acres of grounds, and Blue Hill School (Bishop Holbech Memorial School) and its grounds.

The procedures for the implementation of the *Schools Amalgamation Ordinance* were detailed in the ensuing *1941 Education Ordinance, No 10*. The Board of Education was reconstituted to include six members appointed by the Governor, each to hold office for three years, the Education Officer, ex officio, and the Governor as Chairman. The Board had powers, with the approval of the Governor, to make rules:

(a) for the good government, discipline and routine work of the schools and for prescribing hours of attendance;
(b) for the regulation of the procedures of the Board and for the mode of conducting their business respectively;
(c) for the provision of new schools where necessary and for the replacement, enlargement and improvement of existing schools;
(d) for the acquisition, maintenance and extension of school gardens in connection with the schools;

(e) for the training of prospective teachers and for the provision of suitable short courses for teachers at present serving in the schools;

(f) to determine the qualifications to be required for the issue and classification of certificates to teachers;

(g) for the approval of an establishment of suitable teachers, properly distributed in the schools, and for its increase when necessary;

(h) for the moral and physical instruction and training of scholars and for the practical instruction and training in suitable subjects;

(i) for the provision of free milk and meals to malnourished children in the schools;

(j) for the provision of adequate routine inspections and treatment of all school children by medical, dental and health officers;

(k) for the provision of suitable types of adult education, as determined by the needs which they are designed to satisfy;

(l) for the provision and maintenance of adequate playing field accommodation for the children of the schools;

(m) to prescribe the duties of School Attendance Officers;

(n) to fix the school fees payable by parents of children attending any school;

(o) to determine the ages at which scholars may be admitted to or cease to attend the several schools;

(p) generally for carrying the purposes or provisions of this Ordinance into effect.

Similarly the duties of the Education Officer were detailed. These included having responsibility for the management of education on the island, for the inspection and examination of schools, for the drafting of syllabuses and the training of teachers. Religious Instruction was to be provided daily in all schools, parents having the right to withdraw their children if they wished to do so. School was to be compulsory from the ags of 5 to 15, no child under 13 was to be employed, and no child under 14 was to be employed during school hours. School fees were to be remitted for poor families. An Education Fund was to be established to cover the cost of salaries and books and the rates of school buildings. Such sums of money as were approved by the Governor and the Secretary of State would be paid into it annually.

The schools, as reorganized and renamed, and the head teachers appointed were as follows:

Pilling Central School, Jamestown; Mr William Corker

The Junior School, Napoleon Street, Jamestown; Miss Eliza Smith

The Infants School, Napoleon Street, Jamestown; Miss Mildred Smith

The Gosse Central School, St Paul's; Miss Vida Evans

The Cathedral Junior and Infants School, St Paul's; Mrs Lilian Samuel

Half Tree Hollow School; Miss M. Hartvig

Hutts Gate School; Mrs Lilian Corker
Sandy Bay School; Mr Edward Constantine
Blue Hill School; Miss Evelyn Bagley (pupil teacher i/c)

Pilling Central School, now for senior pupils only, was named after Sir Guy Pilling, the Governor of St Helena from 1938 to 1941. At this stage, both the Seniors and the Juniors from Jamestown moved into the former Garrison buildings in Market Street, the seniors at one end called Pilling Central School, and the juniors at the other end called *Jamestown Junior School*, so vacating the buildings near St John's Church. William Corker retained the headship he had held since 1922, but now his school had reverted to being a mixed one again for seniors only. He was assisted by four teachers and two pupil teachers. The Junior School was now to be led by Eliza Smith, assisted by two pupil teachers. Miss Smith had previously held the headship of the Jamestown Girls' School since 1922. It is interesting to note that in the 1941 Amalgamation Ordinance document both the Junior School and the Infants School were recorded as occupying buildings in Napoleon Street. However, islanders who were children in the schools at the time testify to the fact that immediately following the Ordinance the juniors moved from Napoleon Street to share the upper building at Pilling with the seniors at the former military quarters in Market Street. This left the infants to occupy the Napoleon Street buildings on their own, under Mildred Smith's leadership assisted by two teachers and two pupil teachers.

The *Gosse Central School* was in the buildings of the previous Country Senior School. It was now named after the historian of St Helena, Philip Gosse. Vida Evans retained the headship which she had held there since 1910. The *Cathedral Junior and Infants School* was the new name of the previous Country Junior School, the head teacher being Mrs Lilian Samuel.

Of the remaining four schools in the schedule, *Hutts Gate* remained an all-age school, temporarily under the control of pupil teacher Dorothy Dann, but shortly to be led by Lilian Corker, the wife of the head teacher of Pilling Central School. *Half Tree Hollow*, *Sandy Bay* and *Blue Hill* all became junior schools, with their senior children transferring to the Gosse Central School. From July 1941 Half Tree Hollow was in the charge of Miss M. Hartvig, who had originally come to the island as housekeeper to Bishop Turner but who later moved into teaching. Sandy Bay's head teacher continued to be the veteran Edward Constantine, who had been there since 1904. Blue Hill School, which was no longer called the Bishop Holbech Memorial School, was in the charge of two pupil teachers, Harriet Williams and Evelyn Bagley, who had started in the profession in July 1941.

It will be noted that several of the head teachers were already long-serving members of the island's teaching force and this fact was significant in helping to establish the new system. Others put in charge of schools were comparative newcomers such as Evelyn Bagley. In 1992 she recalled that, just before the Amalgamation Ordinance, she had been very undecided about her future career when she left school at the age of 15, needing to look after her mother. However, the following year, Education Officer Mr Rawlings invited her to become a teacher. Accordingly, while she looked after the Blue Hill School, she also attended the classes once a week for pupil teachers in the pavilion at Francis Plain. Here, Mr Rawlings taught her about class management, at first leaving the content of the lessons she taught to her, although later on she had to submit syllabuses to the Education Officer. Officially at Blue Hill she had only junior children to teach, as the senior-age children were supposed to go to the Gosse School, but many parents did not wish them to walk the distance there, and the pupils kept drifting back to Blue Hill! Consequently, Algernon Broadway was appointed to teach the seniors at Blue Hill for an interim period until they could be persuaded to attend the Gosse School, and Evelyn continued to teach the younger children.[2]

At the time of the major changes in 1941 within the school system, the teachers had the strong support of the new Governor, Major William Bain-Grey, who – like many of his predecessors – interested himself in education in the widest sense.

Nevertheless, in spite of the volume of goodwill towards the new system, it did not have an altogether smooth reception. In addition to the persistence of senior children in continuing to attend Blue Hill School, and the need to appoint a teacher for them, there were also problems at the Pilling School. Derek Fagan, a pupil at the time of the 1941 reorganization, remembers that the changeover was far from smooth. For one thing, the building had been a communal dwelling place and some of the residents were still living there. It was not well equipped for school purposes and the children had to sit in desks cramped together. On the positive side, though, he remembers being taught the basic subjects, and also that the sports equipment was very good; the Hussey Charity School, which he had attended before, had none. Adversely, textbooks were now non-existent, while in the Hussey Charity School the pupils had had one each.[3]

The system also had its influential critics. Although he no longer held an official position within the education system, Canon Walcott continued to express his deep-seated doubts about the handing over of the church schools to the State through the useful medium of the *St Helena Magazine*. Now, in September 1941, he wrote: 'In some respects the new Education Ordinance is a disappointing document and presses heavily, as we are sure it was never intended to do, on the children it is out to benefit and protect.' He was referring to the distances children now had to travel to school – 'the new ordinance, assuming apparently in its respect for children, that our little ones have cherubic wings, has altered the phrase "within two miles" to "within a radius of two miles", which is quite a different matter'. Of Blue Hill he affirmed: 'It will be a discredit to any present or future Board of Education if the school at Blue Hill, which Government has made itself responsible for, is not maintained in its original intention for the benefit of children in the district.'

For some months public correspondence in the *St Helena Magazine* between the Education Officer and the editor continued on the merits and demerits of the new system. May 1942 found Canon Walcott expressing his concern about the 5 to 15 compulsory age range introduced in the new Ordinance: 'It is now generally realized that this alteration was a mistake and that the old rule of 6 to 14 was, in our local conditions, the better one. There were exceptions and some children chose to go at 5 and leave at 15. The mistake was to make the exception the rule, 5 is too young and 14-year-old boys are needed at home.'

Prophetically, in July 1942 Mr Walcott declared: 'What is needed is a properly organized secondary school in some central position.' And in December 1942, critical of the newly reorganized schooling system which had created three elementary central schools, and pursuing the need for secondary education, Canon Walcott wrote in the *St Helena Magazine*: 'So far in St Helena, no opportunity has been given our children to work for a school certificate of a recognized educational standard. Under this new school, the precious hours are frittered away in the carpenter's shop or in the school garden.' Later in May 1943, he shot another 'Canon-ball': 'There are probably more cranks in the educational profession than in any other profession under the sun, and among the cranks are surely the advocates of that system which would use up the precious hours of a short school day in such extraneous things as PT (as they love to call it), domestic science, woodwork, gardening, boot repairing, dancing etc, excellent in their way in the right place at the right time, and of trades at the right age, but not in academies dedicated to letters, devoted to what is generally meant by Education, built upon the foundation of the Three Golden Rs.'

However, the few initial matters concerning the reorganization were sorted out and the schools and their teachers settled down to their new situation. A number of moves were necessary over the next few years in order to share out the teachers appropriately. For instance, Evelyn Bagley was transferred from Blue Hill in 1944 to 'The Cathedral Primary School' which was on the site of the present St Paul's First School. The Senior part of the school was at St Paul's Vicarage, known as the Country School, to which Mr Broadway went as head in 1945. The headship of Blue Hill was taken over for several months by Edward Benjamin. Meanwhile, Miss Bagley was moved to Sandy Bay School for four years, living there with relatives at Wranghams. From here she recalls cycling to school, leaving her bicycle at the top of the valley and walking the rest of the way down to the school. In 1949 George Lawrence became head of Blue Hill and Miss Bagley returned there, taking charge in 1951 when Mr Lawrence went to work in the Education Office. By this time all the senior pupils had been persuaded to transfer from Blue Hill to the Country School.[2] This began Miss Bagley's long period of service as a head teacher which was to last until her retirement in 1985, and it was fitting that it was in the school she had attended as a child.

Meanwhile, at the reorganization following the 1941 Ordinance the employment of former teachers of the Benevolent Society was safeguarded, and they had been accepted into the Government service or retired on a pension from public funds. This enabled a number of the older teachers to retire.

The next decade saw the conditions for several of the schools being substantially improved and some new schools being established. Hutts Gate School had continued to be the only school providing for children in the eastern division of the island and was still seriously overcrowded. Calls for a separate school for Levelwood had not materialised, but in 1945 the long-awaited school was established for seniors, juniors and infants. In the newspaper report of the Official Opening in October 1945, praise came at last from the pen of the editor of the *St Helena Magazine*: 'Here at last is a school building which does the Colony credit and which fulfils a long felt requirement.' Louis Timm was appointed to be Head of the Levelwood School, and he was provided with a residence adjoining the school. It would save some children a long four- or five-mile walk to school, and would also relieve pressure on the schools at Hutts Gate and Sandy Bay. Canon Walcott had the satisfaction, after ten years, of seeing his suggestion bear fruit. The school was opened formally by the Governor on 29 September with 77 children on its books. When Mr Timm left his post for South Africa, the headship was taken over by Arthur Evans.

1946-51: Introduction of Secondary Education

Following the Ordinance, Education Officer Mr Watkins had selected various pupils from each of the island's schools to give them more advanced teaching, using temporary accommodation near to where he was living in Francis Plain House. These lessons are remembered by Ruth Pridham (née Stevens), the present Chairman of the Education Committee (1992), who was one of the pupils involved. Her cousin, Dulcie Robertson (née Stevens), also recalls how, as a 13-year-old, she was chosen from Blue Hill to attend these classes in the Pavilion at Francis Plain, together with one pupil from Sandy Bay (Iva Henry), Hutts Gate (Derek Knipe), Country School (Ruth Pridham), Half Tree Hollow (Wilma Benjamin), and three from Pilling School (including Carlos Netto and Mervyn Reynolds). All of the pupils were roughly the same age, although in addition pupil teachers attended from time to time. In the Pavilion was one large table, around which the pupils sat on long forms or stools. They had full-time school from 9 am to 3 pm each day, with a break for sandwiches at 12 o'clock. Mr Watkins often had to leave the pupils to attend to some of his other duties, and one of the pupil teachers, such as Ivy Constantine, was left in charge. Mr Watkins progressed on from their previous teaching, and gave them a lot of written work to do. This included biology, history, geography and arithmetic, for which he also set examinations. Relaxation came with a game of cricket on Francis Plain, girls and boys together.[4]

But this class was dispersed when Mr Watkins' term of office ended in 1943 and Ruth, for example, returned to her old school at Blue Hill.[5] Dulcie went to the Country School until she left as a pupil at the age of 15, but immediately started there as a pupil teacher under Vida Evans' headship.

Shortly after this, however, it was planned to open the school for selected pupils in premises at Red Gate. This was originally called the St Helena Secondary School, and later the Secondary Selective School. It was established officially on 29 April 1946 under the headship of Miss Penelope Walker, who came from England under the Colonial Development Welfare Grant.

In a letter written 46 years later, Mrs Penelope Porter (née Walker) recalled with pleasure her experiences on St Helena:

It was not until I arrived there in 1946, officially as Woman Education Officer, that I was told that I was expected to start a Secondary School ...

So in April 1946 the Secondary School started with 13 pupils though one had to drop out as it proved too far for her to walk. Our premises were at Red Gate not too far from Plantation House and Kingshurst where I lived. Conditions were very primitive and there was very little equipment of any kind. The children had to walk to school coming from Jamestown, Longwood and Blue Hill. These children were very intelligent being the best children from the various schools. On Saturday mornings a group of Student Teachers came to Red Gate and I taught them.

The following year another twelve pupils came and finally more came in September 1948 so there were almost 40 when I left. I was the only teacher during the whole of my time though I did have the assistance of two student teachers. Eventually the school moved to nearby Bishopsholme when Bishop Lloyd Price Turner moved to new premises. Here we had much more room.

The teaching was very enjoyable and rewarding. The children were keen to learn and very well behaved and I was very fond of them. Bishop Turner came in one morning a week to take a little service. We had lots of pleasure from music though I could not have managed without Keith Yon's very great help. At Christmas we took a bus and went out carol singing.

Two great events were the visit of the Royal Family on their return from South Africa and the visit of an aircraft carrier as the children had never seen an aeroplane. We had an outing down to Sandy Bay and another up Diana's Peak.

For relaxation I played tennis twice a week hurrying down to Jamestown after school. Having no transport I had to walk and run down the steps.

My three years in St Helena were very enjoyable and I am glad I was able to contribute a little to the education there.'[6]

Dulcie Robertson was one of the pupil teachers to assist Miss Walker at the school, initially in a voluntary capacity, and she clearly remembers the first intake of pupils. One of these first pupils was Joan Joshua, now (in 1992) Mrs Thomas, the Head Teacher of Longwood First School. Joan herself recalls the process used for selection for entry – an initial recommendation from the child's head teacher, and, based on an island test, the final selection was made by the Education Officer/Secondary Head Teacher. Mrs Thomas spent four years at the school.[7]

Among the first generation of pupils there were several who were happy to talk in 1991 about their experiences of over forty years earlier. Mrs Ruth Pridham became one of Miss Walker's pupil teachers at the time, spending three days each week studying academic subjects and child development with Miss Walker, and two days learning 'on the job' in the school at Blue Hill. Cecil Maggott, who later became the island's Custodian of Records, particularly recalls the teaching he received from Miss Walker on Shakespeare and John Masefield. Basil George, who was to become the first St Helenian Chief Education Officer, was in the second generation of students at the Secondary Selective School. He has an additional reason to be grateful to Miss Walker, as it was she who introduced her pupils to the value of walking over the island, and this is now one of his favourite pastimes. Bill Drabble, a contemporary of Basil George at Red Gate, now an elected member of the island's Legislative Council, also appreciated the literature lessons and the memorizing which they had to achieve. Mrs Dorothy Hudson, the Assistant Post Mistress, remembering the teaching she had received, recalls gratefully: 'I owe a lot to Miss Walker.'[8]

As successive years of pupils entered the school, they were taught by the same teacher throughout the day, across a wide range of subjects including English, Geography, History, Literature, Mathematics with Algebra, and Science. Vocational classes in typing, book-keeping and dress-making were given to the top form. Unlike all other schools on the island, the pupils wore a school uniform. This was royal blue and white. For a while they also had school dinners which were prepared on site, but this system was short-lived as the Saints (as St Helenians called themselves) preferred to have the traditional sandwiches for lunch.

As described by Mrs Porter, the Red Gate premises became too small within the first two years and the school moved the short distance into a house nearby in the adjoining lane which had been the home of the Bishop, but which he had vacated in favour of the property now known as Bishopsholme, a little lower down the main road. The 'new' school building, adjacent to the building now used as the Motor Vehicle Testing Centre, was able to accommodate the 38 pupils attending the school at its opening there in September 1948. As there were now three cohorts of pupils, two pupil teachers were recruited to assist Miss Walker – Miss Violet Graham and Cyril Lawrence. Mrs Pat Musk (née Benjamin) remembers taking the entrance test set by Mr Thompson, the Education Officer, and then becoming a pupil in this building, where she recalls having lessons on spelling, comprehension and arithmetic.[9]

Meanwhile, the island's major focus had been diverted in 1946 to the effects of a serious outbreak of poliomyelitis, apparently contracted from a person on a recent ship from the Cape. In spite of strong measures to curb the disease, including the closure of schools, several people on the island were affected, some of whom died; others were permanently paralysed in some form. Eric George contracted the disease at the age of eight and, in spite of severe paralysis, pursued a full career in the education service as a teacher, information officer, head teacher and Assistant Education Officer. Cyril Lawrence, Derek Fagan and Patsy Flagg were also victims of the disease but were fortunate to escape long-term ill-effects and, after a promising school life, each has pursued a successful career on the island.

However, in due course the activities of the island were resumed. The second annual competitive Music Festival was held, as was the Annual Sunday School Treat at Francis Plain, which attracted 300 children to participate in football, lunch and sports – the teachers having provided the food.

Meanwhile, in another part of the island, a boost to the morale of the people of the St Paul's area came with the construction of a brand new school building at a cost of £5,500, which was opened by the Acting Governor on 27 September 1947, in the presence of Education Officer Rawlings and Head Teacher Algernon Broadway. The school reverted to its previous name of Country School. No doubt this pleased Canon Walcott who reminisced about the earlier reorganization master-minded by Mr Watkins: 'Then came a new education officer who had an itch for fancy names, and the Country School was renamed the Gosse School after the well-known historian Dr Philip Gosse, and the Town School was diplomatically called the Pilling School, after the reigning Governor of that name.'[10]

Regarding a school at Longwood, it was not until the time of World War II in the early 1940s that plans had really begun to take shape for this area to have its own schools. A little establishment, known as the Bethel School, was the first to appear near Longwood, mainly to relieve pressure of overcrowding at Hutts Gate and to provide more conve-nient schooling for the youngest children. This building was originally the small mission hall constructed by the Baptists on the island in 1932 for the benefit of their members in the Longwood area and it was called 'Longwood Bethel'. The school was along the Deadwood Road, on the site of the present Salvation Army Hall, and it was for the children up to the age of nine years from Hutts Gate. Mrs Edith Timm, now Head Teacher of the Prince Andrew School, recalls starting her schooling at Bethel School at the age of six and going with her two sisters, Lilian and May. At the age of seven she was transferred to Hutts Gate School for the rest of her schooling. An Admissions Register which is still available for Bethel-Longwood School covers the years from 1943 to 1954 and includes the names of 311 children, ranging in age from five to nine years and covering a wide geographical area, including Long-wood, Deadwood, Fisher's Valley, Black Field, Tobacco Plain, Mulberry Gut and Coal Sheds. Most of these people are still on the island today and recall their isolated little school in which they received good individual attention from their two teachers who were sisters – Ivy Duncan and Noreen (Nora) Evans.

During the Second World War various buildings had been put up in Longwood to accommodate the army, but of course when peace came they were no longer needed for that purpose. At the end of the war, the Government decided that the Officers Quarters near the golf course should be converted into a school and so, in 1949, the Longwood School was established there with 60 pupils – a much-needed school in this under-provided but well-populated area of the island. It was only for infant and junior children. All the pupils of senior school age still attended Hutts Gate School. No transport was provided, of course. Mrs Lily Corker was the first head teacher of the Longwood School.

Yet another school was housed in new buildings the following year. This was Sandy Bay School, which was able to move on 27 November 1948 from its dual-purpose room in St Peter's Church to a site which had been donated by Solomons nearby.

In the same year new buildings were provided for Half Tree Hollow School. The 1941 Ordinance had resulted in a recognition of the need for a purpose-built school at Half Tree Hollow, but it was some seven years later that the new building was completed, just below the site of the old school. It was opened officially as a primary school in 1949, still under the headship of Miss Constantine, the seniors having already been transferred to one of the three newly established senior schools on the island – Gosse Central School, Pilling Senior School, or Harford Senior School. The old school building reverted to being a private home, and, in fact, was sold by the Charity to the former head teacher of the school, James Sim. Keith Stevens, in an interview for the 'People Profile' column in the May 1992 St Helena News, recalled the change to the new buildings. His education had started at the old Half Tree Hollow School, and the new building was in the process of being built: 'The school was crowded for the Opening and to mark this historical occasion, Mr Thompson, the Education Officer, had a slide show in black and white on views of the island.' Keith also recalled that on Ash Wednesday the whole school would march to St Paul's Cathedral for the Service. There was only one school bus at that time and it was used for the Secondary School children. He transferred to Country Senior School at the age of 11, where the headmaster was Algernon Broadway,

The Secondary Selective School Building, 1950-88, at the top of Ladder Hill

and he was taught by Mrs Gertrude Gray who 'had such an influence on my life which has lived with me up to the present day'.

R.C.Thompson became Education Officer in 1947, succeeding Mr Rawlings in the post. The efforts to improve the housing of schools continued. In March 1950 the premises used by the Secondary Selective School in the old Bishopsholme became unsafe and were condemned as unfit for the purposes of the school. This time more suitable accommodation was found in the former military buildings at the top of Ladder Hill. Miss Walker had concluded her service on the island in 1949 and in September 1950 the school, under the leadership of Miss Jessie Cardwell, was established at Ladder Hill where it remained until its closure and classes finished in 1988. Mrs Rita Nicholls, now Head Teacher of Pilling Middle School, recalls how she had been selected to go to the school from Jamestown Junior School, having been called into Wellington House by Education Officer Mr Thompson to take a verbal intelligence test. After a short while in the old Bishopsholme, she received lessons in the three rooms of the Colonnade at Ladder Hill. Later the school transferred into the nearby Armoury, where more rooms were available. The site at Ladder Hill had the advantage of the use of a gymnasium, tennis courts and a

Jacob's Ladder, on which SSS pupils climbed to school from Jamestown, and slid back down again after school was over

swimming pool. Being at the top of Jacob's Ladder of 699 steps rising from Jamestown, the school occupied a commanding site, and many of the pupils acquired the art of sliding down the steps by lying across the iron banisters to get home from school. Rita took an active part in the school's activities, particularly in sports. She became head girl, leaving in 1954 to enter immediately into teaching at Jamestown Infants School. There she was 'thrown in at the deep end' and learned on the job, with help and understanding from the head teacher, Mrs Martha George, and by attending Saturday morning sessions with the Education Officer.[11]

Miss Cardwell held the headship post until 1951, but then the position became vacant for two years. During part of this time the school was led by an elderly visitor to the island, Warren Harrison, who was living at the Consulate and then by Assistant Teacher Ronald Chester. Then it was decided that in future the Education Officer should undertake the double role, that is, to include the Headship of the Secondary Selective School within his responsibilities. The first holder of the post was Norman Kerr, who was appointed in 1953 and whose major contribution to education is described in the next section. In spite of these quick changes, the school settled well into the 'new' premises and played an important part in preparing several pupils for future responsible posts on the island.

But, in spite of all the improvements to buildings since the Government took over control of the schools, a major problem confronting the Education Department was the increasing number of teachers who were leaving their posts and emigrating. This concern had been expressed in the Education Officer's Report of 1947, and included in Governor Joy's Report entitled *Information on St Helena Colony, 1947* for transmission under Article 73(e) of the United Nations Charter in respect of 1947, as follows: 'One of the more pressing problems is the emigration of young pupil teachers which is partly due to the general desire always noticed in the island to see the outside world.' In his *Address to the joint meeting of the Executive and Advisory Councils*, both in 1948 and 1949, he included the same concern. Stressing the need for a sound education 'in order that a young man or young woman shall be able to share the life of the community and earn a living in this competitive world', he drew attention to the fact that there was a lack of trained teachers. In 1949, one head teacher, two assistant teachers and three pupil teachers had left the island. He indicated his intention of acquiring two trained teachers from the UK for two years in 1950 – 'but the island needs to be self-sufficient'.

The island also lost another long-serving member of the teaching profession with the death in 1950 of William Corker, the Head Teacher of Pilling Central School. He had been Head of the Government Boys' School from 1922 to 1941, and then continued at Pilling after the amalgamation of schools. Jack LeBreton was appointed to succeed him.

Soon after this, another stalwart left the teaching profession. This was Eliza Smith, who retired in 1952 after a career which had spanned 46 years on the island, starting in 1906. Now in 1992 several of her pupils remember her clearly as 'a good teacher' who set and required high standards.

1952-56: Island Education led by Norman Kerr

In 1952 the island was 'adopted', in educational terms, by the East Suffolk County Council Education Committee, and a significant development of this was the secondment of Norman Kerr in April 1953 as Education Officer at the request of the Colonial Office.

Norman Kerr held the post of Education Officer on St Helena from April 1953 to April 1956. His role included the headship of the Secondary Selective School, where he found that 'in recent years the work has suffered from the vicissitudes of changing premises and staff" – there had been six head teachers since 1949. In July 1953 the pupil numbers were only 30 girls and 8 boys.

In fact, he found that education on the island was generally in rather a poor state and, with the active support of his wife, Margaret (an experienced teacher) and George Lawrence, 'a devoted Chief Clerk', he applied himself energetically to raising the standards. The *St Helena Annual Report, 1952/1953* detailed that there had been 1,269 children at school in 1952; education was free and compulsory from the ages of 5 to 15; there were 11 primary schools and one secondary school; and in the 10-year development plan the aim was to allocate 12% of government spending on education. In the previous year only 9.7% had been spent on education compared with 10.4% on public health and 13.0% on public works.

In correspondence with the author nearly 40 years later, Mr Kerr recalled that as Headmaster of the Secondary School he taught each morning in the Old Barracks, covering a range of subjects – Physical Education, Maths, Geography, History and Science. He had two young teachers to help and his wife taught on most afternoons, on others visiting infants schools to demonstrate teaching methods. As Information Officer – salary £24 per annum – he was responsible for the Library in Jamestown and for organizing the regular news film shows on six evenings each month in different locations on the island. The equipment was taken around in a Landrover. He also was responsible for arranging for the programmes for any important visitor to St Helena. With George Lawrence he compiled a weekly newsletter, since the *St Helena Magazine* had gone out of circulation in 1951. In 1954, at the suggestion of the Governor, 'and in the absence of anyone else', they began to publish *The Wirebird* monthly, which became the official island newspaper for a few years.[12]

On arrival, Mr Kerr had assessed that a lack of reading fluency was causing lower standards of achievement of pupils in all schools, including the Secondary School. A major root cause he diagnosed to be the absence of creative and imaginative teaching methods, and so he made it one of his prime concerns to improve standards. He saw that one of his most serious tasks was to train young teachers. He arranged weekly after-school sessions in the most convenient schools, but the biggest problem was the number of young and 'pupil' teachers who were being tempted from the profession by remunerative offers of domestic employment in the UK. In addition, for three years he arranged residential courses at Country School during holidays for as many as 30 young and pupil teachers, spending the mornings on practical teaching problems, the afternoons ranging over the island in search of endemic plants, and the evenings on discussion. This was a great stimulus to the young people.

By May 1954 he had secured the services of another qualified teacher from the UK, Edgar Wagstaff, who was able to share in the work both at the Secondary School and in teacher training. Mr Wagstaff recalls that, with Mr Kerr – 'a great Education Officer' – he joined in helping the young teachers to get to know their island better by walking extensively with them, including to Blue Hill and to Diana's Peak. In his capacity as the BBC Correspondent, Mr Wagstaff made the first-ever broadcast from the island, when he reported on the visit of the Duke of Edinburgh, during which the Duke had opened the Children's Playground in Jamestown. Mr Kerr and Mr Wagstaff repeated the residential course in each of the following two years. A copy of the programme for the 1955 course showed that it started each morning with physical training at 7 o'clock, followed by lectures and practical work and an introduction by Mr Wagstaff to a new reading scheme. Also included was a session with Dr Clarke of the Medical Department; with Father Flint on Religious Instruction; folk dancing, the preparation of apparatus for use in the classroom, and a film entitled *The Schoolmaster*.

Norman Kerr (centre front) with the Teachers' Residential Course, Easter 1955, at the Country School

In his *1954 Education Report* Mr Kerr was able to describe a year of consolidation. He regretted that, due to shortage of teachers, his pupil teachers were required in the classroom, so they did not have opportunity to observe more experienced teachers at work. Also their training sessions with Mr Kerr had to take place after school hours and on Saturday mornings. Nevertheless, he paid credit to the 15- and 16-year-olds who 'get on with their job of teaching'. He was also able to report that six had taken the qualifying examination to become Assistant Teachers and five Assistant Teachers had qualified to become First Assistants.

J. B. Sidebotham paid a return visit to the island in 1955, his previous one having been in 1939. He was impressed with the progress which was being made and paid high tribute to the work of Mr Kerr. There had been a change in the approach to primary education and the methods of teaching, which included more practical work and use of visual aids; and, at the secondary level, to the application of knowledge to everyday problems of life. In a review of his March/April visit, he included a *Report on Schools*, significant sections of which are reproduced here:

JAMESTOWN INFANTS SCHOOL: In spite of operating in poor buildings, it contained – 'a happy crowd of little people making their first steps in the paths of learning and enjoying it too under the guidance of willing teachers'.

HALF TREE HOLLOW SCHOOL: Conditions at the new school were clearly good. Stating that the children were well and happy, Mr Sidebotham was also able to report that there was an absence of the 'eruptive sores' which had previously troubled the children, of whom there were 150 with a Head Teacher and four student teachers.

SANDY BAY SCHOOL: About Edward Constantine, then in his 51st year as Head Teacher of the school, he wrote: 'The children were being well and carefully taught.' He was impressed that the 70-year-old teacher 'himself guided me down the steep and winding path to the shore of the small bay and showed me much of interest there'. Since 1941 this school had been for juniors and infants only.

HUTTS GATE ALL-AGE SCHOOL: The report noted that there were 135 children, including seniors, at this school, being taught by one master and five student teachers.

LEVELWOOD ALL-AGE SCHOOL: At this school in 1955 there were 70 children being taught by the head teacher, Arthur Evans, and two student teachers. The reports of the progress of the school were satisfactory, except that the poor speech of the children was noted.

One of the pupils at Sandy Bay at this time, Harold Isaac, recalls his school days in the 1950s under the guidance of Mr Constantine and Mr Kerr. In addition to the normal activity at School, Harold describes Ascension Day services at St Paul's Cathedral, the walk there from Sandy Bay, starting at 9.00 am to get there by noon for a picnic lunch, followed by the service. His first educational visit was to Jamestown to the Paramount Cinema to see the film *Where No Vultures Fly*. On Tuesdays the boys walked to the Country School to be taught woodwork by Harold Nicholls. Harold Isaac recalls the days when the stores came to the school from the Government Office, including the arrival of one copy of each of the recent editions of the comic *The Eagle*. This was a real red-letter day.[13]

The two all-age schools were each destined to undergo a major change within the next few years. For many years there had been increasing pressure and need for schooling to be available in both the Longwood and Levelwood areas and also for separate senior schools. With the opening in 1949 of the Longwood Junior and Infants Schools, many of the pupils from Hutts Gate had transferred there. At the opening of the new Harford Senior School in 1957 in purpose-built premises at Longwood, the Hutts Gate School closed. No longer being needed as a school, the premises reverted to being a private dwelling house.

Levelwood All-Age School continued with this structure under a series of head teachers until 1969, when the older pupils were transferred to Harford Senior School. Then Levelwood was for junior and infant children only.

In 1955, under Mr Kerr's leadership, a new curriculum for the schools was made and approved. It included giving attention to fluency, written work, qualities and values, and the study of Scripture; the History and Geography of St Helena, Britain, the Commonwealth and the World; craft, sport and music. In his 1955 Report Mr Sidebotham spoke for many people when he wrote of Mr Kerr: 'For his energy, enthusiasm, and self devotion, as well as for the high order of his professional ability, St Helena has every cause to be thankful.'

Mr Kerr's term of office came to an end in April 1956, but during his three years he had given the education of the island a fresh impetus and a firm base for the future. He had championed the cause of the teachers in his department, and helped them to gain confidence in their own ability by being more knowledgeable and better equipped. He even defended them against unwarranted criticism as in the case of Canon Hall, then the Headmaster of Hutts Gate School, who was rebuked in the newspaper for not attending the Francis Plain Treat Day. In *The Wirebird* of February 1956, Mr Kerr wrote: 'I am grateful for this opportunity before I leave, of expressing my thanks to a fellow Headmaster for his conscientious service at Hutt's Gate School.' Throughout their time on St Helena, Mr and Mrs Kerr's enthusiasm for theatre and folk dancing had been appreciated by the islanders as well as the schools. For instance, to celebrate the Coronation Year they produced an 'Elizabethan Evening', comprising scenes from Shakespeare's *A Midsummer Night's Dream* and some Elizabethan madrigals sung in four parts. 'We found the boys and girls natural actors – the rude mechanicals revelled in their parts and the fairies were superb – we played to packed houses in the Cinema,' reported Mr Kerr. The Kerrs had also organized evening folk dance classes for young teachers and their friends in Jamestown Infants School and at Longwood. As a farewell gesture in 1956, Mr and Mrs Kerr produced the pantomime *Little Red Riding Hood* for which Mr Kerr wrote the script, his wife wrote the songs and composed the music; Eric George committed the score to memory and played it on the piano for rehearsals. Now in 1992 there are many people on the island who remember with appreciation Mr Kerr's whole-hearted participation in whatever task he was undertaking.

1956-60: Development of International Links for Island Education

After Norman Kerr left in 1956, Edgar Wagstaff became Acting Education Officer for almost a year until the arrival of Charles Dixon in 1957. During his period in office, Mr Wagstaff introduced a scheme for free meals at school for the poorer children, financed through UNICEF. Reflecting 35 years later, he looks back on his work on St Helena with great pleasure and maintains a keen interest in island matters.

The *Education Report* covering 1956 paid tribute to the efficient support given by the Chief Clerk to the Education Department, George Lawrence. On his arrival in 1957 Mr Dixon had taken on the same multiple role as his predecessor. He proposed to continue with the policies and practices set up to strengthen the skills of the teaching profession. Like Mr Kerr, he was impressed with the achievements of his pupil teachers: 'Many of the young teachers literally leave school one day, and start as a Pupil Teacher, in full charge of a class, the next. It is greatly to their credit that they achieve such good results.' In fact, 'A Worried Mother' wrote to the *Wirebird* in April 1957 about pressure on her daughter, a pupil teacher who spent eight hours per day and after school on Monday to Friday, Saturday mornings at the Teachers' Class, Sunday at Church and on school studies – 'hours are spent with BOOKS, BOOKS, BOOKS'. Mr Dixon, in his editorial in the same edition, assured her that health need not suffer through study – 'What we know today and in great part the sort of person we are, depends mainly on the ability of the teachers we had. Teachers foster the thinking spirit and have to know a great deal. Pupil Teachers want to do extra work because they want to become better teachers.'

Mrs Muriel Williams, now in 1992 Head Teacher of Levelwood School, recalls being a child at Hutts Gate at the time of the transition to the new Harford Senior School in 1957. Maurice Young kept the headship and was therefore responsible for launching the new school. Muriel, who had started her school life at Longwood Infants School, moving to Hutts Gate for her junior schooling, had passed the entrance exam for admission to the Secondary Selective School, but, like others on the island, was not able to take up the place due to home circumstances. So she now attended the new Harford School, at first fearing but then liking the stern Mr Young. She had progressed rapidly through the earlier classes, and then spent three years in Mr Young's class. He gave her small teaching tasks to do with other children. When it came to the time to leave Harford on her 15th birthday, she chose to remain at school until she was admitted to the full-time teacher training course in the Secondary Selective School, with school attachment at Half Tree Hollow School.[14]

The island was pleased to welcome A.J. Miller, a Fulbright Scholar from Iowa, USA, into the ranks of the teachers for a year. Soon after his arrival in November 1957, he reported in *The Wirebird* that during his first few days on St Helena he had learned much more than he had taught, and that he hoped to explain some of the methods used in the USA to teach children – 'After all, children are pretty much the same all over the world.'

To provide a definite aim to which teachers and pupils alike could work, two examinations were instituted in 1957. These were planned in consultation with the head teachers and Board of Education. The first examination, in English, Arithmetic and General Knowledge for all children between $10\frac{1}{2}$ and $11\frac{1}{2}$ years of age, became known as the 'Secondary Selective Examination', as its results were used to select the most able children to go to the Secondary School. The second was named 'St Helena General Schools Examination' and was administered to all children aged 14+, with papers in English, Arithmetic, History, Geography and General Knowledge. Results of these provided data for the first record cards to be made by the head teachers. In the first year of operation about 40% of the candidates achieved a pass mark of 50%-69%, and a further 10% gained a distinction mark of over 70. This was a promising start.

Another system which had recently been started to improve the standard of teaching was to send one teacher per year to England for training. However, Mr Dixon warned that even if every candidate sent was successful and returned to live and teach in St Helena permanently, it would be some years before marked results were to be seen in the Department as a whole. The first teacher to be sent was Keith Yon in 1953, followed by Ethel Lawrence in 1954, Diana Joshua in 1955, Joan Ross in 1956, Arnold Flagg in 1957, Eric Benjamin in 1958 and Stedson George in 1959. The latter three all attended St Paul's College, Cheltenham, which was destined to become the base for the St Helena Link Committee several years later.

Mr Dixon's *Triennial Report on Education* for the years 1955, 1956 and 1957 ended with a tribute to the Board of Education for providing the element of stability and continuity of policy 'which has been of fundamental importance'. However, in a long article in *The Wirebird* in May 1958 describing education on the island, he regretted the complete lack of interest shown by most parents, who had no conception of a teacher's job and regarded school as a useful place in which to keep the children out of the way. He urged them to accept his definition of education – 'to provide the child with mental, manual and social skills to enable him to have a full and happy life after he leaves school' – and he planned for the department to work as a team 'but we need a forward line – the parents'.

Entry to the Secondary Selective School was not necessarily available to all who might benefit from it. Some children found access to the school too difficult. At one stage transport was provided from Jamestown to Ladder Hill, but not from other areas. Other children could not take up their places because their parents could not afford the uniform, particularly if there were other younger children in the family. For several years, in order to maintain a certain balance of sexes in the school, a given number of places was reserved for boys, although on merit more girls came higher on the entry tests.

Mrs Gay Denbow (née Corker), the St Helena Government Representative in the UK from April 1987 to July 1990, was a pupil at sss. She was among the first group of 13 pupils to stay on at school past the age of 15 and she was enabled to take five subjects at RSA level in the one year. She 'loved her school' and, in 1957, with three of her classmates, Greta Richards, Melina Maggott and Robert Sim, under-took a project entitled 'History of the St Helena Secondary School'. Extra-mural activities undertaken at the school included the establishment of the Junior Red Cross in May 1957; various entertainments including concerts produced by Norman Kerr; carol and other church services; a visit to the ship *John Biscoe* which had called in to St Helena *en route* to England from its five-month expedition in the Antarctic; and sports, including athletics, netball and swimming – the latter describing the mile test which involved swimming in the harbour to the Papanui and back.

In June 1958 Cledwyn Hughes MP visited the island for a month, at the end of which he produced a report entitled *Conditions on the Island of St Helena.* Included was a brief report on the 12 schools, mainly giving the current statistics and highlighting some of the problems caused by lack of teachers. This visit was followed in March 1959 by a similar visit by Aaron Emanuel, CMG of the Foreign and Commonwealth Office, whose *Report on Education, 1959* stated: 'The Education Department is having a very difficult time. It is relying a good deal on pupil teachers who are themselves fresh from school.' He attributed this situation to a number of causes – the failure of teachers going overseas for training to return to the island; the tendency of qualified teachers to leave the island; and the departure of the brighter girls to go into domestic service in the UK. He commented on the discontent felt by some St Helenians that, in spite of the fact that there was compulsory education on the island, the standards had gone down.

In view of the amount of work being expected of the Education Officer, an Assistant Education Officer was appointed in November 1958. Tony Cross took over the responsibility for the training of pupil teachers while sharing the in-service work for teachers with Charles Dixon.

It was realized that the Blue Hill School building was in serious need of repair and a new building was planned. In March 1959 the first blocks were in place for the new school and it was opened five months later on 20 August by Governor Harford.

The end of the decade of the 1950s saw gratifying results in the external GCE examinations, there being 19 distinctions and 39 passes in 1959. The taking of the GCE had been introduced by Mr Dixon, in the first instance principally for teachers to improve their own academic level. Twenty-seven teachers had enrolled in 1957. The UEI and RSA examinations were also conducted on the island, in addition, of course, to the two local examinations taken. One islander, Eric Nicholls, distinguished himself – and St Helena – by achieving 100% on his UEI Mathematics examination, and coming first out of 2,350 candidates. All of these targets were serving as incentives and helping to raise educational standards. At the same time people were seeing the need for opportunities beyond the school-leaving age for pupils who would benefit from further and higher education. Unfortunately, the educational link with East Suffolk had broken down due to the lack of volunteers to serve on the island, so links with other areas were being explored.

Prior to returning to the UK at the end of his three years, Mr Dixon gave a *Review of Education* to the Executive Council in January 1960. He was optimistic on several fronts. The prospects for the future were good. The teachers were taking responsibility for their own work and making attempts to free up their teaching methods. A good start had been made on improving qualifications by the taking of external examinations, these leading to promotions within the profession. Emigration among teachers had decreased. While overseas people were still needed within the system because of their wider experience, more local teachers were taking responsible posts. He wished to see a more systematic teacher training programme. While educational standards were not high, they were very satisfactory compared with other Commonwealth Countries.

7
Towards a New Era:
New Horizons for Island Education
1960-88

The school system is an agency of the larger community charged with the two-fold task of transmitting the heritage of the society and of promoting desirable social change.
Ralph Billing, 1971[1]

1960-66: A Hard Look into the Future

During 1960 five local Teacher Training Scholarships were introduced to enable potential teachers to have a year's training on the island before they started full-time teaching; the Parent/Teacher Association continued their work, including organizing the New Year's Treat Day; plans for a memorial in St James' Church to Canon Lawrence Walcott were made; Tony Cross became Education Officer at the conclusion of three years of service of Charles Dixon; the Chief Clerk in the Education Office, George Lawrence, left after many years of service, and Edward Constantine retired from the headship of Sandy Bay School at the age of 75 after 56 years in the post.

Shortly after taking the helm in March 1961, initially in an acting capacity, Tony Cross submitted a *Triennial Report for 1958-1960* in which he gave a clear statement of policy that education on the island was to be suited to all ages, aptitudes and abilities from 5 to 15 years; it aimed to develop a broader world outlook; to encourage the taking of external examinations; to improve the training of teachers from the age of 16; to make evening classes available to islanders in general; and to develop individual capacities to the full. He embraced within education a wide range of activities including the running of youth groups; liaison with a vocational apprenticeship scheme in the Agriculture and Forestry Department; further education classes and in-service training for teachers. His major concerns were the parochial outlook and narrowness of vision of some of the teachers and their resistance to change. Nevertheless, Mr Cross reported that 'The Island's schools are happy industrious units in which cheerful children are well-taught within the capabilities of their equally cheerful teachers'. The total number of pupils in the islands' schools at the end of 1960 was 1,189, including 816 at primary and 373 at secondary level, the latter including 61 at the Secondary Selective School. Acting for the Governor, the Education Officer became the Chairman of the Board of Education in 1960.

Mr Cross reported that new buildings were completed for Blue Hill School in 1959 and Jamestown Junior and Infants Schools in 1960. The Junior School, which had shared the former officers' quarters in the old barracks buildings with Pilling Senior School, moved to the lower end of the playground, and the Infants' School moved from Napoleon Street into Market Street, across the road from the other two schools. Martha George was head teacher of the juniors, and Una Thomas of the infants. The official opening of the Jamestown schools on 20 January 1961 by Governor Sir Robert Alford and Lady Alford was recorded in *The Wirebird*, the editor commenting that the buildings were 'well-designed with strong emphasis on ventilation and light. The Infant School has the attraction of a paddling pool. It is the intention that the school building in Napoleon Street shall in due course be used as a Community Centre for Jamestown. With its East India Company association it should prove a most suitable structure for such a purpose.'

During the Easter holidays in 1961, education on the island received a great boost when an exhibition of books and materials was staged, through the generosity of the British Publishers' Educational Group. This was followed by the free distribution of two thousand exhibition items among schools and individuals.

Since the role of the Education Officer continued to be a multiple one, including also responsibility for the Information Service and the Library, Alan Johns was appointed to join Tony Cross to assist as Teacher Training Tutor, arriving on 28 August 1961. Throughout his three years as Education Officer, Mr Cross strove to fulfil the educational aims outlined in his first report, and his work on the island is remembered and appreciated by teachers to this day. In his comprehensive *Education Report, 1962* at the end of his term of office, Mr Cross reiterated the need to widen the perspectives and abilities of the teachers. 'The problems are further increased since the teaching staff is drawn from the same environment as the pupils and it is greatly to their credit that many teachers rise high above the general level and command respect in their localities.' He identified the value of including a teacher from abroad within his teaching team, this being Florence Stark who was the second Fulbright Scholar from the USA.

Having had 17 years' teaching experience in California, she arrived on St Helena in August 1961 and spent a year in Jamestown Junior School alongside fellow teacher Mrs Maureen Stevens, participating in using reading schemes with young children. Through this link, a gift of books for the school libraries came from the California Teachers' Association in 1965.

In August 1962, Alan Johns took over the post of Education Officer. Like his predecessor, he had the advantage of having had useful experience on the island prior to taking on the overall responsibility for the Education Department. With much support from the new Governor, Sir John Field, Mr Johns sought to introduce a more progressive system of education. He arranged for vso (Voluntary Service Overseas) young men and women to work as pupil teachers and to assist with evening classes for young adults; the institution of Open Days in schools; increased expenditure on education to improve equipment and materials and the provision of a schools' broadcasting service, Mr Johns being the first radio announcer on Radio St Helena. He stressed the importance of including at least a core of overseas-trained teachers among the work force, made positive efforts to unite the teaching force, involving all concerned in 'friendly critical assessments' and improved the Public Library. He also revised the point of entry to school of each age-group, with infants starting school at the beginning of the term after their fifth birthday, moving to juniors similarly after their seventh birthday, and to senior school similarly after their eleventh birthday. In his *Address to the Advisory Council* in November 1964, Governor Sir John Field urged: 'We must raise standards to participate in the modern world of specialists and technicians.'

The Education section of the *Annual Report of 1962/63* confirmed that since 1962 the vso workers had become an established factor within the Department. Over the next few years several other young people worked within the Department, averaging four each year from 1964 to 1969, the final two coming in 1973. Three of these volunteers married St Helenian people and remained on the island. Barbara Montgomerie, until 1992 Head of the Faculty of Science and Maths at the Prince Andrew School, is the wife of Basil George, now the Chief Education Officer. Cathy Bell, a specialist teacher of music at the Prince Andrew School, is the wife of technical crafts teacher, Keith Hopkins. Caroline Pagett, a former teacher at the Secondary Selective School, is the wife of Hensel Peters.

Three pupil teachers, Beatrice Young, Inez Benjamin and Sylvia George, went in August 1963 to attend Stranmillis College, Belfast.

This procedure was part of the policy established for a teacher to have one year of local training, two years of local teaching, followed by a three year course in the UK to gain a Certificate in Education. Also one primary school head teacher had become the first in a scheme to send senior teachers overseas for short courses of practice and observation in UK schools. By the time of the *1964/65 Education Report* the numbers had increased to six local teachers attending UK three-year teacher certificate courses, including Joyce Harris and Delia Duncan (now Huxtable) and two senior teachers spending one year in Oxford and in London respectively.

'The Aims of Education in St Helena' was the subject chosen by the Reverend M. S. Geen, a member of the Board of Education, in a public speech, reported in *The Wirebird* of August/September 1964. Referring to the acceleration of the process of education in recent years, he gave his answers to the question 'What part has education on the Island?' These included the need for the island's young people to make a living, to train in citizenship for life and to develop their personalities in a spiritual dimension.

Another development was the start of the St Helena Teachers' Association under the initiative of a group of local teachers, including Eric M. George, who chaired an initial meeting on 24 August 1966 at Ladder Hill, and Mrs Martha George, who acted as secretary for the group. Their immediate task was to create a formal proposal to submit to the Governor for the official establishment of the Association. A constitution was drawn up for approval, and an Executive Committee selected, these being:

President:	Mr Eric George
Vice-President:	Mr Stedson George
General Secretary:	Mrs Martha George
General Treasurer:	Mrs Iris Clingham
Members:	Mrs J. P. Flagg (Half Tree Hollow)
	Mrs H. Stevens (Pilling)
	Mrs B. Plato (Jamestown Infants)
	Mrs E. Mercury (Harford)
	Mrs J. Thomas (Longwood Junior)
	Mrs L. Crowie (Levelwood)
	Mrs I. Henry (Sandy Bay)
	Mrs G. Benjamin (Blue Hill)

The Association from the start saw its role as representing all colleagues in the profession. It had an influential voice, since its representative on the Board of Education could discuss issues from the point of view of the teachers. Over the years it has caused the teachers to become more politically and professionally aware, accepting 'ownership' of their work. It has also organized social events for members of the profession. As part of their policy, no senior members of the Department are members of the Association.[2]

Meanwhile during the 1960s the leadership at the Secondary Selective School changed hands a number of times, being held in succession by Algernon Broadway, T. E. Lamin, D. Streatfield, Cliff Huxtable (for two short periods), Ralph Billing and J. Cobbett. Several of today's leading islanders were also involved, each teaching a range of subjects. Cyril Lawrence, now retired from his post as the General Manager of Solomons, had started his career as a pupil teacher doing two days training each week and three days in a school. He shortly moved into full-time teaching at the Secondary Selective School where for him 'it was a question of teaching myself while teaching others'. Rita Nicholls, now Head Teacher at Pilling Middle School, recalls her time as a teacher at sss, saying 'I taught practically everything'. When specialist subject teaching was introduced into the school in the later 1960s, teachers concentrated on one or two subjects – Mrs Mabel Yon on English (later Mathematics), Eric George on English, Stedson George on Geography, Barbara George (née Montgomerie) on Science and Gwen Yon on History and Religious Knowledge – and in 1964 the first three candidates were entered for O levels.[3]

In the light of subsequent developments, probably the greatest achievement of Education Officer Alan Johns was to set in motion the central school project which, 23 years later, materialized in the opening of the Prince Andrew School. Alan Johns provided the impetus when, on 25 August 1965, after making a thorough survey of education on the island, he produced *Recommendations for Educational Policy*. He reported to the Governor, Sir John Field: 'The long term objective should logically be the concentrating of all Secondary Education in one central school with all the necessary trained and specialist teaching staff, facilities, equipment and buildings required.' Among other advantages Alan Johns included: 'It would form a melting pot in which the conditions of prejudice and lack of understanding between different communities would be ameliorated, and it would considerably ease the task of administration educationally.'

By the time he produced his *Triennial Report for 1964-66*, Mr Johns had steered a 10-year development plan through island official channels and it was under consideration by the Ministry of Overseas Development in the UK. Its major proposals included the employment of a small group of expatriate teachers, the centralization of secondary schooling, the provision of a schools' broadcasting unit, the introduction of nursery classes and the expansion of technical training. Reflecting in 1992, Mr Johns readily acknowledged that he was fully supported by Governor Sir John and Lady Field (a former principal of a teacher training college in Nigeria) and that the role played by Ralph Billing from the time of his arrival in 1965 was crucial in planning and administration. 'I think I was very fortunate to serve, for the most part, under a Governor who pressed for change and at a time when events and HMG policies merged to give opportunities in education which had not arisen before.'[4]

1967-72: Island Education Committee Takes Executive Responsibility

By the *St Helena Constitution Order of 1966*, operative from 1 January 1967, there was a new machinery of government. A democratically elected Legislative Council (LegCo) was to take the place of the old Advisory Council which had been appointed by the Governor. Much of the executive work of governing St Helena was now placed in the hands of committees of LegCo. These committees were to decide on policy, and a majority of each was to be made up from people elected to LegCo by the island voters. The chairmen, all from the Legislative Council, were to form the majority of the Executive Council. In accordance with this Order, the Education Committee was constituted as follows:

Chairman:	A. W. Johns MLC [Member of the Legislative Council], Education Officer
Members:	Rt Reverend H. Beardmore OBE ACK MLC
	Major E. J. Moss CBE MC JP MLC
	F. I. Gough MLC
	Reverend M. S. Geen MA

It took over the general management of all aspects of education, these responsibilities being detailed on 6 January 1967 in the *St Helena Government Gazette for 1967-1968*. While taking over the tasks of the former Board of Education, the Committee also now had considerable powers previously exercised by the Governor and certain government officers. For the first time policy was in the hands of the committee – subject, of course to the final agreement of the Legislative Council and Governor.

A link was forged in 1967 between Jersey and St Helena through the Jersey Overseas Aid Committee, which had a particular brief to finance the relief of distress in communities overseas. Through a personal contact, Mr Johns made initial approaches concerning education. However, several years later, following a visit to Jersey by Basil George in 1975/76, an educational programme got under way and St Helena benefited from a travelling library service donated by Jersey. The Aid Committee also later offered to finance the building of the science block of the new secondary school, but this offer was not taken up in view of the recurrent expenditure involved.

In order to promote the development of schools' broadcasting on the island, one of its senior head teachers, Eric George, was sent by the Education Department to attend a five month BBC Overseas Training Course in 1968, dealing both with general and schools' broadcasting. On his return to the island it was decided that, in view of the extent of the development, broadcasting should become the responsibility of the Information Services, with certain time reservations for the Education Department, which was not only producing programmes for schools but also, in the evenings, for adults.

Another of Mr Johns' plans came to fruition in 1968 with the establishment of three pre-primary centres, for children from 3½ to 5 years of age. These were financed mainly from the Colonial and Development Welfare funds and were sited in the Jamestown, Half Tree Hollow and St Paul's areas. A fourth centre in Longwood was opened the following year.

Alan Johns' term of office ended in 1968, but the beneficial effects of his work remained as a long-lasting and well-appreciated legacy to the development of education on the island. Many teachers today remember with appreciation the training he gave them and the high standards he expected of them, not only in school but also in their part in island life.

He was succeeded as Education Officer in 1968 by Ralph Billing who had been an Assistant Education Officer on the island since early 1965. He was therefore familiar with the 10-year development plan which he inherited and supported. Submitting an *Education Report* at the end of his first year in office, he was pleased to record favourable progress with the plan, including curricular development in science teaching and the provision of a science laboratory, with the promise of more to come. Among other developments there had been increasing use of schools' broadcasting, Cuisenaire Mathematics equipment had been introduced and the provision of a third bus now enabled children from Levelwood and Sandy Bay to attend the Country Senior School. This meant that, at last, the island was seeing the end of all-age schools, with the two schools at Levelwood and Sandy Bay accepting only junior age children.

Mr Billing reported further reorganization during 1968 among the senior education staff in order to cover the rapidly developing educational system. Cliff Huxtable had been reappointed Assistant Education Officer, having previously been an AEO in 1966. In the same year, Lily Crowie accepted the new post of Organizer of Primary Schools, having responsibility for in-service work for young teachers and also the supervision of the recently established pre-primary centres.

With these developments, the Education Department published a four-part series on Education in the *St Helena News Review* in February and March 1969 outlining the major advances made in education in recent years. It announced that the aim for the future was 'One central school, which all children over the age of eleven will attend, approximately 500 in all, at which they will be taught by age and by ability'.

For some years the island had been needing a lasting outside educational link. Since the termination of the East Suffolk link through Norman Kerr, there had been a gap, although over the years a number of island teachers had been attending St Paul's College, Cheltenham. Through the auspices of the Ministry of Overseas Development, two tutors, Trevor Hearl of St Paul's College and Colin Roderick of St Mary's College, visited St Helena in 1969, and their subsequent report resulted in the establishment of the 'Cheltenham (University of Bristol)– St Helena Link', a body which was destined to have an important part to play in support of island education.

In 1970, Nicholas Gillett, from Bristol University, came to advise on secondary education teaching methods. Basil George, returning from Leicester University as the first St Helenian to gain a Bachelor of Education degree, was appointed to be Assistant Education Officer in charge of the Secondary Selective School. Ralph Billing now had the support of three Assistant Education Officers, the others being Arnold Flagg and Cliff Huxtable.

With this team at the helm, and in consultation with Visiting Adviser Trevor Hearl in 1971, the department issued a paper to all head teachers for discussion of four major areas which needed to be tackled in order to achieve their aims. These were School Organization, the Curriculum, Teacher Education and Methods of Teaching, and the School Environment. Concerning School Organization, it was proposed to debate the raising of the school leaving age to 16, a system of central secondary schooling, and the extension of nursery schooling. Discussion about the Curriculum would centre on the need to include social, environmental and vocational education. The aims and methods of teacher education would be clarified since 'teacher education is the vital centre of the entire educational process'. The debate on the School Environment would explore effective communication between the school and the community.

While these questions were being debated, schools continued to carry out their tasks. A number of successes were achieved in external examinations, including passes in History and English Literature at the Advanced Level of GCE by Miss Corinda Noaks (Essex), the first A level student on St Helena. The Benevolent Society and the Hussey Charity Trustees added their encouragement by offering prizes for GCE 'O' level passes, particularly in Religious Knowledge, and donating money towards science equipment and Religious Knowledge books.

Education also benefited from a bequest in 1971 from Mrs Helen Gilles, who had made her home on St Helena and had a special interest in music. In the *Minute Book of the Helen Gilles Trustees*, it is recorded that she left money in her will to endow the Helen Gilles School of Music 'To promote musical talent amongst the young people of the island', and she also left her grand piano and her silver flute to be used by musicians. The 'school' took the form of giving encouragement, teaching and awards to young island musicians. Today, 1992, the grand piano is in use in St James' Church, and the flute is loaned to a student of talent in the Prince Andrew School.

In October 1971, Education Officer Ralph Billing echoed some of the debate by concluding his *Education Report* thus: 'The school system is an agency of the larger community charged with the two-fold task of transmitting the heritage of the society and of promoting desirable social change. Effective communication between the school and the community is essential. Teachers must be sensitive to the values and needs of the society they serve. They should attempt to meet these needs and promote understanding of the part played by the schools in community development.'

Mr Billing was also responsible for introducing several more young vso people. Earlier volunteers had included some men to help to fill the great need for men teachers. Volunteers now included several young women over the next few years to teach in the system during the early 1970s. They were distributed among several of the schools, some of them being qualified teachers while others were learning on the job. A number of them were accommodated in Essex House in Jamestown.

Concluding his service to the island, Ralph Billing was succeeded by Cliff Huxtable who took over the role of Education Officer in May 1972.

1972-78: Further Debate and Planning for the Future Structure of the Education System

Cliff Huxtable was a Canadian national and well-known to the islanders. He had developed an interest in St Helena, arriving there in 1966 with no particular post in mind but prepared to use his experience to help in any capacity. A BA graduate, he had had training and teaching experience in Toronto, Regina and British Columbia. At the conclusion of the service in 1966 of David Streatfield as the Head of the Secondary Selective School, Mr Huxtable was engaged as Assistant Education Officer and Head of the school. In particular his task was to strengthen the teaching of science and to introduce it to the other three senior schools on the island.

An important educational development in 1972 was the introduction to the island of the Duke of Edinburgh Award Scheme. With the enthusiastic support of Governor Sir Thomas Oates, Cliff Huxtable established a committee, at first chaired by himself. One of the first tasks achieved by the Duke of Edinburgh candidates was to provide the island with a signpost system. Officers from the Education Department have been associated with the running of the scheme since its inception, particularly Basil George in the early years, and Arnold Flagg whose service to it has spanned well over 16 years.

Regarding pupil development, Mr Huxtable's *Education Report for 1972* recorded that the pupils at the Secondary Selective School were achieving successes not only in the island-based General Schools Examination, but also in RSA examinations. The other senior schools were suffering from the additional creaming off of the more able 14-year-olds to the SSS, and only the top quarter passed the GSE exam. 'Nevertheless, the influence of some determined teachers and head-teachers inspired by UK training, the Cheltenham/Gloucestershire teacher vacation courses, and local further education success, is causing the winds of change to blow in these schools too.' Variability among the Junior Schools, depending largely upon the effectiveness of the head teachers and some outstanding teachers, was an issue. On average, it was reported that the children were two years behind their UK counterparts in reading. Regarding pre-schoolers, Mrs Leonora Pitcairn, a Parentcraft Adviser from the National Association for Maternal and Child Welfare (London), was currently on the island to initiate a programme of parentcraft and child development courses for playschool assistants, senior pupils, teachers and others.

After a few months in office, Education Officer Cliff Huxtable set out for the Education Department a *Situation Report* for September 1972, followed by a *Report on Projected Development 1973-1977*. The *Situation Report* outlined the senior management structure of the Education Department. It comprised the Education Officer; three Assistant Education Officers (in charge of Teacher Education, the Secondary Selective School, Further Education, Library and Radio); two Organizers (in charge of Parentcraft and Primary Education), and eleven head teachers. For the 1,200 children there were 68 teachers, giving a pupil:teacher ratio of approximately 18:1, with a further 60 children in playschools. Six of the teachers were currently on UK training courses, and there were also five teacher trainees and six playschool assistants. The gross annual expenditure per child for 1972 was expected to be between £60 and £70. The schools list in 1972 comprised:

Secondary Selective School (Ladder Hill): 100 pupils
Senior Schools (Pilling, Country, Harford):
  approximately 120 pupils in each
Infant/Junior Schools: eight schools, ranging in
  enrolment from 15 to 170, total 740

A Technical Training Instructor, appointed from the UK, was in charge of the Technical Trades Centre. The qualifications held by educational personnel were reflecting the determination over the past years to raise the standard. The Department boasted one person with BA and Dip Ed; one BEd; three DipEds; nine Certificates of Education, including two vso teachers. Full use was being made of the Cheltenham Link.

Mr Huxtable's *Report on Projected Development 1973-77* included the aim to foster resourcefulness, co-operation, skill attainment and cultural awareness. It tackled the related issues of staff education, the curriculum and the organization of schooling. Putting forward specific proposals for the development of a three-tier system of education, it included a detailed time-scale for its introduction, with forecast that the first year of operation for the modified school system would be 1977.

From the start, Mr Huxtable's prime interest was in organization. He saw as a priority in his role the need to encourage the teachers to prove their worth, to accept ownership of what they were doing, and to be confident to take up opportunities to enrich their teaching – 'and to win victories'. He saw the importance of devolving central authority out to schools, with, of course, the resultant acceptance by the schools of their responsibility for holding that authority. He also wished to expand the overseas in-service training opportunities for teachers, the Education Department being the only major department on the island with a structured programme in this respect. To facilitate this, from 1972 the school year on the island was to run from September to August, so making possible a more ready transference of teachers to the UK.[5]

Following her visit in 1972, Leonora Pitcairn produced a full report in which she included a policy for introducing the teaching of child care and allied subjects to senior pupils, to be examined by the National Association for Maternal and Child Welfare (NAMCW) in London. She also produced a *Textbook for Play School Teacher Training in St Helena*, this being a comprehensive book of information and guidelines about the pre-school child and every aspect related to playschools – staffing, children with special needs, story-telling and music, environment and personal development. Following the advice of Mrs Pitcairn, a Parent-craft Education Centre was opened in 1973. Later in the year nine local pre-school trainees were successful in obtaining both the local qualification and a London NAMCW award. In addition 39 pupils successfully passed the Basic Child Care Examination.

E. J. Dorrell, the Director of Education for Oxfordshire, was sent by the Ministry of Overseas Development to St Helena in October 1974 with the brief to make a general review of the educational system and the Cheltenham Link, to advise on the proposal to establish a comprehensive secondary school, and to assess the island's requirements of overseas staff over the next five years. Identifying certain areas where there was still need for improvement, his December 1974 report entitled *St Helena: The Education System* was also able to pay tribute to the encouraging advances made over previous years. He gave strong support to the proposals for a comprehensive organization at secondary school level. He stated that this was desirable both economically and educationally, but he warned that there were some difficulties of location, whether the site chosen was Francis Plain or Longwood/Deadwood, and of timing, due to the fact that the construction capacity of the island for the next few years was already taken up by developments in agriculture, fisheries and housing. The report stressed the 'need to raise the self-regard of teachers – to participate in decision-making – and the need to be conscious of the importance of their task and to be treated as important partners in the service'.

In his report Mr Dorrell praised the work of the Cheltenham–St Helena Link since its establishment in 1969, when Colin Roderick and Trevor Hearl, of St Mary's and St Paul's Colleges, Cheltenham, undertook the assignment to organize in-service Teacher Vacation Courses on the island from July to September 1969, and subsequently to suggest ways of meeting St Helena's future needs in teacher education and training.

In *An Outline Progress Report, 1969-1974*, Mr Hearl described the services being taken up by the island through the Link. These included sandwich courses tailor-made to teachers' and island needs, comprising two one-year courses in the UK, with 3-4 years' recognized study on St Helena in between. Certificate and BEd Courses were also available for academically and professionally competent teachers. UK teacher exchanges were also being made with selected College of Education courses and school visits being arranged for the island teachers in the UK. An island post was available annually for a male teacher on secondment from the Gloucestershire LEA. Teacher Vacation Courses on St Helena were being led by ODA-sponsored visiting tutors and extended visits made to the island by Specialist Tutors. In addition Link support was given in several ways. These included helping with assessment of Teachers' Assignments, encouraging links between schools in UK and on St Helena, establishing links between island Education Officers and schools and colleges in the UK, corresponding regularly with island staff and extending assistance as requested, providing a briefing and information service with vso, and maintaining the involvement and active interest of Link tutors in the work of educational development and in the welfare of St Helenian teachers in Cheltenham.

Mr Hearl reported that over the five years of the Link's existence it had created an organization which could meet the demands of the St Helenian Government and which had already demonstrated that the island had the educational potential to meet its needs from its own resources.

School statistics published in October 1974 showed that there were altogether 1,258 children in the 12 schools, as follows:

Selective Secondary	116	Half Tree Hollow	148
Pilling Senior	141	Sandy Bay	36
Jamestown Junior	161	Blue Hill	15
Jamestown Infants	74	Harford Senior	143
Country Senior	128	Longwood	147
Country Junior	80	Levelwood	69

The birthrate had declined during the previous four years, with 167 in 1970, 120 in 1971, 122 in 1972 and 116 in 1973.

In 1975 the Duke of Edinburgh Award Scheme gained its first gold awards – these going to three girls, Betty Crowie, Valerie Yon and Alice

Young and four boys, George Greentree, Eric Constantine, David Ward and Gregory Plato. Valerie Yon was able to receive her award from the Duke himself at Buckingham Palace. During the following year, altogether 41 Duke of Edinburgh awards were presented to successful candidates at a Plantation House ceremony. To add to these successes, two St Helenian teachers gained Bachelor of Education Honours Degrees – these, again, being Corinda Noaks and Dan Yon. At the same time Patsy Flagg, the Organizer of Pre-school Education, became the first St Helenian to obtain the NAMCW Part III A award. Progress was also made on the technical front, with the St Helena Government sponsoring 21 young men to take full-time courses at Ladder Hill in Building, Plumbing or Electrical Work.

From 1977 to 1980 Dan Yon held the Acting Headship of the Secondary Selective School, while Basil George undertook responsibility for developing the senior schools. As one of the few island graduates, Mr Yon made a major contribution to raising standards and developing the school, his pupils gaining a high level of GCE results. He played an active part in the Teachers' Association, pressing for improving conditions of service for teachers, and was a founder member of the Heritage Society, playing a key role in getting the museum established. Mr George resumed the headship in 1980. Subsequently in 1992, Dan Yon became the first St Helenian to achieve an educational doctorate, having studied at Toronto on a Canadian University Scholarship.

While the principle of island-wide secondary education had generally been agreed, a number of people were still not totally convinced of the form it should take. These included Education Officer Cliff Huxtable himself. In March 1977 he brought forward an alternative to the comprehensive school proposal for the initial consideration of the Education Committee. Entitled *The Expansion of Third-Level Opportunities*, the alternative acknowledged the rationale for the previous proposals but then said that these same advantages could 'in St Helena's circumstances, be achieved more effectively by expanding practical educational opportunities for all children aged 15 to 17 who have mastered the basic tool skills of language and numeracy'. He therefore proposed that, in addition to the existing opportunities for those aged 15 plus who wished to continue academic studies, the Technical Training Centre should be developed into a small but flexible technical college and further education centre. The college would seek the close co-operation of future employers, in both government and private enterprise. Students at the college, and the 5th- and 6th-form students at the Secondary School, would all be paid allowances. By this proposal comprehensive educational facilities would be available to everyone between 15 and 17.

The members of the Education Committee decided unanimously that they were interested in the alternative proposal and wished to seek wider opinions about it from island teachers and from some of the recent visiting advisers. This started off a thorough debate. A 'Teach-in' for the purpose of considering the proposals was held on 28 January 1978, chaired by the Governor and attended by members of the Education Committee, officers of the Education Department and teacher representatives. The minutes recorded agreement with the notion of a central school organized flexibly in which levels of literacy would be an important factor; it should be planned to permit expansion if the school-leaving age were raised; and the relationship between the central school, technical trades and craft centres should remain flexible, with the aim of integrating services offered to provide courses beyond the age of 15 that would be as varied as possible. 'A purpose-built school would be more efficiently constructed by the Public Works Department than one converted from older buildings.' Following the seminars and the Teach-in, an outline proposal was submitted to London, detailing the island's educational priorities, including diversifying and expanding secondary and post-school educational and social facilities. It was hoped that an Education Adviser from the ODM would visit the island in early 1979 to help clear the way for major action in educational development.

1978-83: The Central School Project Moves Ahead

While the centre of debate was on the progress of the Central School proposal, schooling continued for the 1,200 children on the island. Some improvements were being made in other schools, including in 1978 a much-needed £14,000 extension to Half Tree Hollow School where the population was rapidly increasing.

A major outcome of the public debate on comprehensive education was a return visit sponsored by the ODM in March 1979 of Nicholas Gillett, from the University of Bristol whose previous visit was in 1970. He arrived with the brief to report on the move towards a consensus about future plans for Secondary Education (Central Schooling), on developing community (adult) education, on the place of education in the overall development of the island, and to suggest priorities in education. He held many discussions with individual members of the Education Committee, departmental staff, Heads of Department, District meetings and parents. His nephew, Simon Gillett, who was also on the island at the time as Colonial Treasurer and later as Acting Government Secretary, recalls that in the field of education far and away the most important issue was the campaign for the Central School. There were influential islanders and others who were for and against the proposal. The Foreign and Commonwealth Office were hesitant, not so much on account of the initial capital cost, as of the big increase in annual expenditure. With his uncle, Simon Gillett spent many hours working out what they considered to be the optimal site. 'Francis Plain was the obvious one, but as so many pupils would come from Jamestown the cost of bussing them in and out was clearly a major consideration. We twice walked up James Valley and past the waterfall on the Barnes Road to try and convince ourselves that the distance from roadhead could be walked daily. We remained sceptical ...'.[6]

In his report, Nicholas Gillett stated that the existing provision in the senior schools was not adequate to produce the workforce needed by the island. The interest of boys was not being captured by practical subjects, the necessary space and equipment were lacking, and therefore the schools were failing to turn out people who could undertake practical jobs quickly. He recommended that the Central School Development would be the most effective way of providing these facilities, together with trained teachers in relevant specialist fields.

Not to be outdone, the teacher trainees added their voice to the matter in January 1980, producing for display in the Canister window a description of the Central School Development in terms of Why? Who? Where? When? and How Much?

In his *Education Report of 1979*, Mr Huxtable was pleased to include favourable comment on the progress of pupils and teachers in all schools, on increased use of resources, advances in Further Education and Technical Training, and on the work of the Public Works Department on improving school buildings. A major difficulty being experienced was the chronic shortage of teachers, resulting in the employment of several unqualified supply staff. The Jersey Link again became a useful one, their Overseas Aid Committee supplying St Helena with a consignment of appropriate Readers for use in the primary schools and with remedial groups in the senior schools.

Even though the debate and consultation had been proceeding for several years, the crucial decision of the Legislative Council to go ahead with the central school proposal was still awaited while members sought to make the right decision for their island. It is interesting to note that in his 1982 book entitled *St Helena*, former Education Officer

Tony Cross stated: 'Proposals for a centrally sited comprehensive school, either to replace senior and selective schools or to become the top tier of a three-tier stage system of junior, middle and secondary schools, are held in abeyance at present due to the massive cost of initiating such a scheme and to lingering educational doubts.'[7]

Nevertheless, matters were coming to a head. The plans for a Central School on St Helena were gaining widespread support. A useful step forward was made on 11 January 1980 when the *St Helena News Review* reported that the *Annual Report of the Education Department* contained the proposal for a Central School. The final hurdle to be cleared now was for a formal resolution to be passed by the Legislative Council.

This strategic decision to proceed with the Central School Project was made at the Legislative Council meeting on 13 March 1980 and recorded in the *Minutes* of that date. In his summary Councillor John Musk, Chairman of the Education Committee, declared that the parents had told Nicholas Gillett in 1979 what they wanted for their children: 'No selection, streaming to provide for ability in any subject and to allow for personal interest, the best equipment with the best teachers, closely connected with agriculture and technical training, better opportunities for boys, equal opportunities for everybody, and for every child in St Helena, and consequently going a very long way to help St Helena help itself.' Affirming that financial provision was included in the Development Plan 1980-85 for the creation of the Central School complex on Francis Plain, Mr Musk put forward the notion: 'This Council firmly believes that whatever the future of St Helena is to be, the interests of the Island in education would be best served by the creation of a Central Secondary School.'

Several other speeches were made in support and the motion was put to the Council and passed.

In August 1980 Sir Bernard Braine MP was invited to the island by the Legislative Council and lent his support to the need for action. His subsequent *Report on St Helena* stated:

Since the mid-1970s it has been thought desirable to introduce a central comprehensive school in order to provide a better education for children not academically qualified for selective secondary education. Such a school has not yet been provided. The practical effect of this, and the extent to which a very useful agricultural training scheme and an excellent trades training centre can turn out skilled workers at 18, is being handicapped by the failure to catch the interest of 15 year-old school leavers in practical subjects. Education is being neglected at a crucial stage.

Mr Huxtable's *Annual Education Review of 1981* welcomed the Ritchie Review which revised salaries for teachers, so giving them encouragement in the more responsible role which they were undertaking. In preparation for his own relinquishing of the Education Officer post at the end of the year to come, there had been some redeployment of senior staff in order to ensure continuity in the education process. Mr Huxtable paid tribute to the value of the overseas experience of many island teachers, and also to the major assistance for teachers of children aged 9 to 13 received from R. B. Mather's ODA sponsored visits in 1978 and 1980. Continuing by stating that 'Children's lives are enriched by a variety of means', Mr Huxtable listed the many facilities and opportunities afforded to the children of the island – swimming in the new pool, art, craft, poetry and song-writing competitions and musical evenings, the Duke of Edinburgh Award Scheme, parent-teacher associations raising money for the New Year's Sports Day and for the woodcraft and homecraft centres and guitars, complementary stamp sets from the Post Office to each school, video of the Royal Wedding of Prince Charles and Diana, sent by friends from Bristol, and libraries.

The importance of enriching the lives of the islanders was echoed by Eric M. George in 1981. Making music had for many years been a traditional and popular activity on St Helena, and Mr George's *Report on Music in Schools* gave encouraging news that this continued to be an important element in island education. He described progress in the acquisition of instruments and in vacation courses for teachers and praised the end of term performances, morning assemblies and schools radio programmes. He praised particularly the 'excellent attempts by both primary and secondary schools in the compilation of songs for the St Helena Day Song Competition and the very satisfactory results in the recent GSE Music Exam Paper'.

Meanwhile, in May 1982 after 10 years in office, Cliff Huxtable despairingly produced a hard-hitting *Report for the Budgetary Aid Review (BAR) Team* on the subject of the lack of progress on the Central School Project.

Much has been written and little of substance has happened on the central school proposal since the first proposal was put forward in August 1965. Why is there not yet commitment to proceed? ... Could it be that we do not yet realize the necessity of improved schooling and the promise that it holds for our future? Why is £161,000 to be spent this year on heavy equipment by a society that has more unskilled labour than it knows what to do with? Could not these funds have been better employed building a central school that would be designed to attract and develop the staff that could foster those habits and attitudes in pupils that are so badly needed for self-reliance, enterprise and middle-management?

Cliff Huxtable had served the island for many years. Reflecting several years later, as a successful timber merchant on the island, about his work as Education Officer, he mused: 'I believe I was the right man at that time – to help with the transition from Colonial-type leadership to greater St Helenian participation. The whole Canadian experience was, perhaps, applicable.'[8]

Evidence of the truth of Mr Huxtable's statement came immediately, in that his successor was the first St Helenian ever to hold the post of Education Officer. On 23 December 1982, the *St Helena News Review* rang out the exciting headline: 'Local Man Takes Over a Major Department'. Basil George moved into the post of Education Officer on 26 January 1983.

1983-88: The Fruition of Plans

The Central School project moved ahead. Planners, architects, economists and specialist advisers, teachers and their association, education officers and parent groups all played their part. At a meeting with the consultant group in April 1983, the aims and factors which were to be incorporated into any plans were itemized as:

(a) To equip people for modern management jobs on the island,
(b) To cover the general requirements for jobs both in and outside the island,
(c) To develop people at all levels,
(d) To bring together all children to create a better community spirit and better thinking people,
(e) To provide incentive and encouragement to male teachers,
(f) To cater for the late development of boys,
(g) To provide a basis for the present day technology, and
(h) To develop people who were able to make the maximum use of money supplied by the UK.

By 1983, Education Officer Basil George was seeing what had for 20 years been only a gleam in his eye come to fruition. Giving a *Progress Report*, he said that the three-tier non-selective system (first proposed in 1972) was scheduled to start in September 1985 but warned: 'The over-riding constraint for the success of the new system is the extent of the teacher-training programme; whether suitable overseas staff is provided and whether suitable local staff, particularly males, can be attracted into teaching.' Several people helped to advance the project, including Sir Neil Marten whose task in early 1984 was to report to

Timothy Raison, the Minister for Overseas Development, after talking with the island's Education Committee.

The events of the next five years were dominated by the planning for the three-tier system. St Helena was invaded by advisers on every conceivable aspect of the project. Throughout this period the people of the island kept their heads and played a highly significant part in the preparation for the new system, while at the same time doing justice to their present work. Not only did the local craftsmen undertake the building of the Central School and the adaptations to the existing school buildings to accommodate the middle and first schools, but also, under the leadership of Basil George and his Senior Staff, the teachers of the island took the initiative in the development of the curricula and procedures for their future work.

The greatest impetus to all of this effort came with the visit on 5 and 6 April 1984 of His Royal Highness, The Prince Andrew. An action-packed visit to the island was master-minded by Harry Corker OBE to commemorate the 150th Anniversary of the Crown's control of the island. On arrival Prince Andrew delivered congratulations to the island, saying: 'Distant though you are from Britain, you have a special place in the hearts and minds of the British people.' Anticipating the activities during his visit, he continued: 'The impressions which I will gather will, I am sure, inform the Queen that her Saints are in good heart and that the tough and enterprising spirit which has kept this community going through the good and bad for over three centuries has not changed in any way.'

During the second day of the visit, at the Sports Prizegiving on Francis Plain, an announcement was made by Governor Massingham in the presence of Prince Andrew:

I have particular pleasure in making a double special announcement. As a result of the recent visit of Sir Neil Marten, his successor as Minister of Overseas Development has agreed in principle that we should have our secondary school, our new Central School. But much more important, His Royal Highness has graciously consented that it should bear his name. That means that every generation of island child, boy or girl, of whatever academic achievement, will be able to say – I attended the Prince Andrew School.[9]

The report of the visit in the *St Helena News* of 13 April 1984 said that the loudest cheer of the day was reserved for this special announcement.

This was the highlight of all of the plans, and at this point the long-awaited Central School became a reality.

The days of the former system were coming to a close, and it was time to look back as well as forwards – back at the roots from which the new system could develop. The Prince Andrew School was a successor to the four senior schools, each of which had played an important part in the educational system since the reorganization in 1941.

The school log books of these four previous senior schools provide reminders of the past 47 years and serve to emphasize the extent of the current developments. The available log book of the Secondary Selective School had recorded events from 1946 to 1968, and it gives a good picture of the vicissitudes of this school in its early years of existence, due to a number of circumstances, including changes of site and changes of head teachers. Nevertheless the school had continued to serve the island well until 1988 and educated many of the islanders who are now in leading positions throughout all departments and activities. At the ceremony on 9 August 1988 to mark its formal closure, as reported in the *St Helena News*, Eric George voiced the thoughts of many people when he said:

As the outgoing Headmaster, I wish to thank everyone, including parents, for their support during the existence of the Secondary Selective School and sincerely trust a similar support will be given to the Prince Andrew School, which has so much to offer to all our children, teachers and community as a whole.

Similarly the other three senior schools – Pilling School for Jamestown and the nearby districts, St Paul's Senior School for the west and Harford Senior School for the east of the island – had served to train generations of St Helenians, including several who have entered the teaching profession over the years.

The ending of the former system coincided with other noteworthy endings. For example, in 1985 Evelyn Bagley retired after 43 years of teaching service, almost all of it at Blue Hill School, where she had taken charge in 1951 when George Lawrence, her predecessor, moved to a post in the Education Office. Miss Bagley had been officially appointed to the headship in 1955 and held the post until her retirement, when she was awarded the BEM. Her career was noted for her dedication to her work and her persistence with study and with gaining more qualifications to enhance her teaching. This included spending a year in the UK, and also successfully studying for several O-level subjects on Saturday mornings and during evenings after school.

The year 1985 also saw the departure of Bishop Edward Cannan from the island and from the Education Committee. From the time of the Amalgamation Ordinance of 1941, the Bishop of St Helena had an *ex-officio* position on the Education Committee, maintaining the long-standing traditional links between the church and schools. Like many of his predecessors, Edward Cannan, the 11th Bishop of St Helena, gave valuable service on the committee from 1979 to 1985, and in his book *Churches of the South Atlantic, 1502-1991* demonstrated his strong interest in education in the Colony of St Helena. His chapter on 'Education and Ecumenism' highlights both the important part played in the past in education by Christian societies and churches, including the Anglican, Roman Catholic and Non-Conformist Churches, and the continuing part played now: 'Today the clergy visit the schools periodically for assemblies, and in some cases, by invitation, assist with the teaching of religious education, both in schools and to teacher trainees.'[10] From 1989 the Bishop no longer had an *ex-officio* position on the Education Committee, but ministers from the various Christian denominations are invited into the schools to participate in assemblies and services and to attend school functions.

The Education Advisers who visited the island during the lead-up to the introduction to the three-tier system included several who had been associated with the educational programmes of St Helenians in the UK, and who had both knowledge of the island and the interests of its people very much at heart. Their role at this stage was to work alongside the local and expatriate teachers to advise on various aspects of the new system including the philosophy and running of a three-tier system, curriculum development appropriate for the island and the implications for the pupils and the curriculum of the transition from one tier to the next. Advisers also came to help to plan details of buildings, materials and resources and to help to plan and run in-service training of teachers. Other areas discussed included the dissemination of information to prospective pupils, parents and employers, consideration of specific subject areas, programmes and facilities for children with special educational needs, assessment and testing techniques and school management. The island teachers entered wholeheartedly into this ambitious programme being committed to making a success of this strategic 'beginning' in the history of schools on St Helena.

Peter Scopes, the Senior South Atlantic Education Adviser of the ODA, made a detailed analysis in 1985 of major resources needed such as buildings, staffing, curriculum development, equipment, materials and transport. Clive Warren, the ODA Desk Officer for St Helena, was also tireless in his work for the project, making a number of extended visits to the island. His personal commitment to the project and to the island was unquestionable.

UK Educational Advisers were involved in the immediate run-up to the new system and their principal specialisms were:

Miss Gwen Abbott: Deaf & Partially Hearing Children
Mrs Dorothy Harrison: First Schools; Language/Reading
Mr Vince Davies: Middle Schools; Social Studies
Miss Dorothy Evans: Initial/In-service Teacher Education;
  Mathematics; Assessment & Testing
Mr Brian Frederick: Human and Physical Resources

Miss Abbott, an Adviser on the Teaching of Deaf Children, made two visits to the island in July 1985 and April 1986. Her initial report covered the areas included in her contract which were to identify the needs of partially hearing handicapped children, to draw up a programme for their education over a one-year period and to provide some guidance in communication for teachers and parents of handicapped children. On her second visit she was able to assess the outcome of her recommendations and to give further encouragement to children, teachers, parents and other agencies involved. Among other children needing special guidance were four deaf, mute boys who had been handicapped from birth. Miss Abbott's *Report on Deaf Children on St Helena*, produced in April 1986, concluded: 'Since they [the deaf children] have all, to varying degrees, shown an increase in their ability to communicate with others, the conclusion undoubtedly has to be that the exercise has been worthwhile. One must not, however, lose sight of the fact that these deaf children are a long way behind their peers and there is still much to be done.'

During this time of planning it was business as usual in the schools, except that at times the Education Committee agreed to a part-day closure of schools to enable all teachers to attend planning sessions. Many of these were initially attended by one of the educational advisers, Dorothy Harrison, Vince Davies and Dorothy Evans. The agenda of the Education Committee, while heavily involved with the new system, continued to pay attention to items concerning the present education budget, apprenticeship schemes, schools broadcasting, the libraries, and education on Ascension Island and Tristan da Cunha. In addition the Committee invited the Education Advisers to their meetings in order to keep them informed of the progress of the project.

By 1986 Project 297, as the whole enterprise was called by the ODA, was taking shape after a number of hold-ups *en route*. The projected cost had risen from the original £3 million to £4.8 million. The first headmaster of the Prince Andrew School was to be Scotsman, John Birchall BA, Dip Ed. His teaching career had started in 1971 as an

Assistant Teacher of Geography in a multi-racial school in Glasgow with pupils aged 11 to 18 years. He later became head of the Geography Department in the Glasgow High School for Girls which, during his time, evolved into a mixed comprehensive school. As Assistant Head Teacher of the Kyle Academy from 1979 to 1983 he helped to set up a large brand-new school; and he then moved to the Doon Academy to become Deputy Head and subsequently Head. All of this experience helped to prepare him for his new responsibilities setting up the Prince Andrew School. He took up his post in September 1986 and was deeply involved in all aspects of the school leading up to its opening two years later. Shortly after his arrival the Foundation Stone of the Prince Andrew School was laid on 29 September at Francis Plain. The subsequent report stated: 'Filled with pride, a large crowd of people stood and witnessed the Foundation Stone of the Central School being laid.' The *St Helena News* of 3 October 1986 reported: 'His Excellency Francis E. Baker laid the stone – a red one from the steeple of St James' Church.' The report drew attention with further pride to the fact that 'Our first Island Chief Education Officer, Mr Basil George, is the backbone behind this venture, and our first Island Bishop, The Reverend James Johnson, blessed the stone.'

Mr Birchall worked tirelessly alongside the architects and engineers in connection with the buildings and facilities, and with the teachers and education officers to plan systems for running the school. By 22 October 1986 he was able to outline his plans to prepare for the opening of the Prince Andrew School. Similarly, the head teachers and staff of the three middle schools and the seven first schools were fully involved – not only in planning for their own schools but also in inter-school issues related to curricula, resources, transition and induction procedures, testing, and special educational needs.

On 25 August 1987 Chief Education Officer Basil George presented a working document, symbolically entitled *378 Days along the Water Course Road*, at a joint meeting of the Education Department, the Finance Monitoring Committee and the Governor. This comprehensive statement produced by several senior members of the Department outlined the plans for the implementation of the new system by the changeover date. The sections related to the Education Department's Aims and Objectives; Administrative Considerations; First and Middle School Planning; the Prince Andrew School – Opening on Schedule; Teacher Training and Nursery Education; and the Proposed Structure for Reading/Learning Difficulties in the Three-Tier System.

After much debate, discussion, speculation and planning, the time drew close for the introduction of the new system. During the school term before the launching, children and parents were given opportunity to hear and read about the changes in store and to visit their new schools. The scene was set. The 'play' was about to begin. To quote 92 year-old Mr Hudson, in 1990, as he reflected on his own schooldays in St Helena: 'The people today, they have the option – it depends on the talent to take advantage of it.'[11]

8

The Three-Tier System: The Realization of Decades of Plans 1988-92

The new system is however only a new beginning.
Basil George, 1989[1]

1988: The three-tier system is launched

Eventually, September 1988 arrived and the children of St Helena set off to their new schools. The Prince Andrew School was not yet fully operative, but it was launched at last and pupils from all over the island excitedly entered their school, marvelling at their impressive surroundings and undoubted opportunities.

Basil George, the Chief Education Officer, emphasized that the introduction of the three-tier system of schools marked a strategic new beginning for the island, one of the most significant in its history. 'We have not arrived in education, we have just made a fresh start. But it is a start that lays the foundation for the future.'[2] The anticipation of its approach and the planning for its introduction had occupied the minds of many people, both on and off the island, for many years and, at last, the plans had materialized.

Eleven schools were established and headteachers appointed. Except for John Birchall, all were St Helenian as follows:

The Prince Andrew School:	Mr John Birchall
Harford Middle School:	Mrs Elvina Mercury
Pilling Middle School:	Mrs Rita Nicholls
St Paul's Middle School:	Mr Stedson George
Blue Hill First School:	Mrs Elizabeth Young
Half Tree Hollow First School:	Miss Joyce Harris
Levelwood First School:	Mrs Muriel Williams
Longwood First School:	Mrs Joan Thomas
Jamestown First School:	Mrs Muriel Leo
St Paul's First School:	Mrs Priscilla (Maisie) Thomas
Sandy Bay First School:	Mrs Iva Henry

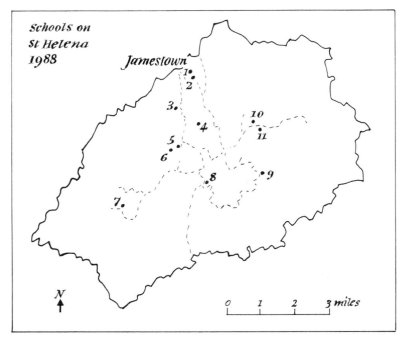

Schools on St Helena at the introduction of the Three-tier system, 1988

1 Jamestown First School
2 Pilling Middle School
3 Half Tree Hollow First School
4 Prince Andrew School
5 St Paul's Middle School
6 St Paul's First School

7 Blue Hill First School
8 Sandy Bay First School
9 Levelwood First School
10 Harford Middle School
11 Longwood First School

The Prince Andrew School would receive all pupils from the age of 12 onwards; middle schools from eight to 12 years; and first schools from five to eight years.

A significant feature of the new system was that, with regrouping the island's children into the three-tier system, the former Jamestown Infant School building was released to be converted into a Teacher Education Centre and also, later, a Learning Support Centre. In addition, since the former primary schools were receiving only four years of children instead of six, there was space to allow the further development of nursery education in all districts, so bringing pre-schooling within reach of all children from the age of three and a half.

The major decision-making body for education for the island was the Education Committee, one of the formal committees responsible to the Governor. It comprised a chairman, at that time appointed by the Governor from the elected members of the Legislative Council, four other members of the Council, the Bishop of St Helena, a representative of the Teachers' Association, and the Chief Education Officer in an *ex-officio* capacity. The committee at the time of the inauguration of the three-tier system in 1988 was as follows:

Chairman:	Mr Eric Benjamin (Lay advocate)
Members:	Mrs Ivy George (Former island head teacher)
	Bishop James Johnson (Church representative)
	Mrs Evelyn Thomas (Former teacher)
	Mr Peter Thomas (Former Clerk to the Government, now with Solomon & Co)
	Mr John Musk (a leading island trader)
	Mrs Corinda Essex (Teachers' Association)
Ex-officio:	Mr Basil George, BEd Hons, Dip Ed (CEO)

Many people had planned and worked hard for a long time to reach this point in the development of the education system. Brief profiles of several of these islanders follow, and they serve to illustrate the demanding path each has trodden to help to bring this about.

The Chairman of the Education Committee in 1988, Eric Benjamin, was a former schoolteacher. He had received all of his schooling on the island, starting at the age of five at Half Tree Hollow Primary School and moving to Gosse Central School for his secondary schooling. Leaving school at the age of 15, he entered teaching and for a few months taught at the school where he had been a pupil, now named the Country Senior School, under Algernon Broadway's headship. He then moved to teach at Half Tree Hollow School under Miss Constantine until attending St Paul's College, Cheltenham, where he took a two year teacher training course from 1958-60. On his return to the island in 1960 he taught at Pilling Senior School, where he shortly took over the headship until 1964. He then came out of teaching to become the Secretary of the General Workers Union, a post he still holds. Over the years his interest in law developed, and in 1986 he began his service as a Lay Advocate for the island. Since 1970 he has been a member of the Legislative Council and the Executive Council, and in that capacity was appointed by the Governor to be Chairman of Education Committee, a position he held until May 1989. Under his chairmanship, many far-reaching and important decisions were made in connection with the

Central School project and the launching of the three-tier system. He saw the establishment of the new system and officiated at the many ceremonies, including the laying of the foundation stone in 1986 and the opening of the first and middle schools in 1988. In acknowledgement of the important part he had played during these years of planning, he was given the honour of officiating at the opening ceremony of the Prince Andrew School in 1989, although at this time he was handing over the chairmanship to Ruth Pridham. Speaking later of his time as Chairman, Mr Benjamin says: 'We were aiming to get the best education we could for our youngsters to take on key positions on the island. We saw human development to be more important than any other development on the island. We saw the development of our human resources to be our most important role. We wished to achieve the best standard we could afford.'[3]

Basil George, the first St Helenian to become Chief Education Officer, was also well qualified for his post. Like Mr Benjamin, he received all of his schooling on the island. He started his schooldays at Jamestown Infants School with Head Teacher Martha George. From here, he progressed through Jamestown Junior School under the leadership of Eliza Smith; thence to Pilling Senior School under William Corker, from where he was selected to be one of the second intake to the Secondary Selective School at Red Gate, initially with Miss Walker, with whom he has kept in contact since that time. 'Miss Walker gave me my knowledge of the island because she took us on walks and excursions during the holidays.' Leaving school at 15, he worked variously as an audit clerk, a labourer in South Africa, and a policeman on St Helena, before he decided that teaching was to be his career. At Harford Senior School he found himself on his first day of teaching facing 32 children, having had no training at all. With the help of his head teacher, Maurice Young, Saturday classes with the Education Officer, and a certain amount of ingenuity and resourcefulness, he taught all subjects to his senior pupils. He taught for a time at the Secondary Selective School while gaining five GCE O-levels by private study to qualify for teacher training in England. There he spent four years from 1966 to 1970 in Leicester gaining a BEd Honours degree. Returning to St Helena, he was appointed to be Assistant Education Officer and Head Teacher of the Secondary Selective School. He returned to the UK for a year to undertake an Advanced Diploma Course at Bristol University in 1976-77, and came back to St Helena as Assistant Education Officer in charge of Senior Schools until 1980 when he returned to sss as Head when Dan Yon left. Mr George was appointed in 1983 to be Education Officer. This title was changed to Chief Education Officer at the approach of the three-tier system. In addition to his educational interests, he has participated in many other island activities, including being a founder member of both the Heritage Society and the Handicapped Society. His philosophy is that education should be built on and integrated with strengths within the island community and culture, to create a sense of identity. As a small isolated community, resourcefulness is at the centre of this culture. In 1987 he presented a paper on resourceful learning as a new approach to classroom teaching. This philosophy underpins both the setting up and the development of education on the island. Coupled with this philosophy is the recognition that the present system of education has been locally developed, with outside help and support, this fact having been instrumental in causing islanders to accept ownership and responsibility for its success.[4]

Under Basil George's leadership, other Education Officers and Assistant Education Officers were appointed for specific areas of work. These were:

EDUCATION OFFICERS
Arnold Flagg (Middle Schools) DipEd ACP CertEd
Edith Timm (First Schools) MEd DipEd CertEd
John Birchall (Headteacher PAS) BA DipEd
Lilian Crowie (Teacher Training) DipEd
ASSISTANT EOS
J. Patsy Flagg (Nursery Education) DipEd NAMCW
Eric M. George (FE/Community Education)

Arnold Flagg, as a very small child, lived on Ascension Island where his father was a policeman and where he was taught to read, but then his family returned to St Helena. He first attended the Jamestown Infants School in Napoleon Street, then spent a short while at Hutts Gate before returning again to Jamestown Infants where Mildred Smith was head. Moving to Jamestown Junior School, which was in the Pilling buildings, he was taught by the severe Eliza Smith and remembers the English, mathematics and craft work she instilled into him. Then it was a return to Hutts Gate, where he left as a pupil at the age of 15 and immediately re-entered the classroom as a teacher. He was assisted in this by teacher-training sessions at Wellington House given by Education Officer R. Thompson. He also took lessons with Canon Walcott and Jessie Cardwell, head of SSS. He moved from Hutts Gate to the Secondary Selective School, then went to the UK to St

Paul's College, Cheltenham, to obtain a Certificate in Education, returning to the island to teach at Harford Senior School under headmaster Maurice Young. In January 1961 he became head of Sandy Bay School until he returned to the UK to take the DipEd at Bristol University in 1962/63. In 1964 he was appointed to be an Assistant Education Officer, and from then until he retired in 1989 he played a prominent part in the Education Department. In addition he has been involved from the start of the Duke of Edinburgh Award Scheme on the island in the early 1970s, and has also held a keen interest in local affairs, becoming an elected member of the Legislative Council in 1989.[5]

Mrs Edith Timm (née Francis) received all of her schooling on the island, starting as a six-year-old at Bethel School, Longwood, where her teachers were the two sisters, Ivy Duncan and Noreen Evans. From there she transferred at the age of nine to Hutts Gate School. Although she was successful in obtaining a place at the Secondary Selective School, she was not able to take up the place as her parents were not in a position to maintain her there, and she remained at Hutts Gate for the rest of her schooldays. From the age of 14½ she did some teaching for the Head Teacher, Canon Hall, and then, on reaching school leaving age in 1951, she left the classroom as a pupil and, like many other colleagues, immediately re-entered the same school as a teacher. After five years she decided to go to the UK on domestic service. While there she was encouraged by her employers to undertake O levels and then to apply for teacher training. She spent two years at Wynyard Hall Training College, Durham, from where she gained a UK teaching qualification and was appointed to a teaching post at a junior school in Middlesborough, returning to St Helena to be married. Subsequently gaining a Diploma in Advanced Studies in Education from Newcastle University in 1970, she came back to the island, but later returned to the UK where she was Deputy Head of a junior school in Inner London.

Mrs Timm was appointed to be an Assistant Education Officer on the island in September 1972. Still keen to achieve more, she gained an MEd from the University of Bristol in 1977, becoming the first St Helenian to achieve an academic award at this level. At the introduction of the three-tier system of schooling, she became the Education Officer responsible for First Schools, later to transfer to the Middle School sector on the retirement of Arnold Flagg.[6] A few years later, in 1992, she again achieved an island 'first' as the first St Helenian to become the head of the Prince Andrew School.

Mrs Lily Crowie (née Francis) attended the Hutts Gate School at the age of six with head teacher Maurice Young. When the little Bethel School at Longwood was opened to accommodate the younger children from the overcrowded school at Hutts Gate, Lily moved there and was also taught by Ivy Duncan and Noreen Evans. While there she had an early taste of teaching when she used to take dictation and to read to the class. However, at the age of nine the pupils had to return to Hutts Gate and this is where Lily received the rest of her schooling. Like her sister Edith, she was not able to take up her place at the Secondary Selective School due to home circumstances. At the age of 15, in April 1949, she took the examination to become a pupil teacher and three weeks later was teaching at her own school, Hutts Gate, now under the headship of Lily Corker. Shortly afterwards, on 14 August 1949, she moved with Mrs Corker to the 'new' Longwood Junior School which opened in the previous Officers' Mess building, and she taught there for the next 15 years. For the year 1964-1965 she became head teacher of Levelwood School, prior to spending a year in the UK at Oxford Institute of Education studying organization and administration for head teachers. She then returned for a brief time to Levelwood before being appointed as a Senior Head Teacher at the Country Senior School, taking the place of Eric George during his year at Oxford. On Mr George's return, in 1968, Mrs Crowie became the Primary Schools' Organizer, this involving advising and assisting teachers of children from nursery age to 11. During the academic year 1977/78 she gained the Diploma in Advanced Studies in Education at Bristol University. In 1985, at the time of key planning for the three-tier system, she was appointed to be an Assistant Education Officer, from which she was promoted to become Education Officer for Teacher Training in 1988. She returned to the UK for a short period in 1989-90 to study teacher training and resource development. Of her role in leading teacher education on the island, she says: 'We want our trainees to be prepared and qualified to become good, confident and knowledgeable teachers in the classroom in general and specialist subjects, bearing in mind their skills and ambitions and the needs of the education department.'[7]

It is of interest to note that Mrs Crowie has followed an entire path through the career structure for teachers on the island, having progressed from being a pupil teacher (1949), to Assistant Teacher (1955), First Assistant (1958), Senior Teacher (1962), Head Teacher (1964), Senior Head Teacher (1967), (Primary) Schools' Organizer (1968), Assistant Education Officer (1985), and Education Officer (1988).

Mrs Joan (Patsy) Flagg (née Leo) began her school life at the old

Half Tree Hollow School under head teacher Miss Perthinia (Teeny) Constantine, with whom she moved into the new building in 1948. There she passed the entrance examination to the Secondary Selective School, starting at Ladder Hill in 1952. She was one of an intake of eight pupils, seven girls and one boy. At the age of 15 she stayed on at school for a number of months during which she and others undertook further studies set by Education Officer Norman Kerr. In April 1956 she became a pupil teacher at Jamestown Infants School in Napoleon Street, where she learned how to teach as she went along, 'sliding in gently, observing and watching other teachers'. She transferred to Sandy Bay School at the end of 1956 for about a year and then went back to Jamestown for four years. Marrying Arnold Flagg in 1960, she returned to Sandy Bay School where her husband became head in January 1961. In August 1962 she went to the UK to accompany Arnold, who was taking the Diploma in Education course at Bristol University. She returned to take up a teaching post at Half Tree Hollow until 1969. With her husband, she spent the 1969/70 academic year in the UK at Nottingham University taking a Diploma Course related to slow learners. In 1972 she was appointed as Parentcraft Education Organizer, following the visit of Leonora Pitcairn, and as such became an Assistant Education Officer. Since then, her role on the island has been specifically geared to educational work with young children both at nursery and first-school level. She sees her present role 'as an enormous challenge and task when I realize how many lives I have in my hands. I am one of many people laying the foundations of the education of young children.'[8]

Eric George had started school at the age of five at Half Tree Hollow School, still housed in the former school building which later became the home of the Sim family. His mother, Dorothy George, was a teacher there. From there he went to the Country School for three years from the age of six, and recalls travelling to school by donkey. His family moved to Jamestown, where he attended the Jamestown Infants School under Mildred Smith's headship in Napoleon Street. A victim of the poliomyelitis epidemic in 1946, he missed some schooling, but then attended the Jamestown Junior School which was in part of the Pilling building, under the headship of Eliza Smith, followed by the Pilling Senior School at the other end of the building, where Mr LeBreton was head. On leaving school at the age of 15, Eric George applied for teaching, and found himself back in Jamestown Junior School, learning from Keith Yon on the job and attending teacher training classes from time to time at Wellington House with Education Officer Mr Thompson. During his early teaching career he taught at the Secondary Selective School and the Country School, having a mid-career break from the profession for eight months, returning to teach at Levelwood School under Ivy, his wife's headship, followed by exchanging roles at the Country School, himself as Head and his wife as Deputy. After a second time away from teaching and involvement as Information Officer for ten years, he returned to the Education Department to promote the development of music in the schools' system. His document *A Report on Training in England (Broadcasting) 1968* helped to establish broadcasting on the island, initially as a responsibility of the Education Department. In 1985 he became head of the Secondary Selective School, holding the post until August 1988, when the Prince Andrew School opened. Thereafter for a few months he remained in charge at the Ladder Hill buildings, where some classes were still being taught pending the completion of the buildings at Francis Plain. Throughout his career Eric George has maintained a keen interest in music and has been responsible for the musical contribution to many island events, including school productions. He has also played a prominent part in the Teachers' Association, having been a founder member.[9]

The internal work of the schools, together with the implementation of the newly devised curricula, continued to be conducted by the teachers themselves, led by the Education Officer appointed for that sector or by a teacher holding a post of responsibility for that area of work. Those appointed to a post of special responsibility for the three-tier system were:

Mrs Joy George (Science, PAS)
Miss Heather George (Aesthetics, PAS)
Mrs Corinda Essex (English, PAS)
Mrs Betty Joshua (Communication Skills, Middle Schools)
Mrs Barbara Plato (Language, First Schools)
Mrs Alice Williams (Integrated Practical Activities, MS)
Mrs Doris Peters (Special Educational Needs, PAS)
Miss Valerie Yon (Special Educational Needs, FS/MS)
Mrs Susan O'Bey (Social Studies, MS)
Mrs Barbara Ann George (Home Economics, PAS)
Mr Anthony Hopkins (Movement, Drama, PE, MS)
Mrs Priscilla Thomas (Mathematics, MS)

In May 1989 a new Constitution was introduced by the Government of St Helena, following the St Helena Constitution Ordinance, 1988. This determined that the majority of the members of each of its committees

The Education Committee in session, 1991. Round the table from the left: Ivy George, John Newman, Valerie Roberts (Secretary), Ruth Pridham (Chairman), Basil George, Cyril Gunnell, Clive Duncan

should be elected members of the Legislative Council, and that the chairman of each of the various committees should be selected by members of the committee itself from the elected members. Following consultation with the chairman of a committee, the Governor could appoint other members, either from members of the Legislative Council or from non-members. At this point, the composition of the Education Committee changed, its members now being:

Chairman:	Mrs Ruth Pridham, Cert Ed
Members:	Mrs Ivy George, former Head; Chairman of the Social Services Committee
	Mr John Newman, former Chief of Police; Lay Advocate
	Mr Clive Duncan, Department of Agriculture and Forestry, Clerk to the Council
	Mr Cyril Gunnell, member of the Social Services Committee
Ex-officio:	Mr Basil George, Chief Education Officer

In view of the new conditions of membership, and for the first time, the Bishop no longer held a position on the Education Committee.

The new Chairman, Ruth Pridham (née Stevens), was also well qualified to take up this important position. She received all of her schooling on the island, starting at the age of five at the tiny Blue Hill School, then under the charge of Caleb John. At the age of 11 she attended the Gosse Central School. Becoming a pupil teacher, she was one of a few young islanders who were chosen by Education Officer Mr

Davies Watkins to receive more advanced teaching and this took place in the Francis Plain Pavilion. At the departure of Mr Watkins this arrangement ceased, and at this stage Ruth returned to Blue Hill, now under the headship of Algernon Broadway, as a pupil. Later, reaching school leaving age, she became a pupil teacher at Blue Hill under the leadership of Edward Benjamin and later George Lawrence. On the arrival of Miss Penny Walker as head of the newly established Secondary Selective School at Red Hill, Ruth spent two days each week at Blue Hill and three days at Red Hill, where Miss Walker taught all the pupil teachers, furthering their academic studies and introducing Child Development. Later, Mrs Pridham went to the UK as an *au pair* and subsequently took a three-year Teacher's Certificate course at St Catherine's, Tottenham, following this with infant and junior teaching posts in Britain. In 1982 she returned with her husband, Gordon, to her native island, to enter almost immediately into serving the community as an elected representative on the Legislative Council, from which she was appointed by the Governor to chair the Social Services Committee until, in May 1989, she followed Eric Benjamin in the role of Chairman of the Education Committee. She has her name firmly stamped on island education because 'Pridham Days' have been introduced, these being the first day of each term which is reserved for special in-service work for teachers.[10]

During the first few months of the new system, each of the middle and first schools celebrated an official opening ceremony. The final one was that of the Prince Andrew School on 5 June 1989. It was attended by John Mark Taylor MP representing Her Majesty's Government, in the presence of the Governor, members of the Executive and Legislative Councils, the Education Committee with the out-going Chairman, Eric Benjamin, and officers, teachers and, last but by no means least, the first Prince Andrew School students. In his speech on this momentous day which had been anticipated for so many years, John Birchall, the first Head Teacher of the school, challenged every member of the school: 'The Island has taken a giant step forward in its Education role for the future of its children and adults. The facilities are there for each and every one of us and we should use them to our full advantage.'[11]

1988: The Prince Andrew School

For the first time in the history of schools on the island, all children aged 12 and over were to be attending the same school. Purpose-built, in a central location at Francis Plain, it brought together all aspects of

The Prince Andrew School (Photograph by David Bentham, taken from High Knoll)

Christmas Lunch, 1991, at Prince Andrew School. This photograph shows the entire population of 12- to 16-year-olds on St Helena. They all attend the one school, with some 17- and 18-year-olds

education for that age range. This would undoubtedly have a significant effect on the island as a whole, not only academically, but also sociologically by mixing this age group from the various communities in different parts of the island. In addition the new school had been planned to provide an important community resource, with all of its facilities becoming available to any islanders who wished to avail themselves of the educational opportunites offered.

Facing the island's sports field, the facilities at the Prince Andrew School comprise a library, classrooms, extensive practical laboratories, technical workshops, maritime centre, agricultural centre, gymnasium, squash courts, weight training centre, playing fields, hall/auditorium, lecture room, music rooms, computer centre, photographic facilities, exhibition areas in the large entrance hall, cafeteria facilities, offices and staff rooms and a centre for senior pupils. The school is sited in a commanding position, facing north and looking over the Jamestown valley to the sea. The grounds were landscaped by Mrs Diana Houghton and they complete an environment worthy of the hopes and expectations which the islanders hold for this school.

The school library was formally named the Trevor Hearl Library in honour of a long-standing friend of the island who, following his initial visit in 1969 as an Education Adviser, has continued to serve St Helena devotedly ever since. This service has taken several forms. He was a founder-member of the St Helena–Cheltenham Link in 1969, which developed into the St Helena Link Committee. Mr Hearl has also succeeded in retrieving many old, rare prints and books written about St Helena, so helping to preserve and foster the heritage of the island. He has become a major source of historical information in the UK about St Helena and, in this capacity has produced journal articles and researched individual queries.

The Harper's Agricultural Centre has been built for the use of the school. It is sited on land near Francis Plain which was bequeathed by the Mary Lloyd Trust to be used for educational purposes. The Centre was built by students from the former Technical Trades Centre and was officially opened by Eric Benjamin, then Chairman of the Education Committee, on 9 November 1988.

Under Head Teacher John Birchall, the school opened in September 1988 with 387 students and 41 teachers, among them seven probationers, one trainee and six supply teachers. The remaining 27 of the teachers had been trained locally or overseas. These included six expatriate teachers from the UK, whose subject specialisms included science, home economics, social studies, technical crafts, mathematics and maritime studies. They were recruited to supplement the work of local teachers and, as required, to provide A level teaching in other subjects to the 96 students who were over the compulsory school leaving age.

Prior to relinquishing his post as headmaster in 1989, John Birchall made a report to the Education Committee and Senior Staff in which he made recommendations for the continued advancement of the Prince Andrew School and education generally on the island. Among his concerns were the need for an employment policy to enable students at PAS to complete their courses and to achieve certificate qualification before being allowed to leave to take up employment, the development of overseas training opportunities clearly defined to meet the needs of the students and the island, greater concentration in the Middle Schools on the curriculum, with extra-curricular activities taking place outside the school day, the production of individual school handbooks, and the further development of liaison opportunities between all sectors and people throughout the educational system.

The school at the time of writing (1992) has been in operation for four years. Terry Ward from the UK was appointed to take over the leadership of the school from Mr Birchall in 1989, an interregnum period of six months being covered by Deputy Head, Mrs Joy George, as Acting Head. Since its establishment the school has become a focal educational centre, meeting centre and resource centre on the island, and runs courses and classes for the community as well as those for its 12- to 18-year-olds.

Mr Ward was pleased to report in 1992 that approximately one-sixth of the population of the island came through the school building during each week, these including the students, teachers and other school workers, further and community education students, apprentices and others on day release courses, and other members of the general public. 'The most thrilling thing about working here is that we are probably the most comprehensive school that there is in the world – there is no alternative. It is truly a community establishment.' The numbers even include about 20 adults who study during the day alongside children in their classrooms, for instance learning computer skills, accounting and biology. The school offers an educational service to other employers, such as the Public Works and Services Department and the Hospital, guided by them concerning the nature of courses offered.

The *Prince Andrew School Handbook*, written for the benefit of scholars, teachers and parents, declares the aims of the school in four categories – social and community, curriculum, pastoral and cultural. The school aims to develop good human relationships and responsible, contributing members of the society. It seeks to extend to adults and children alike all the resources which the school affords for their enrichment.

Scholars are encouraged to stay on at school after the compulsory school leaving age and all students in Year 4 are paid an allowance to enable them to do so. Subject to passing at least one GCSE subject at Grade C or above, Year 5 students also receive an allowance. Students at the school can take external examinations at several levels, including Advanced GCE level, A/S level, GCSE, RSA, City and Guilds, and BTEC, and also the St Helena School Leaving Certificate. The school members are divided into four house groups – Cavendish, Mundens, Dutton and Jenkins – and inter-house activities are keenly contested.

Since 1989 there have been several bursaries and scholarships available for students at school to proceed to acquire post-school qualifications abroad, including first degree and post-degree level and vocational awards. These include the ODA Fee Support Scheme, Commonwealth Scholarships and the Cambridge Trust Scholarship. Opportunities are also taken to send suitable students to Atlantic College in Wales, to undertake an International Baccalaureate to qualify them for entry to higher education.

Terry Ward's philosophy of leadership and management was that of appropriate discussion and delegation of authority within a firm structure. He believed strongly in the need for a broad-based curriculum which would equip the islanders of the future for any eventuality, either on St Helena or elsewhere. 'The Prince Andrew School needs to provide people who can become the greatest overseas earners, as well as those who develop their careers on the island.' Of his teaching staff, he said: 'There are some outstanding individuals who have adapted in an incredible way to all the changes. The capacity for hard work is phenomenal and the dedication incredible. This is the strength of the Education Department. There is only a small pool of people to choose from, who must support each other and continue to work as a team.'[12]

As a physicist and a teacher, he participated in some teaching, both in his own school and in the Teacher Education Centre. He relinquished the post at the end of September 1992, affirming: 'The job itself has probably been one of the most exciting that I've ever been privileged to do – I have enjoyed it immensely.'[13]

His successor at the Prince Andrew School was Mrs Edith Timm, who transferred to the headship from her role as Education Officer for Middle Schools. This marked a strategic point in the history of secondary education because, for the first time, an islander was at the helm of the one community school which caters for all people on the island from the age of 12 upwards.

On the threshold of taking up the headship of the school, she viewed the role as an exciting challenge. Mrs Timm believes strongly that the young people in her school are, indeed, the future of the island. The school has a responsibility to help to develop the potential of all students so that they and St Helena will benefit to the full.[14]

1988: The Three Middle Schools

HARFORD MIDDLE SCHOOL caters for children from the eastern part of the island. The school occupies buildings originally constructed and opened in 1957 as one of the three senior schools on the island. Under the leadership of Elvina Mercury, Harford Middle School opened in September 1988 with 116 pupils, nine teachers and three trainee teachers. During this year Heather George was appointed head teacher-designate, working alongside Mrs Mercury. Miss George took over the full leadership in September 1989. Like all of her colleagues holding headships of middle and first schools, Miss George received all her schooling on the island. She particularly recalls being taught by Mrs Martha George – 'a stimulating lady who made and taught with a lot of visual aids' – and who was well respected by teachers and pupils alike. Miss George did not want to enter teaching but, at the age of 15, was persuaded to do so by her father. Her training should have lasted a year but, due to shortage of teachers, this was cut to six months, during which time she attended classes on Child Development taught by the Education Officer, Alan Johns. During her career she has taken a number of external examinations, including O-levels and RSA subjects. Twelve of these years were at the Secondary Selective School, teaching mainly Geography, Physical Education and Music. She spent the academic year 1984-85 undertaking in-service training in Cheltenham, England.

Miss George herself is musical and creative and this is reflected in the work of the Harford school. In 1984, with a colleague, Miss Pamela Lawrence, she wrote and produced a highly successful schools' musical production entitled *Fibre*, a story based on the island's history, in honour of the Royal visitor, Prince Andrew. Miss George's philosophy as a head teacher is 'to build up a happy, friendly, hardworking school in which everyone is co-operating to the full'.[15]

PILLING MIDDLE SCHOOL, sited in the premises of the former senior school in Jamestown, is led by Rita Nicholls. She too received all of her

Jamestown from Side Path, showing Pilling Middle School and Jamestown First School, at either end of the former military parade ground

schooling and teaching experience on the island except for a one-year course in Birmingham and a term in North Hertfordshire.

The school opened with 89 pupils, most coming from the Jamestown, Briars, Ruperts Bay and Alarm Forest areas, and 10 teachers, eight of whom had been trained locally and/or overseas. The school was additionally resourced for the specialist teaching of science, home economics and technical crafts. The *1992 Pilling School Handbook*, prepared to welcome pupils to the school, emphasizes that the individual child is clearly the central focus in the school, which aims to develop each child to maximum potential academically, socially and physically, in an atmosphere in which all members are happy and caring for the needs of each other.

Mrs Nicholls, a former head girl of the Secondary Selective School, recalls being thrown in at the deep end of teaching, having been offered a teaching post at the age of 15 by Education Officer Norman Kerr. Saturday morning training sessions were arranged for pupil teachers. After several years of teaching, she was encouraged by Education Officer Alan Johns to attend a course at Birmingham University School of Education from 1967-68 for which she produced a DipEd thesis on *Secondary Education in St Helena*. Prior to the introduction of the three tier system, Chief Education Officer Basil George encouraged her to spend some months in Hertfordshire, to familiarize herself with middle school work. Accepting the challenges of the new system, Mrs Nicholls' philosophy is that 'School is part of my home. It is essential to put the children first, before self, and this needs time and dedication.'[16]

ST PAUL'S MIDDLE SCHOOL opened with 153 pupils, seven teachers, three trainee teachers and three supply teachers, under the headship of Stedson George, and in buildings previously occupied by Country Senior School with the new addition of a science block. At the opening of his school in 1989, and proud of the achievements of his ancestors, whom he believes to have been slaves, Mr George was pleased to report: 'I think I am right in saying that Country School was the first Government School to admit slave children.' Certainly, the island schools' census issued in 1818 recorded that there were 63 black pupils at the Plantation House School, 37 of them being slaves and 26 free. The school at Plantation was, of course, an early forerunner of the present school at St Paul's.

The school today is purposeful and active. With 167 pupils, it is one of the largest schools on the island. The pupils come from a wide geographical area, ranging from Blue Hill and Barren Ground, Head O'Wain and High Point, Rosemary Plain and Guinea Grass, New Ground and Scotland, to St Paul's, Knollcombes and Sandy Bay, and Half Tree Hollow.

Stedson George finds that, in spite of this varied background, there are no problems of integration once the children are at school. Following a 'Bridging Meeting' with the head teachers of the contributory first schools, at which the transition of the children into the middle school is discussed, the 41/42 new children are divided into two mixed classes on academic, geographic and personal grounds. He attributes this integration both to the deliberate policy of the school to effect this, and to the fact that today's children are more readily able to travel about the island and to meet other people. It was different when Stedson George was a child, living at Levelwood. 'I went down to Jamestown once a year at Christmas,' he said, 'It was a special treat!' In the past, the children from different areas had different accents, different styles of dress and different expressions, but now all is much more inter-mingled.

Throughout his school and teaching career Mr George has played a lively part on the island. His work in teaching is supplemented by his unofficial role as the island's astronomer. At the time of Halley's

Comet's appearance in 1986, Stedson's broadcasts on St Helena Radio gave valuable knowledge about it to his listeners. As a 14-year-old pupil, he recalls being asked by Education Officer Thompson if he wished to be a teacher and replying 'Yes, please!', to which Mr Thompson replied, 'You are on!' He continued his own schooling at Hutts Gate beyond the school leaving age of 15 as there were no teaching vacancies, and he worked for nothing. At 16 he was given an official teaching job at Hutts Gate, receiving £8 per month which he gave to his mother – except for buying a dictionary. From 1959 to 1960 he attended St Paul's College, Cheltenham, the only overseas student at the time.

Having enjoyed his own schooldays, Mr George's aims for the school reflect this: 'I like happy people. I believe in hard work, but you must enjoy it while you're doing it. I loved school and I want my pupils to like it too. I want the school to make them into people who have learned the skills and developed the ability to acquire knowledge when they want it. Literacy and the ability to communicate are vitally important.'[17] The *1992 St Paul's Middle School's Policy Document* outlines the aims of promoting initiative, resourcefulness, self-reliance and co-operation, and then continues: 'The emphasis in the early years will be on communication, with the aim to have the children talk and write naturally, freely and expressively, to love and appreciate books and reading, and have confidence in their ability to cope with language.'

1988: The Seven First Schools

BLUE HILL FIRST SCHOOL, the smallest of the island's schools, opened with 10 pupils of compulsory school age and four pre-school children, one trainee teacher, one assistant and a head teacher, Elizabeth Young. It occupied the buildings purpose-built for the previous junior and infant school. Like the other ten schools on the island, it assumed a new life in September 1988 when it opened as a First School. Months of planning had preceded this changeover. In order to understand the effects on their children, the parents were invited the previous June to a meeting at which Assistant Education Officer Mrs Flagg and Mrs Young outlined the points relevant to the introduction of the three-tier system. In *Blue Hill School Log Book*, Mrs Young reported: 'We as teachers felt that the meeting was successful and that the parents were interested and receptive, although not very orally responsive.' Perhaps in some minds there was already the concern that the school was going to be very small indeed – and how long would it survive?

From its opening as a first school in 1988 it became expedient to combine with Sandy Bay School for a number of days in each week, but this proved to be rather a cumbersome arrangement in terms of travelling time. By May 1989 it was decided that there was a need to discuss the closure of the school. Called by the Chairman of the Education Committee, Ruth Pridham, herself a Blue Hill resident, and the Chief Education Officer, Basil George, the parents attended a meeting to discuss a matter which grieved everyone present. The parents requested that the school be given one more year of life, until September 1990. This was agreed. In December 1989, when the matter was discussed again, they again were adamant that they wished the school to remain open for a further two terms. But eventually there was no escape from the hard but inevitable decision in June 1990 and the parents received a letter informing them that their children could attend St Paul's First School from September onwards. However, the Blue Hill buildings would be retained by the Education Department 'pending the reopening of the school if numbers increase'.

This marked the end of an era. An all-age school had been established by the church at Blue Hill in 1907 and its history is woven into the earlier pages of this book. In fact, it was the grandfather of a later Head Teacher at the school (Miss Evelyn Bagley) – a gentleman of Scottish descent and persistence – who had petitioned for a school to be opened in the Blue Hill district. From 1930 it became known as the Bishop Holbech Memorial School, to commemorate the fifth bishop of St Helena who had served on the island since 1905 and was due to retire in 1931. The school reverted to its original name on the reorganization of schools in 1941. During its existence the school was served by a number of head teachers, the first of these being Caleb John from 1907 to 1941. His retirement after this long period of service coincided with a reorganization when the senior pupils were transferred to the Country Senior School. However, there was no transport for the pupils and they drifted back to Blue Hill, where the school was now in the charge of two pupil teachers, Harriet Williams and Evelyn Bagley. Acceding to the pressures of allowing them to stay for the time being at least, Algernon Broadway was appointed as headmaster in January 1943 and he held the post until 1945, when for several months Edward Benjamin took charge. Mr Benjamin had entered the profession in 1926, but after many years of service, including his time at Blue Hill, he transferred to running one of the island's now long-established businesses. To quote Mr Benjamin speaking in 1991: 'Now they have O and A levels. Then, we just had spirit-level.'[18] He was followed by George Lawrence who was head from April 1946 until June 1951, when

Miss Bagley was appointed to the headship. She was destined to hold this post for 33 years until 1984. The school log book records major events through the years, including the transfer of all senior pupils to Country Senior School in 1951, although, as on the previous occasion, a few children persisted in turning up at their old school! The log book mentions several major school happenings, such as the opening of the new Junior School building in 1959, and the retirement of Miss Bagley in 1984. It also reflects life in that remote part of the island itself, making mention for instance of the first use of radio in the school in 1967, the installation of the telephone in 1987, and the connection to the main power supply, also in 1987.

Elizabeth Young, who was the headteacher at Blue Hill from 1984 until the closure in 1990, recalled being taught by her aunt, Ruth Pridham, who herself had been a child at the former school. Mrs Young, like her colleagues, was island born and bred. From Blue Hill she went to the Country Senior School. When she left school she wanted to become a nurse, but her head teacher Mr Broadway and Education Officer Mr Dixon, recommended her for teaching. Accordingly, she found herself on 7 March 1960 teaching at Jamestown Infants School under the watchful eye of Head Teacher Una Thomas. She received most of her training on the job, attending Saturday morning classes with Alan Johns, Education Officer, having rushed up the Ladder to get to them. In 1961 the school transferred to the new buildings in Market Street (now the Teacher Education Centre), still with Mrs Thomas as Head. In 1971, Education Officer Cliff Huxtable asked her to move to teach third years at Jamestown Junior School under the headship of Stedson George. She then spent the 1980/81 school year on in-service training in the UK at Cheltenham, returning to teach at Jamestown Junior School. On being invited to take the headship of Blue Hill School on the retirement of Miss Bagley, Mrs Young was enabled to spend a term there to observe, after which she readily took up the post. Commenting on her teaching career, she said: 'This quarter of the century has seen so many changes in approaches to education on St Helena which were definitely not evident when I began teaching some thirty years ago. Then you *taught* children, now we do a lot more *finding out* and *working together*. There's a difference.'[19]

The school at Blue Hill was proud of its standards, giving individual encouragement to its tiny community. In 1990, on the closure of Blue Hill School, Mrs Young took up the headship of Sandy Bay. The Blue Hill Field Centre has been established in the school buildings, thus serving as a meeting or residential centre for various groups such as teachers, trainees, pupils and youth organizations.

Half Tree Hollow School, 1992

HALF TREE HOLLOW FIRST SCHOOL opened in 1988 with 132 pupils of compulsory school age, 16 pre-school children, eight teachers and five trainee teachers. It met in the building previously occupied by the Half Tree Hollow Primary School. An early *School Log Book* records events from 1944 to 1957, such as the Empire Day celebrations; the polio epidemic in 1946; and the arrival during 1949 of a collection of magazines from a London publisher. In 1949 the school moved from its original building at Halfway House, the present home of Grace Sim, daughter of James Sim, head teacher of the time, to the present site. The school was proud of its attendance record, this being 96% in 1957. A second school log book covers the period from 1977 to the present day, including the various extra-mural activities of the school, the visitors to the school, the Parent-Teacher Association activities, and the preparations for the three-tier system.

Being sited in an area which is rapidly developing residentially, the numbers continue to rise, and this is a cause for concern. Already, any children living below Three Tanks are zoned to attend the First School in Jamestown. Miss Joyce Harris, the head teacher, was herself a pupil at the Country School and recalls the teaching of Mrs Iris Clingham, the head teacher at the time, to whom she owes much of her early learning. Becoming a teacher trainee at the age of 15, she trained for one year and attended Further Education classes at the Secondary Selective School every Saturday morning from 9.00 am to 12.30 pm. She recalls the language and mathematics lessons with Algernon

Broadway and teaching method classes with Education Officer Tony Cross on two afternoons each week. As a probationary teacher she was visited by Alan Johns in her classroom – 'a nerve-wracking experience' – but from his critique she derived great benefit. She was able to undertake four periods of training in the UK – 1964-67 at Stranmillis College, Belfast, to gain her Certificate of Education; 1973-74 at Tirlebrook County Primary School, Tewkesbury, to consider the merits of open-plan schooling for St Helena; 1979-80 at Acklam Whin Primary School to study general primary school education with Bob Mather; and 1987-88 in Cheltenham and Hertfordshire to study the management of first schools in preparation for the three tier system.

During her career she has taught at Country Junior School, where she was promoted to Head. From there she became Head of Jamestown Junior School, before being appointed to the Half Tree Hollow Headship, following in the footsteps of James Sim, Teeny Constantine and Ivy Williams. Miss Harris has held the headship for the last 12 years, including the period of the transference to the three-tier system. Her philosophy as a Head is to create a strong and happy school with an enthusiastic staff who will work as a team to develop each and every child to full potential. 'Learning and teaching in my earlier years was very different from today. As a pupil, learning was by listening, remembering and striving and struggling. Today learning is much more fun. Children in my school are given every opportunity to learn through listening and doing – using apparatus and materials to help understand and remember concepts and facts – rather than just listening.'[20]

LEVELWOOD FIRST SCHOOL opened in 1988 under the headship of Mrs Muriel Williams with 24 pupils of compulsory school age, two teachers, and a Nursery Assistant with three children of playgroup age on her lists. Initially the teachers kept their double age-range classes throughout their time at the school, but Mrs Williams and her colleague have now decided to teach the same age range each year, the 3rd and 4th years with the Head Teacher, and the 1st and 2nd years with the Assistant Teacher.

The school originally opened in 1947 as an all-age school. The available *School Log Book* dates back to 1957 and early entries in the book record the highlights, such as the visit on 18 June 1957 to Jamestown of 17 pupils and the head teacher to see the research ship *Atlantis*, the school's first successes in 1959 of three senior pupils in the GSE, the visits to the school of successive Education Officers, the final transfer of all senior pupils to Harford Senior School in June 1970, when Levelwood became a primary school, the visit of Prince Andrew in April 1984, and the preparations and plans for the three-tier system of education introduced in 1988.

By careful budgeting Mrs Williams has been able to create a bright and attractive environment for her pupils, with locally made classroom furniture and plenty of display wall-space, and an attractive and well-stocked garden. One of the major aims of Levelwood First School is quoted in the School's Policy Document as follows: 'We as teachers must consider ourselves as determining each child's future and we must therefore consider what is best for the individual child. We must look at our class of pupils, not as a class of children all to be educated in the same field, but as individual personalities and to be educated in their own field of interest.'

That the school is fulfilling this aim can be seen in the progress of the children. In the past, reading has been a problem due partly to the fact that lack of electricity in several homes prevented children from reading after school. However, this problem is now almost conquered and every child can read and is numerate before leaving Levelwood. Many of the children belong to the Jehovah's Witness Church, as Levelwood has been the home area of many people from this group. The school ensures that the individual's beliefs and practices are respected and there is a happy and supportive relationship with the parents of the children of the school. The PTA has been instrumental in helping to raise money for school projects, the children also helping enthusiastically. To give the children from this comparatively remote area a better knowledge of their island, school visits are arranged, such as a recent one to Jamestown, when each child was given money to spend on books and stationery.

Like most other schools on the island, Levelwood enjoys good facilities and resources on an environmentally beautiful site. Mrs Williams clearly enjoys her work at Levelwood, just as she has enjoyed her previous teaching positions on St Helena. She entered teaching at the age of 15 and was one of the second group to enter full-time training led by Education Officer Alan Johns, helped by Mr Lamin. During the first term of her training she spent one day each week observing at Half Tree Hollow School; in her second term she taught one lesson there each week, and in the third term she taught three lessons each week on one day, culminating in three full weeks at the school with a full timetable. In 1973-74 she went on in-service training organized by Jack Shepherd in Cheltenham, where she was on attachment to Glenfalls

Primary School. She has a particular enthusiasm for helping her pupils to appreciate the natural environmental heritage of the island.

Mrs Williams' philosophy is to see herself as a parent, not a head teacher, and to help the children to determine their future. 'Teaching now is far more demanding than it was. Individuals are more demanding. Before, we catered for the school – now we cater for children.'[21]

LONGWOOD FIRST SCHOOL opened in 1988 under the leadership of Mrs Joan Thomas, with 90 pupils of compulsory school-age, 8 of pre-school age, 6 teachers and 3 trainees. The school receives children from a wide geographical area in the eastern part of the island. Neither of the two sections of the school have totally purpose-built premises. The First School is in buildings which were originally built as an officers' mess during the Second World War. The previous junior school was housed there from 1949, while the infants school had operated in the Golf Club.

All of these buildings have been suitably adapted for their present use. The pre-school children meet in the building which was originally the recreation centre. The lively and happy ethos of the school reflects the aims which, as in all schools on the island, have been devised by the head teacher and staff to suit the particular circumstances of that school. Appropriately, the *1992 Longwood First School Policy Document* carries a picture of the wirebird, which is not only unique to St Helena, but is also a familiar neighbour of children who live in the vicinity of the school. Summarizing its aims, the school seeks to develop in the children lively, enquiring minds, and to develop language and communication skills and creativity, within an environment which is caring and supportive.

The history of attempts to establish schooling in the Longwood area dates back to 1679, when the residents in the eastern country requested a school of their own to save their children having to go all the way to Jamestown. Nothing of any permanence appears to have come of this venture and the story of subsequent abortive efforts to open schools in Longwood – including in the house built for Napoleon, which he never occupied – are woven into the pages of this book. However, the *Longwood Log Book* highlights the major events in the comparatively recent life of the school, including the addition in 1958 of four additional classrooms for the juniors, leaving the original buildings for the infants. From this time, the school was known as the Longwood Primary School. The log book also noted the further extension which was built in 1977. While this was under construction the 70 children occupied the nearby St Mark's Church Hall. Also noted, of course, was the transition from the two-tier to the three-tier system in 1988, giving the school yet another name – the Longwood First School.

Mrs Thomas, the Head Teacher, entered the teaching profession on the island in 1951. Her initial experience as a teacher-in-charge was in 1953 at Longwood, and she has been there ever since, holding the headship of the Infant/Junior School from 1958. She became a Senior Head Teacher in 1970, and with her colleagues played an important part in helping to plan for the introduction of the three-tier system in 1988.

She recalls her own early schooldays at Hutts Gate all-age school, with Maurice Young as a very strict head. At the age of 11, she became one of the first intake of pupils at the Secondary Selective School, then housed at Red Gate. Miss Penelope Walker, now Mrs Porter, was the head teacher, and entry to the school was by test and no interview. On leaving school Mrs Thomas took a clerical post at the Education Office but decided for herself to go into teaching, with the backing of Education Officer Thompson. She became a pupil teacher at Hutts Gate School under head teacher Canon Hall, spending afternoons at training sessions with Mr Thompson. Her long teaching service to the island has given her the philosophy that the major aim of a school is 'to help children to be happy and caring, to progress and to be good citizens'.[22]

JAMESTOWN FIRST SCHOOL occupies the buildings, which had been opened in 1961, of the former Jamestown Junior School, 'across the playground' from the then Pilling Central School, now Pilling Middle School. Its head teacher is Muriel Leo, and the school opened with 95 pupils of compulsory school age, 13 pre-school children, seven teachers and three trainee teachers. Since its establishment in 1988, like other schools on the island, it has become a focal point for the community, encouraging parental involvement with their children's education and participation in school activities. The school is situated in the middle of Jamestown and most of its pupils come from the town itself and from the Briars area, while a few come from the lower end of Half Tree Hollow. Being convinced that the aim of their school is to establish a firm foundation upon which a child will build the structure of his or her future life, Mrs Leo and her staff are concerned about the development of the whole child, physically, mentally, spiritually and emotionally. In accordance with this aim, the *1992 Jamestown First School Handbook* states: 'The general atmosphere should be happy so that the children

Christmas Entertainment 1991, at Jamestown First School

enjoy their work and develop naturally and have an enquiring mind. Conversation should also be fostered. It is the children's school so they must be made to have a pride in their school.'

The log book of the former Jamestown Infants School dates back to 1973, when the head teacher was Mrs Una Thomas. In 1978 Muriel Leo became acting head. Like all other island schools, major events in the UK were celebrated and recorded, including the Queen's official birthday, and several island-wide events were described, for instance the Schools' Gardening Competition in 1976 and the closure of all island schools during an epidemic of 'flu in 1980.

Mrs Leo has vivid memories of her own schooldays with Mrs Martha George, head of Jamestown Junior School, whom she describes as a very good, very strict, outstanding teacher, saying: 'I just learned in that set-up.' With no prior training at all, Mrs Leo was taken on in 1960 as a teacher at Longwood, being visited by Education Officer Tony Cross, and attending Saturday training sessions with him at Ladder Hill. From 1966 to 1969 she took a three-year certificate course at St Matthias College in Bristol; in 1975-76 she was attached to Benhall Primary School in Gloucester working with Diane Baglin; and in 1981-82 she spent a year in Cheltenham on school attachment at Naunton Park Primary School working with Chris Wilday, and undertaking short in-service courses at the College of St Paul and St Mary, Cheltenham. Together with holding headships on the island, these courses helped to prepare her for her challenging role as head in the new three-tier system. Her philosophy as a head teacher is to offer a happy and secure environment for her children, to establish good relationships which lead to high standards and to run a school which serves the community.[23]

ST PAUL'S FIRST SCHOOL, sited on the upper tier but in the same complex of buildings as the Middle School, is led by Priscilla (Maisie) Thomas. It opened with 45 pupils of compulsory school age, 10 pre-school children, four teachers and one trainee teacher in the building formerly occupied by the Country Senior School, and it caters for children from a wide area in the centre and western regions of the island.

The school's Handbook sets out clearly the organization and pro-gramme of the school so that all members, including the parents, can be encouraged to work together for the benefit of the children. An introductory letter to the parents states clearly: 'We look forward to your support and hope that your children will be happy. We welcome all children from the age of 3½-8 years.' In addition to their in-school activities, and like their counterparts in other schools, the children are taken on visits to other areas in order to give them a wider perspective. This is felt to be important because, in spite of the small size of the island, the irregular nature of its territory has in the past prevented ready movement from one area to another. The increasing use of cars is lessening the isolation of remote areas but still children in school are encouraged to explore other parts of the island. Children are also able to participate fully in creative activities, such as singing, dance and drama. Emphasizing the extreme importance of reading – and of the part played by parents in their children's success – the *St Paul's First*

School Handbook concludes: 'We encourage children to take their reading books home, so that parents can help by hearing them read, read with them and to help learn new words. If your children see that you are interested in reading, this will encourage them to read as well.'

Mrs Thomas was from the first keen to be a teacher – so much so that she stayed on at school beyond 15, helping with the teaching but, like Stedson George, receiving no pay for a year. In August 1953 she went on to the established pay-roll as a pupil teacher. Her career from 1968 included several acting headships, until in 1976 she was appointed head of Levelwood Infant/Junior School, a post which she held until the start of the three-tier system in 1988. Her philosophy is based upon the need for commitment. Her own life has been committed to teaching and she has never wished to change it for another job.[24]

SANDY BAY FIRST SCHOOL is based in the buildings of the previous Infant/Junior School, and its Acting Head Teacher at the opening in September 1988 was Hazel Thomas, Iva Henry at that time being in the UK. The school had 17 pupils of compulsory school age, six pre-school children, two teachers and one trainee teacher. Mrs Henry retired in October 1988 and Mrs Thomas led the school until Elizabeth Young was appointed to be head teacher when her own school at Blue Hill closed down in June 1990. Sandy Bay School caters for children in that distant and fairly sparsely populated area of St Helena, but nevertheless is made up of a lively, interested group of children. In the past, it was likely that many of them would not have travelled far away from their home area, but now that family transport is not uncommon, most of them are more familiar with other parts of the island.

The available *School Log Books* cover the period from 1961 to 1976. In December 1960 Edward Constantine, who had been head teacher at Sandy Bay since he was appointed to the post in 1904 at the age of 18, retired. The new head was Arnold Flagg, who was assisted by Iva Henry as the Junior Teacher and his wife, Patsy, as the Infant Teacher. Mrs Henry completed her Senior Teacher's Thesis while Mr Flagg was head of the school. At that time there were 60 children in the school. The log book tells of a number of excursions from the school to such places as Napoleon's tomb and Longwood Old House, to Jamestown to see the film *Battle of the River Plate* and to Sandy Bay beach. About the latter, Mr Flagg reported: 'Everyone seemed quite excited because about 25 of the children had never been to the beach before!' The return journey on this occasion took two hours, as the children were walking. At this time the school was an all-age one, and in 1961 two pupils took the General School Examination and seven took the Secondary Selective Examination. Later visits included going to Lot's Wife's Ponds, High Knoll (to which none of the children had been before) and Plantation House, where Jonathan, the famous giant tortoise, was a favourite. In 1962 Mr Flagg left for other service in Education on the island, and Mrs Henry became Acting Head and then, shortly afterwards, Head Teacher, a post she was to hold until her retirement in 1988. However, even in this seemingly quiet and isolated spot, school life presented challenges. One came from the resistance of parents to the transfer of their senior-age children to the Country School in 1968, when it was decided to make Sandy Bay School into a primary school; the transfer was made in January 1969. The school production of *Snow White and the Seven Dwarfs* was the highlight of 1971. Throughout its existence, the tiny school has received and welcomed many visitors, the names recorded in the *Sandy Bay Log Book* including Education Officers, Visiting Specialist Advisers and Educators – and a helicopter, in 1970.

Mrs Iva Henry had completed a lifetime of service to the teaching profession on St Helena when she retired from the headship of Sandy Bay School in October 1988. She had been a child at the school herself, from the time when St Peter's Church building had a dual role – as a school, with the backs of the pews swinging over to form the tops of desks, and as a church with the pews back as seats. She remembers her head teacher, Edward Constantine, as a strict, knowledgeable and hard-working person who caused his pupils to learn. She also recalls having weekly lessons with Canon Walcott in his Palm Villa house in Jamestown as well as his visits to schools. At the age of 13, Iva taught at Sandy Bay for two months. In August 1945 she received her first monthly pay, amounting to £3 1s 8d, and she taught for four years before her pay exceeded £4. From 1945 she attended teacher training classes run initially by Education Officer Mr Davies Watkins on Mondays, Tuesdays and Wednesdays and on Saturday mornings, these being taken over by Mr Rawlings and later Miss West. From retirement, she looks back on her long teaching career with pleasure, maintains her interest in educational developments and is keen to help preserve the educational heritage of the past.[25]

Speaking of the special nature of her new responsibilities at Sandy Bay School, the succeeding head teacher, Mrs Elizabeth Young, says that she tries to ensure that the children are given a breadth of experiences academically, socially and geographically, in order that they are ready later on to join in the wider world of St Paul's Middle

School and the Prince Andrew School and, with some confidence, to meet and work with people from other parts of the island. The children are encouraged to bring items of interest into school and to share their interests with their parents at home. Most of the children are keen to take work home and this is encouraged.[26]

9
Four Years On
1992

Part of the development is to keep the system dynamic. I am keen to foster closer educational links with the South Atlantic Islands.

Basil George, 1992[1]

1992: Consolidation and Looking to the Future

By 1992 it was clear that the three-tier system had established itself well and had proved itself during the four years of its existence. The teachers were confident in the system they had created, and the pupils were accordingly benefiting. Nevertheless, it was recognised that it was important to assess and review the system in the light of experience to that point. Accordingly, all major aspects of education received some scrutiny. The aims and objectives of the Education Department were reviewed in 1992 by the Chief Education Officer and his senior colleagues, and were re-affirmed on 31 July in *Education Circular No 23/92* to cover the provision of a system of education for children of compulsory school age, such that they developed into 'useful, healthy, moral, resourceful and law-abiding members of their society'. They also covered continued provision for nursery schooling from three and a half years, adult education, school-community links, parental participation, and the extension of 'the social, cultural, educational and sporting opportunities' to the whole community.

The importance of the training of teachers was reinforced by the appointment in May 1990 of Mrs Betty Joshua (née Dillon) as Assistant Education Officer in charge of training. She had had wide experience of the education system on St Helena, in the UK and on Ascension Island. Her own schooling on St Helena was in Longwood Infants and Junior Schools, followed by a short time at Jamestown Junior School before taking up her place at the Secondary Selective School. At the age of 14 years 9 months she took her teacher training in the Colonnade at Ladder Hill for six months with Education Officers Lamin, Billings and John, but the shortage of teachers was such that

St Helena's Senior Education Staff, 1991. Front row l. to r. Lily Crowie, Basil George, Stedson George. Second row l. to r. Valerie Yon, Maisie Thomas. Third row l. to r. Edith Timm, Patsy Flagg, Eric M. George, Joyce Harris. Fourth row l. to r. Elizabeth Young, Muriel Leo, Priscilla Thomas (deputy for Heather George). Fifth row l. to r. Muriel Williams, Joan Thomas. Back row l. to r. Pat Duncan, Betty Joshua

the remaining six months of her training had to be 'on the job' in Jamestown Junior School under the guidance of Mrs Martha George. Here she stayed as a pupil teacher for the next two and a half years. In 1966 she went to St Matthias College, Bristol, for a three-year course from which she gained the Teacher's Certificate of Education. She returned to teach at Jamestown Junior School where at the age of 21 she became Acting Head for a year, followed later by an acting headship of the Country Junior School. Soon after marriage she and her husband took up domestic service in the UK for a short time and then in 1983 went to Ascension Island where she taught for two years before returning home to her own island to serve again at Longwood and Jamestown Junior Schools. On the introduction of the three-tier system, she taught at Pilling Middle School, also holding the Post of Special Responsibility across the Middle Schools for Language. Now in 1992 one of her major aims as officer in charge of training is to try to ensure that teachers help children to take every advantage of what is in the system and that they appreciate that schooldays really can be the best days. She is saddened by the fact that many children are too eager to come out of schooling and asks herself – why is this?[2]

Perhaps some of the answers to Mrs Joshua's question came to light with the introduction on 1 October 1990 of *Education Regulations 1990*, under which the *Education Ordinance 1989* was implemented. This had confirmed the number of school days in each year to be 202 and the length of the school day for children of compulsory school age to be from 9.00 am to 3.00 pm. It also ensured provision for regular inspections and treatment of all school children by medical, dental and health officers of the Public Health Department. To implement the regulations some Attendance Officers were appointed, with the brief to receive reports and investigate failure to attend school and any cases of under-age employment, and to take appropriate action through legal proceedings if necessary. These officers were chosen from the Social Services Department, thus forging a further important link between this major department and education. Cyril Gunnell became one of these officers, responsible for the two St Paul's schools. He pays regular visits to the schools to consult with teachers and to check registers, and is confident that the system is benefiting all concerned, especially the children.

Statistics for schools for the academic year starting in September 1992 were predicted by the Chief Education Officer in an *Education Circular* in May. There were likely to be 1,002 pupils of compulsory school age, 122 of pre-school age, and 110 remaining at the Prince

Andrew School beyond the compulsory age. 105 teachers were approved on the establishment, including 10 headteachers and two PAS deputy heads, but there were currently ten vacancies – these to be filled by supply teachers and second year trainees. The 12 first year trainees were to be joined by a new intake of seven, allowing for inevitable wastage due to off-shore employment opportunities on Ascension Island and the Falkland Islands. 'It would seem that in the Education Department, because of the more attractive offshore benefits for employment, we have to build in a wastage factor in planning staffing of schools. This is however a problem generally throughout the whole of the government service.'[3]

In the circular, Basil George also reported that eight teachers were receiving overseas training during the year, and a recently agreed student scholarship scheme would enable about six students each year from the Prince Andrew School to go to the UK for tertiary education, some for three years, others for one year. Provision was made for 15 Posts of Responsibility within the department, five in PAS for PE, Business Studies, English, Maths and Agriculture; five across the Middle Schools for Language, Maths, Home Economics, Technical Crafts and Science; three across the First Schools for Language, Maths and Environmental Studies; and two in the Teacher Education Centre for Special Educational Needs and Teacher Training. In addition to the Student Scholarship Scheme, other islanders were currently studying abroad – two with Commonwealth Scholarships, one on the ODA Support Scheme, and one, Mr Dan Yon, undertaking a doctorate at Toronto under sponsorship from the Canadian Universities.

Performance criteria were established for teachers and trainees, linked to incremental credits on the salary scale, thus giving encouragement to the members of the profession to become better qualified, to achieve promotion and to strive for high standards. Regular in-service opportunities are provided for the teachers and an 'island first' was achieved during the August 1992 school holidays when a full-time three-day conference was organized for every teacher on the island. This was a Learning Support Conference held at the Prince Andrew School and organized by Dr Tony Charlton and Neil Harvey, visiting ODA Educational Advisers. For two full days immediately prior to the conference, several teachers appointed as Support Staff for Special Educational Needs in the Schools met for special pre-course planning, and then they assisted in leading the ensuing conference. Dr Charlton reported: 'The stigma attached to physical and mental handicap is thankfully passed into history and early identification of those children with special needs is a great step forward. Working closely with the Medical and Social Services, the Special Education Needs Consultative Group, set up in January 1991, now identifies the problems at an early age which will assist those children in obtaining the best use of resources and education to enable them to lead as independent and fulfilling life as possible.'[4]

In this respect a Learning Support Centre has been established adjacent to the Teacher Education Centre in Jamestown, under the direction of Mrs Valerie Yon (née Yon). Children with special educational needs, either from one of the schools or from Barn View, the residential and day centre for handicapped people, are selected to attend on a regular basis in order to receive specialist individual teaching. For the academic year 1991-92 three deaf-mute teenagers were enabled to attend the Royal School for the Deaf in Exeter, largely sponsored by the St Helena Association in the UK.

Discipline procedures across the system were standardized following discussion among head teachers and teachers, and these included procedures for identifying and dealing with possible cases of student abuse.

The Community Education Programme brochure for 1992 looked back over the previous four years, encouraged by the extent of the involvement of large numbers of the islanders, both in academic and skills-based courses and in leisure and sporting activities. Co-ordinated by Assistant Education Officer Eric George, the 1992 programme included a wide range of classes in various branches of Art, Home Economics, Health and Sport, Music and Technical Crafts.

Liaison between other island departments and groups is also being fostered, for instance with the Police Department. Inspector John Clifford, the Police Training Officer, regularly goes into schools, particularly at the first and middle school level, and he sees as his prime concern the establishment of good relationships between the children and the police force. 'Early sessions are devoted to becoming friends. We believe in trying to foster the interest of the kids in the Department – if they are friends with us, we will achieve far more with them.' At the present time he is concentrating on road safety, this being the major concern in view of the increase in traffic, including bicycles. Competitions are arranged, for instance, in the creation of suitable posters for road safety with prizes awarded by the police.[5]

Others interested in the achievements of the island children have instituted competitions, such as the Trust established in the memory of Jean Beadon, which presents an annual prize to the most promising painter between the ages of eight and 18 years. Mrs Beadon was particularly interested in young people, and the Trust, established in her memory, continues to encourage the development of art skills. Similarly, the RMS *St Helena*, under the auspices of the Curnow Shipping Company, staged an art competition, many of the young artists being rewarded by having their paintings hung in the ship itself.

By August 1992 the three-tier system had been in operation for four years – that is, the first students taken into each of the sectors had completed their education there and prepared to move into the next stage. Arrangements for the transition of children from one sector to another were well-established, these including the appropriate transfer of records, preliminary visits to the children's new schools, and bridging meetings to enable teachers of contributory schools to meet with the teachers at the next school, to make a smoother transition for individual children. At these meetings several aspects are considered, such as school achievement, previous school attended, physical or medical circumstances, behaviour and parental wishes, and care is taken to place the child wisely in the new school. For each child a 'Pupil Profile: Record and Assessment' is completed in each school year, recording the child's progress and achievement in a full range of subject areas, including Language Development, General Language, Mathematical Development, Social Studies, Physical Education, Expressive Arts, Science/Health, Intellectual Development, and Social Development. The profile made in the First School follows the child to his or her Middle School, and the final year's profile in the Middle School informs the Prince Andrew School about its new pupil.

The three-tier system stood up well to the initial scrutiny of all aspects of the scheme, and this augurs well for the official evaluation set in motion in 1992 by the Chief Education Officer. This aims to cover the progress of pupils, governors, parents and the community, staff, curriculum, departmental and faculty self-assessment, decision-making and communications; staff development, general environment, resources and statistics.

Regarding the subject of the general environment, Dr Neil McCulloch produced a report in 1992 entitled *The Status and Ecology of the St Helena Wirebird*, in which he stressed the importance of education taking a leading role in promoting knowledge of and interest in local natural history in order to make the local population more aware of their natural heritage and of wider environmental issues. Reports such as this one are taken into account by those who are responsible for the general evaluation of the work of the schools.

The Youth Advisory Committee has been established under the chairmanship of Eric Benjamin MLC and former Chairman of the Education Committee. The terms of reference of the Committee include responsibility to oversee the implementation of the Youth Employment Scheme. At a meeting of the Committee on 26 October 1992 it was reported that under the scheme 183 youths were currently being paid, as follows: 100 in Education (including 94 remaining at school beyond GCSE level, four hearing-impaired boys on apprenticeship with the PWSD, and two technicians at the Prince Andrew School); eight Nursing Cadets; nine on the Agriculture and Forestry apprenticeship scheme; one with Fisheries; seven in Small Industries; 51 with the PWSD apprenticeship scheme; five with Social Services, and two at the Radio Station.

These numbers meant that in total there were 302 young people in the scheme over the three year period to date. The chairman reported that 10 youths were still unemployed and these were directed to the Social Services' Work Experience Scheme, subject to receiving a structured training programme.

There are many occasions within the community life of St Helena in which long-established youth organizations and other associations to take part. These demonstrate the continuing attraction of such organizations among young people, in spite of the increasing world-wide competition from alternative pursuits. There are strong contingents of Scouts and Cub Scouts, Rangers, Guides, Brownies and Rainbows, who meet regularly with volunteer leaders. The history of Scouting and Guiding on the island goes back to early in the twentieth century when Canon Walcott and his wife established the first companies which ever since have played an important role in the educational and ceremonial life of the colony. The Scouting Movement has benefited from the dedication of long-serving leaders: Canon Walcott held the leadership until 1952, then Harry Richards served until his death in 1971, followed by his brother Herbert until 1982. Eric W. George, successor as Group Leader and Commissioner to Mr Richards, had been in the Movement since he joined the Cub Scouts as a child and therefore had personal knowledge of the value of Scouting for young people. Talking about his life as a Scout, Mr George says: 'My aim is to follow Baden-Powell to make this a better world in which to live. Without this help, the youngsters will be deprived. It's a wonderful Movement.'[6]

In 1992 the island celebrated the 75th anniversary of the official recognition of Scouting there, a warrant being signed to mark the occasion. In February 1917, Canon Walcott had reported:

We have made a start with Boy Scouts and Girl Guides in the parish. A great number have joined, and there is much enthusiasm and desire to learn. HE the Governor is our Chief Scout and Commissioner for the island and Mrs Peel has kindly consented to act as Commissioner for the Girl Guides. The Vicar of Jamestown (Mr Walcott), as Scout Master of some years standing will himself act as Scoutmaster of the Jamestown Troop and secretary of the local association; and Mrs Walcott, who has experience of Girl Guiding will act as Captain of the Jamestown Company of Girl Guides.[7]

Speaking at the 1992 celebrations, Scout Master Eric George was proud to report that Scouting over the years had flourished with numbers varying between 40 and 90. At key times, such as during the Second World War, the 'bigger chaps' from the scouts had proved their worth in the service of their country. In the St Helena Rifles, 12 of the first 16 recruits had been Jamestown Boy Scouts and they were praised by their Commanding Officer as being among the smartest recruits. The Scouts had been represented at El Alamein, Italy and Normandy, one being wounded on D-Day, while another went down with his Destroyer in the Mediterranean. During recent years the Scouts had given community service to their island, undertaking such tasks as the redecoration of St James' Church, restoring Canon Walcott's grave and conducting island-wide litter collections. Throughout the whole time, the Jamestown Troop had been the centre of scouting on the island. One of the most popular events was the annual camp, for which Canon Walcott composed a special song entitled 'Scouts' Camp', which began:

When night had fled before the day,
In the new fledged morn we got away;
But first to pile the wagon's load
And then to quickly take the road –
The road to Thompson's Wood.[8]

The Guide movement on St Helena had also flourished over the years and, in fact, there was a demand in 1992 for a further Company to be formed to meet at Half Tree Hollow under the leadership of Mrs Muriel Leo. This increased the numbers of Companies to five, the other four being in Jamestown, St Paul's, Longwood and Sandy Bay. The Jamestown Company had been started in 1921 by Mrs Walcott; Mrs Mabel Peel (née Thorpe), the wife of the Governor Robert Peel, started 'The Lone Patrol' of seven girls in the St Paul's area in the early 1920s; the Longwood Guide Company came into existence in the late 1920s with the support of Jessie Deason and Major Jackson; and the Sandy Bay group followed later in the 1950s. The first Brownie Pack was formed in 1931/32 in Jamestown, and the Rainbows appeared in 1988 under the leadership of Mrs Betty Joshua. Mrs Daphne Francis is the Commissioner and is justifiably proud of the history of Guiding on the island.[9]

Another long-standing youth organization which has played an important educational role is the Church Lads' Brigade. Started in 1895 by Canon Ellis, the first Commanding Officer, it enrolled 96 members but did not last long. However in 1900 the Bishop of St Helena was able to report to the SPG in Cape Town that Canon Porter had restarted the Brigade and already enrolled 130 recruits. Nine years later it was still flourishing under Canon Porter's leadership and described by the Bishop as 'a most valuable organization for our boys'. One hundred boys from Jamestown and St Paul's had just spent three days in training in camp – 'much to their amusement and advantage'.[10]

In February 1913, the *St Helena Diocesan Magazine* described a similar five-day camp at Bamboo Hedge, Sandy Bay, still led by Canon Porter, with the support of fellow Captain C.J.Smith, schoolteacher Edward Constantine and Chaplain Walcott. Numbers fluctuated over the years. By 1928 the Governor's Report on youth organizations indicated an enrolment of 54 all ranks, with 26 in the training corps. James Sim, head teacher of Half Tree Hollow School, was an active member for many years. Numbers appear to have dwindled in the 1950s, and in 1961 Bishop Beardmore started preliminary work to re-form the group in St Paul's Parish. Since then, the Brigade has continued to attract people of all ages and is currently 40-strong and led by Mervyn Yon.

A beneficial scheme which was launched by the Education Department was the establishment of a Book Fund, managed by the Chief Education Officer, which provides sponsorship for those publications which are being produced in the interests of education on the island. Support for this fund has been given by Governor Baker, Governor Stimson and Governor Hoole.

In 1957 author Oswell Blakestone published the St Helena Schools' Song in his book entitled *Isle of St Helena*. This had been given to him by Edward Constantine, 'the schoolmaster from Sandy Bay'. The composer of the song (indicated as JDW by Blakestone) is thought to be George Davies Watkins, the Education Officer at the time of the major reorganization of schools in 1941. The words capture the spirit of education on the island today:

Far out in the midst of the Atlantic swell,
There stands St Helena's Isle
Its schools have a story they are proud to tell
Of a work that is always worthwhile.

Chorus:
So let us sing our own school song,
Sing it in joyful style,
For learning is a pleasant task the whole day long
Here in Helena's isle.

From the time when parents in 1678 were exhorted to be 'friends to their children' by sending them to school, to the present day when the young people of St Helena declare for themselves that 'we are the future of our island', an important story of schooling on the island has developed. This story shows for all time that 'its schools have a story they are proud to tell of a work that is always worthwhile'.

Part II

Ascension Island

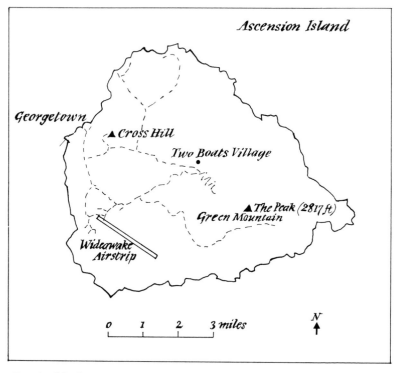

Ascension Island

10
The Working Island:
Schooling with a Moving Population
1815-1992

The Commanding Officer trusts there will be no occasion to call the attention of parents to this essential part of their duty towards their children.
Captain Bate, 1830[1]

For an island like Ascension the school is virtually a palace.
Geoffrey Simpson, 1967[2]

1815-1920: Spasmodic Schooling for Children of the Marines

Ascension Island had been discovered by the Portuguese Admiral José da Nova Gallego on Ascension Day 1501 but it was not occupied until 1815 when it was claimed for the British Empire and a garrison of Marines was established, administered by the Admiralty in London. This occupation was initially directly related to the fact that Napoleon Bonaparte was being held on St Helena. Disaster struck almost immediately when 50 members of the garrison died from a plague caught from a calling ship. The garrison remained on Ascension Island until 1922 although, after Napoleon's death in 1821, farming became more important than the Navy. Georgetown was built in 1820, the Kroomen from the Gold Coast and liberated slaves from other areas supplying the labour force. It is said that some of the Kroomen brought their wives and children and that a school was held for them, but this cannot at present be corroborated. At the time Lieut Col Commandant Edward Nicholls was in command of the garrison, but it was not until his successor, Captain William Bate, took over command of the Marines that records confirm the establishment of a school on Ascension Island. Duff Hart-Davis, in *Ascension: The Story of a South Atlantic Island*, calls Captain Bate 'one of the great figures of Ascension's modest history'. Bate was on Ascension from 1828 until 1835 and was officially in charge of the moral and spiritual welfare of its 200 inhabitants for whom he was 'legally empowered to hold divine service, to conduct marriages and christenings and to bury the dead'.[3]

The history of schools on Ascension Island is undoubtedly one of beginnings and endings. From the 1830s there are some records of schools being established from time to time for a particular group of people, but there have also been periods when the presence of children, particularly those of school age, has been restricted, and the need for organised schooling has not been seen. Clearly a major reason is that this strategically placed island has no indigenous population; over the years its people have been members of changing groups of workers connected with the major 'users' – naval contingents, marines, defence forces, a detachment of the Royal Artillery, a USA taskforce, the Eastern Telegraph Company, the Cable and Wireless Company, the British Broadcasting Corporation, the Royal Air Force, and the United States National Aeronautics and Space Administration. Originally, many Kroomen were employed to serve the people stationed on the island, but since 1921 it has been St Helenians who have helped to look after the welfare of the visiting groups. It is only since the 1920s, when families from St Helena came to Ascension Island, that organized schooling became essential.

Nevertheless, early records do refer to the establishment of a school in 1830 under the superintendence of Lance Corporal Barber and his wife, to be conducted according to Bell's monitorial system as laid down for regimental schools (see page 35). A notice was issued to the effect that 'The Commanding Officer trusts that there will be no occasion to call the attention of parents to this essential part of their duty towards their children'.[4] The fees were to be threepence per week for each child aged three years and over, and twopence for those aged two years or less. At this time the 300 people on the island included 46 African men, 14 boys (junior naval men), 12 women and 14 children. Any newborn children were officially considered to have been 'born at sea' and their birth was registered as at Wapping in England. The presence of children during this period can be further verified by the fact that the dates on children's graves go back to 1830.

It appears that the school did not last long. In 1840 there was 'a testy (sic) order' which laid down that a new school should be opened immediately – 'The Commandant forbids the children being allowed any longer to run riot in the Garrison, and expects that they will be made to attend school. As superior instruction is to be given, a charge of sixpence a week is to be made'.[5] The instruction was to be given by a sergeant. In 1844 there was a new system of command. The HMS *Tortoise*, a store ship, was commissioned to be anchored in the bay. The Captain became the Commander of the Garrison, the command passed

Schoolchildren in the early 1900s, including Janet Jewell (second from left, back row), daughter of Chief Petty Officer William Henry Jewell, on Ascension 1898 to 1903 (Photograph used by kind permission from the archives on the island)

from the Marines to the Navy and the island itself became the 'tender of the guardship'.[6] Statistics of 1844 show that the garrison was 330-strong, including 43 European women and 49 children.

In 1858 William Burnett, the Captain of HMS *Tortoise*, took over charge of the Garrison, and in a letter home to his mother he wrote: 'We have two schools, one in the Tortoise, and one on shore, with not less than fifty old and young attending them and a schoolmistress for the girls.'[7] No records are available to indicate where the on-shore school was held, but it would certainly have been in the vicinity of the naval buildings in Georgetown.

However, the very need for the existence of a population on Ascension Island was called into question at this time. In a chapter entitled *White Elephant?*, Duff Hart-Davis states: 'By the 1860s, however, with Napoleon long dead, the slave trade dwindling and steam rapidly taking over from sail, the full-scale occupation of Ascension became harder and harder to justify.' The records show severe attempts at reductions and economies and these measures queried the presence of women and children. A contemporary wrote: 'All wives and children should be got rid of, or if they are allowed to stay they should be made to pay for the privilege. Such people are useless and frequently mischievous as they foment the slightest rub upon duty between husbands, as would be obliterated at the first mess meal, into a bitter family quarrel, greatly to the obstruction of duty.'[8]

For the next 60 years the major *raison d'être* for any occupation of Ascension Island was as a communications centre for the Admiralty. It is therefore understandable that records concerning education and schools are extremely sparse; few have come to light about the period from 1858 until 1922, when the Admiralty pulled out of Ascension. From ongoing correspondence during 1867-70 between Commodore W.M.Dowell of HMS *Flora* at the island and the Secretary of the Admiralty, it is clear that the envisaged severe reduction of the numbers on Ascension was being effected. In May 1867 Mr Dowell reported that the 112 Africans had been replaced by only 50 Kroomen, and that the number of women and children had been reduced from 111 to 95, 41 women and 54 children. He suggested that the complement of the *Flora* itself could be reduced by getting rid of the Naval Schoolmaster and four boys, the latter being young naval cadets. Among the 203 permanent supernumeraries on the island there were 17 civilian employees, including one schoolmistress. A year later Commodore Dowell received a firm statement from the Admiralty that the reduction plans were to be strictly adhered to. The schoolmistress was still included however, and her salary was to be £16 a year. The school room used was almost certainly in the building adjacent to the St George's Tank. But the need to reduce expenditure persisted, and in August 1868 Mr Dowell recommended that only one married person to 10 single officers and men should be sent to Ascension, as it was too expensive to have families. This policy must have had effect, because by the following August Commodore Dowell's letter to the Secretary of the Admiralty reported: 'There being no duty for the island School-master or Schoolmistress viz Sergeant Jowett and his wife to perform, under the reductions that have lately occurred, I have the honour to inform you that I have permitted an exchange to take place between Sergeant Field and Sergeant Jowett,' the former going away on leave and the latter taking general duties. However, the letter then pleaded that some married men, wives and children should be allowed to come, purchasing their own goods, because they had 'A beneficial effect in keeping the men steady'! Nevertheless, by December 1870 Dowell reaffirmed that there was no need for the schoolmistress to be retained 'the number of children on the island being now very small'.[9]

An interesting pen-picture of the island is captured in *Six Months in Ascension Island*, a diary written in 1877 by Mrs David Gill. Her husband, Professor Gill (later to become Sir David Gill, Astronomer Royale at Cape Town), was conducting research into how far the sun is from the earth. Ascension Island was at that time an ideal place to undertake this research in view of the juxtaposition of the sun, the earth and the planet Mars. However, even in this detailed diary there are no references to the younger generation. After commenting that she was the sixth lady 'on board', she continued that 'a few of the men are allowed to have their wives with them, on condition that the latter make themselves helpful to the community in some way. The male population is under 200 and consists of a company of marines, a few blue-jackets, several St Helena boys who act as servants to the officers, and 70 to 80 Kroomen, a fine race of negroes from the West Coast of Africa.'

By 1880 a plan of the Garrison showed the school room next to the Tank, but indicated that it was vacant, and was to be used for other purposes.

As will be seen, the nature of schooling on Ascension Island through to the end of the century is open to question, but there are indications that it did exist. Certainly a plan of St Mary's Church of 1892 reserved a pew for the schoolmaster. By 1899 there were marine families on the island, which was still run as a ship, but the Eastern Telegraph Company built a cable relay station and brought more St Helenians to the island. The *St Helena Diocesan Magazine* of April 1900 reported that 'We [Ascension Island] have lately, like your island, been provided with the blessings of a Cable communication with the outside world'.

From an article entitled 'Fifty Years Ago' in the *St Helena Magazine* of April 1950 we are able to confirm the existence of a school on Ascension in 1900. 'We have a School presided over by a Sergeant School Master and his wife, and all the children of the island attend, including the Officers' children so they make altogether a nice little party.' Apparently this was a naval school and it was held in the Sergeants' Mess. By 1905 the Admiralty had decided that the command of the island should once more be taken over by a Major of the Marines although, in the event, a Captain Morgan was appointed, later to be called General Morgan. There still did not appear to be provision for civilians, no civil law was in force, only naval disciplinary proceedings.

A map of Georgetown in 1910 clearly marks the position of a school on the site of the present Windmill Cottage, on the far side of the St George's Tank from the flagstaff. No records can be found of this school, but photographs of the time show a one-storey building.

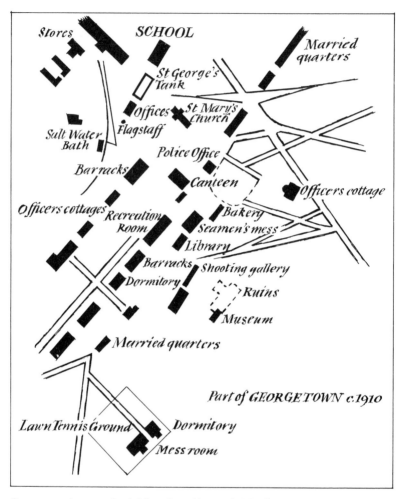

Georgetown, circa 1910 (copied from the archives on the island)

1921-56: A School at Flagstaff for Children on Ascension

From 1921 St Helenians were employed on Ascension Island in preference to the Kroomen, who were giving trouble and becoming violent, and were consequently repatriated to West Africa. The following year, in 1922, the navy departed. Ascension Island then ceased to be a 'ship' and became a dependency of St Helena coming under the control of the Secretary of State for the Colonies. The Eastern

Telegraph Company was the only major concern left and, in practical terms, ran the island, which was becoming increasingly important as a cable station. Duff Hart-Davis describes how 'The Company's Manager became the resident magistrate, the harbourmaster and the lay preacher rolled into one. The Company took over Green Mountain Farm and the garrison hospital and organised their own school.'[10] In December 1923 a special issue of the *Zodiac*, the Cable and Wireless journal, gave advice to prospective employees for Ascension about what they would need there and were warned that 'Living is expensive. For a family of five, 45 pounds a month is a moderate estimate', and that 'There is no school'. This was soon remedied, however, and the Company set about organizing its own school.

A census of 1931 gave the population to be 188, including 126 St Helenians, of whom seven only were children. In addition there were 14 children among the Eastern Telegraph Company families. Any schooling organized was the responsibility of the Company. The official *Blue Books* containing reports from Ascension to the Secretary of State for the Colonies do not include mention of a teacher on the Civil Establishment for several years in the 1930s. By 1935 the population comprised 60 British and 120 St Helenian people, solely the staff and servants of Cable and Wireless, the successors to the Eastern Telegraph Company. Only children of pre-school age were kept on the island, St Helenian children of school age being required to return home to attend school – a situation which pertained for several years. In *Bartlett's Book: A Portrait of Ascension, 1934-1936*, Mr Bartlett, the Manager of Cable and Wireless, wrote that 'Life flows along easily, notwithstanding a certain amount of monotony and constriction. Everyone is ready to make the best of everything and there is little discontent. It is not unlike being in a large ship, for the roll of the sea is never far distant, and the same individuals meet every day.' In 1936 the children were described by Bartlett as 'running foot-loose, bursting with health and full of quaint sayings'. They also wandered about in the hottest sun in this 'veritable paradise'.[11] However, during the Second World War, the voyage to St Helena was considered to be dangerous and some children were allowed to stay. A St Helenian child of the time, now Mrs Pam Hart, recalls being taught by her own mother and by an American on Ascension who was also teaching his own child.[12]

Due to the island's strategic position, Ascension Island's population increased and became more diverse during the war years. The island Defence Force was established in April 1940 and a detachment of the

Royal Artillery was stationed on Ascension in March 1941. By 1942 the United States Government had established an air base on the island. But, apart from families already on Ascension, the civilian population was not increased as the military personnel did not have their families with them. With the exception of the Commanding Officer, this also applied to the Americans at the USA air base.

The Americans withdrew at the end of the war and according to the population census at that time 228 of the population of 292 were St Helenians employed to service Cable and Wireless. By 1948 the total was reduced to 191 including 135 St Helenians, and there were fewer still in 1949, the total being 159 with 113 St Helenians. These fluctuating numbers, particularly within the St Helenian population, meant that any stability in the schooling system was virtually impossible and education could only be directed consistently to the very young children, with the older children staying in St Helena for their schooling.

During the early 1950s this situation still pertained. However, in 1954 the USA established a Space Station on Ascension. This improved the employment prospects for more St Helenian families and, accordingly, increased the size of the child population. From this time schooling was made available on Ascension Island, at least for the younger children. In the St Helena newspaper *The Wirebird* of July 1956 it was reported: 'There is now a small school on Ascension for the younger children, and they are very happy under the care of Mrs Lilian Greentree. This enables parents to keep their children with them longer than previously, until they are ready for their bigger school, for which they must return home.' Mrs Greentree was a St Helenian teacher resident on Ascension at the time. This school became known as the Flagstaff School as it was held in a two-storey building lying between the Flagstaff and the St George's Tank. Being totally dependent upon Mrs Greentree, the school had to close temporarily later in 1956 due to her absence through illness. Larry Henry recalls attending the Flagstaff School on the harbour side of St George's Tank, with Mrs Greentree as his teacher. The school occupied the ground floor and there were offices on the upper floor.

For the next few years children on Ascension were taught by the willing Mrs Greentree, but the conditions under which she was working were far from ideal and there was no structured provision for the older children. The building soon proved to be in an unfit condition and plans were being made to demolish it, so the struggling little school community had to look for other premises. These were found at Clinker Hall on the far side of Georgetown.

Georgetown, 1963 (Photograph supplied by Dr Kenneth Simmons (Head Teacher, 1962-64), and used with his permission)

1960-66: School in Clinker Hall

It was not until 1960 that, under the auspices of Cable and Wireless, an official school was established and a schoolmaster appointed under contract. This was Cyril Eyles, who arrived on the island early in February 1960 for an agreed two-year period. Clinker Hall was being prepared for the use of the school, so temporary accommodation was required as the Flagstaff building had finally been condemned. Accordingly, the May 1960 edition of the Cable and Wireless Journal *Zodiac* describes how, for his first four weeks on the island, Mr Eyles taught his classes in the Bowling Alley. This inauspicious start did not appear to deter the new schoolmaster.

Clinker Hall had been naval quarters. This building has since been demolished but the foundations on which it stood in 1960 still exist near the present visitors' hostel (Clarence House) and tennis courts. The school was officially opened on 29 February 1960. Mrs Greentree was appointed to assist Mr Eyles in the mornings. The juniors, aged seven to 12, attended from 9.00 am until 4.30 pm, while the infants, aged five to seven, attended from 9.00 am to 12.30 pm. Mr Eyles quickly gained popularity with the children, becoming known as 'Mr Chips', 'Schooly' or 'Awkeye', and he reported in the *Zodiac*: 'Never have I met a more delightful group of children, and nowhere are they better behaved or more polite.'

Clinker Hall School, Georgetown (Photograph supplied by Dr Kenneth Simmons, and used with his permission)

Larry Henry was one of the children in the school at the time of its transfer from the building near Flagstaff to Clinker Hall. He recalls that there were two teachers and two classes in the school for the first time. He had mathematics, English and history lessons with Mr Eyles, but there were no facilities to do subjects like woodwork. They did have athletics and sports, however, including the Slippery Pole and relay races. Larry was there for only a short while because when he was ten years old he returned to St Helena with his parents and attended Levelwood School.[13]

For the first time it now became possible for children up to the age of 15 to receive their schooling on the island in a system based largely on British lines. The schoolteachers had to cater for the needs of both the St Helenian children and also the UK children whose parents would be returning to Britain after their tour of duty on Ascension. Inevitably the school population was a moving one since many of the people were only there for a period of time. This fact has been a feature of education on the island over the years, and it continues to provide a challenge to all the teachers trying to ensure that the children are equipped to return into their own educational systems or employment 'at home' when necessary to do so.

The Managing Directors of Cable and Wireless Ltd at Mercury House, London, were responsible not only for employing the teaching staff but also for providing the materials and equipment for the school. Regular reports and resource requests from the schoolmaster were sent via the local Manager, who held the highest civil administrative office on Ascension, the equivalent of the present Administrator. This necessarily meant that they were influenced by his priorities and interpretation of the needs.

John Joshua, now Employment Officer on St Helena, is another St Helenian who has clear memories of his schooldays at Clinker Hall. His parents were working for Cable and Wireless, and he was one of the 21 children at the school in 1961, 13 from St Helena and 8 from the UK. He recalls how, as one of the four children over the age of 11, he was set work in the mornings while Mr Eyles and Mrs Greentree were teaching the younger ones, and then the group of four was taught by Mr Eyles from 3.30 pm to 4.30 pm. All activities in the school were taken by boys and girls together, including football, cricket and tennis. The supply of resources at the school was good, including books and sports equipment. The pupils were required to do homework and examinations and were given formal school reports in the form of a letter, headed 'Cable and Wireless Ltd, Ascension Branch', and signed by C.C.N. Eyles, Schoolmaster.[14]

Mrs Enid Stevens (née Ellick) thoroughly enjoyed her school experiences at Clinker Hall. She went to Ascension at the age of 11 and appreciated the fact that Mr Eyles had a lot of time for senior children. Punishments were not needed at the school because all the children behaved so well. When she was 15 she returned to St Helena where she went to the Secondary Selective School for one year on the strength of a good report about her progress at Clinker Hall.[15]

By the time of Mr Eyles' second *Education Report*, which was submitted in October 1961 to his employers, he was able to record considerable progress made by most of the children, the majority of whom were up to the recognized standard for their ages. With the agreement of the managing body and the parents, he was about to restructure the school into seven groups, two for Seniors (up to the age of 15), three for Intermediates (seven- to nine-year-olds) and two for infants. Mrs Greentree and he were teaching all of these classes between them. Mr Eyles reported that the school was well-stocked with books, and the children were learning how to use them and to discover things for themselves. 'The importance of keeping the children interested and constantly active is the keynote of the school,' said Mr

Eyles. He also undertook some private coaching. The length of the school terms was determined locally according to the circumstances on the island. In fact, Mr Eyles once remarked to his successor that he and the children would work until they could go on no longer without a break, and then request a holiday from the Manager.

Mr Eyles completed his two year contract and, in February 1962, K.E.L. Simmons was appointed to the position of schoolmaster for a period of two years. The outgoing and incoming schoolmasters had a useful overlapping period of fifteen days working together, during which time it was possible for them both to discuss the children's work and progress and to consider carefully the future organization of the school. At the time there were some 24 English families, plus 120 St Helenians working in Georgetown and Green Mountain, and roughly 320 Americans serviced by 100 St Helenian men at the American base. While he found the school itself in good order as he took over from Mr Eyles, Kenneth Simmons was concerned at the condition of the building and furnishings. In later correspondence Mr Simmons (now Dr Simmons) gave a clear description of his school building, Clinker Hall. It was 'an old Victorian naval building of corrugated iron construction with verandahs on most sides and a huge roof space (of the colonial type one sees, for example, in Australian films); there was a central corridor with two rooms and a hall on one side, four smaller rooms on the other (one of which was a store) and another corridor at the far end, making a T-junction with the larger corridor. It was the last of a series of such buildings, most of which had been refurbished as houses for St Helenian workers and their families. A small courtyard holding the water-tank led to a separate toilet block.'

These unusual conditions clearly concerned the new schoolmaster and in June 1962 he prepared for his employers a document entitled *Ascension School: some comments on school facilities and suggestions for their improvement*, in which he sought to address the matters which were in serious need of improvement, stating strongly that 'A school where young people spend a large part of their impressionable young lives, should be attractive and spotlessly clean'. The matters requiring attention ranged from inadequate space and poor facilities for the children and teachers, to the need for an overall redecoration and refurbishment of the entire building.

In his *Schoolmaster's Report* covering his initial period at Clinker Hall from February to August 1962, Mr Simmons described the changes he had made, after obtaining the approval of the Manager and Head

Office, in tightening up the daily schedule in order to reduce the span of the school day with virtually no loss of teaching time. Previously the schedule had included a lengthy dinner break and this, together with working in a tropical climate, caused the children to experience an overlong and exhausting day. He also standardized the school holidays in advance and published the relevant dates for the ensuing year. The school would be in session for 46 weeks, the three terms being divided into six sessions of seven to eight weeks each. Continuing his report, Mr Simmons expressed his gratitude for the goodwill of those concerned who had taken action on the state of the school facilities and effected considerable improvement already, although there were still many things needing attention. He was pleased also to be able to report valuable additions to the school's collection of textbooks, but urged for more still: 'A school, even a small one, cannot have too many library and general reading books.' Mrs Greentree, who had been teaching on Ascension for many years, retired in August 1962 and returned to St Helena. Mr Simmons paid tribute to her as a loyal and co-operative colleague; her work with the two senior pupils had been particularly appreciated. Mrs Simmons had been appointed to be an Assistant Teacher at the school.

Kenneth Simmons and his wife, Marion, both experienced and qualified primary school teachers, had anticipated teaching the primary age range, but they found that increasingly the St Helenian children were remaining at the Ascension Island school until they were 16. Nevertheless Mr Simmons reported that while his wife took the younger children and the less-able older children (under 12), he took the older children and the more able younger children.

In his second *Schoolmaster's Report* covering the period from August 1962 to August 1963, Mr Simmons was able to describe a year of consolidation both in the progress of the children, for whom there were now two qualified staff, and in the improvement of facilities. The number of children in the school had risen to 28, compared with 19 in August 1962, of whom 70% were St Helenian. He was pleased that, for the first time on Ascension Island, he had been able to encourage a St Helenian school-leaver to become a trainee teacher. This was 15-year-old Brenda Crowie who, as well as continuing with her own further education under the supervision of Mr Simmons, was also observing and assisting each morning in the Infants class with Mrs Simmons and in the Junior and Senior classes with Mr Simmons. He was also pleased to report a further improvement in the supply of books in the school and thanked the Company for their generosity. Finally he highlighted the visit in February 1963 of the Governor of St Helena and his wife, Sir John and Lady Field, accompanied by the Manager.

Throughout his two years Mr Simmons concentrated on improving both the conditions in the school and the children's standard of work. As a keen ornithologist, he was pleased when the opportunity arose for him to make a study of the island's seabirds in his spare time. He has revisited the island a number of times in pursuit of this interest and has now been invited to write a book on the birds of Ascension. Reflecting several years later on his experiences as schoolmaster, Dr Simmons comments in correspondence: 'My two years as Schoolmaster on Ascension Island were certainly eventful and interesting but also very demanding and difficult; we enjoyed our time there. I shall never regret spending those two years on Ascension where, for most of the time, we led a contented and constructive life. I am proud of our work at the School and what we achieved there in improving standards.'[16]

Cyril Eyles returned to Ascension in February 1964, having been reappointed to be schoolmaster for a further two years. On his return, he praised the meticulous care with which his predecessor had maintained the records of children's progress, abilities and aptitudes, and the school stock books. The matter of what criteria to use to classify the children into teaching groups was somewhat problematic. Tests showed that in general the children from the UK were mentally superior to those from St Helena, and in addition the motivation among the UK children was higher. If promotion were to be based on age, the less able children tended to keep back the brighter ones. On the other hand if promotion were to be by attainment, some of the less able children, particularly among the St Helenian population, would not be able to progress out of the lower classes. Mr Eyles sought an additional qualified teacher from the UK to help teach the wide range of abilities now in the school. Alan Johns, the Education Officer from St Helena, supported him in this request. In his *Education Report* covering the period from February 1964 to February 1965, Mr Eyles paid tribute to the UK-qualified teacher who had been appointed. This was Mrs G. Ward, the wife of the Assistant Manager on the island, and she had 'literally inspired them and instilled in them such a desire for work that their progress has been quite amazing'.

The British Broadcasting Corporation planned to establish a major relay station on Ascension and building to accommodate the employees at English Bay and at Two Boats began in 1964. By 1966 this brought more families to the island. In addition NASA had established a station on Ascension. The population now rose to 1,400 and, with the increase of major organizations on the island, the Colonial Office in London appointed a full-time Administrator with responsibility to co-ordinate all the separate interests.

Throughout Mr Eyles' second period of office, school for the children on Ascension continued to be at Clinker Hall. But almost from his first arrival on the island in 1960, when he moved his teaching from the Bowling Alley into Clinker Hall, the school had outgrown the little building. Over the years a site for a new school was sought but now, with the influx of children from the BBC families, the overcrowding was even more serious and the identification of a new site more urgent. Two Boats Village, the home area of several of the BBC families, was identified as a suitable place for the school and plans were set in motion for its construction.

1966-73: A New School at Two Boats Village

In his handing-over report to his successor, Mr Geoffrey Simpson, Mr Eyles emphasized again the need for more qualified teaching staff in view of the additional numbers of senior-age children at the school. 'Clearly, the need for a Secondary School is becoming more pressing.' The number of pupils in the school fluctuated due to the transient nature of families' residence on the island. Statistics giving the Ascension Island school population published in successive *St Helena Annual Reports* showed that for the next few years the numbers increased considerably – from 78 in 1966, to 101 in 1967, 125 in 1968, 137 in 1969, 135 in 1970, 131 in 1972, 143 in 1972, and 164 in 1973.

Geoffrey Simpson arrived in February 1966, beginning a valuable period of seven years during which he held the headship. He was able to benefit from a good handing-over period, with Mr Eyles continuing in the capacity of assistant teacher before departing in April. Mrs Simpson, a qualified teacher, was also appointed to teach at the school.

To Mr Simpson came the responsibility for leading his school into its new purpose-built quarters at Two Boats Village in August 1967. At the same time, he was given the title of Head Teacher. The buildings, resources and staff were all funded by Cable and Wireless Ltd. In a graphic article entitled 'Ascension: Opening of New School', published in the *Zodiac* in October 1967, Mr Simpson helped readers world-wide to be able to visualize the setting of the school and to share his excitement:

The School at Two Boats (Photograph supplied by Margot Hutchinson)

The school is pleasantly situated overlooking the new development of Two Boats on Ascension Island. A beautiful view of Green Mountain makes an inspiring break in the monotony of the predominantly red, black and grey landscape. Owing to its height, this area is cooler than Georgetown and rain often sweeps down from Green Mountain in clouds of mist, freshening the air and laying the dust.

From a spacious, trapezium-shaped hall lead off four airy, well-lit classrooms complete with fitted cupboards and blackboards. After walking up the steps of the wide stage, and going through a small entrance, you find yourself in a small quadrangle. Here is the senior classroom/domestic science room, the art and craft room fitted for pottery, painting, woodwork and book crafts, and the science/practical maths room. The children's cloakrooms are fitted with communal wash basins with constant warm water and flush toilets – a far cry from the 'froo' buckets of Georgetown.

After detailing the wide curriculum opportunities afforded the pupils, Mr Simpson concluded:

For an island like Ascension the school is virtually a palace. It is equal in its design and equipment to many of the better junior and infant schools in England. ... Plans for the future are many and we look forward to the school taking its part in the community life of the island.

The pupils of the time also recall helping with the removal and settling in, and their feelings of pleasure and excitement as they experienced all the new facilities. Eddie Fowler, for example, had started at Clinker Hall at the age of 10 and, for two years, had experienced being 'in the tin building with a wooden frame, where the seniors were taught in a wooden hut outside' – but where he had enjoyed the lessons and the sports – and the swimming in the Turtle Pond! As a senior pupil he helped in the removal to the new building, and now he found himself in a brand new purpose-built school, with facilities for such activities as carpentry and gymnastics and Christmas plays.[17] Similarly, Patrick Robinson recalls the move from Clinker Hall, where ceiling fans were tried to relieve the extreme heat within the metal building, to the comparative comfort and luxury of the new airy building at Two Boats. Modern desks replaced the old open-topped ones, and the children were able to enjoy indoor sports in the gymnasium and take part in inter-team competitions. They were taken on walks up Green Mountain – and they were still able to go swimming in the Turtle Pond 'among the turtles and fish'.[18]

The systems, methods and curriculum used in the school were as close as possible to those of the UK to enable the expatriate children to fit easily into their schools at home on their return. There was an audio-visual course for teaching French, a well-stocked library encouraged school and home reading, and a range of sports facilities catered for everything from volley-ball to netball, rounders to soft ball and tennis to cricket. As yet there was no playing field but a hard-surfaced playground was planned. Due to an influx of five year olds, the number at the school was rising to over 100 pupils.

Mr Simpson's *Ascension Island School Annual Report for March 1967-March 1968* expressed satisfaction at the way the school had settled into its new surroundings. The school year of 44 weeks had been split into five terms, each with about two weeks holiday between them in order to accommodate the transient nature of many of the school's members. The rapid growth in numbers necessitated the full use of the rooms by the two infant classes, two junior classes and one senior class. Of the 114 pupils – 68 boys and 46 girls – at the time this report was written, 66 were St Helenian, and 48 from the UK. An analysis of their family status showed 47 Cable and Wireless, 16 British Broadcasting Corporation, 15 Combined Services Overseas, 23 Public Buildings and Works Department, 2 South African and 11 St Helena Government.

Geoffrey Simpson was assisted by Mr and Mrs Randall from the UK and Miss Clingham, a St Helenian Infant Assistant, together with Mrs

Simpson and an unqualified assistant whose husband worked with the MPBW. As his predecessor reported, the teachers were constantly battling against the lack of enthusiasm, interest and competition in the majority of St Helenian children – except in games and light crafts. School activities had included the first School Swimming Sports, an Open Day for parents, displays of Art and Crafts, and a school nativity play.

Mr Simpson's *Education Report* for 1970-71 showed the wide and lively range of activities being carried out in the school, but reiterated the difficulties inherent in a school with a moving population to attempt to keep a balance and fulfil the demands of the curriculum. However, the school had been well-staffed. His staff of eight members included two unqualified assistants and six qualified teachers – including a married couple, Mr and Mrs Jones – Miss Margot Hutchinson, who was destined to become a future head teacher of the school, and Mr Simpson himself taking the 9- to 11-year-olds.

A highlight in 1972 was the Duke of Edinburgh's visit to Ascension, when the school was proud to be able to demonstrate the progress which had been possible in the new purpose-built accommodation.

Miss Hutchinson with Class 2 at The School, 1972-73 (Photograph supplied by Margot Hutchinson)

During that year two more classrooms were added to cater for the increasing numbers.

In his final *Education Report* covering the school year 1972/73, Mr Simpson wrote of a very successful year, both in academic work and in other activities. He was pleased with the results of his pupils on standardized tests, although he still had concern over the lack of motivation of those children whose environment had not surrounded them with the written word. A further challenge was the 'turnover' in the child population, which caused constant organizational problems. Nevertheless, these difficulties had not prevented the normal work of the school progressing, supplemented with activities such as a week-long visit to Green Mountain of a group of boys with their teacher, Mr Jones, to undertake project work and observations on the farm. Arrangements had been made for the first group of children aged 14-plus to take the St Helena General Schools Examination the following August. This would provide the school-leavers returning to St Helena with the GSE Certificate when applying for employment.

In addition to the normal school programme, other events had taken place such as the Children's Sports, Swimming Sports, School Open Day, Harvest Festival Service, and a Christmas Concert in which every child in the lower three classes took part in the play called 'The Fairy Pedlar', and the older pupils presented a Peace Pageant, portraying the futility of war through the ages. And the normal extra-mural activities had included recorder playing, chess and country dancing! Certainly the 154 children at the Ascension Island school, of whom 62% were St Helenian and the other 38% South African and from the UK, had ample opportunity to gain a broad-ranging education.

Mr Simpson paid tribute to his teachers at the school, stating 'I am well satisfied at the moment that we have a staff which is competent and capable of providing the standard of education expected by many of the parents. Our results of children's progress show that this standard is being achieved.' He was also pleased to report the regular contact and good working relationship established between his department and Cliff Huxtable, the Education Officer on St Helena.

Mr Simpson's long contribution to education on the island had been an important one and he was able to hand over a well-established lively school to his successor, Alun Thomas, in 1973.

1973-84: Stability and Development at The School

For the next 14 years, Alun Thomas and Margot Hutchinson held the reins of The School, its title given as the only one serving the island.

The two Head Teachers alternated with each other – Mr Thomas from 1973 to 1977, and from 1982 to 1984; and Miss Hutchinson from 1977 to 1982, and from 1984 to 1987.

Mr Thomas was already familiar with the school, having been an assistant teacher under the headship of Mr Simpson. His annual *Education Report* for the year 1975 reflected the challenges which had faced his predecessors, related to the wide background and experiences of his school population, but he was able to affirm: 'These difficulties are successfully overcome and all pupils are encouraged and accommodated to make progress and develop at their own speed. This means that in many cases, especially in the basic subjects, teaching is virtually done on an individual basis. This caters for the differing interests and the wide range of ability to be found in all classes.' Similarly the school took into its stride the matter of the continual turnover of pupils entering and leaving which, 'though a disruptive factor, is such a usual occurrence that pupils and staff accept the situation, and changes cause minimum inconvenience'. French had been introduced for the 3rd and 4th year pupils, particularly to enable the UK children to be able to keep abreast of their counterparts in the UK pending their return. Good reports were being received concerning ex-pupils of the school who had returned to the UK. Evening classes for any people who wished to attend, given by teachers at the school on a voluntary basis, were continuing, including Maths, History, English Language and English Literature.

He reported on the progress of the Duke of Edinburgh's Award Scheme, inaugurated in 1974. Two candidates had qualified for their Bronze Award, but recruitment of the instructors and assessors needed for the various categories was a major problem, making continuity difficult. This dilemma was encapsulated in an article in the 25th Anniversary Issue of *Award World* in 1981: 'Tiny, volcanic Ascension Island would appear to be an unlikely place to find the Duke of Edinburgh's Award Scheme in operation. However in the one comprehensive school on the island the Scheme has become firmly rooted since 1974. Continuity would appear to be the biggest problem the Scheme has to contend with since the whole population is non-resident in as much as they are on contracts from one to three years. Inevitably instructors and assessors for the various activities are always coming and going with the result that it may be possible for the participants to undertake First Aid in one year but not in the next. However, it does mean that over the years a wide variety of different activities have been undertaken by Award participants.'

Mr Thomas reported that, on their brief visit to Ascension, the Education Officer and the Assistant Government Treasurer from St Helena had both commented very favourably on the quality and range of equipment at the Ascension Island School. And obviously the school 'customers', the pupils, must have been satisfied with their school: 'there was no truant problem whatsoever during the last year', stated Mr Thomas.

Mr Thomas' second *Education Report* covering April 1976 to March 1977 gave the results of the St Helena GSE in July 1976, showing that eight pupils had taken the exam, one with 8 passes, and two with 7 passes. Only one pupil had not achieved any passes. About the curriculum, Mr Thomas reported: 'In spite of the fact that our curriculum is, of necessity, essentially a simple one (because of the lack of continuity of both teachers and pupils), nevertheless a full range of subjects is taught. History, Science, Geography, Scripture, Literature, Housecraft, Gardening, Woodwork, Art and Craft and PE and Games all form part of our weekly timetable, but the main emphasis is on the teaching of reading, mathematics and English.' He was fortunate in being able to report that 'in general the school is well equipped to function normally, without any shortage of equipment or materials'. He hoped that, through liaison with Leonora Pitcairn, the Education Adviser of the National Association for Maternal and Child Welfare in the UK, several of the secondary senior girls would be able to complete their course in child care by taking the examination to gain the NAMCW Certificate in Basic Child Care. Mr Thomas' comprehensive report continued to cover all aspects of the work of the school, including the co-operation with the American Base which had supplied a Christmas cake for the children's party.

Miss Hutchinson's first period of office began in 1977 and was destined to continue for five years, during which she established herself as a valued and well-respected member of the community, participating in many of the island activities in addition to her leadership of The School. In particular she interested herself in the heritage of Ascension Island and assisted in promoting interest in the archives.

In her comprehensive *Education Report* submitted in March 1981, Miss Hutchinson described the past year as a good one. She appreciated the backing that she had had throughout the year from both staff and parents. She added: 'The School generally is fortunate to have teachers whose standards are high. In the Senior School both teachers show concern for the progress of their pupils over and beyond what might be expected of them. It is not always appreciated by non-members of the profession just how difficult it is to teach in a Senior Department of only two classes covering four years within limited facilities for many subjects. In the Primary Department the teachers give their pupils a sound basic education.'

In March 1981 there were 153 pupils on the roll, 118 St Helenian, 30 UK and five South African, with eight full-time teachers, including Miss Hutchinson, and two part-time teachers for Domestic Science and Typing. The South African children were from families stationed on Ascension for five-yearly contracts with the South African Cable Company.

Like her predecessors, she described the recurring problem of lack of determination on the part of many pupils in academic subjects. 'We find this determination is rarely present. The pupils who enjoy these subjects continue to make good progress – those who do not, tend to slide away unless kept well occupied to try to keep up what they have learned already.' To try to redress this situation, she had organized extra group teaching sessions, extended the school day for seniors, and discussed ideas and difficulties with the parents.

Miss Hutchinson's final *Education Report* of March 1982 commented that all of the teachers sent to Ascension during her time as head teacher had been of the highest calibre. Nevertheless, she noted that 'there is a feeling of claustrophobia and it takes a certain temperament to complete a tour of duty without being in some way affected by the isolation'. She advocated more frequent periods of leave to relieve this situation and to help to retain staff and encourage continuity. She paid tribute to the successful work of teachers and volunteers with extra groups for music, country dancing, gymnastics and swimming, but regretted the lack of parental support, particularly of the senior pupils. During the year the school had welcomed its usual large number of visitors, including the Governor of St Helena, accompanied by the Administrator; Cliff Huxtable, the Education Officer from St Helena; Anglican and Roman Catholic priests, and several medical specialists. In addition, a dog handler from the United States Air Force had delighted the children and parents with a demonstration.

Reflecting later on her first 12 years on Ascension Island, Miss Hutchinson summed up the major changes as advances in social skills, language skills and relations between school, staff and parents. Both she and Mr Thomas, with the teaching staff, had worked strongly on each of these.

Handing over the headship of The School on 1 March 1982 to Mr McBride, who was Acting Head pending the arrival of Mr Alun

Thomas in April, Miss Hutchinson said: 'I leave The School with regret, but with many happy memories. I look forward to hearing from my successor that all continues to go well in this school where it has been such a pleasure to teach.' In the event, of course, she was destined to return within two years to take up the leadership reins again.

Reports indicate that the Falklands conflict in 1982 caused the airport on Ascension Island to be the busiest in the world, but throughout this time the work of the school continued and progressed under the second period of headship of Alun Thomas. In 1983 an RAF station was established, the personnel living in a newly developed area, appropriately called Travellers' Hill. Mr Thomas' *Annual Report, 1 March 1982 to 31 March 1983* highlighted the many staff changes which had occurred during the year, inevitably unsettling the school. In spite of this there had been considerable progress, particularly in the Infant and Junior classes. Supported by the Heads of Organizations on the island, Mr Thomas had initiated an Education and Training programme for senior pupils with high grades at GSE level within the Youth in Training Scheme which had been running for several years. The new course included areas of study in electricity, commercial subjects, nursing and trade skills. Mr Thomas hoped that this would stimulate the senior St Helenian pupils to higher achievement. Various representatives of the organizations on Ascension undertook some of the specialist training involved although, as indicated in Mr Thomas' report: 'Further developments have been restricted because of the total involvement of the various departments of the organizations with work associated with the Military presence on Ascension', in view of the Falklands conflict.

Miss Hutchison resumed the headship in 1984. She was not surprised to find that the Falklands War had had a considerable impact, both positive and negative, mainly due to the advent of hundreds of Servicemen. The people who had experienced this period of time likened it to World War Two 'because it drew people together as never before and brought a Dunkirk spirit to the island'. The children had become more assured and sophisticated and the introduction of video had altered the social life on the island. The parents had become more independent and were prepared to speak their mind on school issues.

During 1983 the Chief Education Officer for Educational Broadcasting Services made an official visit to the School and his subsequent recommendations formed the basis of several major changes. These related particularly to the establishment of a Management Group, the introduction of BBC School Radio and Television programmes, greater parental involvement, and a reorganisation of the senior section of the School to give it an identity of its own and to put greater emphasis on technical, scientific and vocational studies. At this time there were 125 children in the School, of whom 44 were in the two senior classes. It was predicted that over each of the next four years this number would top the 50 mark.

Accordingly in 1984 the Ascension Island Services took overall responsibility for the management of The School from Cable and Wireless. A Users' Committee was established, to whom the Head Teacher became responsible. Parents of some of the senior-age pupils were concerned at being required to pay fees of £1,000 per child per annum, the alternative being to leave their children of senior age on St Helena where they would be entitled to the free schooling for all children there. This concern was relieved by a subsequent agreement made by the St Helena Government to pay an annual sum of money to Ascension Island for the education of St Helenian children of senior school age whose parents were provided with family accommodation on the island.

Miss Hutchinson was pleased that the seniors themselves took all the changes in the structure of their curriculum in their stride. They and the staff benefited from being able to concentrate on subject specialisms. Later on this led to many seniors staying on for a further year to study for RSA and GCSE examinations. Looking back on this time, Miss Hutchinson noted that the staff gained great satisfaction from their extra teaching loads and from their increased time given to community groups such as Guides, Brownies, Scouts and Cubs – 'I was pleased to see this involvement – it is very important and leads to good relations with pupils and parents alike'.

Periodic reports were sent to St Helena, including the one given in 1984 by the Bishop of St Helena who, after visiting Ascension Island, was able to report back to the Education Committee on St Helena that he was pleased with the progress at the school.

1985-92: The School: Widening Opportunities
The increase in numbers and the increased activities of the school were such that three extra classrooms and two storerooms were added in 1986. Senior pupils now had opportunity to study for a wide range of vocational Pitman's and RSA qualifications, and these, with GCE subjects, were also available for night school candidates. Extra-mural activities depended on the interests of the staff but included recorder and guitar classes, gymnastics, choir and mathematics. In view of the

financial contribution paid by the St Helena Government towards the education of the senior pupils on Ascension, it was recorded in the *Minutes of the St Helena Education Committee* in October 1986 that of the 126 children on Ascension Island, 101 were St Helenian. In order to help to determine how the annual sum of £70,000 paid in the budget for these children was to be spent, a proposal was accepted at a subsequent meeting of the St Helena Education Committee in April 1987 to establish an Advisory Body, comprising the Administrator, the Manager and the Head Teacher of the Ascension Island School to liaise with the Education Committee.

Coming to an end was Miss Hutchinson's second period of headship. She announced her retirement for the end of the school year in 1987 and tributes were paid to the dedication and commitment she had given to The School and to the island. It was recognised that the community was losing one of its longest serving members, Miss Hutchinson having first arrived 17 years before. She herself said: 'Leaving here will be a great wrench, but I cannot stay here for ever – more's the pity.'[19]

Her successor as head teacher was Mr Keith Sedgwick. *En route* for Ascension Island, he visited St Helena in June 1987 for a holiday and also to further the co-operation between the education personnel on the two islands. While there he was able to visit the schools and homes of many of the pupils who would be joining him at The School at Two Boats during their parents' periods of service there.

A further opportunity for inter-island co-operation was made in 1988 when Basil George, the Chief Education Officer for St Helena, paid a visit to Ascension during which he was able to give a detailed account of the introduction of the three-tier system of education on St Helena, as well as to describe the provision made for all St Helenian children at the first and middle schools, and the wide range of courses at the Prince Andrew School. This would enable the St Helenian parents to make an informed choice about their child's schooling. Further forms of co-operation were considered, including some alignment of the two systems and possible exchange of teachers.

At the St Helena Education Committee meeting on 22 February 1989 it was confirmed that the Ascension Island School would continue to do their local General School Examination at 15, and that the St Helena Chief Education Officer would be able to monitor standards and agree syllabuses. Certificates awarded would be signed by both the Head Teacher and the St Helena CEO. Ascension Island would implement the new ages for compulsory education as determined for St

Helena in the 1989 Ordinance, although the Ordinance itself did not apply to Ascension. This meant that pupils would enter school at the beginning of the school year of their fifth birthday and stay until the end of the school year in which they reached their fifteenth birthday. As Ascension is a dependency of St Helena, regular reports were to be submitted to the St Helena Education Committee, who would receive them on behalf of the St Helena Government. The contribution paid by the St Helena Education Department towards the total costs of Two Boats School was calculated according to the proportion of senior St Helenian pupils to the total school population. For the following year 1990/91 this amounted to £96,111 for the 46 senior pupils, while the costs for the larger number of younger pupils were absorbed into the general total.

Headmaster Mr Sedgwick introduced a number of changes to the Ascension Island Leaving Certificate, including bringing in continuous assessment of English.

At the invitation of the Administrator and Head Teacher in October 1989, Miss Dorothy Evans, ODA Education Adviser to St Helena, made a brief *Report on a visit to the School at Two Boats*, including the following extracts:

I was impressed with the school and felt that the Headmaster, the teachers and the children are all working very well indeed to make the school into a very good learning environment for the 110 pupils. The school atmosphere was purposeful and well-ordered, and the teachers and pupils were keen ...

As on the Island of St Helena, there is concern at the school that many of the senior pupils leave school prior to completing their GCSE courses. Many of them do not recognise any benefit from gaining this qualification. Recently a number of opportunities have arisen for senior pupils at the Prince Andrew School to go abroad for post-school courses, and if these opportunities were made known to St Helenian school leavers on Ascension Island as well, it may encourage some of them to proceed with further study. A climate needs to be created in which senior pupils are encouraged to pursue school education until they achieve their highest potential and so improve the general quality of their lives.

Keith Sedgwick's term of office ended in 1990 and in September Bryan Grey took over the leadership of the school.

An article published on 12 July 1991 in the weekly newspaper, *The Islander*, reported that the school had enjoyed considerable success over the years and was holding the confidence of its consumers. After giving a brief historical statement about schooling on Ascension, including describing the challenges of a frequently changing school population, the article continued with an impressive description of the present educational system. Places for some three-year-old children are available, after which all children enter the Lower School until they reach the age of eight, when they enter the Middle School for three years. St Helenian children remain at the school to go forward for secondary education, while the expatriate pupils leave to attend boarding schools in their own country. Examinations taken by the Senior School are covered by School Leaving Examinations set by St Helena and Ascension and also by GCSE in their final year. RSA and Pitman's examinations can also be taken by the pupils. The article continued to describe the other opportunities open to the pupils, these including several lunchtime clubs such as Chess, Recorder and Guitar lessons and Choir.

From the next school year, History was going to be available at GCSE level, in addition to the Maths, Science, English Language and English Literature already offered. Education courses in Computer Studies, Drama and Gardening were given in an extended school day, and evening classes for everyone on the island were offered in such subjects as French, Woodwork and Aerobics. As the reporter concluded: 'School days are the best days of your life – so the saying goes …!'

Liaison between the employers on the island and the school attempted to assist the school leavers in finding suitable employment. For instance, Patrick Robinson of Cable and Wireless reported in 1992 that it was the Company's policy to employ at least two school leavers each year and to train them on an apprenticeship scheme. Night classes were run in connection with the school in subjects such as computing, typing and electronics.

The Islander carries frequent bulletins on the school and on other additional educational opportunities open to the young people on Ascension, including groups of Beavers, Cubs, Rainbows, Brownies, Girl Guides and Scouts. These are run by many volunteers who seek to enrich the lives of children whose parents work on this isolated but strategically important speck in the South Atlantic.

The School at Two Boats has now been in operation for 25 years and has continued to develop under the leadership of a succession of head teachers, starting with Geoffrey Simpson in 1966 and, since then under Alun Thomas, Margot Hutchinson, Keith Sedgwick and Bryan Grey. Each of these head teachers and their respective staff have played a significant part in the story of the school. Regular visits to the school have been made by the BBC Senior Education Officer Eric Twaddell. An article written by him for *Air Waves*, the BBC Northern Ireland Staff Magazine, describes the educational facilities as experienced by the BBC families on the island. The article was printed in *The Islander* on 20 November 1992 and it captures something of the uniqueness of contemporary school life on Ascension Island:

There is a large number of BBC staff and their families who, along with other companies and the RAF working on the island, have approximately 130 children at the school ... As the BBC Education Officer, I have been fortunate to visit the school on five occasions – usually for a week at a time ... Just like schools here [Northern Ireland] there is a great uneasiness with all the changes in education but, on Ascension, staff feel even more isolated in their remote school ... I have helped to run courses as part of in-service training, as well as helping with teacher assessment and recruitment ... Financial restraints also make it necessary to appraise the requirements for all young people on the island and to make recommendations to the BBC for future planning ... The school is an ideal setting to enjoy teaching. It is a well equipped modern building where there are no discipline problems ... The quality of life – during and after work – would be hard to equal anywhere in the world – although it's like living in a goldfish bowl!

In another article, written for *The Islander* of 13 November 1992, Mr Twaddell reported the successful completion of the training of nursery teacher Tammy Yon on the island, culminating with the presentation of her Teacher's Certificate. This marked an important achievement on Ascension. Miss Yon, a St Helenian, had started at The School at Two Boats in 1979 at the age of six when her father had returned to work for Cable and Wireless. She received all of her subsequent schooling there. In 1988 she worked at the school as an assistant to Miss Linda Russell who helped her to undertake a part-time Montessori course, through distance learning on the island. In addition she made one visit during the summer of 1992 to the UK for a practical course. Cynthia Bowers, a St Helenian trained teacher, has been teaching full-time in the secondary sector of the school since 1987.

Certainly, some of the early pioneers of schooling on Ascension Island in the early nineteenth century would have marvelled at, and envied, the opportunities available now, not only for the young people on Ascension Island but also for their parents.

Part III

Tristan da Cunha

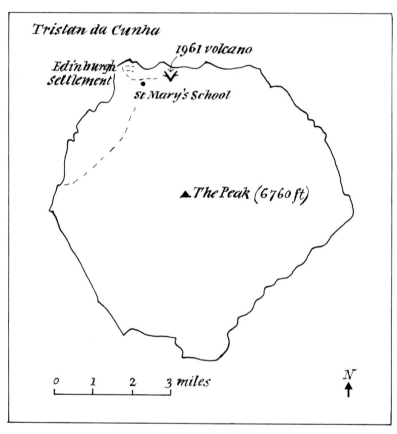

Tristan da Cunha

11
The Remotest Island:
Early Schooling Provided by the Church
1816-1942

It seemed impossible that so diminutive a person could be clever enough to be all the big, important, impressive things that the captain said he was – not only a parson but a schoolmaster and a doctor into the bargain!
13-year-old Henry Glass, 1851[1]

1816-81: William Glass and his Family

The education story of Tristan da Cunha is traced back to the year when a Scottish soldier, with his Cape-born wife and family, chose to return to the island after other military personnel based there during Napoleon's exile on St Helena had left. This was in 1816. From this time there were children on Tristan, being brought up to know the essentials for life on the island. Formal schooling was, however, not introduced for a further 30 years after this, when the Society for the Propagation of the Gospel (SPG) took responsibility for finding a minister for the small community.

William Glass had been born in Scotland and was a corporal in the Duke of Wellington's army when Napoleon was exiled on St Helena. As one of the Royal Artillery drivers, he was stationed on Tristan with the garrison, whose role was to prevent the French from using the island to facilitate an escape by Napoleon. When the army contingent was withdrawn in 1816, William Glass returned to Tristan with his wife, Maria, who was the daughter of a Boer Dutchman, and their two children. They were allowed to retain many of the provisions left by the garrison including two cows and a bull, some sheep and lambs, two turkeys and a supply of food and tools!

In *Tristan da Cunha: The Roaring Forties*, Allan Crawford states that William Glass 'can be regarded as the founder of the present community'.[2] Glass was a literate man with strong Christian beliefs, and he read his Bible daily. By 1820 the Glass family had been joined by three shipwrecked men and a further three men who came on a passing ship from India. As the small population grew over the years due to others joining this isolated community, William Glass conducted prayers each Sunday. By doing so he assisted others in understanding the Christian religion and so can be described as the first educator on the island, if not the first teacher. He was very keen that his children should be educated. Brander's *Tristan da Cunha 1506-1902* records that in 1820, three years after he had settled on Tristan, William Glass allowed a Captain Todridge to take his five-year-old son William and three-year-old daughter Mary back home with him to England to have them taught, but that Captain Todridge had to send them back after a year as he could not afford to have them.[3] Thereafter, William Glass took advantage of anyone visiting the island to do some teaching.

Brander also records that in 1824 Augustus Earle, an artist and naturalist, became marooned on Tristan for eight months. In a subsequent account of his experience he spoke of the courtesy and care which had been bestowed on him, particularly by Mr Glass:

Since my arrival I have been unanimously appointed chaplain; and every Sunday we have the whole service of the Church of England read, Mr Glass acting as my clerk. I am also schoolmaster to the elder children who are pretty forward in reading and their parents are so anxious for their improvement that it gives me the greatest pleasure to be able to assist them in so laudable an undertaking; though, to be sure, we are sadly at a loss for books, paper, pens, and all other school materials. Their parental exertions (poor fellows) would not avail much; the state of literature being but at a very low ebb amongst them; but what little information they have they all endeavour to teach the children.[4]

In desperation, in 1826 William Glass sent two (or perhaps three) of his children to school at the Cape, where they remained until 1832. In 1827 the St Helena authorities allowed five women, one of them with four children, and one man to go to settle on Tristan, and these people helped to build up the small community.

Meanwhile, another itinerant teacher arrived at Tristan. Around 1830 a certain Benjamin Pankhurst, 'a strange character', visited Tristan, being in disgrace with his family and taking himself to distant parts to try to 'reform himself'. He was received well on Tristan and, being well educated, was employed by William Glass to teach the children – 'a work for which, if severity is the highest qualification, he was most admirably qualified; for no poor child dared take his eye off his book, even for a moment, in his presence'. Pankhurst stayed on the island for nearly two years, shortly returned again for a few months,

Aerial view of the settlement at Edinburgh (Photograph supplied by Father Brendan Sullivan)

then departed for good, but 'By his departure, Tristan had lost its teacher'.[5]

By 1834 there were several parents on Tristan who were getting very concerned about the lack of schooling for their increasing families. These included children of the Glass, Swain, Riley, Cotton, Peterson and Taylor families. Signed by William Glass and marked by Richard Riley and John Taylor, the following advertisement was placed in a Cape Town newspaper dated 17 January 1834:

> We the undersigned, being three of the senior principal inhabitants of the Island Tristan d'Acunha do hereby agree to furnish any respectable middle-aged people (as man and wife) who are willing and capable to undertake the office of schoolmaster and mistress.[6]

The advertisement continued to describe the benefits and conditions for the newcomers. Sadly, there were no applicants.

In the later 1830s the islanders met a clergyman on Tristan for the first time. The Reverend J. Applegate visited them and, while he was there, baptised 39 young people aged between a few months to 17 years old – so the population had certainly increased rapidly during the few years of the settlement. The need for some kind of schooling was becoming urgent, particularly to the education-conscious William Glass. But it was not for several years that some positive progress was made on this. Eventually, it was through another visiting minister in 1848 that things started to happen to make others aware of the needs of this tiny remote community. The Reverend John Wise was a passenger aboard the ship *Augusta Jessie*, which called at Tristan. He was able to go ashore and found that, due mainly to the ministering work of William Glass over the years, there was a flourishing group of believers on the island. The Reverend Wise baptised 41 children into the Anglican faith. William Glass, now proclaimed Governor of Tristan, was keen for the islanders to have their own resident clergyman, and the Reverend Wise agreed to follow up this request in the UK. He wrote to the Society for the Propagation of the Gospel praising Glass' efforts to instruct the little community, lamenting the lack of educational books, and hinting that a teacher would also be a great blessing to the island. A nameless gentleman in England heard the appeal and 'resolved to send to the people of Tristan a teacher who should instruct them not only in temporal but also in spiritual things'.[7] His gift of £1,000 enabled the SPG to set up a fund for Tristan and to make an appeal for a clergyman to come forward. The appeal was heard: 'In London a young ex-warehouseman named William F. Taylor, who had not yet taken holy orders, with idealistic fervour applied for the post. As soon as he was ordained, he set forth on a rough voyage to the South Atlantic, where he was to stay from 1851 to 1856.'[8]

Accordingly, the Reverend Taylor arrived at Tristan on 9 February 1851. Nancy Hosegood, author of *The Glass Island*, gives a delightful account of the first impressions formed by Henry Glass, then aged 13, of his new minister-schoolmaster. Henry had accompanied his father, William, to the boat bringing Tristan's first minister, and he 'stared unblinkingly and unbelievingly at the bright eyes, bushy grey beard and long dark coat of the man the captain had introduced as the Reverend William Taylor. It seemed impossible that so diminutive a person could be clever enough to be all the big, important, impressive things that the captain said he was – not only a parson but a schoolmaster and a doctor into the bargain!'[9] William Glass lent the parson the principal room in his own house to be used for a church, school and parsonage.

Three months later, in April 1851, the Reverend Taylor wrote a letter to the SPG in which he said: 'There will always be a good supply of the rising generation, for the island is prolific enough of them. For such a little flock a teacher must be always sadly wanted, as I have already found.' Of his work as a schoolmaster, Mr Taylor later reported: 'I began school and found that half a dozen of the young people could read fairly – one or two very well. But of writing and arithmetic, all even the eldest were entirely ignorant ... I commenced a day school for the younger children and an evening school for the elders, some forty scholars altogether. My greatest difficulty was the want of proper books.' By 1852 another house had been provided for him and this became known as Church House.

Meanwhile, in 1851 HMS *Herald* called at the island, and the Commander, Captain Denham, subsequently produced a report of his observations during his visit. The Reverend Taylor introduced the Commander to the children who were at school in one of the cottages. Captain Denham wrote:

And certainly on entering the door so perfectly an English rural scene presented itself as made it difficult to believe that one was in another hemisphere. But so it was at that isolated and rarely visited spot, six thousand miles from the mother-country. In the cottage, seated, or standing in classes, were eighteen girls and ten boys, all clothed like English yeomen's children, all ruddy and happy looking, and attentive to their instructress, whom the clergyman introduced as Mary Riley. She had greatly assisted Mr Taylor in a part of his charge; however, she was about to be claimed in matrimony by James Glass, a son of the Governor.'[10]

According to Henry Glass, Mary Riley 'taught them lessons, but only reading and writing and no stories'. Henry did not know who had taught Mary, herself because 'there wasn't anyone born on the island who'd been to school except his eldest brother, William, and his eldest married sister, Mary, who had gone to America.'[11] Two years later, in 1853, William Glass Senior died and the islanders lost the leader who had been the founder of their community. Peter Green was recognized as his successor. Green was an educated man from Holland who had been on the island since he was shipwrecked there in 1836.[12]

In 1856 the Bishop of Cape Town, Dr Gray, was concerned to hear rumours of overpopulation on Tristan and resolved to see the situation for himself, having in mind the probable benefits of bringing the islanders away. As it happened the situation had improved, since Mrs Glass with her 24 children and grandchildren had removed themselves to America. During his brief visit of four days, Dr Gray visited the school, where 16 children had been assembled for him to examine. He reported that 'the greater number could read very fairly, write neatly, and do simple sums in arithmetic from addition to long division. They understood what they read, and several had a fair knowledge of the Catechism.'[13]

Great excitement surrounded the royal visit in 1857 of Prince Alfred, Duke of Edinburgh, who was received by Peter Green. The Reverend J. Milner, chaplain of the royal ship, took the opportunity to leave a large quantity of elementary school books, catechisms and slates. He urged Mr Green to appoint someone to act as a school master or mistress, but Mr Green replied that he himself was the only man qualified to do so, although there were several women who could read and write and able to fulfil the role.[14]

Mr Taylor had been on the island for six years, undertaking several roles – minister, schoolteacher, doctor and general adviser. One building served as both the church and the schoolhouse. (This house was later occupied by Peter Green and his descendants and now bears a name-board, 'Mabel Clark' – taken from an American barque which foundered near Tristan in 1878.) The Reverend Taylor's wide-ranging ministry among the people was much valued, not least because he was prepared to share their spartan life-style and to work tirelessly for them. The effort took its toll, and it was as a sick man that he had to leave the island in 1857. Allan Crawford records that at this time there were only 28 people left on the island; 45 were leaving in the same boat as Mr Taylor, most intending to settle in the Cape.[15]

No one came to Tristan to replace the Reverend Taylor for many years, so there was no formal schooling during this period. On the departure of Mr Taylor, the church-school building had been taken over by Peter Green. He had sought to keep some of the work of the school and church going, but more in the form of a social centre for the island. Various sources describe a second islander who undertook some teaching during this long interregnum – Mrs Frances Cotton, the wife of Cornelius Cotton. The latter was a son of Alexander Cotton, who remained on the island at the time of the major exodus in 1857. Details given in a list of the inhabitants of Tristan later on, in October 1875, describe Mrs Frances Cotton, aged 39, as a St Helenian who had come to Tristan in 1870 and who would be content to stay if she had the means to educate her children properly. Describing her as 'a character in her own right', Peter Munch says in *Crisis in Utopia, The Story of Tristan da Cunha* that, in spite of a serious shortage of books, 'She started to teach the children of the island, gathering them in her own house on Sundays, and from what we can glean from the scant reports, she seems to have done it in competition rather than co-operation with Peter Green's efforts in the same direction. She also read prayers for those who wanted to come to her house on Sundays, which of course tended to draw attention away from Peter Green's house as a community centre.'[16]

An incident in 1871 brought to a head discussions about the sovereignty of Tristan da Cunha and also had the effect of furthering the interests of education. Two German brothers had visited Tristan da Cunha and then sailed to neighbouring Inaccessible Island and settled there. Eventually, in 1873 they were taken off by HMS *Challenger* and a report of this expedition drew attention in England to the matter of sovereignty of this group of islands. The report ended with the statement: 'Should this group of islands be made a dependency of the British Crown, a resident clergyman or schoolmaster might be appointed to act as Governor.'

Following a series of high level communications between the Admiralty, the Earl of Carnarvon and Henry Barkly of Government House, Cape Town, a Captain Bosanquet of HMS *Diamond* was sent in 1875 to ascertain the 'true condition' of the island and its people. He made a long report in which he said that education was at a low ebb, although a few children were being taught by Peter Green and others by Mrs Frances Cotton, but the unanimous desire and urgent need of the people was for a resident minister, 'and, if such could not be had, for a schoolmaster or Scripture reader'.[17] He listed many items needed, including school books, children's and other books.

Shortly after these discussions, Tristan and its neighbouring islands became part of the British Empire. Up until this point the pleas of William Glass and Peter Green had been private ones – but now they could make their requests for clergymen and schoolmasters to their Government in London.

The following year, 1876, some supplies reached the island, including 18 spelling books and 2 lanterns for Mrs Cotton's infant school and Peter Green's adult school.[18]

Several efforts were made to acquire a suitable person to go to Tristan as resident minister. In July 1876 the Bishop of St Helena wrote to the SPG to recommend that a Mr Brady, a 24-year-old St Helenian schoolmaster, should be appointed – 'a good religious man, exceedingly useful to me in church work, very desirous to go to Tristan d'Acunha. He would in many respects be far better able to settle himself contentedly on the island than an Englishman, or anyone brought up in a higher social position. His father was a sergeant of some regiment formerly stationed here, his mother is a white or very nearly white St Helena woman, very respectable – he has had a fair

English education, his manners are good and he is studious. He would keep a day school for the children as well as minister to the people which is very desirable.'[19] Unfortunately this seemingly faultless young man did not, in the end, fulfil either the medical or the academic requirements of the post. Two years later another candidate put forward by the Bishop was Mr Whitehead, who planned to take his 14-year-old son with him to Tristan and leave his wife and four younger children on St Helena. But he, too, was found unfit for the job.[20]

1881-1909: Early Friends of Tristan da Cunha

After almost a quarter of a century without a pastor, a minister was found and appointed by the SPG to go to Tristan. This was the Reverend E. H. Dodgson, whose famous brother, Charles Lutwidge Dodgson (Lewis Carroll), wrote *Alice in Wonderland*. A warm welcome from the people of Tristan awaited him and his wife as they went ashore from the *Edward Vittery* early in 1881. Undeterred by losing much of his luggage into the sea as it was being unloaded due to the schooner breaking up on the rocks, Mr Dodgson later described his initial activities as follows: 'Of course nothing could be done about a church for the first Sunday – the day after my unexpected arrival, so the services had to be in one of the dwelling houses, but the following week I had the best and most central house given up to me for a Church and a School.'[21]

On arrival he found that 'Mostly the women can read a little, and some can write, but there is only one who can do both with any likelihood of being intelligible'. He continued: 'There were about forty children in the school, divided into four classes. The first two classes came under my jurisdiction, and I found that two of the elder girls, sisters, were able to be pupil teachers, so I gave one the third class, and the fourth class (infants) to the elder sister. After a time I persuaded one of the women to have an infant school in her own house, so that all the children in the other school might know their letters, read little words, and be able to count up to ten. Some of the children came rather irregularly at first, but the parents realized the need to be regular or not at all, and then children came along quite regularly and got on well.'[22]

By March 1881 he had assessed the situation and was able to send a letter to the Secretary of the SPG describing his first impressions: 'As far as I can judge at present the number is 105 all told – seventeen different families and one castaway. The younger children have been more or less schooled by a Mrs Cotton, but the elder ones, particularly the boys, have been allowed to run wild, and I shall have to take them in hand. It is quite delightful to see such a friendly, cordial feeling existing amongst the whole population.'²³

He immediately set about his two major tasks as minister and school teacher, and in January 1882 wrote to the SPG giving them a progress report. He first thanked them for sending some materials by HMS *Diamond* – 'It is an immense relief to my mind to have such a stock in hand of school materials, instead of having to beg a few things at every opportunity from passing ships. As to slate pencils, we had been reduced to a very limited number of pieces, averaging about one inch in length, and we have not been able to write in copy-books at all.' After describing the do-it-yourself making of blackboards and easels, he declared: 'I really think that we shall have every mechanical assistance in our school which you have in England, with the exception of a frame of balls for teaching addition and subtraction – as the mental powers of the children are so entirely in abeyance, I find that ocular demonstration is the only way at present of getting them to understand anything, and even then teaching a new rule is very apt to drive old ones out of their heads. However, Rome wasn't built in a day, and I have good hopes that patience and perseverance will in time mend matters.' He had about 50 scholars in the day and 20 at night – 'we have not the slightest need of a School Board Officer to enforce attendance!' About discipline, he was optimistic that he had this problem in hand – 'really now we have almost reached the standard of English school discipline'.²⁴

After three years on Tristan, the Reverend Dodgson had lost much of his initial optimism and excitement about the prospects of his work. There were then 97 people on the island and he reported to the SPG – 'The children have certainly improved considerably in mechanical knowledge of the three Rs, but only three of them show the smallest improvement in intelligence. I attribute this to the unnatural state of isolation in which they are living. It is simply impossible for you to realize the mindlessness of the children and young people and also of the grown-up people – a greater or lesser degree according to the length of time they have lived here.' And in despair he concluded: '... there is not the slightest reason for this island to be inhabited at all. It has been my daily prayer that God would open up some way for us all to leave the island.'²⁵ In this he differed seriously with Peter Green, who reported to the Admiralty that the majority of the people of Tristan would definitely not wish to leave the island.

Shortly after this, in 1884, the Reverend Dodgson left the island on leave because of ill-health and depression. During his leave he continued to press for the total removal of the people from Tristan, saying that then and only then would he resign his office as Vicar of Tristan. However, a shipping tragedy happened in November 1885 in which 15 men from the island lost their lives, leaving the island people mourning and devastated. When the Reverend Dodgson heard of this he immediately set about finding a way to get back to minister to the people in their sorrow. This he did, remaining on the island for a further three years – 'I shall remain and do all that I can for the people.'[26] This was the time when the island gained a lifelong friend in the person of a London solicitor, Douglas Gane. To help the people in their sorrow he set up a Tristan Fund which gave much support to the islanders over the ensuing years.

During this time the Reverend Dodgson continued his ministry and his teaching. In his later report for 'The Church Abroad', he recalled his teaching experiences: 'There was of course no payment of money for the school teaching of the children but I calculated how much firewood I should want in the winter months (June to September) and each father or mother had to provide me with a certain number of cartloads of wood for firing each month, according to the number of children which they had in the school. School teaching is very monotonous work, but it is interesting to watch the steady improvement of all the children – some quick and some slow – both in learning and behaviour.'[27]

By 1890 he had to be invalided home, after which he wrote to the SPG: 'I have not the slightest intention of going back to Tristan da Cunha. The intellect of the Tristanites is now so dwarfed by reason of their utter isolation that I do not think that I or anyone else could be of use to them. The only thing is to get them all away so that no more children may be brought up there.'[28]

Throughout the history of Tristan da Cunha there have been times when the islanders have made a mass exodus, to take up their lives elsewhere. This fluctuation in the size of the population has, of course, had far-reaching effects upon the numbers of children and the schooling provision required, both immediately and in the longer term in relation to future childbirth. These fluctuations are shown in the chart opposite.[29]

After the Reverend Dodgson had left in 1890, the Tristanians were once again left to their own devices for 16 years without a minister. Peter Green, now aged 81, continued to be the main spokesman for the island, although it was a long-standing principle that all islanders held the same status. His house was still the community centre of the island.

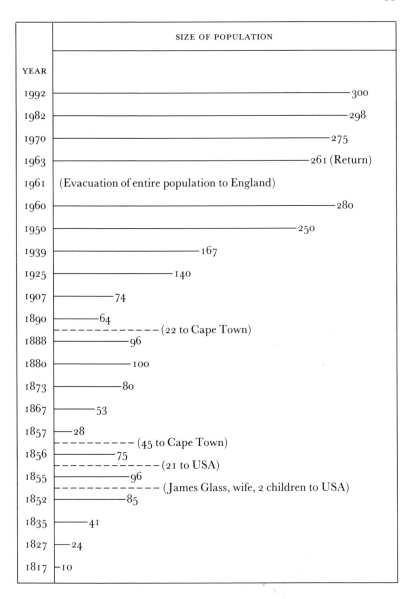

YEAR	SIZE OF POPULATION
1992	300
1982	298
1970	275
1963	261 (Return)
1961	(Evacuation of entire population to England)
1960	280
1950	250
1939	167
1925	140
1907	74
1890	64
	(22 to Cape Town)
1888	96
1880	100
1873	80
1867	53
1857	28
	(45 to Cape Town)
1856	75
	(21 to USA)
1855	96
	(James Glass, wife, 2 children to USA)
1852	85
1835	41
1827	24
1817	10

Various contacts with the outside world carried news of progress and conditions on the island during this period. In 1892 the Bishop of St Helena, who was responsible for Tristan, tried to visit the island but, due to rough seas, was not able to land. However, 13 islanders came on board his ship to go to the Cape, and of the three young men, three young women, three widows and four children, he reported to the SPG in Cape Town that 'Their intelligence and religious knowledge and good conduct are all fruits of the Reverend Dodgson's work of four years ago'.[30] The population had reduced itself to 50, of whom only nine were young men fit to man a boat.

The following year, 1893, a long despatch was written to the SPG by Commander Rolleston from HMS *Racer*, which had called in to Tristan. The population was then 52, comprising 15 men, 18 women and 19 children.

The only education for the children is imparted by Mrs Swain, a native of St Helena, and a widow, having lost her husband in a boating accident some seven years ago when 15 men were drowned. She teaches the children in the evenings and on Sundays conducts a service for them in her house, for all of which she receives some small remuneration in kind. I am told that they learn to read and write, but the presence of a minister or clergyman who would undertake this duty and act as head of the community would, I think, confer on it a great benefit. In conclusion, there are no complaints or individual desire to leave, but parents undoubtedly feel that their children should receive a better education than the place at present admits, and if means were offered would send or bring them to the Cape for that purpose.[31]

This suggestion led to an initiative taken by Joseph Chamberlain, Secretary of State for the Colonies, who enquired of the Governor of the Cape whether there were any institutions which could receive the Tristan children free of charge to their parents, to give them an education.[32] An arrangement was made with the Sister Superior of the All Saints Home, Cape Town, to board, lodge, clothe and teach them for £12 per year each, but when it came to making the arrangements there were not enough places for them and the plan came to nothing.

In 1895, Captain Rolleston sent another report to the SPG saying that teaching was still being given by Mrs Swain and also by Mr G. H. Cartwright, a mate of the ship *Allenshaw*, but the education was of the simplest kind and many of the children could neither read nor write.[33]

By 1898, the elderly Peter Green sent a despairing letter to the Secretary of the SPG: 'Since the leave of Mr Dodgson nearly 9 years ago now we are without any spiritual adviser on the island with 72 inhabitants. Our children grow up without any other education than our poor self can give them. We are thirsting for the Lord and our children need education.' Peter Green died in April 1902, without a satisfactory outcome to his letter. The island was in dire need. At this time there were 74 people on Tristan, including 19 men, 26 women and 29 children. To quote Brander: 'Undoubtedly all the older people who had profited by the ministrations of the Reverend Dodgson were fairly well educated for their station of life. One generation, however, born in and after 1884, had lost the opportunity of securing school-learning. Mrs Swain taught a few of the children to read and conducted a Sunday School; some of the mothers were able to teach their own children, but very inefficiently. These difficulties of educating the children seemed to have been largely responsible for the migration of almost half the population in the years from 1889 to 1893.'[34]

In 1903, the Governor of South Africa made an offer to take the Tristanians off their island to live in his country, but his offer only stood if the entire population would agree. In February of the following year this was the subject of a referendum on the island. From the 17 families there, ten voted to remain and seven to go to South Africa, so the matter was dropped.

A further educational initiative came from the British Government in 1904 when they offered to send a schoolmaster to Tristan if the inhabitants would contribute £75 a year towards his salary. However, the answer was given that this was impossible, 'as only five shillings had come to the island during the whole of that year'.[35]

But a solution to the problem was soon to come. On 31 August 1905, the Reverend J.G. Barrow wrote to the SPG from his home in Great Malvern to offer his services: 'Knowing that the Islanders of Tristan da Cunha have for 15 years been wanting clergyman or schoolmaster, my wife and I have decided to go and live amongst them if we can get to them. We have contemplated this step for some time, taking a special interest in the islanders because years ago my mother was shipwrecked off Tristan and cared for by them.'[36] Margaret Mackay tells the story of how Graham Barrow's mother, as a four-year-old child, was shipwrecked off Inaccessible in 1821, and of how 'the tales of her adventures and hardships became her small son's favourite bedtime stories. She always wanted to repay the Tristanians.'[37] Suffice it to say that, after further correspondence and a delay in waiting for a ship, the repayment became a reality some 85 years later. In 1906 the Reverend and Mrs Graham Barrow landed on Tristan.

The Barrows moved into the house of Betty Cotton (the sister-in-law of Frances Cotton), while the men started to prepare it for use as a church and a school. As recalled later, in the *St Helena Diocesan Magazine* of October 1935, they found a population of 75 – 14 men, 22 women, 21 boys and 18 girls. Both of them entered immediately and fully into the life of the island. So, after a very long gap, the islanders once again had the advantage of a school for their children and very soon the Barrows had 36 scholars whose ages ranged from three years to 30. Both Mr and Mrs Barrow participated also in running the church and organized other profitable activities for the islanders. Mrs Barrow taught sewing as well as other subjects and 'she found the women and girls of the island well skilled in knitting and in making use of the wool from their own sheep'.[38] Knitting was an important task undertaken by the women on Tristan. The wool from the fleece was washed and laid on walls to dry and then the older women carded it. The unmarried women (spinsters) then spun the wool into single threads using large wheels and wound it on to bobbins, before plaiting it into two-ply thread. Thereafter everyone knitted the traditional white socks, jumpers and cardigans. If any coloured wool became available from an old garment or bundles brought by a ship, this would be used as decoration – particularly by the engaged girls who knitted socks for their intended husbands.

Mrs Barrow's book, *Three Years in Tristan da Cunha*, gives an interesting diary of their activities on the island and throws light on all aspects of life there as it was at that time. Her entry for Tuesday, 8 May 1906 was: 'We are settling down to our daily routine. I go up to school each day at 10.30 now and take Class II in writing for half an hour, before the infants.' At that time there were 39 children on the island. A month later she wrote: 'The elder infants are getting on nicely; the parents of some are teaching them at home, and they are beginning now to read small words. Most of the girls bring their knitting, and during the interval sit on stones and knit away till the bell rings for them to go in again. I used to take mine, but devote the time now to ruling slates.' And a few days later, after describing the patience needed to teach infants, she wrote: 'The four older ones can read short words quite easily. They each have a book and read round in turn. The four can actually add 2 to a number, and Arthur Repetto can even add four and five together.'

It is of interest to note that the Roman Catholic community on the island had its beginnings in 1908 with the arrival of two sisters from Ireland, one of whom, Elizabeth Smith, had married Robert Glass and had become a schoolteacher during her time in Cape Town. When they returned to Tristan, Elizabeth's sister, Agnes Smith, travelled with them, and there married Robert's brother, Joseph. Elizabeth and Robert had nine children, and Agnes and Joseph had three children. After Joseph's death, Agnes remarried and she and her second husband had a further seven children. Records have not shown whether Elizabeth, the schoolteacher, continued to teach on Tristan.

The Barrows left Tristan in 1909 on leave, and intensive efforts to find transport for them to return to the island failed, so once again, Tristan was plunged into a long interregnum of 13 years without a minister or schoolteacher.

1909-27: The Reverend Rogers brings back Schooling after a long Interregnum

Before the Reverend Barrow left Tristan, the Bishop of St Helena had appointed Arthur Repetto as Reader, with authority to take church services in the absence of a minister. However, in 1911 Mr Repetto died, so once again the islanders were left bereft, because no one else could be recommended to take Mr Repetto's place. This meant that, once again, there was no official schooling for a long period. In fact, communication with the island was extremely sparse at this time, and then only through an occasional whaling ship calling in. Friends of the island, such as the Reverend Dodgson, were anxious about the islanders' welfare. The world was approaching war. Late in 1913, the Bishop of St Helena reported that he had received a letter from Mrs Repetto, the widow of the Reader, and he was not encouraged by the news of the islanders. In December of that year he reported to the Reverend Dodgson that 'it is now five years since Mr Barrow left, and they must have increasing need of religious teaching as well as ordinary education'.[39]

Once the war started, the situation got even worse. The Bishop's report to the SPG said that no news had been received during the year from Tristan and that no visit to the people would be possible until the war was over. Eventually, some three years later, channels of communication began to open. The Bishop reported to the SPG on 14 June 1918 that at the end of 1917 he had received a letter from Robert Glass on Tristan, seeking authority to baptize and to conduct marriages. Some islanders had refused ministrations by Mr Glass as he had not been appointed by the Bishop. At the time of the death of Mr Repetto, no one had been appointed as a successor because 'those who were worthy could not read, and those who could read were not worthy. They manifestly need a good leader, to uphold the right and denounce the wrong. I have no doubt that they need another visit such as Mr and

Mrs Barrow gave them, for spiritual ministration, for teaching, for the education of children, and for setting forth a right standard of life. Mr Barrow strongly urged that a married man should go with his wife, so as to influence the women for good; Mrs Barrow's work in this way was, I believe, very valuable.'[40]

But by February 1919 they were still no nearer to sending anyone to Tristan, and in desperation the Bishop of St Helena repeated to Bishop King at the SPG: 'I hope that as soon as possible they may have the spiritual ministrations and teaching, as well as the education of their children which they need, for it is now 10 years since their last missionary came away.'[41] Nevertheless, in spite of the desperate situation, the Bishop declined the offered services of a priest in the USA nearly two years later because of the cost of getting him and two ladies in his family to Tristan.[42]

The people on Tristan da Cunha were certainly paying a price for their isolation, but still they resisted all attempts to bring them away from their island home. As on previous occasions, they continued to live their lives buoyed up by their unique community spirit and mutual help.

Douglas Gane, the firm friend whom Tristan da Cunha had acquired in 1884, continued to be very active in helping to send much-needed items of food and materials to the island. His abiding interest had started when he visited the island *en route* to the UK from Australia. When, in October 1921, he heard that the Bishop of St Helena had informed the SPG that a Reverend and Mrs Martyn Rogers were keen to go to Tristan da Cunha to lead the ministry and to teach on the island, Mr Gane took a leading part in the campaign to find a way to get them there. For several months efforts were made by many people to find a passage for them to get to the island. With others, he took up the Rogers' cause, and eventually he was able to report 'It looks as if we are closing in on the Citadel, but, as Milton says of the requirements of the teacher, it wants sinews almost equal to those which Homer gave Ulysses'. Shortly afterwards, writing to Messrs Samuel and Co Ltd of Bishopsgate concerning the Rogers' passage to Tristan, he stated: 'I have asked for the services of a clergyman schoolmaster for the education of the children as the want of the means of education is the islanders' chief privation. Considering that the place has been without a clergyman for more than twelve years, the finding of a man for the post is a satisfactory achievement.'[43] Their efforts were rewarded and the Rogers' plan to get to Tristan began to take shape.

Throughout the subsequent period of service of Mr and Mrs Rogers on Tristan, Mr Gane was very supportive and was instrumental, with Mr Rogers, in awakening the awareness of people in Britain and in other parts of the world of the existence and needs of this isolated island. In terms of securing resources for Tristan, his contribution to education was outstanding.

While awaiting a passage to Tristan, Mr Rogers spent time finding out more about the place to which he was going. Having spoken to the Barrows, he became very concerned about the safety of his young wife on the island, as there appeared to be no guarantees at all of security of life or property. While most of the islanders were honest, it appeared that there were other more recent arrivals on the island whose practices were less so. In a letter to the SPG, Mr Rogers enquired whether it was the duty of the Colonial Office to appoint a missionary who was also a resident magistrate, and he required some assurances in this respect. In the event, he received from Winston Churchill, Colonial Secretary in Downing Street, a letter to take with them, addressed to the Inhabitants of Tristan da Cunha, as follows:

I am sending this letter by the hands of the Reverend Henry Martyn Rogers who has been appointed by the Society for the Propagation of the Gospel as clergyman and schoolmaster at Tristan da Cunha.

Since the departure of Mr Barrow, whose work with you I know was gratefully appreciated, His Majesty's Government have felt much concern at the prospect of your children growing up without any educational facilities: and I understand from the report received from the Commanding Officer of HMS *Dartmouth* which visited your island last year, that it is your own desire that a clergyman should come and live among you. It is therefore with great satisfaction that I learnt that Mr Rogers and his wife had come forward to undertake the work which you will realise must necessarily involve much personal sacrifice on their part. It is, I understand, their hope to remain among you for three years, and I am confident that you will do your utmost to make their stay with you a happy one and to take full advantage of the instruction and assistance which they will be able to give you.

I have it in command from His Majesty the King to inform you that he is glad to have this opportunity of sending his wishes to you. His Majesty feels sure that the manhood of the island can be relied upon to contribute their utmost by diligence and industry, to their common prosperity. It is the King's earnest hope that peace and contentment may for ever reign within the boundaries of the Island.

(Signed) Winston Churchill 12th July 1921[44]

On 8 March 1922 the Rogers sailed for Cape Town on the first lap of their journey. Their luggage had reached unexpectedly high proportions and included the parts of a three-bedroomed bungalow, a harmonium, church and school material, and clothes and food for three years.[45] After a brief stay in Cape Town, they embarked on a Japanese ship, the *Tacoma Maru*, which conveyed them safely to the island, arriving on 1 April 1922. Unexpectedly, the Educational Department at Cape Town had presented them with a wireless set 'as a tribute to the self-sacrifice of Mr and Mrs Rogers in going to such a lonely place, an exposition of the true Christian spirit'. In addition they were given some meteorological equipment in the hope that it might enhance the value of Tristan as a weather station.[46] These gifts were to have a profound effect for good upon the life of the island.

On arrival they acquired the largest room on the island, part of Andrew Hagan's two-storey house, as the schoolroom and church. On 24 April 1922 the school was started with 42 scholars between the ages of three and 30 years, and it became known as St Mary's Church Room. From then, 'St Mary's' was also the name of the school. Night classes were started for young men, but soon had to close because there was no lighting. Mr Rogers started the 1st Tristan Troop Penguin Patrol and also cricket and football games. The first island Council – 'Our Parliament' – was started, comprising the head of each of the families, with the Padre in the chair.

Six weeks after arrival, on 15 May 1922, writing from 'The Parsonage', Tristan da Cunha, Mr Rogers sent a full and interesting letter to the SPG, with the intention that news of the island should have a wider audience:

Dear Sir, There is much to be thankful for, a real desire for instruction, both in religious and secular education. We have started a Church of England Day School, with evening classes twice a week, which has about 60 scholars, out of an entire population of less than 140. The Sunday services are attended by the entire population. I have a Communicants' Roll of 50 persons, all adults of course. I give daily Religious Instruction and have a large Sunday School. There are many children here, some babies just born, and a few very old folk. Please pray for us all on our lonely island.[47]

This was the first of a number of documents by which Mr Rogers, with the ready support of Mr Gane, was able to raise people's awareness of the island and its needs. Help from all sides began to come for the island, both in kind and in money. Mr Gane continued raising funds with the purpose of keeping communication open with the island, sending needed commodities and preparing for the needs of a successor for the Rogers in due course. This publicity did not entirely please the Bishop of St Helena, who felt that it detracted from the major contribution which the SPG was making towards the welfare of the island. Nevertheless, the islanders were aware of a strong tide of goodwill from well-wishers. National newspapers, including *The Times*, the *Guardian*, the *Daily Mail* and the *Church Times*, published articles about the island, and gifts of books, food, clothing, church wine etc began to arrive at the island on any available ship. On the island itself, plans went ahead to build a new Church and School – 'a great step, a venture of faith, but folk here are great contrivers'.[48] In the interim, the church and school continued to meet in the room which had been lent to them by Mr Hagan.

The islanders were delighted with the birth of Edward, the first child of Mr and Mrs Rogers, during their first few months there. Writing to the SPG in December 1922, Mrs Rogers reported: 'We find the children are progressing quite a lot in school. They are fairly quick at writing and reading but find Arithmetic very difficult. My little son, Edward, the only English baby ever here, is the islanders' pride and joy.' She added a postscript: 'I should like to write more but I am so busy with extra choir practices for Xmas and we are getting up a school concert and I have baby too.'[49]

At the close of the year the Reverend Rogers wrote an article for publication by the SPG entitled: *A Permanent Church and Missionary's House for the Island of Tristan da Cunha*. After giving a brief history of the island, he explained the present position that the islanders met three times each Sunday for services and were keen to have their own church. This was the fourth time they had attempted this in their history, but previous attempts had failed due to lack of money and resources: 'They value a resident missionary here both as a minister in religion and a schoolmaster. They so badly desire to see the children well taught and school held continuously. I am most concerned for the Church. We shall use it as a school also. I have a flourishing day school but that is overcrowded also.' He appealed for donations and gifts in kind.[50] Coincidentally, Douglas Gane produced an article for the *Empire Review* and had 500 copies made as a brochure. Donations poured in.

In March 1923 a further report from Mr Rogers was received by the SPG. The work was encouraging on the whole; the building of the church and priest's house was progressing slowly; the attendance at church, day and Sunday school averaged at 100%; but the general moral tone of the people was poor. The population was 139, and there were 30 families, and 73 children and unmarried adults. He concluded: 'I think it would be the salvation of this place if the Union of South Africa would take it over, send a magistrate, put up a wireless station and administer the island kindly and firmly.'[51]

Shortly afterwards Bishop Holbech of St Helena paid a visit to the island during which he confirmed 63 people out of a total of 127. But even this did not endear Mr Rogers to him as the Bishop disapproved of the publicity used to attract gifts for the island.

On 15 June 1923 a letter written to a Mr Balfour of Ireland by one of the islanders, Mrs Andrew Swain, expressed the pleasure of the whole community with the completion and dedication of the building and with the work put in by the Rogers: 'We had service in it last Sunday when the Reverend Rogers dedicated the church to St Mary and blessed the ground. There was not a man, woman or child that did not attend the service. We are all very fond of the Rogers and their little son who is growing a fine boy. How we shall miss them when the time comes for them to go again. I am sure the children shall miss the Reverend Rogers for they love him very much and you will see him going along the beach of an afternoon with a crowd of children behind him.' She continued that he was also a great friend of the Boy Scouts and was teaching them to play football: 'It is the first time that they have seen a football.'[52]

By July 1923, writing for the first time from St Mary's Vicarage, Mr Rogers reported officially that the beautiful new St Mary's Church was complete – except for some cruets. Religious instruction was being given daily in the day school and children were attending day services voluntarily. The main content of the teaching programme was the three Rs. In addition, a branch of the Mothers' Union was meeting regularly and the Scouts were in correspondence with a troop in England.[53]

The Rogers' three-year period of service was already drawing to its end and consideration was being given to a successor. Remembering the difficulties they experienced in getting to the island, Mr Rogers' mother and Mr Gane began negotiations for getting them off. In the meanwhile, the Reverend R.A.C. Pooley heard of the need for a minister for Tristan and offered himself in two year's time, to allow him opportunity to complete his medical work.[54]

After three years of much activity and progress, the Rogers departed from the island in February 1925 amid tears and cheers from the islanders. The exertions had taken their toll on Mr Rogers, who was ill. No successor had been identified, but Bishop Holbech resolved that for the time being he would not select one in order to leave time for the island to settle down to its previous quiet and settled existence, less in the glare of publicity. In fact, he declared: 'I have no intention of seeking another priest for Tristan for some time to come.'[55] But the islanders were already asking for the Rogers to return and Mr Robert

Glass, the island's spokesman, wrote to the SPG to try to get this to happen, saying: 'He was always a hard worker at the island in trying to teach the young ones to read and write and they did get on well at school and also at Church.'[56]

While these negotiations were taking place in 1925, other matters related to life on the island were being discussed. One was a proposal, known as a Group Settlement Scheme, to settle some of the young Tristanians permanently in South Africa. This idea had the backing of a number of people, including Mr Rogers and Mr Gane, and was prominent in people's minds for a number of years.[57] Another concerned a proposed scheme for the future administration of the island, which was mentioned in correspondence between the Department of Public Education in South Africa and Mr Gane in London. But no progress was made on either of these fronts at this time. The Reverend Rogers, recovered from his illness, was ready to go back to Tristan. He made considerable efforts to get authority to do so, even offering to return largely at his own expense, but the Bishop was not inclined to agree at that time. Reluctantly, Mr Rogers submitted his resignation from the Tristan post, but still offered to be an intermediary in South Africa should the scheme to resettle Tristanians there materialise.[58] Ironically, the Bishop's agreement for the Rogers to return to Tristan came too late, as Mr Rogers died in May 1926.

Shortly afterwards, in August 1926, the Bishop agreed that another priest could be sought to go to Tristan the following year. Mr Pooley's interest had not waned in the interim since his original proposal to the SPG. He was offered the position and began his work on the island early in 1927. Compared with previous occasions, the interregnum between ministers this time had been short.

1927-42: A Succession of Ministers provide Schooling during difficult times for Tristan

Before taking up his post, the Reverend Pooley, who had a particular interest in medical affairs, made firm arrangements to convey adequate medical supplies to the island. The Rogers had been very popular, so any successor had a hard act to follow. Nevertheless, Mr Pooley quickly established himself, and his early report of April 1927 to the SPG (now reporting to London) was encouraging and optimistic, stating that all was well on Tristan. He was grateful for the supplies which had been sent. Out of a population of 151 people there were 51 scholars in the day school, ranging in age from five to 21 years, divided into two classes. They were being taught by himself and Philip Lindsay, a young theological student who had travelled to the island with Mr Pooley to work alongside him, mainly with the children and the Boy Scout troop. 'We teach the 4Rs – Reading, Writing, Religion and Arithmetic (later on). We have enough slates and books for all pupils. The teaching of Mr and Mrs Rogers bears fruit.'[59] Mr Pooley also reported that brass memorial tablets had been dedicated, the one to the Reverend E. Dodgson, 1880-84 and 1886-89, and the other to the Reverend M. Rogers 1922-25, both remembered and much-loved by the island.

In April 1927 Philip Lindsay sent a letter to Mr Murray at the SPG giving news of his early experiences on the island: 'Hard work has been and still is the main item of the day's work.' Feeling that he was doing the lion's share of this hard work, Mr Lindsay reported: 'We started school last week and when I tell them that I am going to bring a cane the parents usually say – that's right, Mr Lindsay, knock it into them! Very, very few can write properly, and a less number than that can read, as can be seen from the fact that when I first arrived I used to go round to the house reading their letters for them.'[60]

In his second report sent in August 1927 Mr Pooley recalled again the work of the Reverend Dodgson and the Reverend Rogers: 'Both were men of great sympathy with the poor folk here.' He continued to report: 'A rectory has been built recently and is much appreciated. The next work to tackle is the School House, 30 ft × 12 ft. We need wood and tar for the purpose. The missionary does the work of government in teaching 50 scholars and in holding a night class for adults. The question of good laws and management of the island's food supply is also being undertaken with marked success. Offences of theft are punished. The men recognise the priest teacher as leader.'[61]

Mr Pooley's third report was sent to the SPG in February 1928. A meeting had been held of all the heads of houses to consider the advisability of building a school. They had all agreed to build one and hoped to complete the work by Easter 1928 – but only two days a week could be spared for the work, and they were also short of wood. 'This building will be used for dancing and meetings. It is badly needed. In five years great progress has been made here. Mr Rogers built the little Church in 1923. Now in my time a Rectory and School have been set up.' He anticipated that the building would be finished by the end of March 1928. In conclusion he wrote: 'The missionary is doing the work of state here by teaching, doctoring, surveying and acting as magistrate. These worthy folk need all the help possible.'[62] But Mr Pooley, like his predecessor, was becoming depressed and ill due to the isolation and the absence of communication with the outside world. In a letter to Mr Murray, spg, in February 1928, he wrote that not a single cargo vessel had visited the island on its own account since 1925. He asked to be able to leave the island in 1929 rather than later.[63]

Buoyed up with this prospect, he found renewed determination to fulfil his ministry on the island, and in his report of December 1928 his depression seemed to have lessened: 'School continues for 10 months in the year. We have shortened Matins to start the proceedings and the children are free after two hours, with an interval for play at 10.45 am. The older girls and one man attend at a different hour from the small children. Mr Lindsay helps me much. It tries one's patience a good deal when tackling 30 lively youngsters at lessons. My old school, the Edinburgh Academy, sent us many useful books to use and we have plenty of slates and pencils. Progress is slow but satisfactory. The absence of desks makes it harder for the children, who lie on the floor sometimes with slates in front of them.'[64]

It was arranged for Mr Pooley to leave the island early in 1929. His place was to be taken by the Reverend Augustus George Partridge who set sail for Tristan on 4 January 1929. Mr Lindsay would continue to assist the new minister. Shortly after, on 23 February, Mr Lindsay informed the spg: 'We now have our school house and a great help it is; during the day it is a school and after that it is anything, dance hall and general play ground for one and all' – for the 156 people of the island.[65] A month later he wrote of his pleasure at the arrival of Mr Partridge.

Mr Partridge took an instant liking to the island and its people and to his fellow worker. Within a few days his daily notes were indicating that he wished to stay at least two years, possibly three, and that, apart from the failure of the potato crop, 'all goes extraordinarily well'.[66] Of his work as a schoolteacher, he made an early reference: 'Monday begins the regular routine: Up at 6.30 am, medical work from 8-9 am, breakfast, matins 9.30 am, school till 12. SOME SCHOOL! They want to do everything by rote to a sing-song, even the multiplication tables – but ask 4 times 7 and everyone gazes blankly!'[67]

In a later official letter in May 1929 he said that he and Mr Lindsay got on famously, and he sent a message to Mrs Rogers that the anniversary of the death of her husband had been marked by a service at which there was 'a church full of weeping people who all send their love to her'.[68]

The time was approaching for Mr Lindsay to leave the island but, reporting in September 1929, Mr Partridge did not think it necessary for a replacement to be found as he would be happy on his own. He said that 'life goes on with the same happy monotony' and that 'All is as in

Rogers' time and the people love it'. Of the children he was teaching he reported: 'Most of the children are under the age of 14 years. It is difficult for them to learn but they have good memories.' He also instructed the young men in carpentry and decorative painting, and he taught domestic science to the women. Nevertheless, he wished to take some UK leave soon and recommended that his place could be taken by Reverend Pooley while he was away since 'Tristan liked Pooley very much and would welcome him back.'[69] Mr Pooley was keen to return.

The earlier plans for a group settlement scheme for six youths gained ground in 1929. Douglas Gane organized a petition which he sent to the SPG in August, and which was sponsored by the Tristan da Cunha Fund, the Royal Geographical Society and the Royal Empire Society, concerning 'the training for the livelihood of young islanders on the African Mainland'. He secured a number of eminent people to sign it, and hoped to secure General Baden Powell's signature too.[70] But others, including Philip Lindsay, had reservations about the group scheme. What were their employment prospects, and how would the consequent imbalance of young men and women affect the future of the island? At the same time he indicated his wish to return to the island if it were humanly possible.

The Group Scheme did not get a promising response from the SPG, who asked Mr Gane in September 1930 to go to discuss the matter with them. They saw the need of 'a small philanthropic committee in South Africa to be responsible for the maintenance of the scheme, and the training, placing and aftercare of the young people'.[71] It was possible that the Government would cover half the costs, but who would cover the rest?

Meanwhile Mr Partridge was still thriving on Tristan, proposing to the SPG that he should stay until 1932, then have leave while Mr Pooley took over for a year, and then return for a further three years. He added that he had been trying to persuade the young people to leave the island, but only three would do so. He was worried that the present system was pauperizing the people, who had 'no idea of values and although so dependent upon the charity are frightfully wasteful and terribly careless'.[72]

Throughout its history there have been well-wishers to the island who have offered their services – some for a lifetime – but for the most part these advances were not taken up. Early in January 1931 such an offer was made by two young men who had recently been in the RAF. They offered to go to the island to give whatever skills they had acquired while in the RAF, whether it would be school teaching, missionary work, wireless, agriculture or to fulfil any other need. At the time, the island was not able to take up this offer.

By 1931 even the Reverend Partridge was feeling the effects of loneliness and the lack of conversation and he sought leave. To add to his problems, according to a report subsequently published in the *St Helena Diocesan Magazine* in March 1932, he was finding difficulty in attracting children to attend school: 'The children will not come to school as they see no use in it. They know it in their heads, they say, and the parents have no control.'

Meanwhile, back in the UK, the Reverend Pooley had heard from one of the islanders to the effect that since Mr Lindsay had left there had been no school at all. In a letter to the SPG he hoped this was not true, but if it was, then – 'If Mr Partridge cannot or will not conduct the elementary school, he has no right to be there. I am very distressed to know there is NO SCHOOL.'[73] Mr Pooley urged that an advertisement should be made for a chaplain to replace Mr Partridge, and a little later he offered to go to Tristan himself at his own expense. Mr Partridge took leave in 1931, but had to make arrangements to return to the island earlier than expected due to a proposed visit there of a Brazilian meteorological expedition. In the event this was cancelled, but Mr Partridge proceeded with his protracted journey, getting to Tristan in May 1932 to take up his interrupted work.

In 1932 Mr Partridge was appointed HM Commissioner and Magistrate for the island, and his parsonage was referred to as Government House. At the request of the Colonial Office he inaugurated a headman for the islanders, who was to be the chairman of the island Council. He left the island in May 1933, having appointed William Repetto to be Chief Islander as Chairman of the island Council, with authority to perform marriages. Mr Repetto 'held the fort' until the arrival in February 1934 of the Reverend Harold Wilde.

On his return to the UK Mr Partridge spoke at a meeting of the SPG in London about his work on Tristan, and this was reported in the *St Helena Diocesan Magazine* of November 1933: 'Imagine and realize that on this plateau there are thirty-three thatched cottages, one tiny church, one hut which we call the schoolroom, a few sheep and a few cows and bullocks, and 164 people, of whom 42 are children under the age of fourteen.'

The *St Helena Diocesan Magazine* of June 1935 reported that the islanders were pleased to welcome an unusual visitor – a 17-year-old girl from Hollywood, who received almost a royal welcome. She was amazed at the versatility of the minister: 'Not only is the clergyman the shepherd of his flock, he is also the postmaster, doctor, schoolmaster, and even runs the hospital!'

Although not officially given the title HM Commissioner, Mr Wilde controlled the island strictly for over six years until August 1940. Acting also as the storekeeper and postmaster, he set up a storehouse where all items delivered to the island were taken to be sorted and distributed appropriately.[74] He regarded his task as schoolmaster to be somewhat of a challenge and was reported in the *St Helena Diocesan Magazine* of January 1936 as saying: 'The school is a case of making bricks without straw. We have the room and the children but no school materials. I have about a dozen pieces of white chalk to write with, heaps of pencils, an assortment of odd reading books (no two alike) and no writing books. We all enjoy the school, and the children are progressing quite nicely under the circumstances, but, I ask you, what could any man do without tools? What can I improvise?' A report on 10 January 1936 to the Secretary of State for the Colonies in London from the Master of ss *Auditor* said: 'Under the driving influence of the Reverend H. A. Wilde, the younger generation is being instructed in the three big Rs and the morals of the people raised to a higher standard, but they are reluctant to adopt new ideas. Perhaps when the younger generation, now being educated, are grown up and read about modern methods of production, they may become more self supporting. At present they are too illiterate, too hidebound to make any effective alteration in their mode of living.'

Nothing daunted, Mr Wilde persisted with his task and in an article dated May 1936 which he wrote for the *St Helena Diocesan Magazine*, published in August 1936, he was able to affirm: 'As for the children, every child possesses a Bible, the gift of the Bible Society, and this is our only reading book.' But Mr Wilde read other books to them and 'since last year we have finished *Alice in Wonderland*, *Robinson Crusoe*, *Robin Hood*, *Grimm's Fairy Tales* and *A Christmas Carol*. The children are very keen and never miss school, whatever the weather. It seems such a pity to lose their enthusiasm for want of the necessary equipment – chalk, writing, reading and arithmetic books would be a godsend to me. I have taught them two of my mottoes – You never win by giving in – and – Any old thing won't do. In fact the children are doing so nicely that now the older folk are asking to be taught, and they want me to start a night school.' The indomitable minister was giving them lectures on Wednesday evenings and 'so far I have talked on First Aid, Egypt, Shakespeare, War Reminiscences, Coal and Oil, Things to make for the home, and the Cost of Living in England. The lectures are quite voluntary, but no one misses, and they all say how they enjoy these evenings.'

In 1937 a Norwegian Scientific Expedition led by Dr Erling Christophersen made a thorough study of Tristan and Gough Island. The group included Allan Crawford, who became another lifelong friend of the island, not only as an author of books on Tristan, but also as President of the Tristan Association in the UK for many years. The subsequent comprehensive *Report of the Expedition*, published on 29 June 1938, included observations on environmental, biological, botanical, sociological, physiological and educational aspects of life there. Of the latter, Dr Christophersen reported: 'Regarding illiteracy, it is impossible to give any definitive figures as the knowledge of reading and writing varies greatly. However it is fairly correct to state that approximately 35% of the grown-up men, and 50% of the grown-up women can read and write, while most of the bigger children know letters, and many of them can read and write fairly well. School for children between 6 and 10 years of age was started this year, and school was also given for children above 10.'

After all of this exertion, Mr Wilde needed leave by 1937 and the islanders were reported by the *National Geographic Magazine* to be sorry to see him go but pleased that he intended to return. During his absence Will Repetto was unanimously elected by the islanders to be in charge.

Mr Wilde returned to the island after his leave and reported that he was enjoying the hard work to the full. In a long letter to the SPG in May 1938 he reported: 'You will be glad to hear that now we have got our schoolbooks and now I hold three periods a day. The Juniors 9-12, Middle School 2-4, Senior School 6-8, so that keeps me out of mischief.' After war broke out in 1939, he expressed his willingness to remain on Tristan until it was over. But his strong rule was proving to be a fairly turbulent time for the 167 islanders, and a considerable number of them transferred to the Roman Catholic community. Mr Wilde left his wide-ranging role in 1940 and a successor was sought.

A point of interest is that in 1939 Peter Snell of Cape Town, who had had educational and other links with Tristan over the years, was called the Administrator for Tristan, this being the first mention of this title.

As had happened so often in the past, the task of finding a successor to Mr Wilde took a number of years. Philip Lindsay, Mrs Rose Rogers and Mr Wilde himself were all keen to return to Tristan, but these offers were not taken up. The war went on and little or no news came from the island, except that which was relayed by occasional ships.

One of these was a merchant cruiser which rescued some Tristan men stranded on Nightingale Island in 1941. The ship's chaplain, the Reverend A.J.Tempest Lewis from the Cape Town Seamen's Mission was on board and returning home reported that the church and schooling were at a low ebb on Tristan. There were neither church services nor school sessions. Mrs Repetto, now a very old lady, gave some simple religious instruction but that was all. Mr Lewis was 'impressed by the number, brightness and the educational needs of the children. The older boys are becoming dull and reluctant to exert themselves', and he said that there was urgent need for a clergyman.[75]

12
Island Education Moves into a World Setting
1942-92

The Tristan islanders have seen what is on the other side of the fence, and on closer inspection the grass is not as green as they thought it might be.
The Return to Tristan, 1963[1]

1942-53: Industry and an Administrator come to Tristan

Amid great secrecy in 1942, a Meteorological Station was established on the island, to be run by the British Admiralty in co-operation with South African Engineers and Air Force personnel. An advance party arrived on the island with a large amount of equipment, to be followed by the major contingent of officers and their families together with a doctor, chaplain and nurses. The chaplain was the Reverend C. P. Lawrence, appointed to serve as minister to both the islanders and the naval group. The commanding officer was Surgeon Lieutenant Commander E. V. S. Woolley, who also acted as magistrate. One of the members of the contingent was Allan Crawford, who had earlier visited the island in 1937 with the Norwegian Expedition. Several of the officers brought their families with them, and accommodation was built to house them and the station. For the first time there were living quarters in the settlement with running water, electricity, a sewage system and a telephone system. In his *Story of Tristan da Cunha*, Peter Munch described the naval garrison HMS *Atlantic Isle* – named by the islanders as 'The Station' – and added 'Most of the Officers brought their families along, which led to the establishment of a regular school, with a teacher added to the number of station people, and with compulsory attendance by the Tristan children as well. This was a new and closer contact with the outside world for the island.'[2]

This enterprise brought a much-needed boost to the island. One of Dr Woolley's first tasks was to convene the Island Council and, as reported in the *Tristan Times* of 6 March 1943, it decided that a school should be started in the near future. This was warmly welcomed as there had not been a school for many years. By 5 June 1943 the

Reverend Lawrence was able to report to the SPG that the school would open in two weeks' time. It had been built by South African naval personnel, assisted by islanders working for one shilling per day. With the help of local voluntary labour the furniture for two out of the three schoolrooms had already been completed. Education was to be compulsory for all children. A parents' meeting was called by the Padre on 27 June, and initial gatherings of the groups of Seniors, Juniors and Infants during the following week. Five teachers were provided by the station, including the Reverend Lawrence and Dr Woolley himself. Morning school was to be held for the smallest children twice a week, and there was to be 'compulsory' education on two evenings a week from 5.15 to 7.30 pm for the women and girls under 24 and the unmarried men.[3] D. M. Booy, in his book *Rock of Exile*, gives a narrative account of how several of the group of naval telegraphists enrolled as assistant teachers at this time. 'Lessons now took place in a vacant room at the station; the old school-house behind the church, built as the people would say "in the time of Father Rogers", had passed from school-house to council chamber and dance-hall and finally into disuse.'[4] He continued later: 'Most of the children learned fairly quickly once they overcame the initial shyness imposed by the strange classroom. They studied elementary arithmetic and how to read and write. The biggest obstacle was that the English they were being taught to read and write was so different from the language they spoke.' Describing the children's fascination for stories, Mr Booy said: 'This was a new magic we had brought into the lives of the young people.'[5]

Throughout the story of schooling on Tristan, visiting teachers have noted the particular language style of the islanders, seeking on one hand to preserve its special characteristics, and on the other to teach standard English. For example, many years later, Miss E. Harvey, a teacher from Norfolk, reported: 'For the first two days I found the Island speech difficult to understand. Often Islanders ask a question in the form of a statement, only the lifting of the voice showing that a question is intended. "Sidney, what time it is?" or "Good morning Teacher. How you is?".'[6] She found that many words were pronounced differently – 'rop' for rope, 'sop' for soap, 'larning' for learning, 'coating' for courting. She was addressed as 'Missarvey'. Jim Flint, a later head teacher, commented: 'In the islanders' Dickensian speech Vs become Ws and extra Hs abound – one islander told him – "Hi didn't was want to went hout hin the dark." The children simply spoke two languages – School English and Island English. An attempt to change something which I believed worth preserving played no part in our

English course.'[7] Another challenge to the teacher was that the children had no real grasp of the size or appearance of such things as roads, rivers, railways – which they knew only from pictures.

By August 1943 the Padre had announced plans for the building of a new School House and Parish Hall, and every man was to give one day a week to the work. The stone from the old Mission House was to be used. While on Tristan, the Reverend Lawrence discovered that the deep sea around the island was rich in crawfish. Not only had he and his fellow officers helped to bring a much-needed boost to the social and educational life of the island, but he personally also unlocked the door to a flourishing industry for this previously impoverished community. After the end of the war the naval contingent was withdrawn but the benefits which it had brought continued. Plans to develop the crawfish industry were proceeding. In 1945, the SPG appointed a chaplain to go to the island to succeed Reverend Lawrence and also a qualified school teacher to continue the good work established by the naval station. These two people were the Reverend and Mrs Alec Handley.

Prior to going to Tristan the Handleys made what preparations they could. After talking to Dr Woolley, Mr Handley reported: 'He gave us good news of the school. The furnishings are good and adequate and they were made by the naval personnel. Mrs Handley has already received quite a generous response to her requests to Educational Publishers and has also had some £15 to help with school materials. There are 40 children of school age and 250 native islanders.'[8] Mrs Handley was a trained teacher who had studied modern methods of teaching in Britain and had taught backward and handicapped children. She was also preparing to teach weaving to the women of the island and was eager to travel there to get started.

They encountered a long delay and various frustrations on the way but eventually landed on Tristan in February 1946 and immediately took up their roles. They quickly found themselves well accepted and loved by the small community and threw themselves fully into the life and work of the island. Shortly after arrival Mr Handley reported to the SPG: 'The Church life of the islanders must be like it was in the 15th and 16th centuries. All moves around the church and the school. The change in the people's lives owing to the naval occupation was only temporary and they have reverted to their former way of life. I think our greatest source of influence comes through the school children and our successors should be able to carry on this side of the work. The priest or his wife must be a qualified teacher. The future of the island depends on the children.'[9]

Mrs Handley (1946-49, 1950-52) and children at St Mary's School (Photograph supplied by Mrs Handley)

Sending a long report back to the SPG, by the ship which came to Tristan in May 1946 to take off the naval personnel, Mrs Handley wrote that the school occupied most of their time. During the mornings she taught the 15 juniors while her husband took the 14 seniors, and in the afternoons she taught the 20 infants. The morning timetable included worship, religious instruction, arithmetic, reading, spelling, handwriting, poetry, speech, grammar and composition; and in the afternoons the infants had worship, religious instruction, speech, songs, number, writing and reading. Of her infants she reported: 'All twenty of them seem to be at twenty different stages and I teach them in three groups equivalent to three classes in an infant school and I feel as tired as three people put together at the end of an afternoon.' In spite of this, she wrote: 'After the ship has gone we shall have evening school three times a week for the adults and those over 16 years of age. Reading, writing, singing and sewing will be the subjects.'[10] Unfortunately her letter had to report the accidental loss overboard of her trunk containing school paints, brushes, drawing paper, plasticine, books and illustrations!

Mrs Handley found her pupils to be intelligent. During the war, the children had been taught by naval ratings who were on a two-hour rota for teaching in the school but, although they had done a valuable job, they were not trained teachers. Much of the teaching had been rote learning, committing facts to memory with little understanding. When Mrs Handley explained the 'Why?' of facts, she found that the children loved to have the mystery explained. In their own time the boys liked to play football, with their donkeys and at catching small octopuses on their toes, while the girls played at making house – and knitting their socks and jumpers. At first, throughout the day, the girls all wore white cloth scarves on their heads called 'kappies' (word derived from the Dutch), made from discarded household materials, but when Mrs Handley supplied the girls with combs from England, they took their kappies off.

Mrs Handley's hard work paid dividends, as is shown by this original piece of work written by pupil Lars Repetto in October 1946 (Lars is now, in 1992, the Accountant of the Fishing Company on the island), which gives a remarkably good picture of the school, which by then was in the naval building:

OUR SCHOOL

Our school is made of wood and the roof is made of corrugated iron. It is fifteen feet wide and sixty-six feet long. Inside the building is divided into two class-rooms one bigger than the other. There are windows on the north and south sides. There are six electric lights in the large room and four in the smaller room. Each of them has a big cupboard. In the large room there is a kitchen dresser underneath. In the large room there are two blackboards and one in the other. The scholars sit on forms which easily hold three children but generally only two sit on each. There are desks the same size. Neither the desks nor benches are fixed to the floor.'[11]

A little later on in his book, as a writing exercise, Lars wrote what was obviously Mrs Handley's philosophy for herself and her pupils: 'Make up your mind that you can do well and say to yourself, I can, I will.'

In April 1947 the Archbishop of Cape Town visited Tristan and reported: 'The Reverend A. E. Handley and his wife are doing quite excellent work. He handles the community with sympathy, firmness and tact. He has to do everything and his medical knowledge is invaluable. Mrs Handley has created an excellent school. She is a most competent and patient teacher and I am assured that the whole life of the children has been revolutionized by her efforts. No praise could be extravagant for what Mrs Handley is doing.'[12] In addition to her teaching she had also started up Guides and Brownies, whose uniforms were made from materials left over in the Naval Canteen. Their hand-knitted hats and socks were made mostly by the children, who were described by Mrs Handley as 'born with knitting needles in their hands'.

Tristan da Cunha lost a long-standing friend in 1947 on the death of Douglas Gane who had been associated since the 1880s with the island. In a letter to the SPG in September 1947 Irving (later Sir Irving) Gane wrote: 'I think it can be fairly said that my father was largely instrumental in putting Tristan on the map and bringing the problems of the inhabitants to the notice of the public generally.'[13] Irving Gane himself had taken up the cause which had been so dear to his father and had become the Honorary Secretary of the Tristan da Cunha Fund.

Throughout 1947 matters were coming to a head concerning an important development on Tristan da Cunha, this being a project to establish the Lambert Bay Fish Canning Company. Discussions had been proceeding between the Colonial Office, the SPG and the Company to determine the conditions under which the enterprise was to be established. Reverend Handley was asked to be the representative on the island of the Colonial Office during the local discussions. Among other matters the company wished to create the post of Manager/Chaplain to be held initially by the Reverend Lawrence who had been the naval chaplain on the island during the war and who had first realized the abundance of crawfish around its coast. Clearly this would affect the work of the SPG chaplain, but discussions ended with all parties in agreement, and the project which was to have such a profound effect on the island was launched.

Throughout their first two years on Tristan, the Handleys' work continued to be highly valued. Mr Handley was asked by the SPG to remain an additional year in order to cover the transitional period while the company was getting under way. But, sadly, this was not to be, as he died very suddenly in February 1948 at the age of 52 among the people he had taken so much to heart. The *St Helena Magazine* of May 1948 paid tribute to him: 'Mr Handley toiled on the beach with the menfolk. He taught adults and children in day-long classes as they dug the potato patches to discover the causes of potato rot. He was agricultural adviser, postmaster and government administrator.' The islanders grieved: 'All our childer have losted the friend who was all in all to them.' After her husband's death Mrs Handley chose to remain there alone, saying: 'I shall stay here until some other clergyman comes. It is my duty. The islanders need me.' In December 1948, the *Tristan da Cunha Newsletter: News from the Island* (published by the SPG) added its tribute: 'The Island has lost a well loved and deeply respected priest, teacher and leader. His [Alec Handley's] memory will live on and the work that he accomplished so successfully and so devotedly will continue to bear fruit in the lives of those to whom he ministered. Mrs Handley has continued to run the school, to organise the Mothers' Union and the Brownies, to care for the sick (assisted by Mary Swain) and to do the scores of other jobs which she has no time to mention in her brief wireless messages to England. In addition she has cared for the spiritual life of the islanders by conducting services and giving addresses. Mrs Handley has been chairman of the Island Council since the return to Cape Town of the Reverend C. P. Lawrence, and has also run a Women's Island Council.'[14]

Meanwhile, some influential people away from the island were continuing to voice doubts about its future. An article in the *St Helena Magazine* of April 1948 quoted comments of the Archbishop of Cape Town after his recent visit to Tristan: 'No one has yet found a satisfactory answer to the question – what is the future of the islanders?' He noted that despite their industrious, healthy lives, they could not produce enough to make trade a paying proposition. 'They have ambition to see the world, and can learn only from books and pictures.'

At the end of 1949 the responsibility for the control and management of the Tristan School was regularized. It was to be conducted by the SPG for children from five to 15; the SPG chaplain was to be Manager and Official Correspondent; the Head Teacher was responsible for the internal conduct and discipline, and the preparation of syllabuses based on the English and Welsh system of primary and secondary modern schools; in consultation with the Head Teacher, the chaplain was to determine hours of instruction and length of terms, and to be responsible for religious instruction, taking part as he wished; the Head was responsible to the chaplain in his capacity as Manager of the School.

Mrs Handley took leave from her wide-ranging responsibilities and returned to England on furlough in 1949. Miss E. Harvey, head teacher of the Church School at Gooderstone, Norfolk, was given leave of absence for a year and sent by the SPG to run the Tristan school. In Gooderstone she had been secretary of the Parochial Church Council, superintendent of the Sunday School and organist at the Parish Church. She settled happily into her life on Tristan.

Meanwhile, the Reverend Luard, who had been appointed to work as Chaplain on Tristan at the end of 1948, had had to return home due to personal circumstances, and the Reverend Lawrence, the Station's chaplain during the war and the new Manager/Chaplain for the Fishing Company, became acting chaplain pending a full appointment. His additional tasks included regular visits to the day school. Eventually, in September 1949, a new chaplain sailed for the island, the Reverend Dennis Wilkinson, to be followed shortly afterwards by his wife and their two small children.

Miss Harvey reported enthusiastically in the *Tristan da Cunha Newsletter* about her year's activities: 'I find the islanders charming people. I have met with nothing but kindness from them since I came here. They value education (larning as they call it) very highly. One man said to me only the other day "I want Margaret to stay at school as long as she can. Larning's a thing no one can take away from her". This is the usual attitude of the parents, and the children are a joy to teach, because they want to learn. Mentally, I find these children well up to standard. Arithmetic presents the greatest difficulty, but English is well up to standard. I have never before taught children so well disposed to their teacher.' The *Newsletter* continued to say that Miss Harvey's work on Tristan was well appreciated and a tribute was paid to her by the Reverend Wilkinson, who spoke of her zeal and the tremendous amount of work she put in. 'The Society and its supporters owe Miss Harvey a big debt of gratitude for her year of loyal and devoted service on Tristan.'[15]

During her leave Mrs Handley decided to offer another term of service on the island and this was gladly accepted. She returned to Tristan, travelling to the island on the same ship as the Administrator, Hugh Elliott, in January 1950. The newly created post of Administrator of Tristan da Cunha had been established, with magisterial powers, to administer the laws introduced on the establishment of the fishing industry on the island. Of the Canning Company, the *St Helena Magazine* of January 1949 reported: 'The island [Tristan] is about to enter a new phase of life and the title "the inaccessible island" will no longer be able to be applied to it. Under new conditions the 230-odd inhabitants will have to adapt themselves to a new mode of life. They will become wage-earners and their standard of living, and indeed their whole life, will be drastically altered.'

Accordingly, in 1950 Tristan welcomed Mr Hugh Elliott, later by inheritance to become Sir Hugh Elliott. Since Tristan was part of the Colony of St Helena, the Administrator was responsible to the Governor of St Helena. He quickly gained the respect and confidence of the islanders through the procedures which he instituted for their welfare and, indeed, for their future prosperity. He participated in the island activities and, like the whole island community, was impressed with the work of Mrs Handley. He kept a personal diary of his experiences on Tristan da Cunha and his entry of 26 June 1950 stated: 'I attended the Girl Guide party after supper for an hour or two. Mrs Handley, as usual working like a Trojan, managed to organize a number of team games, songs and dances – including perhaps ten pairs of girls who ventured to try the Scottish Country Dance Waltz. The island girls are very much less self-conscious than the boys who sit around apparently enjoying themselves but quite unwilling to try anything new!'

An artist of no mean distinction, Hugh Elliott was responsible for designing the first official Tristan Island stamps (although Allan Crawford had earlier created the now-famous potato stamp) and so starting another lucrative industry on the island. For his first year, Mr Elliott came alone, his wife planning to join him the following year. In her book entitled *Voices and Echoes*, Joan Alexander states: 'When Hugh Elliott took up the post, Elizabeth, his wife, might have been hand-picked for this assignment. Not only was she a trained nurse and midwife, but she enjoyed the simplicity of the people and their way of life.' She took their youngest of three children, Clive, aged four, with her to the island. Mrs Elliott, like her husband, kept a day-to-day personal diary of her life on Tristan. In addition to her constant nursing and midwifery activities she also helped at the school where she taught the infants' class. Her diary for Monday 21 May 1951 recorded: 'I started teaching in the school – the infants for an hour a day – they were very good and I quite enjoyed it.' On 21 June she wrote: 'I had a noisy hour with the infants at school. They certainly are far from the repressed little things they were reputed to be but I suppose it is the educational awakening which makes them be more like other children in the world'.

In March 1950 education had become compulsory for all children on the island from five to 15, although, because of the broken nature of their past schooling, boys were permitted to leave school only when they were 16. In addition, boys aged 14 to 16 were permitted to work only in their free time from school – during afternoons, Saturdays and school holidays.

A difficult period of expanding opportunities for the Tristanians ensued, including accustoming themselves to a different lifestyle with new resources, a money system and opportunity to earn money and spend it. Under the guidance of the Administrator, an island Council was chosen, ten of its members being islanders and the other two being representatives of the Company. During this time Mrs Handley continued to run the school, helping the children also to accommodate themselves to their changing island.

However, by 1952 she decided that the time had come for her to leave the island where she had played such an important part and made so many friends. She left in October, all the islanders being sorry to see her go. The *Tristan da Cunha Newsletter* of December 1952 spoke for the island: 'It will be difficult to think of Tristan da Cunha without Mrs Handley for her association with the island goes back over many years. Successive numbers of this news letter bear witness to the wide range of Mrs Handley's activities inside and outside the school. She leaves behind her a memory which will long remain green, and also one cannot doubt, a corner of her heart. Long, self-sacrificing service has forged bonds of affection and friendship which will endure through the years.' The truth of this is apparent. Now, 40 years later in 1992, Mrs Handley, lively and active at the age of 80, recalls her time on Tristan da Cunha with fond memories, saying at her home in Cheltenham: 'I had a very happy time on Tristan. The children wanted to learn. It was easy teaching because there was no resistance. They did their best all the time.'[16]

The ship which took Mrs Handley from the island brought the next chaplain, the Reverend David Neaum, with his wife and three children to succeed Mr Wilkinson who had spent three years on Tristan. Mrs Handley's place as head teacher of the school was taken by R. J. Harding, whose wife was also appointed to teach in the school. While the appointments were made and sponsored by the SPG, it was a grant from the Colonial Development and Welfare Funds which enabled there to be a second qualified teacher from the UK. The number of children in the school had risen to nearly 60 and was continuing to rise, with excellent attendance, following the age-old tradition on the island.

1953-63: The Volcanic Eruption Interrupts Developing Management Structures for the Island's Education

During this decade, education on the island was led by expatriate Education Officers who normally held office for up to three years. The system in 1953 was that the SPG supported the chaplain and was responsible for appointing the teaching staff for the school, while they were supported partly from the Colonial Office and partly from the Development Company. The head teacher was assisted by from three to five island teachers and, later, one additional expatriate teacher. Other expatriate people, such as the wives of the Agriculture, PWD or Medical Officers, taught in a voluntary, part-time capacity offering whatever skill, expertise or enthusiasm they had. The school buildings were progressively less and less adequate for their purpose; the need for a new building was apparent, and after several years it materialized. The attendance at school by the children was excellent, but the teachers found it difficult to raise the general standard of work. A matter which was continuing to exercise the minds of successive Education Officers and teachers was – what should be the aims of education on Tristan?

One who was ready to accept this challenge was the new teacher, Ronald Harding. In the few months since the departure of Mrs Handley, the Reverend Wilkinson, followed by the Reverend Neaum, had taken charge of the school. On arriving at the end of 1952 Mr Harding set about his task enthusiastically, and by November 1953 he produced a comprehensive *Education Report* in ten sections, each covering a major aspect of St Mary's School. He explained that social changes which the island was experiencing made the report desirable, necessitating a re-evaluation in order to offer a 'full and fitting educational programme'.

Mr Harding reported that, compared with children whom he had taught before, the island children were backward. He attributed this to outdated curricula, equipment, books and accommodation – and not to absenteeism, since the average attendance was 99.6%. There were only three teachers for the 65 children, who needed to be divided into three age-based classes, each of two or three divisions. He needed more books for private reading and wished to introduce teaching of subjects like handwork, woodwork, physical training or science. The Agricultural Officer was prepared to assist with Horticulture instruction and the Development Company with basic mechanical training. Further education off the island should be available to broaden the horizons of the people. He drew attention to the fact that the school, built in 1942, was originally part of the Army/Navy Quarters, and it was also doubling as the Village Hall. It was now totally inadequate, not least because of the constant need to remove the furniture and equipment for regular dances. He added that the school furniture was inadequate. The blackboards were builders' board, stained with Indian ink (perhaps the very ones created this way by the Reverend Dodgson in 1881). The total working space for each child was one square foot, with no locker accommodation. And finally, a radio would 'bring the rest of the world into the classroom and break down the feeling of loneliness and isolation'.

Noting Mr Harding's voluminous 57-page report, the *Tristan da Cunha Newsletter* of March 1954 quoted his aim 'to show the children how to live, and enjoy living, more fully, it being essential so to equip the rising generation that it is able to grasp and use the opportunities now offered for the first time'.

In his report, Mr Harding set an agenda which was to spread through many years. Many of his successors as Education Officers found the need to re-echo his statements in their own way within the circumstances of their own time.

By March 1955 the SPG was able to report in the *Tristan da Cunha Newsletter* that the school had made great strides while the Hardings had been in charge: 'Much has happened since Mr Harding submitted his monumental report in November 1953 and many of the improvements he suggested have been carried out.' There were now sufficient teachers to divide the 59 children into three classes, with the appointment of a pupil-teacher in addition to two full-time teachers. The 26 seniors, 23 juniors and 10 infants continue to maintain a 99% attendance record. Not only had all rooms in their ex-Navy quarters been relined, but also a new floor had been fitted, and new equipment had arrived – 50 desks, infant desks and chairs, a teacher's desk, a new blackboard, sports equipment and textbooks. In addition it had been recognized that a school with over 60 pupils of ages ranging from five to 15 needed more than two full-time teachers. From the Administration Fund it had been possible to appoint a pupil teacher, the first holder of this post being Trina Glass. 'This wise appointment not only means that the school will be more efficient but also that an opportunity has been given to one of the brighter pupils to help forward the development of the Tristan community.'

The Hardings played an important role in the general life of the island, in addition to their work in the school. They started a club for boys and girls, bringing together the older Cubs and the boys and girls of Scout and Guide age.

In view of all the recent changes, the Standing Committee of the SPG decided in 1956 to review and formalize the management structure of the school and its relationship with the chaplain. The first of their draft proposals, which was that the chaplain or his wife was to be a trained teacher and appointed to staff the island school, with the assistance of only one trainee teacher, was met with immediate objections. Mr Harding and Chaplain Bell, among others, affirmed the total inadequacy of this provision. The other proposals, relating to the appointment of future chaplains, the establishment of a School Council and the conduct of the school, were accepted. The latter followed closely the procedures agreed in 1949. The new School Council was to advise the Manager on the well-being of the school, in consultation with the Head

Teacher, and its members were to be the Chaplain as Chairman, the Administrator (if willing), one station parent and four island parents nominated by the island Council. The Head Teacher would be present at all meetings except occasions determined by the School Council.

Mrs Stableford, the wife of the Agricultural Officer on the island, wrote an account for the St Helena *Wirebird* in January 1957 of the recent visit of the Duke of Edinburgh, describing the excitement of the occasion. 'The children went to their places at school for the Duke to inspect some of their work, much of it being displayed upon the walls. The children also did a few of their dances.' Later the Sea Scouts, Girl Guides, Cubs and Brownies all went on parade for the Duke's inspection. While on the island, the Duke laid the foundation stone of the new Prince Philip Village Hall, which became the social centre for the community, freeing the school from being used for social occasions.

Mr Harding left in 1957 after five years of energetic and valuable service to education on Tristan during its period of great change. In the *Tristan da Cunha Newsletter* of April 1957 his achievement was acknowledged: 'The School has made remarkable progress since Mr and Mrs Harding were appointed in 1952. From the start Mr Harding had a very clear idea of what St Mary's School should be and it was not long before he had put it all down on paper in his challenging 1953 report. His plans did not remain pious hopes. As the months passed we saw them gradually becoming realities, until today much of what was once a blue-print has become part and parcel of a vigorous and still-developing school. Although in all this Mr and Mrs Harding have received assistance from many sources and encouragement from a numbers of persons, the greatest credit must go to the determination and clear-sightedness and ceaseless activity of Mr Harding.'

On the departure of Mr Harding, the SPG announced in the 1957 *Tristan da Cunha Newsletter* that it was 'endeavouring to recruit for August 1957 a woman teacher of about forty years, who is competent to teach boys and girls to the age of fifteen'. This teacher would be responsible for the school and work with Mrs Bell, the chaplain's wife, and Miss Trina Glass. Pending the new teacher's arrival, the chaplain would help to keep the school going. The recently-established School Council would assist this team.

Further tribute came in the *Tristan da Cunha Newsletter* a year later in April 1958 from the Reverend Bell: 'The first thing that comes to mind is Mr Harding's whole-hearted and full-time devotion to the children and school. It was always noticeable that he was fully dedicated to his job, and often spent most of the holiday periods in working on

COW HIDE
MOCCASINS

These drawings are taken from a booklet produced by the children of Tristan da Cunha on their return to the island in 1963 after the volcanic eruption. They were inundated with requests for penfriends from other parts of the world, and wrote and illustrated the booklet to help to meet the demand. Thanks are due to Jim Flint, the headmaster of the school at the time, for supplying the booklet.

OUR CHURCH

AT WORK ON THE HARBOUR

THE VOLCANO ERUPTING

LONGBOATS GOING TO NIGHTINGALE

improvements for the school. I think that everyone would readily recognize that the whole school has been splendidly revolutionized and equipped during his headmastership, so that it is now a good deal better in furniture and stock than many a church school in the countryside of England.'

The search for a new teacher was successful and Rhoda Downer duly arrived in 1957. The islanders and Miss Downer immediately liked each other. The *Tristan da Cunha Newsletter* of April 1958 reported: 'Miss Downer is a great favourite with the young Bells, who pop in and out of her house and give her much happiness. The station folk (mostly young married couples) bring her into their social activities and she is always welcome in the Chaplain's home.' By December 1957 her report to the SPG described the wide range of ability among her pupils: 'It means endless preparation of individual work, great pressure during lesson-time, and quantities of marking afterwards. As there will be 25 in the class in January, I shall need all my ingenuity to play fair by each child.' Like her predecessors, she had initial difficulty in following some of the island speech. Reporting in February 1958 to the SPG she told the Secretary that she was well settled in: 'I am thoroughly at home now with the children, though sometimes I have to make them repeat sentences, slowly, before I can be sure of the meaning. They have two distinct languages, and they have forgotten school speech during the holiday.' In addition to her teaching she was also giving extra tuition to Trina Glass, her young assistant, including training in teaching methods.

The *Tristan da Cunha Newsletter* of June 1958 reported that Mrs Bell, who was now undertaking regular work at the school, was enjoying every minute of her teaching with the Infants and with Trina Glass, and that 'during the first part of 1958 foundations were laid for future development and the breaking of new ground in the Senior classes', including needlework and fair-isle knitting for the girls and handwork and gardening for the boys.

Miss Downer's work on the island continued happily, both for her and for her young charges. She gained great pleasure from the wild life of Tristan and sent lively letters back to the SPG describing her experiences observing the wide range of birds, including a penguin which she nicknamed Percy. Following in the footsteps of Mrs Handley many years before, Miss Downer officiated at Matins and Evensong during an extended illness of the chaplain, Mr Bell. Of the school, Miss Downer reported to the SPG in June 1959 that 'ninety-five percent of the children work to capacity all the time and are eager to learn'.

During this year, 1959, the need was felt again to make more formal the management structures for the school in view of the changing relationships and control held by the major concerns on the island. An *Instrument of Management* was devised and agreed, by which a Board of Management was established, with two Foundation members – the Church of England chaplain and a communicant member appointed by the chaplain – and two Colonial Office representatives – the Administrator and a person appointed by the Administrator. The Board was to meet once a term under the chairmanship of the Administrator. The Colonial Office would cover the cost of all salaries and building needs. The Head Teacher was to be appointed by the SPG, in consultation with the Colonial Office, and be under contract with the SPG. Assistant teachers were to be appointed by the Board, and the Head Teacher was to be responsible to the Board for the internal organization and running of the school. The Foundation members were to oversee the worship and religious instruction and the withdrawal of any child as required by a parent.

It seems hardly surprising that in May 1960 the SPG received a gentle letter from the Colonial Office querying whether the SPG should have so much control if they were not actually providing any money. Nevertheless, they were confident that a mutually acceptable compromise would be found.

Writing in the Administrator's 'Tristan Topics' reported in the July 1960 *Tristan da Cunha Newsletter*, Miss Downer included some interesting observations about teaching children at that time on such an isolated island: 'General Knowledge, History and Geography lessons are treated almost as fairy stories, though they now see travel films. Many books well-loved elsewhere hold no attraction, for poetry and literature mean little to those who have never seen trees, heard singing birds or gathered wild flowers. The children have a good sense of rhythm, and learn new airs easily, but few attain a sweet tone. They are acquiring a keen sense of pattern and colour, and are original in design. Hockey, Cricket and Rounders are played on sloping ground with many outcrops of rock. We may be held up by the passage of a bullock cart drawing building stone; or the English teacher may miss a stroke if a child remarks casually – there's a whale.'

Miss Downer's period of service was due to end in March or April 1961 so, once again, the SPG was looking for a replacement teacher. However, much to the children's later pleasure and relief, she was destined to meet several of her young charges again shortly afterwards when they were evacuated to Britain in 1961 at the time of the volcanic eruption. At that time she helped the Tristanians to settle in to their unfamiliar surroundings, and they were pleased to have their kindly former teacher to do this.

Miss Downer was succeeded by Miss Edith Bennett. Like her predecessor, she settled readily into her teaching in her unique surroundings. Like all teachers who have the unusual privilege of working in such an isolated community, she soon entered into island life, specifically by helping the children to equip themselves for their future lives there. Little did she, or anyone else, realize that other far reaching events were about to overtake the people of Tristan da Cunha. During a series of earth tremors which started in August 1961, many properties in the eastern side of the island became unsafe. To quote the *Tristan da Cunha Newsletter* reporting later, in October 1963: 'There had been warning enough that something unusual was on hand.' A letter dated 8 October 1961, written by one of the children at the school to a friend in England, said: 'We are having a lot of landslides which is cause by a heavy shaking, which starts on the six of August and are still going on yet. We have had a large landslide just as I am writting this letter.'

A large bubble of earth near the village had taken on the shape of a volcanic cone, and early on Tuesday 10 October it erupted. 'All the people were splendid,' continued the *Newsletter* article of October 1963, 'They were calm, and did all that they had to do without any panic or grumbles.' Miss Bennett left her classroom just as it was and, with all the men, women and children from the island, was evacuated to Nightingale Island and thence to Cape Town. Like the islanders, she met this challenge calmly and with courage, not knowing what the future would hold for any of them. She had continued with her work in her classroom until the last possible time, the date of 9 October 1961 which she had written on the blackboard remaining until the islanders' return some two years later.

On arrival in Cape Town, William Repetto told the friendly waiting crowds: 'When it's over, we'll go back.'[17] They were all confident that the evacuation would be for only a short time, but this was not to be the case. When it became clear that they could not return to Tristan for a considerable time, if at all, the islanders were all taken to Britain, arriving at Southampton on 3 November 1961 and cared for temporarily at Pendell Camp, a disused Army Camp in Surrey. This had been prepared within the previous few days for their arrival, some of the helpers coming from the senior classes from nearby schools. Many visitors had come to welcome them, including some familiar faces of administrators, clergy, teachers and friends who had been on the island. Sir Irving Gane reopened the Tristan Fund to help supply the islanders' needs. The administrator, Mr Wheeler, and the chaplain, the Reverend Jewell, remained with the islanders to help them to settle. Margaret Mackay reports: 'The seventy-two children were at the camp's prefab school. Father Jewell led me to the classroom where the elder half, the 10- to 15-year age-group, were having their lessons under their former Tristan teacher, the kindly Miss R. M. Downer. The girls were allowed to knit the perennial white stockings (with wool brought from home) while we talked.'[18]

Peter Munch captured some of the initial reactions of the Tristanians' arrival in England. 'The islanders stood out conspicuously among the English. They did not come entirely unprepared, however. For almost twenty years they had at least had some contact with the Outside World through the Station and its changing population. And they had received some measure of formal education through the school on Tristan, particularly in Standard English, resulting in some adaptation of their local dialect.'[19] Nevertheless, a considerable measure of culture shock was inevitable, not only in adjustment to English life and customs, but also in such matters as dress. They had been used to wearing their own homemade clothes, using basic designs and materials. Now they saw the choices available to their English counterparts.

The children were allocated a large room in the NAAFI building where there were many toys, books, puzzles and gramophone records to play with. The *Tristan da Cunha Newsletter* reported that at first most of them were apprehensive and overwhelmed, but soon 'after school hours we would find groups of these children dancing to the gramophone or pushing dolls out in their prams'. Several of the children enrolled as Guides or Brownies in nearby troops or packs.

Meanwhile permanent new homes at Calshot on Southampton Water in Hampshire were being completed for the Tristanians in the married quarters of a disused RAF Station. They transferred there in late January and shortly afterwards the children started to attend local schools. Their reactions and progress at school are well documented, both in the *Tristan Times* (October 1963) and in a long study undertaken by the Department of Psychology at University College, London. The latter reported that the Tristanians' initial arrival at their schools was noteworthy. 'The scene in the playground of the junior school was particularly striking, both during the morning and the dinner breaks. The Tristan children, as a whole, tended to be physically small and thin. They shivered in their thin, inadequate clothes, still with the Tristan molly caps and white knitted socks with coloured bands round the top. They huddled together in mute, wondering and rather frightened groups, eyeing their new companions apprehensively. The Tristan girls in the secondary school group were easily picked out too, partly because of their style of hair dressing, partly on account of their long mid-calf length dresses which stood out from the school uniforms of short skirts and blouses worn by the other girls. It was to be some time and involve considerable efforts on the part of others before the Tristan children adopted the clothes and took on the general appearance of the other school children.'[20]

The study predictably identified the major problems which faced the Tristanian children, particularly during the first six months. First they had to adjust to the longer journey to school, albeit local, and the separation from home and from their brothers and sisters, where differences in age made this inevitable. They were also changing to much larger classes and schools, and had to adapt to different teachers and to strange children. And also there were considerable differences in curricula and teaching methods.[21]

Many fundamental and less tangible factors continued to create problems for the young island children – such as differences in pronunciation and idioms of speech, in reluctance towards changing into standard wear for PE, and in the need to adapt to a range of specialist teachers covering a wide range of subjects, some of which were totally unfamiliar to the Tristanian children. 'Even those in the junior school felt somewhat at sea and relied a good deal upon each other for surreptitious help, which might have been called cheating if it had not been so open and naive.'[22]

According to the study, several of the children did make progress during their time in the English schools, particularly in reading. In general, though, the Tristan children had so many 'hurdles to jump' in these unfamiliar surroundings that their attainments did not reach those of the UK children. The study was of the opinion that: 'The acceptance of changed standards and demands was on the whole more striking among the secondary school children than among the juniors, who contrived in their tightly-knit groups to preserve the somewhat lethargic approach to self-improvement that had characterised most of them on arrival. One of the main stumbling blocks in both schools continued to be language, both oral and written work, in which they were still handicapped when they left in October 1963.' The study concluded: 'Taking the group as a whole they remained for the most part closely integrated, rather passive, peace-loving children, not outstanding in ability, content with their own company and their own ways of life.'[23]

Without doubt most of the children and their parents were waiting for the day when they could go home. To quote the *Tristan Times* of October 1963: 'They could not conceal their homesickness and their longing to return to their beloved island.' They would not have much longer to wait. Writing later, Dr Hilary Jones said: 'The Tristan Islanders have seen what is on the other side of the fence, and on closer inspection the grass is not as green as they thought it might be. For two years they were offered our modern industrialized society on approval. But their final decision was quite unanimous. They are grateful for the experience in England but in reality they are quite satisfied exactly where they are.'[24]

1963-74: Life begins again on Tristan da Cunha

In preparation for the return of the islanders to Tristan after the evacuation for two years, the Africa Sub-Committee of the SPG considered a new draft constitution for the school at their meeting in March 1963, as recorded in the *Minutes*. Its name was confirmed as 'St Mary's School'. The Head Teacher was to be responsible to the Administrator for the running of the school, appointed by the Secretary of State for the Colonies with the advice of the SPG, contracted to the Government of St Helena, paid by the Tristan Administration, and a communicant member of the Church of England or of a Church in full communion with the Church of England. Assistant teachers were to be appointed by the Administrator in consultation with the Head Teacher and paid by the Tristan Administration. The Chaplain, licensed by the Anglican Archbishop of Cape Town for Tristan da Cunha, was to be responsible for conducting school worship and religious instruction at times agreed by the Head Teacher, parents having the right to withdraw their children from these if they wished, and to have alternative provision made if possible.

The Head Teacher appointed, now by the Government, was Jim Flint, who had been teaching in Epping, Essex. He had opportunity to get to know many of his future charges before starting to teach them as he travelled to Tristan together with the main party of islanders returning after the eruption. He even surprised himself in applying for the post, but his interest in the island had been aroused when he had taught his class of children in England about Tristan and the volcanic eruption.

Two advance parties of Tristanians, the second with Administrator Peter Day, had done what they could to prepare for the arrival of the large proportion of islanders who had chosen to return to their homeland. Apart from the canning factory and one homestead, all the

Children on Tristan with the School Crest designed in their Art lessons, 1963

other buildings in the small community had survived the eruption, but had, of course, been affected by being abandoned for two years. The *National Geographic Magazine* in January 1964 described the return and captured the general thankfulness of the islanders, quoting one of them who said: 'Our fourth day on the island, Good Friday, was devoted to rest and worship. In the absence of a chaplain, Administrator Peter Day – Great Britain's representative on the island – conducted the simple yet moving service.'[25]

Mr Flint arrived on the island to take up his post in November 1963 and, in an unpublished document written later, he tells a graphic story of the condition of the school. 'It [the school] was well stocked with textbooks, stationery – and mice! In the absence of other food they had found the glue in book binding palatable and the spines of many volumes were ruined. The classrooms had a *Mary Celeste* atmosphere, work done in pre-volcano days hanging on the walls and a blackboard still bearing the date "October 9th, 1961". One desk contained the rock hard remains of a half eaten sandwich.' During the first three weeks relays of cleaners went into the school to scrub floors, wash desks and clean windows, and it was ready for the 45 children to start school on 28 November. 'On the very first day one boy ran away, as the other children had predicted. It was, it seemed, a regular habit and, after four months of holiday, the prospect of school once more was too much for him.' However, the next morning he was back in school and his little escapade was ignored.[26]

For the short term before Christmas the children were in three age groups, being taught by Mr Flint and three pupil teachers – Gerald Repetto, Rosemary Green and Caroline Swain. Mr Flint found that the majority of the children were easily stimulated to learn to read and write, but had less enthusiasm for other subjects, for which they saw no particular use. 'Why do we want to know about Japan, sir?' queried one girl at the beginning of a geography lesson. Nevertheless, he decided to keep the syllabus approximately to the work which pupils of similar age would be doing in an English school, as it was by no means certain that the return to Tristan would be permanent. If the harbour plans failed the children might well have found themselves completing their education in the English school which they had recently left. At the same time he felt it important to preserve the particular way in which the islanders spoke, rather than force them to use English English; island English was part of the heritage of the people.   After Christmas, when Jim Flint had had opportunity to assess their ability, the children were graded into four classes and four new infants were added to the roll. The infants attended school in the mornings only, but the junior, middle and senior classes attended all day. Father Keith Flint, the Chaplain, [no relation to Jim Flint] took charge of the teaching of Scripture, and he also taught the pupil teachers in an after-school lesson. Mrs Penny Day, the wife of the Administrator, took successful cookery lessons with the girls, but the boys' gardening lessons met with less success due to high winds and pests. To bring up the standard of reading, particularly with the junior children, extra classes were held after school on four days each week.

The visit of the Governor of St Helena on 20 April provided a highlight in the school year, with a very satisfactory showing of work and pictures done by the children. In his first year's *Report on Education 1963-1964* the Headmaster felt that generally speaking the children seemed alert and interested in their work, though some suffered from lamentably short memories. By the end of the year only six children were seriously backward in reading. The Seniors had become very interested in a game of their own invention – a mixture of rounders and cricket played on the tennis court, which was originally the Quarter Deck of the wartime Naval Station.

In the next school year, Gerald Repetto left and Pamela Lavarello returned for a term to the teaching role she had had prior to the eruption, and then her place was taken by Trina Repetto. Films were now used in the senior class for the first time. With the recent world-wide interest in Tristan, so many requests came from children abroad for pen friends that it soon became impossible to find anyone to reply. To avoid disappointment the Tristan children wrote and duplicated a booklet entitled *South Atlantic Island*, to send in response to these requests. After introducing the reader to 'The small windswept islands of Tristan da Cunha', the young writers say: 'Tristan has had many books written about it which will give you far more information than this one, but so far this is the only one written by the people of Tristan themselves. We hope you will find our story interesting.' After a few geographical facts and figures, the booklet gives a brief history of early settlers, followed by short sections on the Garrison, the wreck of HMS *Julia*, the seven families on the island, the new Bedford Whalers, the Second World War, recent history, the volcano, 'Our Tristan Houses', livestock, the potato patches, fishing, 'Tristan Today' and 'Work since we came back'. The booklet is illustrated by the children's own sketches. The events of 1961 make colourful reading:

THE 1961 VOLCANO

When the volcano erupted near the Village we were in School. We went to the potato patches for the night but had to come back next morning to get out to the fishing ships by Longboats. The Volcano was smoking and big red rocks were flying out.

We went to Nightingale Island 25 miles away. Next morning a ship arrived and took us to Cape Town. From South Africa we went to England.

For 3 months we lived in Surrey and for a year and a half at Calshot near Southampton.

An Expedition to Tristan said that the volcano had stopped erupting and our houses were safe. So in November 1963 we all returned to Tristan.

One house had been burnt and the beaches were buried under the lava but we were all happy to be home again.[27]

In his last report before leaving on 10 December 1965, Mr Flint pointed out that, compared with the seniors, the younger children were poor at expressing themselves, so he had placed an emphasis on oral work, such as discussions.

Reflecting on his life and experiences on Tristan, Mr Flint recalled that games and handwork were clearly the most popular subjects with the children at the school. A natural swimming pool had formed itself in the heart of the lava field, not only with a shallow and a deep end, but also with underground heating from the lava! For anyone swimming too deep the water became too hot. Sadly a storm destroyed the

St Mary's School, 1965

pool after about six months, so swimming had to be from the beach 'but the cold waters of the South Atlantic were a poor substitute for our lava-heated lake', wrote Mr Flint. In one of the art lessons in school the children designed their own school badge 'and a mixture of their ideas were incorporated into the brightly painted shield which we added to the school gate. On a background of blue sea and sky, an open book of learning is surrounded by four stars – the shape of the Southern Cross which shines most nights above the cliffs, and also symbolizing the long-standing link between school and church. The letters SMS appear above the badge on an outline of the island, and the motto sums up the school's aim to give its pupils "Wider Horizons".'[28]

Thinking of the future, Mr Flint forecast: 'Now that the Tristans are settled once more on their island, a school syllabus which gave a grounding in the basic subjects followed by courses emphasizing cookery, needlework, woodwork and agriculture would seem the most practical for the future needs of the community. A major part of any future Agricultural Officer's job might be the running of a model farm with the senior boys and incorporating the neglected forestry work into the school curriculum.' Writing *Some Thoughts on the future of Education on Tristan da Cunha*, Mr Flint emphasized that it would be through the children that any long-term changes in agricultural and conservation practices would be effected and that therefore it was vital that the curriculum should reflect the need to ensure that the islanders' existence in future would not become entirely dependent on the factory and store, and that the most economic use be made of the resources of the island. Otherwise should the crawfish industry diminish, the islanders may need to abandon their homes and their way of life.[29]

Jim Flint's work on Tristan was clearly a highlight of his career. The island and its welfare are still, in 1992, of high interest and importance to him.[30]

When Mr H. Burton joined St Mary's School as Head Teacher in 1966 there were 40 children in the school between the ages of four and 15. His colleagues were three local teachers, two of them pupil teachers in their first term of teaching. The children were divided into four classes – seniors (11-15), juniors (9-11), middle (7-9) and infants (4-7).

His comprehensive *Report on Education 1966* referred to the long document produced by Ronald Harding some 12 years before. Mr Burton described the poor condition of the school building and the shortage of equipment, and to emphasize his point he remarked: 'There is an adequate supply of paint, but no paint brushes and a good supply of pens and nibs but no ink!' He was concerned that the reports made on the progress of the children served little purpose because they went only to the Administrator and not to the parents. Nevertheless he and his teachers were aiming to ensure that each child would be able to make as great and as useful a contribution to the life of the island as lay within his/her capabilities. Unfortunately it was not possible to run an evening school as there was no lighting. In acknowledging the report, the administrator addressed the head master as education officer, the first specific use of this title.

The subject of education on Tristan featured as a regular item in the *St Helena Annual Reports*. In 1967 it was reported that the 49 children at school during the year had maintained their excellent 99% attendance, pupil teachers from the island had gone to St Helena for training, and plans for the new school building were approved. Several major worldwide bodies had taken an interest in Tristan and supported island projects financially. For instance, the Gulbenkian Foundation sponsored the playing fields and children's playground, donations from Canada and the British Council promoted the development of the new Public Library and the school library, and the local Fishing Company provided the Youth Club with equipment.

J. M. Lewis followed as education officer for a few months, but he found it difficult to acclimatize to the island and chose to return to the

UK before the end of his contract time. Ian Fleming took over and submitted the *1968 Education Report*. He recommended that the island should explore the possibility of using a 'mode 3' type of CSE examination particularly relevant to the local situation for selected islanders and expatriate children, and also a liaison with appropriate authorities for taking the 11+ (presumably for those expatriate children who would be returning to the UK), and the GCE. However, Mr Fleming also soon left the post to become the island's Administrator, and the school was left in the charge of a local team of teachers.

The *St Helena Annual Reports for 1968* and *1969* recorded a stability in the number of children in the school being taught in four classes. One local teacher had returned from training in St Helena to join other local colleagues at the school, and there was also a VSO volunteer in the school to assist with the teaching. Materials for the largely pre-fabricated school had now arrived on the island and it was anticipated that, at last, construction would begin.

The long-awaited new school building was still far from being completed, the predicted date of opening being postponed until 1975. But other activities were proceeding with more success, including the Public Library, which was receiving regular donations of books from the Renfurly Library in London. Several youth organizations were similarly flourishing, including Cubs, Brownies, Girl Guides and Sea Scouts.

Before Kenneth Schurch arrived to take up the post in June 1971 the island had been without a UK education officer for over a year. During this time a dispute between the school staff and the Administration had resulted in the appointment of a local Acting Education Officer, but further disputes arose causing concern among the parents and the Education Committee, and the work of the school became seriously unsettled. However, these matters were resolved after Mr Schurch's arrival in June 1971. Mr Schurch well remembers his introduction to teaching on the island. Poised to start his first lesson, he saw a large rat appear from a hole in the floor, run across the room and disappear down another hole. Nothing daunted, he continued with his lesson.

Mr Schurch's *Report on Education 1971* recorded that there were 52 pupils in the school, including seven expatriates, being taught by three local teachers and the headmaster, and the island minister assisted with religious instruction and school assemblies. During Term 3 the normal excellent attendance record had been lowered to 91.28% due to an influenza epidemic following the visit of the MFV *Tristania*. Like his predecessors, Mr Schurch had to report on the poor condition of the building: 'The fabric is in a state one would expect in a wooden building which has been standing since 1942,' but he was able to strike a note of optimism, saying that 'During December, part of the site chosen for the new school was again bull-dozed flat'. A new curriculum was in course of preparation and two adult education classes had been conducted by three expatriates, including Mrs Schurch. It was hoped that, alongside the Sea Scouts, Guides and Brownies, there would soon be a youth club as well as participation for the first time in the Duke of Edinburgh's Award Scheme. The island Library was straining its shelf space to the limit with 3,000 books, thanks to the Renfurly Library and the Cape Town Library, but the main clients were the children. Special teaching was being given to an island child with hearing and speech difficulties.

In spite of all its diverse responsibilities and difficulties the school had staged a highly enjoyable production of *Alice in Wonderland* – a most appropriate choice for Tristan, remembering the work there decades before of the Reverend E. H. Dodgson, the brother of its author Lewis Carroll.

Meanwhile, in a study published in 1971 concerning the problems and opportunities of the isolation of Tristan da Cunha, three researchers – Lewis, Roberts and Edwards – discussed the future in relation to the important role of education. After describing the bleakness of the island, the researchers suggested that the relatively low level of attainment of the children could be due to two main factors – inbreeding, and the lack of mental stimulation for the young minds. But, that on one side, they stressed the need to ask the question 'What sort of education is best suited to the realistic needs of the Tristan islanders?' They urged strongly that there was a need for a specially imaginative type of education, especially devised for their isolated circumstances. 'It should be based on rural studies, or the modern concept "ecological studies". The foundation should be a showpiece school farm, where gradually, over a few years, the benefits of rational practice would become obvious. It is usually prudent in the long run to invest in the children – that is, of course, if the country can afford to wait a decade.'[31]

Mr Schurch's last *Education Report* before his departure in 1973 expressed regret that, regarding the new school building, 'the only visible progress which has been made is the laying of the foundations, the first stone of which was laid in August'. However, in spite of this, the work of the school had proceeded apace and, in addition to all the regular subjects, cookery had been reintroduced into the curriculum, and also included were an improved gardening course, rural studies, animal husbandry, and rural science. The school had relied heavily on the teaching input of the chaplain and several expatriate people – Mrs Schurch taught cookery; Mrs Loretta Richardson, English; Mr Jack, gardening; Drs Mantle and Jenkins, biology; and Mrs Claxton, dancing. The newly formed youth club was struggling, due to lack of members, but the Duke of Edinburgh's Award Scheme had got off the ground with one candidate, Wendy Swain. That year the island had been entertained by a production of *Snow White and the Seven Dwarfs*.

Like others before him, Mr Schurch (now Dr Schurch, Deputy Head of the Lord Williams' School, Thame, Oxfordshire) looks back on his experiences on Tristan with particular pleasure. It was very early in his career that he had applied for the post, so naturally in hindsight and with the benefit of a career in teaching he feels he would probably now undertake some of his work differently. Nevertheless, he had tackled his wide-ranging task on the island wholeheartedly and with energy. He maintains a lifetime's interest in the island and its people and is still in touch with a number of islanders.[32]

When she took over as Education Officer in June 1973 Mrs M. E. (Loretta) Richardson had the advantage of having been on the island for several months. Her *Education Report* at the end of 1973 stated that the 56 children were being taught in four classes:

Mrs Marlene Swain, with 18 infants
Mrs Yvonne Glass, with 8 middle year children
Miss Asturias Repetto, with 13 juniors
Mrs Richardson, with 17 seniors

The building was now described as derelict, but the completion date for the new school building seemed to be receding further and further away. In spite of this, the wide-ranging activities of the school proceeded, including swimming – 'on fine days the whole school now goes in the water and at least two teachers join them'. During this year the now-traditional end of year production entertained the islanders with *Cinderella*, in which every child in the school took part. Sadly the youth club was disintegrating and the one Duke of Edinburgh candidate had left the island.

In her final *Education Report* produced at the end of 1974 Mrs Richardson was able to affirm that the new school was nearly completed and she hoped to move in by Christmas. All the activities of the school had been progressing satisfactorily during the year and, despite much opposition, a flourishing playgroup had been established, run by two expatriate helpers. Mrs Richardson thanked many people for their support and concluded: 'The future of education looks bright for the youth of Tristan. There can be no doubt that a pleasant environment engenders happier children, not to say staff.'

1975-82: A New School for Tristan

The successor to Mrs Richardson, Nigel Humphries, had spotted the advertisement for the post of Education Officer for the island of Tristan da Cunha in the *Times Educational Supplement* in June 1974. It had made quite clear the extent of the job:

To be in charge of the island school which has 50 all-age pupils (5-15 years); to teach the senior class; to be involved in youth work; to initiate evening classes for adults; to co-operate with the Chaplain in the religious education of children; to organize the Library; to take part in local broadcasting; and to assist with the education of expatriate children.

Nothing daunted – in fact, challenged – by the task he applied for the post and was successful. He arrived on the island early in 1975 and, in addition to the published tasks, found himself also to be Entertainments Officer, Clerk of the Court and the main Radio Announcer. Shortly after settling in he had the distinction and the excitement of moving into the new school building. The move itself was not without incident because on the day scheduled for it, Friday 6 June, there was a violent north-east wind and torrential rain, so it was postponed until the following Monday when, at 1.30 pm the school moved and at 5.00 pm it was declared open. After assembly the next morning, the first lessons began. But Mr Humphries was not the only excited one, as described in his *1975 Report of Education*: 'On the day when the children moved in, Monday 9 June, they sat spellbound for nearly two hours at the sheer delight of the bright airy comfortable classrooms.'

His description of the school is included here in its entirety, as it not only gives a graphic visual picture but also indicates some of the challenges of the move:

The new St Mary's School is situated on a gentle slope to the east of the village, overlooking the playing field and the sea. The classrooms and hall are situated around a central quadrangle laid out to grass. There is a colonnade around which gives adequate protection from bad weather. At the entrance way to the east are toilet and cloakroom facilities. The hall is a particularly fine feature of the school, being equipped with a raised stage, lighting and mechanically operated curtains. A hatchway leads in from the domestic science room enabling the service of refreshments when the need arises such as at youth club.

During the latter days of the school's construction it became evident that the child population would be well above the 50 catered for. A peak of 70 would be reached towards the end of the year. It was decided that the school would have five classes instead of four. The woodwork room which was the same size as a standard classroom became Class II and the library-cum-staffroom became the woodwork room. Additional shelves were placed in the head teacher's office to accommodate excess books, but most books are in the classrooms apart from teachers' books and handicraft books.

Due to the increase in the school population and subsequent additional class, a new member of staff was appointed at the time of the move to the new school. The post was advertised and the candidates sat an examination and were interviewed by the Education Committee.

Mr Humphries was keen for the level of teaching to be improved and in general for the standing of the teachers to be strengthened. A number of staff changes were introduced. One teacher left the staff, and Mrs Marlene Swain took over the new post of Senior Mistress in the school. The 67 children were grouped as follows:

Class I: 14 reception infants, with Trina Repetto
Class II: 12 infants, with Yvonne Glass
Class III: 14 lower juniors, with Marlene Swain
Class IV: 12 upper juniors, with Anne Green
Class V: 15 seniors, with the Education Officer

He listed the members of the Education and Social Welfare Committee:

Education Officer (Chairman)
Chief Islander Albert Glass
Councillor Harold Green
Councillor Lars Repetto
Councillor Mrs Pamela Lavarello

This Committee met at regular intervals at the new school or the Council Chambers to discuss matters of school business, acting in an advisory capacity, and they also participated in the interviews for new teachers. Mr Humphries paid tribute to 'the work and wisdom of this group who have the interests of the school at heart'.

After reporting fully on the curriculum and activities in the school, Mr Humphries concluded gratefully: 'The building is conducive to advancement in learning and an encouragement to the teachers. The Department has enjoyed a most fruitful year of change and looks forward to a year of consolidation and steady progress in 1976.' A matter for concern was the difficulty in finding suitable candidates to enter teaching. He made a study of the likely numbers of children on the school roll over the next five years, forecasting that the number would fluctuate within the 60s, from 69 in 1975 to 65 in 1979.

Mr Humphries' confidence in the school was well-founded, his *Education Report for 1976* showing steady progress on all fronts. However, he identified some deficiencies in the system of having only one teacher to a class with a wide range of ability. 'Certain pupils would benefit from a more advanced course, justifying the appointment of a suitably qualified teacher for Maths, English and General Science to O-level, leaving the Education Officer free to concentrate on other problems, especially reading, and the running of the school.' During the year he had taken UK leave and had made some useful visits to UK schools. Also during the year, the nucleus of a museum had been started on Tristan.

The *1977 Education Report* was the final one submitted by Mr Humphries, who by the time of his departure would have served three and a half years on Tristan. He had been joined in May by Miss Christine Stone as Senior Teacher, with a responsibility for the senior class and the teaching of science. The customary comprehensive report described steady and consistent progress throughout the year, but one problem was highlighted: 'By the time children reach the Senior Class, environmental factors are a great problem. Very few Tristan homes have any books. The Tristan vocabulary in general use is very limited and then in a dialect based on the spoken word and not the written. Such deficiencies are very difficult to overcome. This is coupled with an innate lack of drive for a goal, that has yet to be seen'. A system of awards improved motivation and a Speech Day had been held in June, the Administrator, Mr S.G. Trees, presenting certificates for excellence, good work and progress; the Fursey Cup for unselfish service; and the Day Cup (given by former Administrator, Peter Day and his wife, Mrs Penny Day) for endeavour.

The traditional theatrical performances had been given and 'some Tristan children are becoming quite gifted little actors and actresses'. Each class had produced a play for the Christmas Concert, involving them also in the making of costumes and scenery. Further Education had moved forward apace, there being fifteen students taking between them English, Maths and Art. The Youth Club, too, had had a successful year, the members organizing a rich programme of outdoor games, rambles, badminton, table tennis, monthly dances and feature films. Interest had been taken in the island Archives, these including a Tristan oxcart and wheelbarrow, and maps of Tristan and its neighbouring islands. The overseas programme was giving opportunity to three islanders to go to the UK; D.Rogers was taking a course in Agriculture, another young man in the Post and Telegraph Department was preparing to go abroad, and a boy with severe hearing loss was about to join Boston Spa School for the Deaf, where he would learn carpentry and garden skills.

Mr Humphries concluded: 'During the last three and a half years there has been much change, and that for the better. There has also been a marked change in attitudes and ideals. If the present system is maintained, it will be with confidence that Tristan da Cunha will be able to accept more responsibility in the running of their affairs, and welfare, with islanders becoming much more equipped to do so.' He produced some 'Handing Over Notes' for his successor, describing succinctly all the organizational and management matters related to the school and to the wide role of the Education Officer.

Nigel Humphries' period of time as Education Officer for Tristan da Cunha was a challenging and important part of his career. In his home named after the island, he enjoys recalling his experiences and maintains a lively interest in its affairs.[33]

J.Whittington succeeded Mr Humphries. In his January 1979 report he said that he was impressed with what he found when he took up his role as Education Officer in September 1978. 'The four local teachers have all shown themselves to be hard-working, enthusiastic and interested in the education of the children in their care; ideals missing in many highly qualified teachers the world over. The children are hardworking, polite and sympathetic to each others' difficulties. The atmosphere of the school is very pleasant. It is one of quiet industry with an undertone of cheerfulness.'

However, echoing the thoughts of leading teachers a century before, he felt concern that the school's horizon was one of uncertainty, as it lacked a school policy for the future, and challenging questions must be faced. He asked: 'What is the aim of education on Tristan? Is it necessary to teach school subjects to a higher level to children who are unlikely to leave Tristan, to children who, when they grow up, will become fishermen, housewives and subsistence farmers? Is it right that through a better education the expectations of the children be raised to the point where they may wish to leave the island and seek their living abroad?'

He identified a need for island teachers to be given opportunities for overseas training, so that the lack of continuity provided by expatriate teachers on their comparatively short periods of service would be offset by island teachers taking responsibility for subject areas and interests.

He believed that a Tristan Certificate of Education or a CSE would be far more worthwhile and appropriate than GCE O-level. He concluded his report:

Education on Tristan da Cunha is at the cross-roads. It can either leap forward or it can sit back and stagnate. I believe that for the good of the children on the island and for those islanders who wish to avail themselves of the advantages of a reasonable education, it must leap forward. This inevitably means money must be spent on education, more money. It means that the teachers must be prepared to go abroad for further training, it means that everyone connected with education must work harder, from the Education Committee to the youngest pupil. But it also means that the children of Tristan will be better equipped not only to understand their life on Tristan but also the workings of the outside world. There is no reason, given a sound education policy, why many posts, at present filled by expatriate officers, could not be filled by qualified islanders in the future.

By the time he produced his *Education Report for 1979*, Mr Whittington's idealism of the previous year had been influenced by his further year's experience, and he felt that some of the uncertainty had been dispelled. It had been agreed informally that the aim of education on Tristan was to equip the child for life in the twentieth century and not merely to allow him to get by on Tristan. More formal discussions were pending with the teachers, Education Committee, Island Council and the Administrator, to produce a written policy to give guidelines for the future. Miss Short had been appointed as Community Development Officer, leading a newly formed Community Development Committee. This had taken over certain areas of responsibility previously held by the Education and Social Welfare Committee. Mr Whittington had had a very encouraging year, but stressed that improvements noted would only continue if in-service work for teachers received a high priority.

During 1980 Mr Whittington was away from the island for two periods and each time on his return was disappointed at the lax and undisciplined condition of the school, but he was pleased on other fronts – agreement on an Education Policy, a three-year contract for a trainee to become equipped on the island to enter a teacher training course in the UK, generous grants to increase the number of reference books and to convert the entrance hall into a resource area, and progress related to Tristan's involvement with the St Helena Link Committee in Cheltenham.

In his last *Education Report 1981* Mr Whittington was gratified that many islanders were becoming involved with community activities, including taking the sole charge of the senior and junior youth clubs, and the Scouts, Guides, Brownies and Cubs. A Liberal Studies programme had been launched for anyone to attend, each session taught by an islander or an expatriate volunteer according to their chosen subject or expertise. The results of the CSE examinations taken in May 1980 had been gratifying, with eleven subject passes across English Language, Religious Studies and Geography. He reported that the subject list would be widened to include Maths and General Science in 1981.

1982-92: Widening of Opportunities at Home and Abroad

Mrs Marlene Swain was Acting Education Officer for the brief time between Mr Whittington's departure in 1981 and the arrival of J.H.Cooper in March 1982. In his first *Education Report* submitted to the island Council in December 1982, Mr Cooper stated that there were 66 children, in five classes, with six teachers, including one from the UK, and two local teachers with the 9- to 11-year-olds. However, he made a forecast of school numbers, drawing attention to a significant decline over the next five years, which would have an important bearing on the school.

	SCHOOL	PLAYGROUP
1983	56	6
1984	49	8
1985	36	10
1986	33	(unknown, 5+)
1987	34	(unknown)

Nevertheless, he reported 21 passes in GSE subjects taken in May 1981 by the current school leavers, with particularly pleasing results in Science of seven passes, five at Grade 3 or above. Of nine candidates taking GCE English Language, two had achieved a Grade A, one each at Grades B, C, D and E, and three ungraded. Mr Cooper was also able to report that Marlene Swain had gone to England to spend a year at a school in Bristol, as arranged by the British Council.

Mr Cooper's *Education Report* for 1983 welcomed 'the most exciting event of the year', which was the offer of free education at Denstone College in the UK for up to three candidates per year from Tristan. This had arisen following a visit by a party of boys and a master, Michael Swales, from Denstone College, an independent secondary school in Staffordshire. They were visiting Tristan after an expedition to Inaccessible Island and the visitors joined their Tristanian counterparts in undertaking projects for their local studies. It was clear to the visitors that there was no further education beyond GCSE, and this would handicap the island in the long term. So in order to repay the islanders for their generous hospitality, the offer was made for young people from Tristan to continue their education up to A-levels. This offer was taken up readily, and by September two sisters, Lorna and Valerie Lavarello, were on their way.

Commenting in 1992 about the success of the scheme over the ensuing years, Michael Swales explained that the link owes its origin to the Gough Island Scientific Survey of 1955-56. Mr Swales was the vertebrate zoologist on that expedition, which spent some six weeks on Tristan before going on to Gough Island. During that time the islanders and visitors became well acquainted, and the visitors realized that the educational achievements of the children fluctuated according to teaching strength at the time. Subsequently, Mr Swales organized and led the Denstone Expedition to Inaccessible Island in 1982-83, four of the islanders participating in the expedition and some of the visitors involving themselves in teaching on Tristan. While on Tristan, they were also asked to advise on the setting up and the initial implementation of a GCSE syllabus for 'Tristan Studies', this being based on local topics including history, geography, biology and crafts. In this way, a close liaison was built up between the Denstone visitors and the islanders. Of the subsequent take-up of places at Denstone College, Mr Swales reported: 'The Tristanians showed themselves to be highly adaptable, hard-working and very capable. So they suffered few ill effects and overcame the culture shock involved in coming to England and into an English public school remarkably quickly. All have achieved well also and gone on to apply the new skills learnt.'[34]

A further overseas link was established in 1983, this being through correspondence and the exchange of local information with the Hervé Bazin School near Orleans in France. Monsieur Bazin was the author of *Tristan*, a book based on the real-life experiences of the islanders around the time of the volcanic eruption.

As a former primary school teacher, Mr Cooper's concern in his *1983 Education Report* was the level of provision for the lower-aged children compared with that for the seniors. He determined to redress the balance in the areas of reading, mathematics and general English, including remedial work. He paid tribute to the stimulus provided by his colleague, Richard Grundy, and sought continuation for the post of Senior Teacher. During the year a new Education By-law had been introduced in September 1984 which legalized visits to neighbouring Nightingale Island by schoolchildren during term-time, this enhancing their CSE Tristan Studies work. In conclusion he stressed again the vital importance, to the future of the school, of teacher training for local staff.

On her return home to Tristan after her year in the UK, Marlene Swain reported in the *Tristan Times* of May 1984: 'You don't realise what you are missing, until you leave home and go to another country. The things I took for granted on Tristan, I didn't appreciate until I went to Britain ... I longed for a bit of the peace and quiet of Tristan ... It took me only a year away from home to realize how lucky we are to be living on Tristan da Cunha.' Meanwhile, Lorna Lavarello was sending back news of her life at Denstone, describing her pursuit of A-level studies in the fully occupied day from early morning to late at night, with both formal and informal activities.

Mr Cooper's final *Education Report* in 1984 traced the decline in the birthrate and the consequent plans to reduce the number of classes to four. Mrs Swain would remain on the teaching staff but as a floating teacher. The 1984 CSE results across eight subjects (including Tristan Studies) were extremely gratifying, with 42 passes, including six at Grade 1, and only four unclassified results. Another islander was at Denstone College. The local Government had decided that places at Denstone should be given only to islanders who had a definite post on the island when they returned. This was an attempt to bring qualified people back to Tristan, the particular need being for nurses and teachers. He urged for more opportunities to be made available for Tristanians to take off-island training in order to be able to return with new skills and techniques – particularly with the localization of some island posts. Once again it had been the turn of *Snow White and the Seven Dwarfs* to provide the major school production for a delighted island audience. Mr Cooper concluded his final report on a high note: 'The general policies now operating, with more children taking examinations while still at school full-time, and more local staff teaching examination courses, providing a continuity impossible with changing expatriate teachers, should lead to continuing improvements in external examination results. I see every reason at the moment for the general standard of education on Tristan da Cunha to continue to improve.'

S. V. Townsend took over the role of Education Officer in 1985, and he recorded in his *1985 Report on Education* that his initial reaction to his new post had been one of disappointment about poor standards of work, record keeping, teaching and the school building itself. The local teachers were keen but lacked training, and only two could participate in teaching examination classes. He felt that staff training was essential, together with careful discussion about the aims and objectives of education on Tristan. The traditional egalitarian way of life meant that the local people were reluctant to take leadership roles, only two being willing to lead the Brownies and Guides. Mr Kerr was leading the youth work, including the Sea Scouts.

By the time he wrote his second *Education Report* in 1986 most of the ills had been remedied, and he was far more optimistic. A structured teacher training programme was being developed; the CSE results had shown improvement; the first candidates had embarked on the new GCSE course; a small basic microcomputer had entered a Tristan classroom for the first time; but still the reticence of local teachers to assume responsibility was a cause for concern. 'I am concerned for the immediate future of the school without an expatriate senior teacher. Local staff still need to be encouraged to exercise responsibility both in school and in extra-curricular activities.'

A long-awaited swimming pool was completed in 1985 and was formally opened on 23 November. This was very much welcomed and special times were set aside for the use of the school. It had been a long time since some islanders had enjoyed swimming in the heated water of the natural pool warmed by the volcano in 1963.

In an article which he wrote for the *Tristan Times* in May 1987 entitled 'St Mary's School – Twelve Years On', the Head Master gave a full account of the diverse activities of the school, ranging over a good range of CSE passes; the introduction of a two-year in-service training scheme developed in consultation with Peter Scopes, Senior Education Adviser to the ODA and the St Helena Link Committee based at Cheltenham; recreational activities, including swimming in the new pool, and athletics; the Duke of Edinburgh's Award Scheme; and a Youth Group, Scouts, Guides and Brownies. Mr Townsend's article concluded: 'All in all, those responsible for the provision of the new school on Tristan can rest assured that twelve years later it is still being put to good use.'

Mr Townsend's final *Education Report* in 1987 explained the introduction of the Tristan Certificate for the Tristan Studies programme in future. One islander was undertaking nursing training in the UK and four young men were attending the Trades School on St Helena. There had been some delay regarding launching the UK teacher training programme, and the pursuance of a local programme of training needed to be followed up subject to available staffing. Highlights of the school year had included a highly successful Sports Day and a production of *Charlie and the Chocolate Factory*.

In conclusion, Mr Townsend urged that serious consideration be given to the provision of further education and training for employment, this being particularly important to the girls, who were leaving school with better qualifications than the boys.

When James Kerr took over as Headmaster from Mr Townsend in 1988 he had already spent a considerable period of time working in the school. He also had the advantage of considerable experience of living on a remote island, having spent some of his childhood on St Helena while his father, Norman Kerr, was Education Officer there. On assuming the role of Education Officer himself, James Kerr knew what he wished to achieve in terms of school organization, staff training and curriculum reorganization. A key matter he was discussing with the Education and Social Welfare Committee, and subsequently with the island Council, was the proposal for the localization of the post of Education Officer at the conclusion of Mr Kerr's term of office.

In preparation for this, Mr Kerr worked closely alongside island teachers, other workers and expatriates in all aspects of educational work in order to prepare them to undertake future responsibility. Emphasis was given to curriculum development and staff training, health education, extra-curricular activities, sport, school reports and records, stock ordering and resources, library and building maintenance.

Mr Kerr's 1988 *Education Report* gave the results of the locally set and examined subject of Tristan Studies, for which four students gained passes and were awarded a certificate. Further plans were being developed for Mrs Marlene Swain and Mrs Anne Green to go to the UK for in-service training with the North Hertfordshire Education authority; one pupil, Iris Green, was taking A-levels at Denstone College, and Mr Kerr was investigating the possibility of sending students to St Helena for GCSE, A-levels or vocational training, in view of the introduction of the three-tier system of schooling there.

In October 1989 Mrs Marlene Swain, Assistant Education Officer and also Education Officer-designate for Tristan da Cunha, submitted the annual *Education Report* in the absence on leave of Mr Kerr. Discussions were proceeding and progress being made on all aspects of the previous report submitted by Mr Kerr, and in addition Mrs Swain was able to report on the widening educational opportunities being taken up by Tristanians going to the UK to study for A-levels or to train for teaching, electronics or nursing. Advantage had been taken of the expertise of visiting specialists during the year, and also an experimental Tristan Examinations Board had been officially recognized following its assessment of the Tristan Island Studies.

On his way back to Tristan after his leave in the UK, Mr Kerr visited St Helena in order to discuss and develop inter-island communication and liaison. He attended the meeting of the Education Committee on 31 January 1990 and discussed particularly the role which St Helena and the Prince Andrew School could play for senior and post-school students from Tristan. Possibilities included Tristanian students attending Prince Andrew School for GCSE and A-level courses, and for selected post-school students to go to St Helena for the two-year teacher training course or work experience. Mr Kerr stressed the need for occasional visits from the St Helena Education Officers to Tristan after December 1991 when the localization of the post of Tristan Education Officer would take effect.[35]

Mr Kerr's *Education Report* of 1990 described the first year of the two-year plan to localize the Education Department. Mrs Marlene Swain and Mrs Anne Green completed an eight-month training programme in Hertfordshire, UK, and on their return to Tristan Mr Kerr handed over the day-to-day running of the school to Mrs Swain, as Education Officer-designate and to Mrs Green, as Deputy Head, while he concentrated on teacher training. There were 41 children in four classes and a pre-school group; seven full-time staff and two part-time. Mr Kerr launched an island teacher training course, all teachers agreeing to attend two sessions per week. The school and public libraries had been amalgamated, with the continued support of the British Council and the Renfurly service. Extra-curricular activities continued also, with several islanders taking leading roles. Mr Kerr was pleased with progress towards localization.

Having spent extended times on Tristan, John Bailey, Dentist, his wife and their two children speak warmly of their experiences on the island. The school was able to offer a wide programme of subjects and activities, having adequate facilities and resources. Further educational opportunities were being taken up, including overseas training courses. Within the school the children were divided into two houses, Nightingale and Inaccessible, competing enthusiastically against each other in sport, drama and classwork. Pre-schooling was provided for children from the age of three and a half years. Out of school activities included Scouts, Guides, Cubs and Brownies and, of course, there was Sunday School. So the provision for children of school age was as wide as could be expected within the small community on Tristan.[36]

In the *1991 Report on Education*, the final one to be given by an expatriate Education Officer on Tristan da Cunha, Mr Kerr described the intensive work which had been carried out in teacher training and

St Mary's School, 1990 (Photograph taken by Jim Forsey, RMS St Helena)

At work in St Mary's School, 1990 (Photograph taken by Jim Forsey, RMS St Helena)

in helping Mrs Swain to undertake the management aspects of the role she was taking over from January 1992. Out of the current population of approximately 300, the number of children had gone down to 37, including four expatriate children who would be leaving the island shortly. Reading and mathematics tests recently administered had shown disappointing results, but were useful in highlighting the children's needs. The school had acquired its second computer during the year. The staff training sessions during the year had included some child psychology; the teaching of reading, handwriting, spelling and mathematics, marking, and the use of computers. Curriculum development sessions had dealt with the Tristan Education Policy and also policies related to mathematics, English, reading, marking and handwriting. A staff handbook had been devised to include documents from the courses. Extra-curricular activities were still proceeding well, including music lessons – in violin, guitar and keyboard, Adult Education Maths, Ladies' Keep-Fit, various fund-raising activities, participation in the English Schools Athletics Association's 'Milk in Action Award', and Sports Days. The Education Officer himself did a series of Sunday radio broadcasts on educational matters, including advising parents on encouraging their children to read. Particular interest was being shown by Tristanians in going to attend the Prince Andrew School and to undertake nurse training in St Helena. He was also able to report that four Tristanians were currently training in the UK – M.Repetto and R.Glass at Denstone; Ian Lavarello on radio training in Hertfordshire; and D.Rogers on an Agriculture course.

Concluding his report, Mr Kerr affirmed: 'I believe the staff, under the leadership of Marlene Swain, are capable of some self help and I hope they will continue the staff training and curriculum development sessions. They will eventually need some help from outside. I think that the best answer would be for a visiting specialist in a certain field to visit the island for a 1 to 3 month period every two or three years to investigate the current practices, make recommendations, train the staff concerned and help with the purchase of new equipment if needed.'

The time had come for another important 'beginning' in the history of education on the Island of Tristan da Cunha – the time when the key post of Education Officer was to be held by an islander for the first time since that post had been created. Mrs Marlene Swain became Education Officer and Head Teacher of St Mary's School in mid-January 1992.

Postscript: Twelve months later, in correspondence to a friend, Mrs Swain affirmed 'It has been a year now since I took up the post of Headmistress of the school. I have enjoyed every moment of it and I have my staff to thank for it as they have supported me all the way.'[37]

Part IV

The Falkland Islands

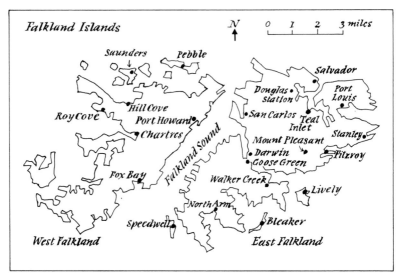

The Falkland Islands, showing places where schooling has been conducted

13
The Scattered Islands:
Education at School and at Home
1843-1969

With education it seems a case of doing all you can and in every way possible to school the children, a right which is theirs as citizens of a part of the British Empire.

F. McWhan, 1952[1]

1843-79: Schooling for the Early Settlers

The first sighting of the Falkland Islands occurred in August 1592 on the travels of Captain John Davis. However, the islands were not occupied until 1763, when the French took possession although the British were occupying the Port Egmont settlement on Saunders Island on West Falkland. Shortly afterwards the islands were bought by the Spaniards and held by Spain until the British Government commandeered them in 1832.[2] The strategically important position of the Falklands, particularly in times of war, was soon realized. In a document of 1840 from the Colonial Land and Emigration Commissioners to the Secretary of State for the Colonies, the islands were described as 'the Key to the Pacific, a Station and Depot for our Naval Force. It would appear to us that the Falkland Islands would be able to support a small body of Colonists of frugal and industrious habits.'[3] The Lieutenant-Governor of the Falklands, R.C.Moody, advised Lord Stanley in London: 'The settlers best adapted to colonize these islands would be from among the industrious population of the Orkney and Shetland Islands, accustomed to a hardy life, and as much seamen as landsmen.'[4] Accordingly, the Falklands developed as a British colony administered by the Admiralty. In 1843 a group of British settlers arrived, principally from Scotland and England. They became the first permanent community in Stanley and a Civil Government was established there. Since this was a small outpost of the British Empire, a colonial chaplain was appointed. This was the Reverend J.L.Moody, brother of the Governor, who was responsible to the Governor for supplying the islanders' spiritual and moral needs.

The chaplain accepted the responsibility of providing some form of education for the children of the families. In 1846 he sought financial assistance from the Government to establish a school in Stanley, emphasizing 'the extreme necessity of educating the rising generation in order that having been taught in their infancy to fear God and honour the Queen when they grow up they may become good Christians and loyal subjects'.[5] This school materialized and was housed in the Long Room of the Army Barracks situated in the dockyard in Stanley. Twelve children registered for the first class. The schoolmaster was a young man of 19, named Mr Brown, who had come from a merchant ship. He was paid £20 per year, plus rations, while the pupils were charged 6d per week. The colonial chaplain determined the course of instruction. Records indicate that another of the early teachers was a pensioner who had gone to the islands with a group of Out-Pensioners from the Royal Hospital, Chelsea.[6] He was not a qualified teacher but, with the guidance of the chaplain, he taught a basic curriculum. Although the chaplain was Anglican, the curriculum had no religious bias in order to avoid offending any of the settlers who were of several different denominations.

Within a year the little school had to move its premises to a building where the Speedwell Store is now sited (1992). Mr Brown was succeeded by another ex-merchant service man, Mr Hardy, who enjoyed considerable success with his teaching. The number of children increased rapidly over the next few years and in 1856, with a roll of 62, the school had another move, this time into the west wing of the newly constructed Exchange Building. The fees by this time had been reduced to 3d per week, as many parents could not afford 6d.

Meanwhile, in 1854 a small private school was opened in Stanley by Mrs Montague, the wife of a former magistrate. This was the first of the few private schools which have existed on the Falklands from time to time but, with the exception of a Roman Catholic school later on, their lives have been short.

In 1859 the Reverend Charles Bull MA, became the Colonial Chaplain with the additional role of Inspector of Schools. A qualified schoolmaster from England, G. Clarke, was appointed to teach at Stanley and he too succeeded in gaining general approval as 'an able and zealous teacher'.[7] At the same time, aware of the religious diversity of the islanders, Governor Moore issued a despatch which made it clear 'that no proceedings whatever can be permitted in the school which would offend the religious prejudices or feelings of persons not belonging to the Anglican Church'.[8] Nevertheless, shortly afterwards, in 1860, it became necessary for a public notice to be issued which allowed parents to withdraw their children from religious instruction and Bible reading if they so wished. In 1861 the Governor forbade the reading of the Bible in school, but apparently the determined chaplain continued to insist on having daily readings there, although he conducted his denominational teaching only in the church. This developed into a confrontation with new Governor Mackenzie in 1865, which resulted in the Reverend Bull asking to give up his duties as Inspector of Schools and the work in the school becoming secular only.

Mr Clarke continued enthusiastically as a teacher for many years and in 1870 Governor D'Arcy described the school as being very satisfactory. However, as the child population grew and the settlers became more scattered over the islands, so the problem of how these children could receive schooling became more acute. In his *1870 Report to the Secretary of State for the Colonies* the Governor put forward a possible suggestion by comparing the Falklands with the remoter parts of Scotland: 'In Scotland I am told such requirements are met by a mounted Schoolmaster who goes from cottage to cottage regularly remaining at each shepherd's hut a week leaving a task behind him to be learnt by his return.' Actually it was over 20 years before his suggestion was taken up and became an important and indispensible feature of schooling on the Falkland Islands.

In the meanwhile, however, the needs of the 'Camp' children, as the children in the outlying parts of the islands were called, were partially met by the opening of a school in Darwin in 1870 by the Falkland Islands Company, which had been established to manage land distribution and use. The settlers in Darwin erected a building to serve as a church and a school and the company appointed a schoolmaster from Britain. For many years this was a Scottish teacher with an MA qualification.

By 1871 the intrepid Reverend Bull succeeded in causing Governor D'Arcy to reinstate him as Inspector of Schools and to allow religious activities to take place in the schools again.[9] By 1872 the infant children were being taught in a school of their own, which had been set up in the mortuary. Over the years this school was destined to have several venues, including the Exchange Building, the Broadcasting Studio and the Barracks.

In 1872 the older children were being taught by Mr Clarke while his wife took the infants. Bell's System, the monitorial system which enabled larger numbers of children to be taught by their own senior members, was introduced. On Mr Clarke's death in 1874 the islands' gaoler, Mr Hocking, became temporary schoolmaster until a qualified successor came from Britain. This was J.W.Collins, a graduate of Edinburgh University. Although his work as schoolmaster helped to raise the educational standards, sadly he transgressed the law and departed from the islands three years later. His successor in 1877, Mr Taylor, lasted two months.

However, at this point, a noteworthy 'friend' of the Falkland Islands arrived. This was the Reverend Lowther E.Brandon who, in addition to his church responsibilities as colonial chaplain, took on the role of schoolmaster for the next 18 months, later to become Government Schools' Inspector. His service to the islands was to span over 30 years, during which time he helped to maintain and mould a system of education able to cater for the unusual circumstances of this colony, roughly half of the children living in Stanley while others were scattered all over the islands. Even after 25 years in the job he was reporting that 'the circumstances of the Colony in regard to education are peculiar'.[10] Cawkell, Maling and Cawkell state: 'It was Brandon who laid the foundations of education as we know it today in the Falklands.'[11]

In his capacity as Inspector of Schools during most of his time on the islands he submitted a thorough report each year on the state of education, having checked for himself not only the work of the schools, but also, whenever physically possible, he inspected the work of the travelling teachers and the small settlement schools. He campaigned tirelessly for compulsory education as far as it could be enforced in territory like the Falklands and, while despairing of some parents who failed to help their children to receive the schooling which was their right, he did not give up the battle to try to secure it for them.

1880-94: Efforts to bring Schooling to every Child

During the 1880s Governor Kerr was concerned that, even in Stanley where schooling was readily available, there were still many children who were not availing themselves of it. The schools already established were progressing reasonably well year by year for those children whose parents realized that education could benefit their offspring. However, in his annual report of 1885 he said this non-attendance was a matter for regret and he speculated upon the idea of introducing compulsory education, as already introduced in Britain. In the event this was not introduced for a further ten years.

A peat slip in 1886 badly damaged the Exchange Building in which the main school operated and it was moved to the loft of the dockyard store. This was clearly not suitable or convenient as a permanent site and in his report with the *1887 Blue Book* to the Secretary of State for the Colonies, the Governor requested that a new school house be built as soon as possible, but no ready answer came. From 1887 regular reports were provided by the Governor on the progress of education on the Falkland Islands, these for many years being produced by the Reverend Brandon in his capacity as Government Inspector of Schools. The 1887 report gives a clear indication of both the achievements and the challenges of making provision for this unique population. After stating that the numbers of children on the school rolls were 92 in the Infant School and 95 in the Senior School, he reported that the average attendance was only 65 and 70 respectively, but this still represented a slight improvement over the previous year. He drew the attention of the Governor to three matters:

(i) There are many children in Stanley of school age who seldom or never enter the schools and are receiving no education at home; this will continue through the neglect of their parents until education is made compulsory;

(ii) Children in the Infant School vary in age from 5 to 13 years. Proper attention cannot be given by the schoolmistress and her assistant to 90 children. During 1886 and 1887 a second assistant was paid by private subscription;

(iii) The state of education in the country parts of the islands is deplorable, nothing whatever having been done during the year either by Government or the lessees of Crown lands towards the education of the children scattered throughout the islands, with the exception of the school established at Darwin by the Falkland Islands Company, where the few children resident in Darwin receive instruction.

By the next year the *1888 Blue Book* indicated that the situation was still much the same. Out of the 600 children in the Falklands under the age of 15, 300 were living in Stanley, 150 in the Company 'Camp', and the remaining 150 were scattered over the rest of the islands. The Stanley School rolls showed that there were 95 seniors and 109 infants and 'the usual routine of school work' had been carried out in the Government Schools despite an extended closure due to a measles epidemic. But the Reverend Brandon had to report that an average of 25 children were attending so irregularly 'only now and again at long intervals, that practically they are receiving no instruction'. To add to his concerns, the Darwin school had been closed for the greater part of the year due to the absence on leave of the schoolmaster. Brandon had visited West Falkland and six of the small adjacent islands and examined 50 children 'all of whom were receiving some instruction from their parents, but in many instances it is but little they can do, owing to the defective education of the parents themselves'. The plight of the 'Camp' children continued. His recommendations repeated the request to make education compulsory; sought additional money to pay for a sewing mistress for the seniors and a junior assistant for the infants – particularly to cover those periods of the year when many Camp children came to Stanley while their fathers were out of work between October and March, so swelling the school numbers by 70 or 80. He suggested that it would be useful to find out how other island communities in the world coped with similar difficulties. He drew up regulations to exempt certain deserving parents from paying school fees – and to save Mr Brandon himself digging into his own pocket to pay for them.

The year 1889 saw the opening of a small Roman Catholic private school in Stanley run by the Reverend P. J. Diamond. This was outside the jurisdiction of Mr Brandon, who urged that the school be required to submit fortnightly reports to the Colonial Secretary. It attracted 41 pupils, including some Protestant children. Fearing further erosion of numbers in the Government Schools, the Inspector suggested that there should be separate boys' and girls' schools in Stanley 'as parents have a most decided objection to sending their girls to a mixed school'.

During 1890, due largely to the untiring efforts of the Reverend Brandon almost since his arrival on the Falklands, sufficient support and funds had been raised to lay the foundation stone of the new church which was so much needed. This was on the same site as the old church, which had been damaged by a second peat slip in 1886. The event gave rise to celebrations including sports for the children and a dance for the grown-ups.

Attendance at school had been 'fitful' during 1890, partly due to a two months' closure of the Stanley Schools during an epidemic of whooping cough but also due to excuses such as 'taking father's breakfast' and 'helping to rickle peat'. Mr Brandon despaired of convincing some parents of the value of education, and once again he pressed for the idea of a peripatetic schoolmaster to be considered seriously and also for education to become compulsory for those within access. His efforts achieved a measure of success in 1891, when compulsory education for five- to 13-year-olds in Stanley was intro-duced and it was decreed that fees could be remitted for those in financial need. However, it took another four years to introduce compulsory education across the islands because the Ordinance to bring this about was not passed until 1895.

Yet another private school was established in 1891 by a Miss Prior, who had 19 pupils, 13 girls and 6 boys. A night school was also opened to cater for any islanders who wished to avail themselves of some education. Eventually, in February 1892, the new church was completed and consecrated as Christ Church Cathedral. The Reverend Brandon became Dean and his assistant, the Reverend Aspinall, became Canon. But all of this activity in his capacity as the leading churchman on the islands did not diminish Dean Brandon's efforts on behalf of education. These included his Camp visitations to each house at least once a year acting as an unpaid agent between Stanley and the Camp – 'bringing delight and happiness into lives that were lonely and isolated; bringing much else besides – papers, books, commissions of all kinds'.[12]

The *1893 Blue Book* reported that another denominational school had been established in Stanley, this time by the Baptists. This meant that there were now five day schools in Stanley, one night school and a Company School at Darwin. A bright spot this year for Dean Brandon had been the financing by the Falkland Islands Company of 'travelling schoolmasters' for the education of children of settlers and shepherds in the Camp. This included Lafonia, Bleaker, Lively and Speedwell. Educational provision on the Falkland Islands was certainly multiplying, but there were still many children who either could not, or would not, avail themselves of the opportunity of taking it.

The school statistics, as given in the Governor's *1894 Blue Book* were as follows:

	BOYS	GIRLS	AVERAGE DAILY ATTENDANCE
Govt Senior School	34	31	44
Govt Jun/Inf Dept	38	48	34
Roman Catholic School	20	12	30
Baptist School	30	23	43
Miss Prior's School	20	15	
	142	129	
Stanley Schools Total	271		

The Governor continued to pay tribute to the Falkland Islands Company 'who in a praiseworthy public spirit have ministered to the educational requirements of their employees by engaging and maintaining itinerant teachers whose roll of pupils amounts to 37', and he announced that the Government were soon going to follow suit and appoint itinerant schoolmasters on West Falkland.

1895-1901: Camp and Compulsory Education come to the Falklands

In April 1895 the *School Attendance Ordinance* was passed by the Falklands Legislative Council. It made education compulsory for children from five to 13 years of age unless there was a reasonable excuse which satisfied the Police Magistrate. This excuse could be the passing of an examination by a child of ten or over as prescribed in the Schedule, or alternatively being provided with some other form of instruction, or on account of illness. The Chief Constable was to keep a list of all the children in Stanley and the Head Teacher of the Government school was to supply him with a list of non-attenders. These laws were to apply to any other Government school established elsewhere on the islands. Those parents who were genuinely unable to pay fees were to be granted remission. The curriculum included reading, writing, arithmetic, geography, history, drawing and music. Some in the Roman Catholic School were learning Spanish, enabling them to emigrate to South America should they wish.

The lack of trust between the varying religious denominations which had led to the establishment of the Roman Catholic and the short-lived Baptist School, now threatened to give the Government schools an Anglican label. Governor Goldsworthy decided to settle the matter in 1895 by abolishing religious education entirely in the Government schools. With an agreement between the various clergy a form of morning prayer in school was allowed to continue.

At the instigation of the Governor, the teachers at the three Stanley schools met in 1896 to draw up a synopsis of their work. This was in readiness for standard examinations to be used in twelve months time using printed papers from the Education Department in England. In his report accompanying the *1896 Blue Book* the Governor saw the rivalry between the Government, Baptist and Roman Catholic Schools as wholesome because it was 'accentuated by efforts to make these quasi-voluntary schools to improve their curriculum and the appurtenances of their schools and to put them on a par, as far as possible, with the Government Elementary School'. 1896 statistics show that there were 60 children at the senior (mixed) school in Stanley, 32 boys and 28 girls, with an average attendance of 54.5% and 47.8%, and 69 children in the infants' school, 36 boys and 33 girls, with average attendance of 24.7% and 27.6%. In spite of the comparatively low attendance figures, Dean Brandon was pleased that they showed some improvement.

In 1897 the Falkland Islands Government also carried out their promise to employ itinerant teachers but, as no local teachers could be found for this, two teachers from the UK were specifically appointed to cover West Falkland. Dean Brandon reported: 'Elementary education has been finally brought within reach of the most remote shepherd's hut so that no further excuse exists for the lamentable condition of illiteracy in which whole families had unavoidably to be raised.' At first the number of visits which could be made by an itinerant teacher on horse-back to a remote area was few, to some only once a year. The teacher would live in the home of the child for two weeks or more, receiving free board in exchange for his teaching. In addition to instructing the child, he also gave help to the parents who would be responsible for seeing that the child continued with the work set until the teacher returned, but this was 'in the often forlorn hope of sufficient parental time and ability to ensure its completion before the next visit'.[13]

In his 1897 report Dean Brandon expressed his hope that there would soon be some more advanced classes for young people over school age, and also some technical instruction in trades. Another educational development of this period was the establishment of small settlement schools for the children clustered in outlying areas at large farms where several families were employed. It was often the farm's book-keeper who would be given the task of teaching the children. However, when a cargo ship arrived, the school would close for the day – much to the delight of the pupils – because their teacher needed to revert to his prime task of checking the stock which had just arrived. These settlement schools were widely scattered among the islands and in general had to be self-reliant.

The Baptist minister departed from the Falklands in April 1898. This led to a rapid decline in numbers to only 13 children at the Baptist School and its brief life ended. Thereafter the published schedule of schools comprised:

Govt Primary School: 4 instructors, 190 pupils
Roman Catholic School: 62 pupils
Private School (unaided): 12 pupils
Darwin School: 26 pupils (Trained teacher Mr A. Moir MA)
East Falkland Travelling Teachers: 36 children
West Falkland Travelling Teachers: 60 children

A comprehensive *Education Report* covering progress in 1901 was submitted by the long-serving Dean Brandon for inclusion in the Governor's Annual Report for the Colonial Secretary of State. He reminded his readers of the peculiar circumstances of the Colony in which half the child population was scattered over the 15 islands – the children of shepherds, navvies, managers, masters. Except for those living in Stanley and Darwin, families could be separated from each other by a ride of at least one, two or three hours. There were now only three schools in Stanley, two run by the Government and one by the Roman Catholic Church. The Baptist School and Miss Prior's School had closed. The two Government Schools were run by a schoolmaster and a schoolmistress trained in England, assisted by two local young people who were uncertificated but trained on the islands. The Private School run by the Roman Catholic Church now received a small government grant and the priest was assisted by a teacher from Buenos Aires. Of the school in Darwin, Mr Brandon reported that the children were taught by their store-keeper, who was a trained schoolmaster with an MA degree from Aberdeen University. The system of itinerant teachers was becoming well established and accepted and was producing encouraging results. 'Though a primitive arrangement the children get on very well indeed; the master, while residing with the family, teaches new rules etc which the parents keep up while he is absent. In fact the advantage was so marked that the teachers have gradually increased from one to four, and the Falkland Islands Company are speaking of appointing another teacher for the children in their Camps.' The full cost of education during the year, excluding that provided by the Company, had been £635 14s 5d. The children in Stanley had paid fees – 6d per week for seniors and 3d for juniors – but no fees had been charged for the Camp children as the teacher had received free board and lodging. Schooling in Stanley was now compulsory up to the age of 15, and all schools followed the same syllabus based on that used in British primary schools. Stanley Schools had been examined by the Government Inspector of Schools while the work of the travelling schoolmasters had been examined by the church clergy, themselves itinerant. The Government schoolmaster received £170 per annum plus £35 school fees and free residence, while the schoolmistress received £40 per annum plus approximately £30 school fees. The travelling schoolteachers received £5 per month for the first year of service, rising by £5 per year up to £80 p.a. and a free passage to and from the Falklands. Altogether, reported Mr Brandon, there were six men and three women teachers employed.

The syllabus of the senior school in Stanley included singing, drawing and a little physical drill, but as yet it had not been possible to include any agriculture, cooking, domestic economy, handicraft or

manual skills, except for girls' sewing. There was no secondary education as the population was too small; the Government schoolmaster ran
a night school in the winter although he had no aid from the Government. Mr Brandon was able to conclude by reporting that there were
no blind, deaf or dumb children on the Falklands, nor any who needed
any special restraint in terms of behaviour.

1902-35: Ups and downs in Island Education

An itinerant teacher for North Camp in East Falkland was appointed
by the Government in 1902. This brought the number of travelling
teachers to four, including two in West Falkland and one associated
with the Darwin School appointed by the Company. By 1904 the total
number of children receiving instruction in the Falklands was reckoned
to be 410, although it was difficult to ascertain the exact number in
Stanley because several children were drifting between the Government School and the Roman Catholic School. The total included a
further 9 children, 2 boys and 7 girls, who were being taught privately.
In his *1905 Blue Book* report the Governor stated: 'There is not a single
"camp" child, capable of receiving education, who is not being taught,
either by the travelling teachers or privately – children of the sheep
farmers or managers – except one family on Bleaker Island and one
family on Speedwell Island where the parents are doing what they can'.

The foundation stone of the first major purpose-built government
school on the Falkland Islands was laid by Mrs Allardyce, the wife of
the Governor, in November 1905. It was to be the senior school and
was on a site behind the Cathedral. It was opened by the Governor in
1906. From this time onwards the Education Department was in
existence and an Education Committee selected, whose members' role
was to monitor schooling throughout the islands.

In the same year came the disendowment on the Falkland Islands of
the Anglican Church; it was still forbidden to include religious
instruction in the school curriculum. This did not apply, of course, to
the private Roman Catholic School, St Mary's, but this school received
a highly critical report in 1907 from a visiting HMI, H. M. Richards. As a
result, its numbers declined and the Catholic authorities decided no
longer to accept the grant-in-aid, in order to be free of such inspection.

Having served the Falkland Islands as colonial chaplain since 1877,
Dean Lowther Brandon retired in 1907. Throughout his time he had
campaigned vigorously, tirelessly and fearlessly for the betterment of
life for the islanders and his personal contribution to the cause of
education was highly significant:

Dean Brandon outside the old school house in Port San Carlos with his riding cape on and maletos over his shoulder, 1905

There has never been in the Falkland Islands, and it is unlikely there will ever be, anyone quite like Brandon. An Irishman, short-sighted, deaf, none too robust, but with a forceful and redoubtable personality, he spent thirty strenuous years in the islands, working continuously for the welfare, material as well as spiritual, of the Falkland Islander. When he gave up the chaplaincy in 1907, he left behind him not only a church developed and expanded out of all recognition, but a record of social service that will never be surpassed ... In his work for youth the Sunday School occupied a pre-eminent place. Brandon's Sunday Schools – he held two each Sunday – were no ordinary Sunday Schools. They were run on day school lines, with examinations twice yearly and prizes at the end for the children who had done best ... He started a Penny Savings Bank at the Government School, the precursor of the present Government Savings Bank ... To widen their horizons he opened a Children's Library. For those who had left school he started an adult library run by his wife, a night school at the Parsonage, and reading circles ... He promoted sports and recreational activities of all kinds ... He founded, edited and printed the Falkland Islands Magazine ... Brandon believed in mixing amusement with his instruction ... his magic lantern became in time as famous as Brandon himself. No entertainment was considered complete without it.[14]

Brandon's successor as colonial chaplain and dean, and as Government Inspector of Schools, was the Very Reverend Cyril H. Golding-Bird MA. In his first and only report he announced the opening of the newly created Government School. This, he maintained, bore comparison with any school of similar purpose in the UK, including outdoor provision for physical exercises. Mr Golding-Bird's successor in 1908 was the Reverend Canon E. J. Seymour, who was extremely pleased with the work being done in the Stanley schools. Of the work with the older children his *1908 Annual Report* stated that: 'The lessons are made interesting to the scholars and everything is being done to bring the school up to a high educational level'. He continued: 'The infants are being carefully and systematically taught, and appear to be interested and happy in their lessons.' He was pleased, too, with the work of the itinerant teachers, but stressed that it was only 'where the parents co-operate with teachers that good results are attained'.

The 1909 Public Education Ordinance raised the school leaving age to 14 and made provision for the employment of pupil teachers. Altogether 428 children were receiving education in one form or another, 222 boys and 206 girls. The Reverend Seymour held the role of Inspector of Schools until the approach of the First World War and under his kindly supervision the value attached to education was considerably enhanced. The raising of the school-leaving age led not only to an increase in the number of children on the school rolls but also to a marked improvement in attendance, and the *1911 Education Report* stated that: 'In both these cases, statistics point to the fact that the methods and tuition are duly appreciated alike by parents and children.' A new classroom had to be added on to the Government School in Stanley to accommodate the additional numbers.

Concern was still felt by the Anglican Church at the absence of religious instruction in the government schools, and in 1912 Bishop Blair raised the matter with the Secretary of State for the Colonies. He indicated that unless the situation was changed the Church of England would consider setting up its own school on the islands, independent of the Government. This did not, however, receive the general backing of the islanders themselves, who preferred matters to be left as they were, and nothing came of this proposal.

The outbreak of war caused considerable disorganization of the educational system on the islands. Three of the itinerant teachers joined the volunteer force and were recalled from their country 'beat' to Stanley. The Government School in Stanley closed for an extended period during 1914, and for a period of six weeks all the women and children were evacuated to various parts of East and West Falkland.

The somewhat tenuous link between education and the church was becoming weaker and, in fact, was severed in 1916 when the role of Schools Inspector transferred from the Dean, the Colonial Chaplain, to the Colonial Secretary. This coincided with the appointment as Superintendent of Education of A. R. Hoare, who was destined to be in charge of education on the Falklands for the next 25 years. Like Dean Brandon, Mr Hoare served the cause of education well, retaining his determination and enthusiasm throughout his long period of service to improve and enhance the educational opportunities available to all the islands children.

Meanwhile, when describing the severance of the formal links between education and the church, it is important to place on record the key part which the church had played over the years since the colony's original settlers formed the first community on the Falklands. From the start the church had been instrumental in forwarding the cause of education. This was particularly due to the work of its chaplains, most of whom had also carried the role of Superintendent of Schools. They had attempted to raise and maintain standards in spite of many setbacks, including the sheer difficulty of reaching some of the children, of convincing some parents of the value of education and of finding people able to do the teaching.

For the remainder of the war years the Camp programme was severely affected, as it proved to be impossible to fill the vacancies left by the men in the forces. This meant that many Camp children received no education during the war. In fact, the 1918 report showed that only 19 Camp children were receiving schooling from just one teacher, instead of the previous 90 children with five teachers.

At the end of the war, matters improved with the arrival of four more travelling teachers from the UK and with the provision of training for pupil teachers at the Government School in Stanley. However, after the setbacks occasioned by the war years, the travelling teacher system came under considerable criticism over the next few years, particularly from Mr Hoare, the Government School Superintendent and head teacher. In 1923 the Governor's *Blue Book* reports that 'the system of sending uncertificated and untrained teachers round the country to spend from 2 to 6 weeks during the year at each place could only be regarded as an inadequate makeshift, but it has served its turn well'. A scheme to attempt to improve the situation, proposed by Mr Hoare, received the approval of the Secretary of State for the Colonies. By this, a Government Hostel was to be set up in Stanley where children from the outlying districts could receive board, lodging and education for a cost to their parents of £1 per month. Should parents prefer their children to reside with relatives or friends in Stanley, a government subsidy of £2 per month for each child would be paid to the host. So on 1 January 1924 another landmark in the history of education in the Falklands was made with the opening of the Government Hostel in Stanley. It had accommodation for 16 senior children from the outlying areas.

However, the response to the system by the end of the first year was disappointing. G. R. L. Brown, reporting for the Colonial Secretary, had hoped that the attractions of the new scheme would bring a large number of children from the country districts into Stanley and that it would be 'unnecessary to continue the unsatisfactory system of employing travelling teachers, beyond one for East Falkland and one for West Falkland. This has in practice not been realized and additional pupil teachers are being trained with a view to the ultimate engagement in "camp" teaching.'[15]

At this time the total population of the Falklands had risen to 2,197, with 1,219 males and 978 females. There were the two elementary schools in Stanley, one run by the Government and the other by the Roman Catholics; four travelling teachers were being employed, two by the Government and two by the Falkland Islands Company; and the Company also paid for a resident teacher at their station in Darwin. 340 children were being taught, as follows:

	BOYS	GIRLS	TOTAL
Government School	104	76	180
Roman Catholic School	17	43	60
Govt Travelling Teachers	27	21	48
FIC Teachers	27	25	52
	175	165	340

The following year things looked a little more promising concerning the take-up of the hostel places, as there had been eight or nine children there for most of the year. Also the number of boarders in private homes had varied from 10 to 13. But throughout the years from 1926 to 1929 the providers of education were on an uphill task and each annual report registered disappointment that the parents in outlying parts of the Colony were not appreciating the benefits of the scheme. The number of children receiving schooling reached as high as 394 in 1927 and the attendance at school of those registered maintained a reasonably good level of well over 90%, but there was still a hard core of parents who were resisting taking advantage of formal education for their children. By August 1929 the decision was made to terminate the hostel scheme as the numbers did not justify it.

Other aspects of education were a little more encouraging. A Continuation Class for a two-year course of more advanced study was set up at the Government School in Stanley, the syllabus including woodwork and shorthand. This was also offered in an evening class which was well-attended. Football for the boys and hockey for the girls had become very popular, due to the efforts of the qualified instructor of Physical Education and Gymnastics who had been appointed the previous year. Good reports were being received about Falkland Islanders who had moved to England and who were proving to be well able to hold their own in their new schools there, as well as two boys who had left school to join the Royal Navy and were well up to standard. Three itinerant schoolmasters were still being employed for West Falkland plus one for East Falkland.

A Falkland Islander who prefers not to have her name mentioned started school at this time. She recalls receiving all of her schooling at the Government School in Stanley. The Infants School and the Senior School each had a single-storey building. In the Infants School there was the 'Baby Class' and two other classes, all three sections meeting in the one long room. The room was heated by a big free-standing peat-burning stove. The Senior School had a large central room called the Hall, and five other classrooms. The school year ended with a display by the children, each class participating in such activities as gymnastics, folk dancing, one-act plays or swinging Indian clubs. The Governor attended these and distributed prizes. She, the islander, was spellbound by the teaching of poetry and literature by teacher Miss Oldham, and of Welshman John Davis who taught music and singing she says: 'He despaired of we island Children, saying we were all tone deaf.'[16]

In addition, out of school activities were popular among the young people, including Scouts, Guides, Rover Sea Scouts, Cubs and Brownies. There were opportunities to join in Highland dancing, amateur dramatics, badminton, riding bicycles, horse riding, fishing and picnics, and the islanders were also able to benefit from the recently established public library.

1936-49: Widening Educational Opportunities On and Off the Islands

During the ensuing two decades those responsible for providing education pursued with vigour the task of trying to give all the children on the Falklands a fair and equal opportunity of receiving instruction. The Headship of the Government School in Stanley continued to be held by A. R. Hoare throughout the 1930s, and he also held responsibility for the education of the Camp children and the overall superintendence of education. Alongside the teaching provided within the normal school system, various other schemes were tried to enhance educational provision. For instance, an attempt was made in 1936 to introduce schooling by correspondence for children in outlying areas. The scheme lasted only four years, due mainly to the irregularity of the mail to and from the remoter areas, which depended upon the arrival of the inter-islands' steamer.

The Continuation Class at the Government School in Stanley was still providing teaching for pupils beyond the school-leaving age. A fee of one shilling per week was charged for this, while the fees for younger children were 6d per week for Standard 1 and above and 3d per week for Standard 2 and below. The staff list of 1937 for this school comprised a Headmaster, Assistant Master and Assistant Mistress, all of whom held either a UK Board of Education Certificate or a Scottish Education Department Certificate, and five locally trained teachers –

the 2nd Assistant Master, another Assistant Teacher and three Supplementary Teachers.

Some reorganization concerning the management of education took place in 1939. Mr Hoare became the Director of Education and T. D. Evans was appointed to be the Head Master of the Government School, the first time these two roles had been separated. For his last two years in office Mr Hoare continued to work tirelessly to improve the educational provision for the Camp children. For instance he took advantage of the visit to Stanley of all the Farm Managers from West Falkland for the 1939 Stock Show to meet with them and his new colleague, Mr Evans, and to involve them in drawing up proposals to improve the educational provision in West Falkland, thus enlisting their increased support and interest.

Owen McPhee, a Falkland Islander, recalls his experiences as a child at the Government School in Stanley at this time:

One of my first memories is of the big boys cooking potatoes in the open peat fire to eat at playtime. Sometimes the potatoes would burn in the hot ashes and the teachers would smell them. On such occasions the potatoes would be confiscated. The school day started with hymns and prayers at assembly. This was followed by maths, spelling, reading and English. We had games twice a week and handwork/woodwork once a week. Outside activities varied depending on the season – football, rounders and cricket during the summer and sleighing in the winter if there was enough snow. During the summer most children were expected to help with rickling and carting the family's peat supply. For a time I helped to deliver the local paper before school and this took me about an hour to deliver the forty copies. On Friday evenings there were silent picture shows in the Catholic Hall with music provided by the music pupils from St Mary's School.

When I was nine I moved to the school hostel (the building known as the Church House next to the old Senior School). The hostel children had to help with the various chores such as setting the table or collecting the peat. This was a fairly small hostel for children whose parents worked in the Camp. Some of the children had lost their mothers and their fathers worked on the farms. On Saturday the hostel children used to go caddying for the golf players.

Special events during the school year included the annual prize giving and also PT demonstrations (our PT instructor also trained the Falkland Islands Defence Force). The Governor of the time wrote and directed a pantomime – Zachariah Fee – which included a lot of school children – all the rehearsals were held out of school hours.

Mr McPhee went on to describe his work as a teacher:

During the Second World War I spent a few months as a travelling teacher on West Falkland. This involved travelling from farm to farm or to remote shepherds' houses on horseback, such journeys sometimes taking 3-4 hours. I also helped for a few weeks at Port Howard when the Stanley children were evacuated there.

After serving in the Falkland Islands Defence Force I went to Teal Inlet to work as teacher/book-keeper. There I taught a mixed class with ages ranging from 5-14 which made it very difficult to keep everyone occupied all the time. The one-roomed schoolhouse was in quite a poor condition so I spent a lot of evenings repairing and decorating it. The schoolhouse would be used for a church service from time to time when a minister visited – sometimes I would provide the music on my accordion.

He left Teal Inlet when the number of children was too small to warrant a full-time teacher, but he returned there several years later when his own children attended school in the same old schoolhouse, to be taught by Mr Tony Nelson (now Publisher of South Atlantic Books). Mrs Marjorie McPhee, Owen's wife, is proud of the achievements of their two sons, one of whom is now an electrical engineer and the other an airline pilot. They both received most of their schooling at home on the farms, first at Teal Inlet and later at Douglas Station. It was usually left to Mrs McPhee to see that all homework was faithfully done and, at times, to teach much of the work herself![17]

Mr Hoare retired in 1941 and Mr Evans was appointed in his place, his role reverting to that of Superintendent of Education. In January 1942, on the entry of Japan into the war, Mr Evans found that one of his first tasks was to mastermind the arrangements for the evacuation of the Stanley children to five large centres in the Camp areas. Two teachers who had had experience of evacuation work in England, Miss H. Brown and Miss P. F. Ryder, assisted in this. The 209 children, 34 mothers and 14 teachers were divided between the settlements at North Arm, Port Howard and San Carlos, and the remaining 50 went to the 'Cookhouse' at Walker Creek, given by the Falkland Islands Company. Families were kept together and children housed with relatives or friends whenever possible. Resources such as textbooks, stationery and sports equipment were shipped to the various centres and each was expected to cope with any unforeseen circumstances which might arise. Of the Walker Creek centre in charge of Mr and Mrs H. L. Baker, the Governor's *1942 Report* stated: 'It was interesting to note the progress of this self-contained unit, it being the country's first experience of a boarding school. The delegation of some measure of authority to senior children has promoted and fostered a healthy public spirit.' All the evacuees returned to their homes in October 1942.

Falkland Islander Mrs Joan Bound recalls her own schooling around the time of the war. Living on a large sheep farm at Goose Green, she was one of 20 children between the ages of five and 14 at the settlement school. There she was taught by a Scotsman, Mr Honeyman, whom she describes as 'a remarkable teacher'. He was also book-keeper for the farm, which involved administering the farm's store. He gave her an appreciation of Bible stories which he made very exciting. She recalls sitting in a group around the peat stove and open grate listening to him reading stories about Shackleton. Outside school time he ran a train club, taught country dancing and ran a children's newspaper costing one penny. He also produced plays such as *The Lady with the Hat*. His wife was very supportive of all the activities with the children, and Joan recalls with pleasure the mushroom cakes produced by Mrs Honeyman at party time. Every morning in school Mr Honeyman started the day with world news, including events of the war which he had been able to extract from the radio as there were no newspapers. Mr Honeyman tested his pupils through general knowledge quizzes and these included questions on both local and world matters. Joan Bound left the Goose Green School at the age of 12 and for 15 months went to school in Stanley, where she lived with her aunt. However, she was caught up in the wartime evacuation of Stanley and found herself back in Goose Green again for a few months before she returned to Stanley. From the Stanley School she won one of the two scholarships to go to the British School at Montevideo, where she took her School Certificate. Throughout her schooling she remained grateful for the good grounding she had received from Mr Honeyman at Goose Green: 'He made you learn. You had to learn. He wouldn't accept anything less.' Mr Honeyman retired to New Zealand, but he clearly passed on his love for the Falklands to his daughter who is now following in his footsteps as a teacher there.[18]

The Roman Catholic School closed during 1942. It had been run successfully by nuns from a teaching order in Argentina since 1907, and it remained in the care of the Order until the Sisters returned to Argentina in 1942. Throughout its existence the school had maintained a high proportion of female pupils, and this was a major feature which attracted some Protestant parents to send their children there.

The *1943 Report on Education* was produced by the Acting Superinten-dent, H.L.Baker, the Assistant Master in the Government School. At the end of Mr Evans' term of office the following year, Mr Baker became Superintendent, a post which he held until 1949. A large contingent of the armed forces continued to be present on the Falklands and co-operated well with the civilians, including in education. Free evening classes were organized by the Army Education Officer and the

Superintendent of Education for members of the forces and civilians together. These were in a range of subjects including English Literature, History, Modern Languages, Mathematics, Science and Commercial Subjects. Co-operation also extended to the use of buildings, the girls giving up the use of their domestic science room to the Navy, and later the Navy letting the school use their drill hall for PE, when the school gymnasium had to take the place of the burned-down town hall. A Schools' Broadcasting Programme for the benefit of the Camp and settlement children was started in October 1944. Each afternoon the programme lasted for an hour and comprised four parts, including reading for infants and juniors and a range of subjects for older children. The scheme survived for four years, but due partly to technical problems and partly to the fact that the children would not listen to the programmes, it was discontinued. However, the potential of the scheme was recognized, to be re-introduced when the initial difficulties had been sorted out.

For the first time in the Falklands a candidate took and passed a subject in the General School Certificate Examinations after having private tuition. In 1945 extra encouragement was given to 14- and 15-year-olds from the Camp to take advantage of the Continuation Class which had been set up in Stanley to enable pupils to stay on at school for further teaching: they were to receive a maintenance grant while in Stanley. However, like other systems tried before, this one also failed due mainly to the fact that the Camp children were not educationally ready and able to take up the offer. It was abandoned after a short while.

Greater success was being experienced with the settlement schools, some of which received teaching from a travelling teacher, while others appointed their own teacher. Sometimes this was still the station's book-keeper, but records show that in some schools the manager's wife was also called upon to do the teaching. In order to give support to these various attempts to reach the Camp children, a supervisor of Camp Education was appointed in 1944. Surprisingly, this job was found to be 'unnecessary' and was terminated in 1951.

As there was no opportunity for 'grammar school' education, two bursaries were awarded annually from 1943 to give opportunity to two scholars who qualified by examination and selection to go for a more advanced education for three years abroad. At first these children went to the British School in Montevideo in Uruguay, but from 1950 it was decided to send the scholars to England instead. This was partly for financial reasons and partly for preference. An arrangement had been set up whereby selected children from the Falklands would be able to take up places at one or more of the boarding-grammar schools in Dorset and this scheme proved to be very successful. Mr Baker's *Education Report* in 1946 indicated that several settlement schools were still running strongly. These included full-time schools for Teal Inlet and Salvador, part-time schools for San Carlos and Fox Bay, a full-time school running for half the year at Chartres, and another for the other half year at Roy Cove. In addition to these Government schools the Company was still maintaining the part-time settlement schools at Darwin and North Arm. There were now four pupil-teachers on the establishment. The Senior and Junior Schools in Stanley were progressing well and a house system had been introduced, the names selected being those of dependencies of the Falklands – Georgia, Graham, Orkney and Shetland. He also reported other items of interest, namely that a hobbies period had been introduced into the timetable, a concert had been produced and presented, Remembrance Day had been honoured, a system of free milk for children had been introduced, a measles epidemic had affected the school at the end of the year, and a further two pupils had successfully taken a Cambridge School Certificate examination and passed.

The *1949 Education Ordinance* required parents to have their children educated wherever a recognized school or teacher was available. It also required regular medical inspections to be made at the schools. Provision was made to raise the school leaving age to 16 'when the time was ripe'. A regulation was passed that school fees for all children up to the school-leaving age of 14 were abolished. A charge of one shilling a week (later 2s 6d) was charged for attendance at the Continuation Class, but as it was seen to be unfair to charge people showing keenness to extend their education it was decided to reimburse those who obtained an average mark of 60% or over in their examinations.

Mr Baker, who had served education on the islands faithfully from the wartime evacuation of Stanley children, resigned his position as Superintendent of Education in August 1949. D. M. Honeyman became Acting Superintendent. In his *Education Report for 1949* Mr Honeyman outlined proposals on policy and future aims for education, stating that: 'Generally the system of employing travelling teachers is not only economically unsound but has failed entirely to achieve its purpose.' He drew attention to the time wasted between visits to the Camp children because on each visit there had to be a long period of revision. The Government plans for the future were to centralize education by initially withdrawing the local travelling teachers and giving them further training in teaching methods in Stanley; appointing six qualified teachers to replace the local untrained personnel; building eight new school buildings – four in West Falkland and four in East Falkland; and bringing all Camp children to board at one of these school for four days' teaching each week, for a boarding charge of 1s 3d per day. At the age of 11, the children would be transferred to the Junior School in Stanley. A Junior-Secondary School was to be established in Stanley for 100 pupils between the ages of 12 and 15, the main emphasis being on practical subjects, and a hostel for 30 pupils would be built. While most children would work towards a Local School Certificate, there would be special instruction for those wishing to take the Cambridge School Certificate.

This Report also gave details of the teachers' conditions of service. Local pupil teachers would receive £90 per annum plus a cost of living bonus. After passing an examination at the end of one year, they would become Assistant teachers at £110 per annum plus cost of living bonus. The men teachers would rise through the incremental scales to a maximum of £360 per annum at Grade I, while the maximum for the women would be £220 per annum at Grade III.

Further information was given on a number of issues. The Montevideo scheme was to be discontinued and the bursaries to be allocated for further education in the UK, some technical training was now being given in evening classes, a new infant school was to be built with funds from the Colonial Development and Welfare Scheme, and the Education Department was to take over the work of the Information Officer. A number of out-of-school activities were available to the young people in the Stanley region. While the 1st Company of the Boys Brigade was celebrating its fifth anniversary in 1949, a Junior Contingent known as the Life Boys was being set up. A Girls' Club was started up by some of the senior girls for the benefit of their younger friends from 12 to 14 years of age, the activities including games and physical training.

1950-69: Challenges, determination and progress in education

During these years every effort was being made to give a sound education to the children of the Falklands whether they lived in a town or a country area. This was due in no small measure to those people who, in spite of persistent setbacks, steadfastly kept to their central task. These included the school teachers, the travelling teachers, the settlement teachers, the ministers, the government officials, the Company managers, the overseas schools, the parents and, last but not least, those children whose school life was probably among the most unique and adventurous of any in the world.

The planned eight settlement schools were still in the course of construction during 1950, but by 1951 the Governor was able to report on six in East Falkland – Darwin, North Arm, Teal Inlet, Douglas Station, Fitzroy and San Salvador, and three in West Falkland – Pebble Island, Fox Bay and Hill Cove. Sadly, three of these had to close temporarily during the year owing to the lack of teaching staff. Some parents were also being recalcitrant, the report indicating that only nine children had been sent to these schools.

Through the co-operation of the Falkland Islands Company and J. L. Waldron Ltd with the Government, finance was secured for the building of two boarding schools. It was hoped that more children would be encouraged and enabled to attend school. The Government would take the responsibility for resourcing, staffing and running of the schools. In the event these buildings were not completed for a number of years. The East Falkland school was officially opened in 1956 with 39 boarders – almost up to capacity – and a number of day children also attended this school. The second school in Port Howard in West Falkland was opened in 1957. There was still no secondary or higher education in 1951, though the Continuation Class remained available to any 14- and 15-year-olds who wished to continue their schooling. A similar opportunity was given to others to receive this teaching at evening class but, apart from young Government employees for whom the course was compulsory, the attendance otherwise was very disappointing.

Forrest McWhan, for 30 years Minister at the Tabernacle, wrote a personal account of life in the Falklands at that time. His 1952 book, *The Falkland Islands Today*, includes a description of the education system. After detailing the provision made – two schools in Stanley, two overseas scholarships, travelling teachers, small settlement schools, attempts to set up schools' broadcasts, a boarding school at Darwin in East Falkland, and plans for a similar school in West Falkland – he commented: 'With education it seems a case of doing all you can and in every way possible to school the children, a right which is theirs as citizens of a part of the British Empire.'

Since the closure of the Roman Catholic School in 1942, children of all denominations had attended the same school and were taught together. However, the *Falkland Islands Gazette* of 1 June 1951 described the arrangement which had been made whereby the clergy could teach the children of their own denomination once a week. Attendance at these classes was strictly voluntary and depended upon the parents' wishes in the matter.

In 1951 the Government had decided that the infants school, which had been accommodated in makeshift buildings for about 80 years, should have its own purpose-built premises. Accordingly the Foundation Stone was laid that year, but it was June 1955 before it was officially opened by Sir Miles Clifford. The *Education Report of 1955* described the new buildings as spacious and modern and able to house the lower age classes from the senior school as well as the infants for whom it had been built. The Report also stated that a school for 40 boarding pupils and 20 day pupils had been opened at Goose Green in East Falkland and plans were in hand to open a similar school in West Falkland.

It is interesting to note that the standard of education obtained on the islands in the mid-1950s was described as higher than in Secondary Modern Schools in Britain. 'That this is so astounds newcomers to the town who tend to think that, because children live in a remote corner of the world and lack so much in their environment, their capacity to learn must in consequence be deficient. The contrary is the case. Falkland Islands children are very intelligent, as the man who knew Falkland Islanders better than any outsider is ever likely to know them, pointed out more than half a century ago. Dean Brandon wrote in his *Inspection Report for 1894*, "The children are well fed, well clothed, well housed, not over-worked and as a rule well looked after. Teachers have first class material to work on and education ought to be above the average in primary and national schools in England." '¹⁹

The number and qualifications of the teaching force fluctuated from year to year according to the people coming and going from the islands. By 1959 there were 27 teachers, of whom 12 were certificated, 10 were uncertificated but had completed the Secondary School course, 3 were locally trained but had not completed the Secondary School course, and 2 were untrained. In the same year there were 317 children receiving teaching, of whom 53 were in the Infants School for children from 5 to 7 years, 109 in the Senior (all-range) School for children from 7 to 14 in Stanley, 77 were in the two Boarding Schools in the East and West Falkland, and the other 78 children were in the two full-time or eight part-time settlement schools or were being taught at home by one of the ten Camp teachers. There were still seven children, two boys and five girls, who were not receiving any school education at all in spite of financial inducements to parents in the form of boarding allowances, overseas bursaries and tax-free grants in an Overseas Education

Allowances Scheme. By 1959 the Falkland Islands Government was spending 10.8% of its total expenditure on education, this having risen from 7.9% in 1953.

As an inducement to parents to allow their children between the ages of 11 and 18 to go abroad for their education, the Government had introduced a scheme in 1957 whereby the parents would receive a grant of £150 tax free for the first year of study abroad for their child, followed by up to four more years with a tax-free grant of £100 per year for overseas study. The *Falkland Islands Report* for 1960/61 reported that the take-up of this offer was encouraging and by 1960 13 children were benefiting from this scheme. In addition, bursaries had been awarded to pupils who had reached a satisfactory level of education and who wished to train to teach within the Department of Education. Clearly the Island of South Georgia was in a system of its own, there being one girl of school age in 1960 and a boy and a girl in 1961.[20]

A glowing tribute to the travelling teachers and to some additional vso workers together with a graphic account of their work is included in the 1962/63 Report: 'The children in outlying houses are taught by Travelling Teachers, each of whom is assigned an area which he covers by horse, Land Rover or by aircraft. The Travelling Teacher stays a week or a fortnight with each family in turn and leaves homework to tide the children over until he returns six or eight weeks later. The Travelling Teacher has an interesting though arduous and sometimes thankless task. Only young men of spirit, initiative, a certain physical toughness and an ability to mix can successfully carry out this unique post. The Travelling Teachers have been strengthened by members of the Voluntary Service Overseas, three boys and one girl in late 1962 and four boys and a girl in 1963. It is impossible to speak too highly of these young people, whose sole thought is to be of service to others; without them in 1962 many children would have received little tuition, for there was a serious shortage of Camp staff. Board for all Camp Teachers while on duty is fixed at a maximum of 35s per week.'[21]

John Leonard throws interesting light on the life and work of the Camp teachers, having been one himself. As a representative of the Baha'i Faith, he had arrived on the Falklands in February 1954. Immediately he was aware of the shortage of travelling teachers and, after some time spent becoming acquainted with the islanders, his application was accepted. Recalling his experiences nearly forty years later, he wrote:

There was always a shortage – it simply varied from acute to not so acute. Continual travel from one place to another; never having a home of one's own;

having to adjust continually to other people's habits and outlook; never being able to settle down to one's own music and books, for example; and very poor pay, were just a few of the discouraging features. On the other hand, there were the children – several hundred of them, each of whom had just as much right to be educated as any child on earth, and whose start in life was being seriously stunted.

My first beat was enormous; it took six months to get around. My first stop was a large settlement named Hill Cove, with a population of about fifty people. They had not had a teacher for over a year, so the day I flew out in the tiny, 6-passenger seaplane in use in those days, the entire settlement were on the jetty to inspect the new teacher. Nothing whatever had been said to me about teaching methods. The idea was, there were some books around – use them. Hill Cove actually had two settlements, about a mile and a half apart with children in both, and I was expected to divide up my time between them. In one, my pupils were a six-year-old boy and a five-year-old girl – brother and sister – neither of whom had been exposed to school before. Frankly, I don't know which of the three of us was the most terrified.

Somehow I began to learn what was needed. Gradually my schoolroom, such as it was, began to fill with words, cut-outs, that sort of thing. A great deal depended upon the willingness of the mother to see to it that the children did the homework I left for them.'[22]

In an article written for the *Guardian* in 1986 entitled 'Education in the Falkland Islands: A Fresh Start', John Leonard further described the unique circumstances in which the travelling teachers worked and reiterated the importance of the mother's participation:

To gain a real feeling for the problems of education in the Camp, it is best to fly over the islands. One travels for miles over seemingly empty space – the land mass on both East and West Falkland Islands is unexpectedly large and incredibly vacant. Here and there one spots an isolated house, still less frequently a small farm settlement – reminders that people really live in this great open area. Rivers and streams intersect the land in every direction; lakes and ponds punctuate much of the landscape, but there are no paved roads to be seen anywhere, and even the farm tracks end before they have decently begun. Children live in many of these lonely spots.

Inevitably the measure of the child's achievement was what the mother could provide. An educated mother, interested in furthering her children's education, could almost work miracles, and a few did. But the lot of a farm wife in those days was far from easy. Faced with a routine close to slavery, it took an exceptionally dedicated mother to see to her children's education as well. Under the circumstances, one might have expected the arrival of the travelling teacher to be an occasion for rejoicing, and in a few homes this was so, but for many it meant simply an added problem in a lifestyle which already contained enough problems. There was another mouth to feed, more laundry to be done, another body to fit into the Saturday bath routine. For father, it meant saddling up a spare horse when the time came for the teacher to move on, and escorting him halfway along the 'track' to a rendezvous with the teacher's next host. And in the home he had just left, mother might well be taking a brief, discouraged glance at the homework prepared for her children during the teacher's visit, knowing how hard it would be to get them to apply themselves to it; knowing how incapable she would be of answering their questions; and knowing, too, that in all probability they would not have done more than ten per cent of the work by the time the teacher returned. Under such conditions, education was largely of the 'no frills' variety. The attainment of literacy and basic number skills were the main objectives; anything else was a bonus.'[23]

In addition to giving praise for the work of the travelling teachers, the 1962/63 Report continued to describe the successful programme of evening classes offered in Stanley from May to October, these including English, arithmetic, advanced mathematics, Spanish, dress-making, art, book-keeping, shorthand, basketry and electronics. The take-up of these classes, two of which led to an RSA examination, fully justified the provision of the class. Education continued to be free, of course, for all day children. Boarders at the Darwin school had to pay a nominal fee of £4 a term although it was now catering for as many day pupils as boarders since there were two nearby settlements. News of the West Falkland school at Port Howard was less good though, and it had had to close as a boarding establishment due to lack of support. It was now a full-time settlement school instead, with a teaching staff of two.

By 1968/69 the Report was able to include mention that several pupils had obtained O-level and, for the first time, A-level successes in the General Certificate of Education. Preparation and teaching for this had been through special tuition as there was still no secondary or higher education available in the Colony. Within the normal school system candidates had successfully taken RSA examinations in commercial subjects and some City and Guilds examinations. The school leaving age had been raised from 14 to 15 and it was now compulsory for children to attend school from the term in which they became five until the end of the term in which they became 15. Attendance was compulsory for all children of school age living within one mile of a settlement school and for all children between the ages of seven and 15 who lived within two miles of a settlement school. For children beyond these limits the travelling teachers were supplied. These teachers attended training sessions each year at Darwin Boarding School.[24]

14
The Falklands on the World Map
1970-92

It is possible that some aspects of the Argentine occupation may be put to direct advantage of the community.
Prospects for the Falkland Islands, 1983[1]

1970-82: More Setbacks and Advances

This period of time was to prove to be perhaps the most momentous in the islands' history. From the time of the early settlers, many of whom had come from the harsh life of the Scottish islands, the people on the Falklands had met and overcome hardships and challenges. They were certainly going to need all their resilience and courage in the years to come.

The 1970s started off in a dramatic way with the burning down of the building in which the senior school had been operating since its opening in 1906. However, as with other crises over the years, the Falkland Islanders met this one with minimum difficulty, finding alternative accommodation for two classes at 44 Davis Street while the other classes met in surviving rooms in the old building. Plans were set in motion for rebuilding.

The year 1970 saw the closure of settlement schools in Chartres and Fox Bay East, each of these areas now requiring travelling teachers. The only remaining 'book-keeper/teacher school' was at Hill Cove. With rising costs, the amount paid by parents of children at the Darwin Boarding School rose from £4 per annum for the first child in 1970 to £36 per annum in 1975. There were competitive scholarships and allowances for children whose performance merited support, and places were still available in a boarding grammar school in Dorset, the British School in Montevideo, and, from 1971, in the Argentine. The first two scholarships to Argentina were taken up in 1971. With encouragement from the islands' Education Authority, the numbers of senior children going overseas for education increased. By the time of the 1972/73 report 41 children were involved, including 24 in the Argentine where the potential number was described as unlimited.

From 1970 to 1974 the range of educational provision on the Falkland Islands remained comparatively stable under Mr Draycott, who served a total of 11 years as Superintendent. The two schools in Stanley for Seniors and Infant/Juniors were under joint administration. The boarding school at Darwin catered for up to 45 boarders, also taking some day pupils. There were two settlement schools in West Falkland and as many as 38 houses across East and West Falkland. Each travelling teacher visited between four and six houses in rotation, spending two weeks at a time at each one. Mr Draycott was succeeded as Superintendent in 1974 by B.S. Stocks.

Major educational statistics for the period from 1970 to 1975 were given in lists supplied by Mr Stocks from the *Annual Reports 1970-1975*:[2]

	CHILDREN RECEIVING EDUCATION IN THE FI			TEACHERS		CHILDREN ABROAD
	total	EF	WF	MALE	FEMALE	
1970	383	299	84	22	12	24
1971	361	293	68	19	12	24
1972	335	268	67	15	14	27
1973	311	254	57	19	9	41
1974	311	260	51	20	10	45
1975	313	261	52	21	11	51

For East Falkland these figures include the Stanley Schools, the Darwin School boarders and day pupils, and the Camp, including settlements. The number of pupils in West Falkland is comprised of Camp children, including settlements.

Throughout these five years there was still no official secondary education, although it was still possible for students to have special tuition to take GCE O- and A-levels and certain subjects with the City and Guilds and the RSA boards. The expenditure on education rose appreciably from £60,737 in 1970 to £97,964 in 1975, the latter representing 11.18% of the Government budget. This proportion had changed considerably over the years from only 7.9% of the budget in 1953, so reflecting the increasing importance put on education.

A number of major challenges facing the Education Authorities included the difficulty of maintaining the size of the teaching force, particularly in the Camp. Illness among the teachers from the UK caused problems of continuity in the Stanley and Darwin schools and low recruitment of travelling teachers brought problems in the Camp. The contribution of Voluntary Service Overseas workers each year, particularly to help as travelling teachers, attracted the admiration and gratitude of the Governor whose annual reports continued to praise their courage and initiative. John Leonard noted that the task of travelling teacher was becoming a little less difficult as horse travel was gradually replaced by vehicles and then by flights, where feasible, in the tiny seaplanes which serviced the Camp. At least the teachers could now carry adequate equipment. Another positive development was the introduction of seminars for Camp teachers, so diminishing their sense of isolation and establishing a pool of knowledge from which all of them could draw. Increasing use was being made of broadcast lessons which had been introduced in 1965, much of the educational material being provided by Deutsche Welle of Cologne, West Germany or by the New Zealand Broadcasting Corporation, or purchased in Britain.[3]

In the *1974/75 Report* it was stated that an Adviser for Education in the Camp had been appointed, particularly to work on the production of taped lessons for Camp children and to visit other Camp teachers. The five vso workers during 1975 included one young lady volunteer. Funds had already been allocated for the setting up of a Library/ Resource Centre, but plans for the new boarding house had had to go back to the drawing board pending the arrival of an architect, as requested from the oda.[4]

Since 1951 a system of weekly denominational teaching periods had been in operation, but in 1976 this matter was brought up for debate by the Superintendent of Education, who was concerned about standards of teaching. A new scheme based on the Cheshire Agreed Syllabus was accepted but this soon faltered, since non-denominational teaching was not acceptable to all clergy. 'In the event, formal religious education in the schools did not survive much longer although clergy of all denominations continue to pay informal visits to the primary and junior secondary schools in Stanley.'[5]

A major change in the organization of the two Stanley Schools occurred in 1976, when they became administratively separate, each under the charge of a head teacher. There was still a high level of co-operation between the schools, specifically in terms of the use of specialist facilities. A Parent/Teacher Association was formed in the Junior School and it was likely that the Senior School would soon follow suit. The supply of teachers for the Camp children was reported by the Superintendent for the *Governor's 1976 Budget Address to Legco* to be unsatisfactory and the outlook bleak. However, the Falklands Islands Company policy of employing book-keeper/teachers was healthy and there were now six full-time schools operating on this basis.

By May 1977 the teaching situation in the Camp had not improved. The Acting Superintendent put strong recommendations forward that the Government should be responsible for all schools, including those in the settlements, and added: 'In the long term, it was good to hear that Government had finally decided to educate all children over 9 years old in Stanley. The plans for a new hostel to accommodate these children have been fully aired and it is to be hoped that a start can soon be made of this building.'[6] The staff of the Darwin Boarding School were assured that there would be no run down of the existing facilities there during this period.

Twelve months later, the new Superintendent of Education, T. E. Lamin, stressed that 'Alongside plans for our new hostel it is essential that we consider plans for giving all of our children a broader and more relevant education'. It was hoped to establish workshops and facilities for the teaching of rural studies and home economics. Mr Lamin added: 'The Staff of the Secondary School have recently begun a programme of reappraisal of the school's curriculum, which will shortly be studied by the Education Committee. It is to be hoped to introduce all of our children to courses more relevant to living in the Falklands whilst offering those with special ability opportunities to take examinations which will lead to further training.' During the year some O-levels had been taught in the school for the first time.[7]

During the remainder of the decade, with the general policy of strengthening education in the Falklands, a number of strategic procedures were introduced. In co-operation with local employers, day release classes were held for young employees and Government trainee clerks, the latter attending the school for two and a half days each week to take courses in Maths, English and Commercial Studies.

An important development during 1978 was the establishment of a link with the Faculty of Education at Brighton Polytechnic under which the Falkland Islanders would benefit from both teacher training and from advice on resource provision. Through the Brighton link it became possible for two members of the Education Department staff at Brighton to conduct courses on the Falklands, Jim Randall teaching Environmental Studies and Joan Bird taking a course on Pre-School Education for Mothers. It also became possible for islanders to undertake courses at the Polytechnic in Brighton.

Dr I. Griffiths was sponsored by the ODA to advise the island Education Department on the use of video in education, this being of particular value to Camp teaching. To help with the difficult task facing the teachers of children in remote areas, qualified teachers from the system were sent during holiday times to discuss the work being done in settlement schools. Other forms of co-operation with the local community came through the involvement of the Senior School pupils in Community projects, for instance visiting and helping the elderly people in Stanley, restoring the children's playing field, building and learning to use canoes, and repairing part of their own school.

All was not plain sailing as the decade drew to a close, however, and Superintendent Mr Lamin had to report considerable setbacks and few advances in his *Education Report, 1979-1980*. The long-awaited new Stanley School was still not ready, so the plans to close the Darwin Boarding House in 1979 did not materialize. To add to the problems, fire in the Darwin building engine shed necessitated finding alternative provision for the Darwin boarders. Some were boarded with relatives or friends in Stanley, while others had a programme of correspondence lessons and additional visits by travelling teachers. Nevertheless, all of these occurrences served to strengthen the determination to focus secondary schooling in Stanley.

By the turn of the decade, schooling on the Falkland Islands was on a firm footing for all sections of the community, and the islanders in general were appreciative of the educational opportunities which were afforded to them, both at home and abroad. Communications were comparatively straightforward with the UK and between certain of the islands, although the position and nature of others ensured that they would remain isolated. Mr Lamin's term of office ended and in 1981 he was succeeded by J. T. Fowler as Superintendent. But the purposeful endeavours of the people were soon to be interrupted by an event which would attract world-wide attention and temporarily shatter the comparative equanimity of this remote South Atlantic Colony.

1982-88: The Falklands Conflict and Its Aftermath

By 1982 the decision had been made to centralize all secondary education in Stanley. However, a different matter was to cause a delay in further planning – the Argentine invasion of the Falklands on 2 April 1982. 'With less than twelve hours warning the peace and tranquillity of a unique way of life in the Falklands was shattered. These lonely and beautiful islands were invaded, occupied, liberated.'[8]

The schools in Stanley immediately closed during the period of the invasion, and some children were able to be taught in private homes in that time. Stanley House, the boarding hostel, was occupied by troops until the end of the year and reopened in 1983. In his *Guardian* article of 1986, John Leonard paid tribute to the intelligence and capacity of the

Falkland Islands children: 'Dramatic evidence of their calibre was demonstrated in the class preparing for GCE examinations when the Argentine invasion took place. Although the schools were closed during the occupation, and many of the teachers had returned to England, some of those who remained undertook to coach the children who remained in Stanley. Despite the rising fear and tension as the war progressed, and the chaotic conditions immediately following it, the class sat for their O-levels the following January. Two of the girls who had remained in town took and passed six O-levels each – one with six As, the other with 3 As and 3 Bs. These two, joined by a third qualifier, travelled the following August to England, to commence a two-year A-level course at the Thomas Peacock School. At the end of their first year there, the girl with six O-levels had taken the school prize in English Literature, while the other one captured the school prize in Physics, a subject she had not studied previously.' Mr Leonard also noted the impact of the war on the children as assessed by two of the teachers. 'An awful lot of them had suddenly grown up. In lots of cases they were children in body, but they weren't children in mind any more,' said Mrs Jenny Felton. David Evans, the Head of Stanley Junior School, believed that the war and its aftermath was generally a stimulation to the children. 'A lot more is happening now; the pupils are happier because more is going on around them. The place has really woken up.' One of their postwar reactions was, however, more troublesome. 'There was a period after the war when we had a lot of ganging – gangs fighting each other. I think that was a reaction to the war. We came down heavily on them and it stopped, but it took a while.'[9]

After the devastation and trauma of the conflict, there needed to be some positive outcomes. *Prospects for the Falkland Islands*, produced by the Falkland Islands Office in London in 1983, expressed optimism:

The future seems to hold a number of overlapping and related phases. The most constant factor will be the children. They will probably recover from the traumas of the invasion months very quickly. They are remarkably resilient, pragmatic children and will be the key factors in helping all concerned return to normality. However their normal exuberance will be restricted by the consequences of military activity.

It is possible that some aspects of the Argentine occupation may be put to direct advantage of the community. For example, the television equipment could be used for educational purposes including video, for children in Stanley and Camp. The immediate tasks of putting the schools back on to their feet may not be too daunting and all teachers and children will rapidly, willingly and enthusiastically respond to the challenge.

Certainly island students, now undertaking higher education in the UK, demonstrate the success of their earlier schooling throughout the time of the conflict.

The Falkland Islands' Appeal was set up in Britain to help those who had suffered losses during the conflict. Through this the Education Department acquired some new equipment in June 1983, including several 'two-metre' sets to enhance the opportunities for Camp children to link up by radio with their teachers. The whole system of travelling teachers had been thrown into disarray during the conflict and it proved to be very difficult to recruit more travelling teachers, given the conditions of the contracts. However, in 1984 changes were made in the procedures for recruitment, including shortening the contract to one year, and there was a flood of applications from people of high calibre through the Falkland Islands Office in London. Having led education through the turbulent period since 1981, Mr Fowler came to the end of his term of office as Superintendent and he was succeeded in 1985 by David Smith.

Eventually the buildings materialized. On 11 May 1985 Prince Andrew declared open the well-designed hostels built to accommodate the girls and boys from the Camp, and the Stanley schools could cater for all those children who wished to go to town.

This did pose problems, however, for the teachers who found themselves dealing with children at widely varying levels. At the Junior School, David Evans set up full-time remedial work with the aim of hearing every child reading every day following the philosophy that 'Once they start to read fluently, that's the key to everything else'. Mr Evans had gone to the Falklands on his first teaching contract in 1969 and had been there ever since, although he had a break to try his hand at sheep farming from 1972 to 1980. During that time he was elected to the Legislative Council and, as a member of the Education Committee, played a key part in the decision to provide a strengthened GCE programme on the Falklands to obviate the need to provide overseas scholarships for this purpose.

The Senior School's building, however, was 'proving increasingly inadequate to cope with the increased numbers attendant on the closure of the Darwin Boarding School in 1979 and the decision to centralize the provision of secondary education in Stanley'.[10]

The comprehensive *Annual Education Report* submitted in February 1986 by Superintendent David Smith gave details of the progress of Camp children compared with those in school in Stanley. In standardized tests in reading and arithmetic the seven year-old children from the Camp were the equal of their peers in Stanley, and he felt that great credit should be given to both the Camp mothers and the teachers. The ten year-olds remaining in Camp and not receiving full-time education in settlement schools, however, showed some tendency to lag behind. He felt that this strengthened the argument to encourage the Camp children to go to Stanley for their secondary education. The recent extended sub-division of areas had created a need for more travelling teachers and radio lessons, and he was putting in motion the setting up of a VHF repeater for Camp Education. He had also explored the New Zealand system of education by correspondence but felt that it would not be suitable for the Falklands.

Within his report on the provision of education at secondary level, Mr Smith stressed the importance of offering an appropriate curriculum for each of the pupils and of defining very clearly its aims in providing any particular course for them. Among these aims, he identified the importance of islanders being equipped to hold a considerable number of posts in the Civil Service, currently held by expatriate officers. But while providing schooling for academically able pupils, it was essential that the school should not neglect its other pupils for whom at present the facilities were inadequate. He looked forward to the new building which would be purpose-built for teaching a wide range of subjects such as drama, cookery, needlework, metalwork, woodwork and other technical studies, typing, office practice, book-keeping, and work with computers. 'It is hoped that the enriched curriculum resulting from the new building will give pupils knowledge and skills which will enable them to contribute to and profit from the process of economic development in these islands.'

Looking at population trends, Mr Smith speculated that provided the net immigration from outside the islands did not increase very rapidly, the existing school building would suffice for the next few years. He recommended that when the Stanley Schools became overcrowded, the system be changed to a three-tier organization, with a first school for the five- to eight-year-olds in the present Junior/Infant School; a middle school for the nine to 12s in the present Senior School; and a new upper school for the 13 to 16s.

The Senior School headmaster at this time was Jeremy Baylis who had prevously been an Army teacher, and knew nothing about the islands until he joined a combined services' scientific expedition to Elephant Island in the Antarctic in 1976, travelling in the HMS *Endurance* which called in to Stanley harbour *en route*. He was immediately attracted to Stanley and within two years had applied successfully for a teaching post there, arriving with his family in 1978. Straightaway he found he was enjoying the challenges of the work on the Falklands. Mr Baylis became Head of the Senior School immediately after the Argentine invasion. By 1986 he was still encountering problems, among them lack of space for all the courses required. He was also concerned to find a way of motivating the Camp children to undertake the more advanced education opportunities as taken by the Stanley children. He hoped that 'with the passage of time, academic success becomes more the norm, and because it becomes a more acceptable goal to the rest, the thing gathers momentum', and also that, with assessment of course work and the option of including local studies in the newly-introduced CSE programme, more children would enjoy more success.

John Leonard concluded his 1986 article for the *Guardian* on education in the Falklands by describing the opportunities which were existing for islanders to take up higher education abroad: 'The outlook for the islands must inevitably be far brighter as a result of such a programme – spotlighting as it does whatever talents and abilities exist among its youth, regardless of their background or financial resources.' Within the £31 million development aid provided for the Falklands by the British Government after the war with Argentina, it was planned to provide overseas training at higher education level. Administering the aid, Mrs Caroline Armstrong of the British Council stated: 'I would see it as maximising the potential there is here; perhaps encouraging more islanders to take on key roles, so that they are, on a day to day basis, very much shaping the destiny of the islands.'[11] This certainly echoed the aims of education as outlined earlier by Superintendent David Smith.

One other problem in the Senior School was the absence of a foreign language, which was often needed for entry to UK universities. Spanish was the obvious choice to be introduced, but this was a highly emotive matter in view of the recent experiences with the Argentine. Spanish had been taught in the Senior School as far back as 1969 and, in fact, teachers from the Argentine had been sent to teach it. Also, since the early 1970s there had been the unlimited opportunities for Falkland Islanders to go Argentina for their secondary education, although this system had virtually died out before the conflict. But now the islanders were predictably reticent and cautious and, since the conflict, 'the question of language teaching was quietly left in abeyance'. However, in 1986 Mr Baylis had high hopes that a teacher of Spanish would soon be coming from the UK.

Mrs Eileen Murphy took over the role of Superintendent of Education and submitted the annual review for 1987 to the Governor for his *Budget Address to the Legislative Council*. She gave credit to the teachers for undertaking extra work during a year of serious staff shortages. However, energetic action had resulted in the recruitment of teachers for both the Infant and Junior School and as many as seven new teachers for the Senior School, with three more expected soon. But problems still remained in recruiting travelling teachers for Camp Education, for which the difficult work needed people of a limited age group. Other challenges facing the Department were the introduction of the GCSE, and the development of systems to ensure a balance between 'reasonable freedom and controlled activity' at the Stanley Hostel.

However, the most serious problem was the shortage of space due to inadequate buildings. The 1954 school, built for 70 to 80 infants and juniors, was now having to accommodate 155 pupils. Regarding the seniors, Mrs Murphy concluded her report by stressing that: 'The CEO wishes finally to emphasize her belief that the most urgent need in education for all Falkland Islands children is a new Senior School. She is preparing a paper on this subject for the consideration of His Excellency and for Honorary Members of the Education Committee and Legislative Council.'[12]

This clearly put in motion a further significant step towards the creation, a few years later, of a brand-new, purpose-built secondary school of which the Falkland Islands could be justifiably proud.

1988-92: An Island Director of Education

The year 1988 was a milestone in the history of education on the Falkland Islands because it marked the first time that an islander held the position of Director of Education. Mrs Phyllis Rendell was appointed to the role in June 1988, having previously served on the islands as a teacher from 1972 to 1975 and since 1982, when she returned to the Falklands from the UK. She was born and brought up on the islands, receiving her schooling in Camp before going to boarding school in Britain. She gained her formal teaching qualification in the UK. From 1984 to 1988 she ran the Camp Education Unit, and, reflecting later on this work, stated: 'My aim was to give Camp children the same standards of teaching as Stanley children. We found funds to employ qualified travelling teachers. A second aim was to bring education to every child on every day of the school year, not just when travelling teachers were on the farms. We did this through two-metre radio and relay repeaters. Now every child has either a radio lesson or a teacher with them for thirty-nine weeks of the year.'[13]

On assuming office in 1988 Mrs Rendell updated and reissued a concise but comprehensive document entitled: *Education in the Falkland Islands*, the major features summarised as:

(a) Free and compulsory schooling for all children from five to 15 years, and voluntary further education up to 16.

(b) Government provision of teachers, equipment and supplies for all education, including settlement teachers from 1990.

(c) In Stanley: Primary school, 12 teachers, 170 pupils.
Senior school, 14 specialist teachers, 135 pupils.
(Including local UK-trained, UK and New Zealand teachers.)

(d) Internal and external examinations: GCSE (in 16 subjects), RSA, Pitman's, SMP Mathematics and AEB, but no A-level

(e) Funding for suitable students to take A levels (at Peter Symonds' Sixth Form College, Winchester) and further and higher education in the UK.

(f) A Camp Education Unit to support a team of six travelling teachers, setting work for children between their teacher's two-week visits in each seven weeks; daily radio lessons from Stanley or the schools at Fox Bay and Goose Green and other settlement schools.

(g) Purpose-built dormitories (opened in 1985) in the Stanley Hostel for up to 85 nine- to 16-year-olds; boarding fees £66 per term for the first child, £44 for a second child, and no fees for a third or subsequent child.

(h) A public library and heated indoor swimming pool (to be completed in October 1989), administered by the Education Department.

But – perhaps the most significant information of all – Mrs Rendell reported: 'Plans are going ahead for a new community school to be operational by 1992. It will include facilities to expand technical and vocational courses, and a sports hall will be available for community use.'

During Phyllis Rendell's first four years of office, she led progress and developments on a number of fronts, supported by the Education Committee and other colleagues. Dr David Burgess was appointed head of the Stanley Senior School in May 1988, and held the post for the final years of the life of the old school and for the transition into the new Community School. He came to the Falklands having had previous overseas experience in El Salvador and Nepal. An able administrator, he restructured secondary education on the Falklands, giving it greater breadth and a higher profile, thus helping to plan and prepare for the establishment of the new Community School in 1992. Mr Richard Fogerty was appointed to run the Camp Education Unit in

1988 and, to quote his predecessor Mrs Rendell, in 1992, 'the system has gone from strength to strength over the last four years'.[14] Further and Community Education had benefited from the appointment of a Community Education Officer, whose responsibilities included the oversight of evening and apprenticeship classes, and who also worked closely with the Senior School concerning careers and work experience programmes and with youth organisations. One disappointment to Mrs Rendell was the difficulty in attracting Falkland Islanders into the teaching profession, partly due to the need to go off the islands to the UK for training for a period of up to six years. Talking on St Helena radio in July 1991, Mrs Rendell explained: 'Most of the teachers at present come from the UK, although it is hoped that improved salaries for teachers may encourage more islanders to take up the profession.' Nevertheless, over recent years there had been a supply of teachers from New Zealand, both for the Camp and the Stanley Schools. In 1989 the first islander for many years returned as a trained teacher – in Mathematics. The year had also seen the narrowing of the gap between the salaries of contracted and locally-employed teachers; improved promotion prospects for local people with the introduction of responsibility posts, and the visit of an Educational Psychologist to give help and support to teachers of children with special educational needs.

During this time the management of education was structured on a more formal basis. The terms of a new *Education Ordinance* were debated fully by Staff and the Education Committee, and approved by the Legislative Council to become operative on 1 January 1990. Three major executive groups were established: the Education Board, the Library Committee and the Scholarships and Awards Committee. The Director was an ex-officio member of the Board, chaired by an elected member of the Legislative Council. The Board was responsible to the Governor and Executive Council for educational matters on the islands, including policies related to staffing, curriculum, buildings, term dates, overseas training and departmental budgets. The Director was also to hold the chair of the other two committees.

The major matter on the educational agenda for the Falkland Islands was undoubtedly plans for the new senior school in Stanley and a further committee was set up to monitor progress, this involving consultation between the architects and specialist senior school staff. The actual project commenced on 15 September 1990. In her 1990 *Education Report*, Mrs Rendell stated that £10 million had been allocated for the new school and a site selected adjacent to the swimming pool. Archivist Jane Cameron described the ceremony of the unveiling of the foundation plaque: 'HRH The Duke of Kent unveiled a foundation stone plaque when visiting the islands on 2 October 1990 and HRH The Duke of Edinburgh expressed keen interest in the project when he viewed the site on March 1991. Islanders will have much to be proud of when the school finally opens its doors to students and the community in 1992 ... There will be something for everyone included in the facilities.'[15] These were to include a large multi-purpose sports hall, a playing field and athletics track, the public library and a coffee shop. Expanded educational provision would include facilities for vocational courses for school leavers, a day release scheme for apprentices, and adult day and evening classes.

In her 1990 Report, Mrs Rendell explained that the enhanced provision aimed to fulfil the Education Department's Statement of Policy:

1. To promote the development of pupils to their maximum potential, preparing them for adulthood.
2. To provide a broad and balanced curriculum, relevant to pupils' needs as well as to the requirements of life in the Falkland Islands and elsewhere.
3. To promote the cultural, educational and sporting opportunities available to both school age and adult members of the community.
4. To foster respect and a caring attitude for the welfare of others, in all pupils.
5. To provide the above to pupils in as positive and enjoyable a manner as possible.

By 1991, the Director of Education was able to report on the name chosen for the new school. This had aroused considerable interest and debate, and the name – The Falkland Islands Community School – had been chosen after a considerable time earlier in the year collating suggestions for a name from both the public and interested parent groups. 'Suggestions were presented varying from those wishing to retain the present name and others wanting the name to reflect the facilities that would be available in the new complex. Ultimately Executive Council agreed on the name Falkland Islands Community School.'[16]

Meanwhile work went on as normal in the existing schools on the islands. The 1989 *Education Report* explained that, with the introduction of GCSE work, the Senior School had gone through a period of considerable reorganisation in which subject-based rooms were allocated for each specialist teacher, and candidates from Years 4 and 5 and some day-release students had been entered for public examinations. Staff committees had been working on curriculum development, the production of handbooks and a school magazine. The Friends of Stanley

Senior School, the parent/teacher association, had had a successful first year of existence.

The Stanley School Hostel had accommodated up to 47 pupils and during the year a new programme of activities had been introduced to help cover the wide age-range and varied behaviour patterns of the pupils. These included introducing tutor groups, regular homework hours, and activity records to be completed by houseparents. Two fruitful days of discussion were held with all of the people responsible for running the Hostel to clarify their aims and objectives. The Educational Psychologist visiting the Falklands had held two useful meetings with the Hostel staff.

By 1991 the Senior School had a population of 136 pupils, and 33 were accommodated in Stanley House. The school had begun to work with the International GCSE Board at Cambridge, in addition to the Southern Examining Board, and a new Agriculture GCSE Course was being taught jointly by the school's own teachers and members of the Agriculture Department. In the outdoor pursuits programme, pupils had carried out geographical, scientific and historical research at Goose Green and Port Louis. The Community Education Officer had set up a resource centre in the Senior School, giving information on local career opportunities. The Evening Class and Apprenticeship Class Programme had continued. With the ending of British Council funding for island education, the Community Education Officer took over the role of advising other government department staff and the public on suitable overseas educational opportunities.

Meanwhile, the Camp Education Unit had continued its policy of providing a basic primary education for Camp children to enable all 10 or 11 year-olds to transfer as smoothly as possible to the school system in Stanley. At the end of 1989 only two children had not transferred. At the same time, population trends were increasing the number of isolated single family units while the settlement populations were decreasing, thus boosting the need for travelling teachers. For instance, the Goose Green school population dropped from 12 to 4 children, while within the sub-division of Hill Cove the number of farms with young children rose from 18 to 22. It was anticipated that 1990 would see a further increase following the sub-division of Port San Carlos. To help with this situation, the education department was looking at ways of making full use of improved communications, including the new telephone network. In 1989 a school was established at Mount Pleasant, with links to the Camp Education Unit but with a military-sponsored teacher on contract. Camp statistics over the previous few years showed a decline in pupils, but a slight rise in teacher locations:

A Camp child in her own classroom, 1992 (Photograph supplied by Phyllis Rendell)

	PUPILS	TRAVELLING TEACHER LOCATIONS	CAMP SCHOOLS
1987 (April)	70	18	6
1988 (Feb)	67	21	5
1989 (Feb)	55 + 3MPA	22	5 + IMPA*

* Mount Pleasant

By the time Phyllis Rendell wrote her 1991 *Education Report*, Camp Education was catering for 63 children. The number of locations requiring a visit by a travelling teacher had increased to 29, but every effort was being made to encourage children to visit other farms when a teacher was there. During Farmers' Week, twenty Camp children had attended classes in Stanley Primary School. (Farmers' Week is an annual occasion when farmers from all parts of the Falklands gather in Stanley for trade, mutual support and social purposes. The farm children accompany their parents and can take advantage of the school facilities.) Mrs Rendell reported that the Camp Education Managers were supporting a policy of centralisation of all education facilities in Stanley and the need for an island-wide primary curriculum was highlighted.

By 1991, the Primary School comprised the Reception Class and six year classes for 147 children. To give more room to the overcrowded younger children, plans were made to move the infants into the main building and the older children to the prefabricated block. The Director reported a year in which there had been a continuing concentration on a specific area of the curriculum, at present mathematics.

Regarding pre-school education, disappointment had been recorded in the *Penguin News* of 15 June 1990 by the Nursery School teacher, that a decision had been made by the Councillors not to establish the Nursery School as part of the Falkland Islands' education system. This school had been running for two years and had been attended by 45 children, of whom 75% had been local. Little progress had been made on this front by 1991, when Mrs Rendell reported that, although the Education Department did not have direct involvement in the Stanley Nursery School, it was ready to offer advice as required. However, the Camp Education Department continued to provide pre-school materials for young children on farms and in other isolated areas, and pressure was growing across the islands for the provision of a wider service for young children. It was hoped that this might be possible in the near future.

Meanwhile the Library Committee, formed in 1989, was charged with promoting the Library's usefulness, and moderate interest had been shown. But the swimming pool had been an instant success, and it was officially opened in February 1990 with international swimmer David Wilkie as the chief guest.

A further significant development early in the directorship of Phyllis Rendell was the move towards inter-island co-operation. In her interview on St Helena Radio during a visit in July 1991, Mrs Rendell spoke of the hope which she and Mr Basil George, CEO St Helena, hold

Young People at work, 1992

for future educational co-operation between the Falkland Islands and St Helena, for their mutual benefit.

Within her 1991 Report Mrs Rendell continued to comment on the progress during the year of all aspects of the educational system on the islands. Anticipation of the new school was uppermost in the minds of many Falkland islanders.

1992: The Falkland Islands' Community School Opens in Heritage Year

The year 1992 was a strategic one, as the Falkland Islanders had a five-fold celebration. Not only was it the 400th anniversary of the first sighting of the islands by Captain John Davis (14 August 1592); the 100th anniversary of the consecration of Christ Church Cathedral (21 February 1892); the 100th anniversary of the establishment of the Volunteer Defence Force (13 June 1892); and the tenth anniversary of the liberation of the Falklands Islands (14 June 1982) – but also it marked the official opening of the new Falkland Islands Community School.

With a motto of 'Desire the Right', a Souvenir Brochure entitled *Heritage Year 1992*, was compiled by Nikki Summers in which it was stated:

The real celebration of Heritage Year however is the Falklands people: their hard work and the dedication that has been put in over the years to make the islands what they are today – a self sufficient and caring community with a belief in the future.

Clearly, education had played an important part for one and a half centuries in reaching this point, and the belief in the future was based on the confidence that the rising generations would equip themselves through education to absorb and foster this heritage, and to carry it into the future. The Governor of the Falkland Islands, W. H. Fullerton CMG emphasized this in his message in the brochure:

There have been many improvements in the infrastructure. The largest single element in all of them is the new Stanley senior school now under construction which will also have facilities for the community as a whole. The emphasis given to the quality of this school is perhaps more indicative than anything else of the outlook the islanders now have for the years ahead. The islands have a promising and exciting future, one which should be increasingly attractive to young people and in which education should play a greater role.

Lord Shackleton was invited to perform the Opening Ceremony at the new school. Created a Baron in 1958, and a former Leader of the House of Lords, he has had important links with the Falklands since 1976 when he produced an *Economic Survey of the Falkland Islands*. This he updated in 1982. He was awarded the Freedom of Stanley in 1988. Unable to be present himself at the Opening of the School, he was represented by his daughter, the Hon Mrs A Burgel, who unveiled the plaque. Through a live satellite link Lord Shackleton formally opened the school on 17 August 1992 saying:

Falkland Islands Community School, 1992 (Photograph supplied by Phyllis Rendell)

The splendid new school does represent definite evidence of belief in the future of the Falkland Islands. Former Councillor and Chairman of the Education Board, John Cheek, has done so much to promote the concept of a new secondary school and indeed the whole Council deserve credit for making such a brave decision to invest in education in this way. The Director of Education, Phyllis Rendell, has worked extraordinarily hard on the project and her enthusiasm for the promotion of the concept has been contagious.'

After congratulating those responsible for the construction of the buildings, including the local Director of Public Works, Brian Hill, and the Clerk of Works, Tom Robertson, Lord Shackleton concluded:

The community school offers something for everyone and represents determination on the part of the Falkland Islands people to build for a secure and prosperous future.

The Falkland Islands Community School opened its doors to its first pupils in September 1992. The comprehensive and careful planning by many people had come to fruition. One of these, David Burgess, completed his term of office as Headteacher of the school in December 1992. His place as Head was taken by Mrs Judith Crowe who was Head of a school in Lincolnshire before taking up her post on the Falkland Islands.

Writing in 1992, Mrs Phyllis Rendell explained her philosophy in tackling her major and responsible task as Director of Education for the Falkland Islands. After describing two key objectives in her work – to

English class in session at the Community School, 1992 (Photograph supplied by Phyllis Rendell)

promote the Falklands in the curriculum; and to introduce a policy of equal salaries for equal qualifications within teaching, to encourage more young islanders into the profession – she stated:

As Director my main aim has been to see a wider curriculum at secondary level. The Headteacher, David Burgess, has done much in this field since 1988 and the culmination of our efforts has been to open the Falkland Islands Community School this year where excellent facilities are available to develop vocational courses. I have always believed that able islanders are well catered for and can go to UK for higher education but we have a useful band of practical young people who need to develop their skills. With training, they could do many of the jobs here that outside contractors come in to do. This is an exciting area to develop, for instance through day release classes for apprenticeships. So much of this has been achieved on St Helena and I learnt a lot from my visit to Prince Andrew's School.[17]

The islands were now provided with wide-ranging facilities for the educational and recreational benefit not only of school age children but of all other islanders. This was a far cry from 1846, when a school was opened for the recent settlers on the Falklands by the colonial chaplain, the Reverend J. L. Moody, in the Long Room of the Army Barracks in the Dockyard in Stanley.

There is no doubt that the early pioneers in education on the Falkland Islands, ranging from the far-sighted educationalists such as Dean Brandon to the intrepid travelling teachers who took education to remote Camp areas, would marvel at today's provision for the people of the islands and would be proud that their work of the past has helped to lay its foundations.

Part V

Schooling in the
South Atlantic Islands:
the Future

15
1992: Educational Opportunities and the Future

Yes, we are the future of our Island.
St Helena School Song, 1988[1]
Eric George, Susan O'Bey

The school is an ideal setting to enjoy teaching.
Eric Twaddell, 1992[2]

It took me only a year away from home to realize how lucky we are to be living on Tristan da Cunha.
Marlene Swain, 1984[3]

The Community School offers something for everyone and represents determination on the part of the Falkland Islands people to build for a secure and prosperous future.
Lord Shackleton, 1992[4]

The story of education on each of these South Atlantic Islands has pursued a pathway strewn with adventures, difficulties, hazards, successes, failures, beginnings and endings. Throughout the existence of schooling on each island, there have been successions of people who have added their own contribution to the story, and who have helped to lay the foundations of the present systems of education which are giving the future leaders the skills, knowledge, aptitudes and enthusiasm to prepare for their roles on their island, or to apply what they have learned to life elsewhere.

In terms of education leadership, the senior officer on each of the islands of St Helena, Tristan da Cunha and the Falklands is, in 1992, one of the islanders themselves. Since 1983 Basil George has held the post of St Helena's Education Officer, this being designated Chief Education Officer in 1985. In this capacity he has led the planning, introduction and implementation of the three-tier system. On Tristan da Cunha, Marlene Swain became the island's Education Officer and

Head Teacher in January 1992, taking over from Jim Kerr. She had held an acting role in this capacity on occasions in the past but now is appointed in her own right to the leading position. Like Basil George from St Helena, she received all of her schooling on her own island and has taken opportunities to go to the UK during her teaching career to gain wider experiences which were to stand her in good stead for her leadership role. In 1988 Phyllis Rendell became the first Falkland Islander to hold the leading role in education when she was appointed to be Director of Education. She had prepared for her important task, having received her schooling both on the Falklands and in the UK, and having gained wider educational experiences in the UK. This local leadership marks a significant step forward in the progress of each island and pays tribute to those educators of the past who have helped to mould the systems which produce island leaders.

Clearly, the education system on Ascension Island has developed differently from that on the other three South Atlantic islands, having been the direct responsibility of the major organizations using this island, which has played a strategic role in international affairs.

It is not surprising that there are other points of similarity between the stories of education on these islands. Each has developed important educational links abroad, realizing the vital importance of keeping open the door to outside ideas and new opportunities. Through past links with East Suffolk and Jersey, and with the long-standing St Helena Link Committee based on the Cheltenham and Gloucester College of Higher Education (formerly the College of St Paul and St Mary), St Helena has been able to take full advantage of further, vocational and higher education opportunities for their school-leavers, and in-service and degree courses for their experienced teachers. In addition over the years, through the Link, St Helena has welcomed many advisers sponsored by the ODA to range alongside the local teachers in their work and to run appropriate courses. The island has also been able to gain from the provision of educational resources from North Hertfordshire Education Authority, through the Link. Tristan da Cunha has enjoyed outside links in the past with the Hervé Bazin School in Orleans, France, with Denstone College in the UK and with the Prince Andrew School on St Helena where students have been able to receive additional and further education. Teachers have attended courses in Bristol, Cheltenham and Hertfordshire. The Falkland Islands have experienced a number of overseas links, for instance in the UK with Brighton Polytechnic, the Thomas Peacock School and Winchester Sixth Form College, and in the British School, Montevideo,

Uruguay. On Ascension Island the Two Boats School has a large proportion of both UK and St Helenian children, and the important outside influence comes from the ever-changing population. Each island has experienced its own challenges, brought about by the changing circumstances of the island itself. Each has had the uncertain advantage of having episodes within its history in which it has been thrown into the world's limelight. St Helena gained world attention through its famous prisoners over the years and as a once important, heavily used port of call for many ships. Ascension Island has for several decades earned world recognition as a strategically important centre for international and satellite communications. Tristan da Cunha claimed the world's attention on a day in October 1961 when the devastating volcanic eruption seemed to mark the end of a community living on such a remote island. And the people of the Falkland Islands found themselves in the middle of the bitter conflict between the UK and Argentina which could have marked the end of the type of existence which the islanders had developed for themselves. The common feature about each of these major events has been that the outcome of hardships and almost insuperable problems has been the birth of a new spirit of determination within the islanders themselves to build for a firmer future.

Domestically, the story of education on each of the islands has borne similarities with others in the group. Rugged terrain has caused problems in the past in getting schooling to children in the remoter parts of St Helena and in the Falkland Islands, but the importance given to education has increased over the years and now education is available to every child. The buildings and facilities made available for schools at times in the past on all four islands have frequently been less than adequate, and teachers and pupils have persevered with their work in very difficult circumstances. But, far from daunting the people concerned, these hardships seem to have created a resourcefulness and determination not found in people elsewhere whose lives have been cushioned against such circumstances.

Each of the islands has been proud of its British heritage and the nature of education has evolved from being heavily modelled on the British system, to the present structures and curricula which include local studies and skills to satisfy the needs of the island and to take it into the future. Since none of the islands at present offers higher education it is inevitable and essential that students who are academically capable of doing so should be able to gain the entry qualifications in order to enter higher education in the UK or elsewhere. For this and other purposes and where appropriate the curriculum covers work allied to the UK syllabuses for GCSE or A-levels.

The future may well hold opportunity for more inter-island links between these four South Atlantic islands in terms of consultation, teacher exchange, participation in courses on another island for pupils, teachers and education officers and in general mutual support. In the past, the distances between the islands and the difficulties of travel and communication have impeded progress with this form of co-operation, but these obstacles are gradually being lessened. As Basil George, Chief Education Officer on the island of St Helena said on 10 July 1991:

Educationally the islands would benefit from more interchange. Each has in common the development of an education system for a small isolated island community. The school has an important function both for human resource development and providing a focus in the cultural life of the local community. All islands have reached a stage of development where it is important that representatives get together to decide for themselves how they see closer links could be fostered for the benefit of all concerned.

The unfolding of the story of these four South Atlantic Islands has demonstrated clearly that the sheer remoteness and the courage of the small communities have helped to mould generations of people who have developed an intense loyalty and love for their homeland. Schools have played an important part in building up this heritage. Long may they flourish.

References

Notes on References used in the text

Blue Books Annual Returns from the Governor to the Secretary of State for the
   Colonies, giving full details of government departments, employees,
   statistical and financial information for the year just completed (St
   Helena, 1838-1942; Ascension Island; Falkland Islands)
Education Ordinances: Governmental legislation, approved by the UK Secretary of
   State, introducing laws and regulations for education.
EIC In-Letters, Vol 1-42, 1804-34: Letters received by the Governor of St Helena
   from the Court of Directors in London
EIC Out-Letters, Vol 1-28, 1706-1825: Copies of Letters from the Governor of St
   Helena to the Court of Directors in London
EIC Register and Directory: Official List of the names and appointed positions
   world-wide, of employees of the Company, including the St Helena Civil
   Establishment
St Helena Annual Report: Report produced by the Governor for the Secretary of State
   summarising the major work and developments within each Government
   department (usually despatched with the Blue Book)
Hussey Charity: A bequest from Rebecca Hussey for the benefit of liberated Africans
   on St Helena
St Helena Calendar and Directory, 1834-56: Annual publication printed on St Helena,
   listing Government employees, including the school establishment
St Helena Gazette, 1845-date: Annual data about Government Departments and
   employees. From 1845 to 1851, these also served as a local newspaper.

Abbreviations used in the References

ADM   Letters to the Admiralty from the Officer i/c Ascension Island
BenSoc   Benevolent Society
CDR   East India Company Court of Directors' Report (India House)
CLEC   Colonial Land and Emigration Commissioners
CLR   (see SPG: CLR)
CMG   Companion of (the Order of) St Michael and St George
COL   Colonial Office List, 1862-1966, Annual lists of Government employees,
            occupations, salary etc
CSIL   Colonial Secretary's In-Letters, 1839-1908
CSOL   Colonial Secretary's Out-Letters, 1839-99
EIC   East India Company
GovDesp   *Governor's Despatches* to the Secretary of State for the Colonies, 1837-1909,
            1927-63: Copies of letters reporting on matters related to island life,

people, buildings and systems, enclosing relevant letters, documents and extracts.

JNM   Janisch, H. R., *Notes and Memoranda on St Helena Records, Vols 1-132, 1678-1836*: Extracts selected in 1879 by Governor Janisch from the St Helena Records (Consultations), including a detailed index of Vols 1-132

LegCo   Legislative Council

MBE   Member of the (Order of the) British Empire

OBE   Officer of the (Order of the) British Empire

ODA   Overseas Development Administration, (MOD, Ministry of Overseas Development)

PAS   The Prince Andrew School, St Helena

PersInt   Personal Interview

PWSD   Public Works and Services' Department, St Helena

SHDM   *St Helena Diocesan Magazine*, 1899-1937: Monthly newspaper

SHG   *St Helena Guardian*, 1861-1923: Weekly newspaper

SHLE   St Helena Letters from England, 1673-1701: Documents sent by the EIC Court of Directors in London to their appointed Governor on St Helena

SHM   *St Helena Magazine*, 1937-51: Monthly newspaper

SHN   *St Helena News*, 1988-present: Weekly newspaper

SHNR   *St Helena News Review*, 1958-86: Weekly newspaper

SHR   *St Helena Records*, Vols 1-136, 1678-1836: Reports and documents of the Consultations of the Island Governor and Council, with copies for the London EIC Court of Directors, the Governor, and for record purposes.

SHW   *St Helena Wirebird*, 1955-66 (also called the St Helena Weekly News)

SPG: CLR Letters sent to the Society for the Propagation of the Gospel in Cape Town from their appointed clergy at home and overseas are included in *Capetown Letters Received* in Rhodes House Library, Oxford.

SPG-LR   (As above) Correspondence with SPG in London

SSS   Secondary Selective School, St Helena, 1946-88

VSO   Voluntary Service Overseas

Introduction

1 George, E. M., & O'Bey, S., *Prince Andrew School Song*, 1988
2 Eliot, T. S., *Little Gidding*, Part V
3 George, B., Speech, 12.5.1989

Part I: Island of St Helena

Chapter 1: 1661-1810

1 SHR, Vol 1, 2.11.1678
2 SHM, Dec 1938, re July 1674
3 SHLE, 20.2.1677
4 SHM, Dec 1938, re Sept 1678
5 SHLE, 20.3.1677
6 SHR, Vol 1, 2.11.1678
7 SHLE, 24.3.1679
8 JNM, 1679, 1680; SHR Vol 1, pp79,104
9 JNM, 1683; SHR Vol 1, p336
10 JNM, 16.1.1682, pp221,231

11 SHLE, Feb 1683, Vol 2, p45; SHDM, Jan 1924
12 SHR, Vol 3, 25.1.1688
13 SHR, Vol 6, p60
14 SHR, Vol 9, p58
15 SHDM, Nov 1925
16 SHR, Vol 11, 21.3.1714, p393
17 SHR, June 1722
18 SHR, 30.11.1725
19 SHDM, Jan 1924
20 Ibid
21 SHR, Vol 84, 29.6.1795, 20.7.1795
22 SHR, 23.6.1806
23 SHR, Vol 113, 2.8.1813, p316

Chapter 2: 1811-34

1 SHR, Vol 125, 12.2.1824, p181
2 Chaplin, A., *St Helena's Who's Who*
3 SHR, Vol 113, 10.5.1813, p143

4 Evans, K., *The English Educational
System*
5 SHR, Vol 64, 1781
6 SHR, Vol 100, 8.11.1803
7 Gosse, P., *St Helena, 1502-1938*, p267
8 SHR, 12.5.1823
9 Brooke, T. H., *History of St Helena*,
p104
10 Gosse, P., op.cit., pp278-9
11 SHR, 23.11.1818
12 Hearl, T. W., *Library Requisition List*,
1820
13 SHR, Vol 125, 12.2.1824, p172
14 Brooke, T. H., op.cit., p404
15 Brooke, T. H., op.cit., p412
16 SHDM, Feb 1834
17 Brooke, T. H., op.cit., p117
18 Robson, T., *St Helena Memoirs*, c.1830
19 Jackson, E. L., *St Helena, The Historic
Island*, p73

Chapter 3: 1834-67
1 Crown Ordinance No 24, 1839
2 Benevolent Society, *Schools 1835-
1852*, 2.6.1835
3 Ibid., 19.4.1836
4 Ibid., 2.7.1835
5 Jackson, E. L., op.cit., p73
6 Benevolent Society, op.cit., 7.8.1838
7 CSIL, July/August 1839
8 Curtis, S. J. & Boultwood, M. E. A.,
*An Introductory History of the English
Educational System Since 1800*
9 Benevolent Society, op.cit., 9.6.1845
10 Ibid., 1.7.1845
11 GovDesp, Vol 2, 3.9.1844, p156
12 GovDesp, Vol 3, 17.8.1850, p313
13 GovDesp, Vol 4, 13.10.1852
14 Foote, Lieut. A. H., USN, *Advocate*,
10.6.1852
15 SHG, 8.8.1861, 21.11.1861
16 St Helena Record (newspaper),
3.1.1861
17 CSIL 48, 30.11.1865, p601
18 Ibid., 9.6.1865, p285
19 GovDesp, Vol 7, 12.5.1865, p161
20 Ibid, 14.3.1866, p244
21 SHG, 14.2.1866
22 GovDesp, Vol 8, August 1866, p1
23 BB, Education, 1965
24 CSIL 51, 18.12.1866, p93
25 CSIL, 8.5.1867

Chapter 4: 1868-1903
1 SHG, 18.6.1874
2 SHG, 21.1.1869
3 SHG, 22.12.1870
4 GovDesp, Vol 9, 24.8.1871, p27
5 SHG, 28.12.1871
6 SHG, 18.12.1873
7 SHG, 13.8.1874
8 SHG, 22.10.1874
9 Dir-Gen., Military Educ., *Third
Report on Army School and Libraries*
10 Map of Jamestown, 1880 (owned by
N. Thorpe)
11 Board of Education *Minute Book*,
5.7.1877
12 Ibid., 6.6.1878
13 SHG, 3.1.1884
14 SHG, 7.4.1884
15 Jackson, E. L., op.cit.
16 SHG, 3.2.1887
17 CLR, Vol 116, p370
18 SHG, 18.2.1892
19 SHG, 5.5.1892
20 Sterndale, R. A., *Sancta Helena: An
Island in Extremis*, (attached to 1894
Blue Book)
21 SHG, 9.7.1896
22 GovDesp, Vol 16, 15.3.1897, p148
23 Ibid, 4.9.1899, p376
24 SHPM, 20.2.1900
25 Boer Prisoners, *De Krijgsevangene*,
1.7.1901
26 Boer Prisoners, op.cit., 29.6.1901
27 SHG, July 1902
28 GovDesp, Vol 17, 29.4.1902, p140
29 St Helena Govt., *Ordinance*,
17.1.1903; GovDesp, Vol 17, p244
30 GovDesp, Vol 17, 27.2.1903, p272
31 SH *Annual Report* to Secretary of State
for Colonies, 1903

Chapter 5: 1904-41
1 SHG, 29.8.1907
2 PersInt, Grace Sim, 8.8.1991
3 Ben Soc *Committee Minutes*, 7.6.1956
4 Ibid, 1904, 1905
5 PersInt, Henry Benjamin, 27.7.1991
6 PersInt, Harold Isaac, 2.7.1991
7 PersInt, Constantine Family
members, Phyllis John, Oliver
Constantine, Delphia Stevens, July
1991

8　Constantine, E., *Personal Writings*, 1904-1960
9　Constantine, E., 'What my life as a schoolteacher has taught me', SHW, Oct 1958
10　Thomas, J., *Two Great Educationalists in St Helena in the Early 1900s*
11　PersInt, Charlie George, 15.8.1991
12　Castell, R., *St Helena*, p123
13　PersInt, Ruth Pridham, September 1991
14　SHG, 29.8.1907
15　Thomas, J., op.cit.
16　PersInt, Phyllis John, July 1991
17　PersInt, Muriel Young, Aug 1991
18　PersInt, Cavell Duncan, 17.8.1991
19　PersInt, Maisie Benjamin, 27.7.1991
20　SHDM, April 1921
21　PersInt, Martha George, Heather Abel, Arnold Flagg, July/August 1991
22　PersInt, Bill Drabble, 23.8.1991
23　PersInt, Bert Quinn, Sept 1992; SHN 11.9.1992
24　SHDM, Dec 1924
25　PersInt, Phyllis John, July 1991
26　SHDM, March 1929
27　SHDM, August 1932
28　SHM, July 1939
29　Hussey Charity Trustees' *Minute Book*, 14.7.1939
30　*Education Ordinance Agreement*, 7.7.1941

Chapter 6: 1941-60
1　SHW, May 1957
2　PersInt, Evelyn Bagley, 1.8.1991
3　PersInt, Derek Fagan, 26.7.1991
4　PersInt, Dulcie Robertson, August 1991
5　PersInt, Ruth Pridham, September 1991
6　Porter, P., Personal Correspondence, 25.8.1992
7　PersInt, Joan Thomas, 10.10.1991
8　PersInt, Cecil Maggott, Basil George, Gwen Yon, Bill Drabble, Dorothy Hudson, July/August 1991
9　PersInt, Pat Musk, 9.9.1991
10　SHM, November 1947
11　PersInt, Rita Nicholls, 9.10.1991
12　Kerr, N., Personal Correspondence,

June 1991, Oct 1992, Jan 1993
13　PersInt, Harold Isaac, July 1991
14　PersInt, Muriel Williams, 10.10.1991

Chapter 7: 1960-88
1　Billing, R., *Education Report*, Oct 1971
2　PersInt, Eric M. George, 2.8.1991
3　Several PersInt, July-Oct 1991
4　Johns, A., Personal Correspondence, 20.9.1992
5　PersInt, Cliff Huxtable, 6.8.1991
6　Gillett, S., Personal Correspondence, June 1991
7　Cross, T., *St Helena*, p106
8　PersInt, Cliff Huxtable, 6.8.1991
9　Massingham, Gov, *Speech*, 6.4.1984 (recorded by St Helena Radio)
10　Cannan, E., *The Churches of the South Atlantic, 1502-1991*, p164
11　Hudson, Mr, Taped Interview, PAS Library, 1990

Chapter 8: 1988-92
1　SHN, Basil George, *Speech*, 12.5.1989
2　Ibid
3　PersInt, Eric Benjamin, 9.11.1992
4　PersInt, Basil George, Dec 1991
5　PersInt, Arnold Flagg, 22.7.1991
6　PersInt, Edith Timm, 18.9.1992
7　PersInt, Lilian Crowie, Nov 1992
8　PersInt, Patsy Flagg, 24.9.1992
9　PersInt, Eric M. George, 2.8.1991
10　PersInt, Ruth Pridham, Sept 1991
11　Birchall, John, *Speech*, 5.6.1989
12　PersInt, Terry Ward, August 1992
13　Ward, Terry, *Broadcast Interview*, St Helena Radio, 23.9.1992
14　PersInt, Edith Timm, Dec 1992
15　PersInt, Heather George, 3.10.1991
16　PersInt, Rita Nicholls, 9.10.1991
17　PersInt, Stedson George, 1.10.1991; 10.8.1992
18　PersInt, Edward Benjamin, 7.8.1991
19　Young, Elizabeth, Personal Correspondence, Oct 1991
20　PersInt, Joyce Harris, 2.10.1991, 4.12.1992
21　PersInt, Muriel Williams, 10.10.1991
22　PersInt, Joan Thomas, 10.10.1991

23 PersInt, Muriel Leo, 8.10.1991
24 PersInt, Maisie Thomas, 7.10.1991
25 PersInt, Iva Henry, 28.7.1991
26 PersInt, Elizabeth Young, August
    1992

Chapter 9: 1992
1 George, B., *Education Circular*,
    31.7.1992
2 PersInt, Betty Joshua, Nov 1992
3 George, B., *Education Circular*,
    22.5.1992
4 SHN, 4.9.1992
5 PersInt, John Clifford, Sept 1992
6 George, Eric W., Statement on
    Scouting, 1992
7 SHDM, Feb 1917
8 PersInt, Eric W. George, Dec 1992
9 PersInt, Daphne Francis,
    19.10.1992
10 CLR 117, 1909

Part II: Ascension Island

Chapter 10: 1815-1992
1 Hart-Davis, Duff, *Ascension: The
    Story of a South Atlantic Island*, p69
2 Cable and Wireless Journal, *Zodiac*,
    October 1967
3 Hart-Davis, Duff, op.cit., pp57,68
4 Ibid, p69
5 Ibid, p92
6 Ibid, p87
7 Ibid, p96
8 Ibid, p133
9 ADM, 123/75, *Letters*, Dowell
    8.5.1867; 2.8.1869; 2.12.1870
10 Hart-Davis, Duff, op.cit., p172
11 Bartlett, L. S., *A Portrait of Ascension
    Island, 1934-1936*, p18
12 PersInt, Pam Hart, 6.1.1992
13 PersInt, Larry Henry, 6.1.1992
14 PersInt, John Joshua, 4.1.1992
15 PersInt, Enid Stevens, 6.1.1992
16 Simmons, Dr K. E. L., Personal
    Correspondence, June 1991-Feb
    1993
17 PersInt, Eddie Fowler, 6.1.1992
18 PersInt, Patrick Robinson, 6.1.1992
19 Hutchinson, M., 1987

**Part III: Island of Tristan da
Cunha**

Chapter 11: 1816-1942
1 Hosegood, N., *The Glass Island*,
    pp70,71
2 Crawford, A. B., *Tristan da Cunha:
    The Roaring Forties*, p30
3 Brander, J., *Tristan da Cunha, 1506-
    1902*, p132
4 Ibid, p111
5 Ibid, p131
6 Ibid, p133; Capetown Newspaper,
    17.1.1834
7 SPG, *Letters Received*, early 1850s
8 Mackay, M., *The Angry Island*, p78
9 Hosegood, N., op.cit., p70,71
10 Brander, J., op.cit., p150
11 Hosegood, N., op.cit., p72
12 Munch, Peter, *Crisis in Utopia, Story
    of Tristan da Cunha*, p95
13 Brander, J., op.cit., pp166/167
14 Ibid, p195
15 Crawford, A. B., op.cit., p37
16 Munch, P., op.cit., p69
17 Brander, J., op.cit., p220
18 Ibid, p235
19 SPG: CLR 116, 22.7.1876
20 SPG: CLR 116, 2.10.1878
21 Dodgson, E. H., *Eight Years at TdaC*,
    The Church Abroad; SHDM March
    1908
22 Ibid; SHDM April 1908
23 SPG: CLR 116, 1.3.1881
24 Ibid, 31.1.1882, p231
25 Ibid, 25.3.1884, p245
26 Ibid, 20.6.1886, p295
27 Dodgson, E. H., op.cit.; SHDM, May
    1908
28 SPG: CLR 116, Vol 5, p336
29 Sullivan, Fr B., Statistical
    Population Chart, 1992
30 SPG: CLR 116, Vol 5, p401
31 Ibid, 23.5.1893, p408 (Also Brander,
    p295)
32 Brander, J., op.cit., p305
33 Ibid, p303
34 Ibid, p313
35 SPG: CLR 116, Vol 6
36 Barrow, Rev J. G., Letter, 31.8.1905
    to SPG
37 Mackay, M., op.cit., p145

38 SHDM, April 1909
39 SPG: CLR 118, Vol 7, 21.2.1914
40 Ibid, 14.6.1918
41 Ibid, 20.2.1919
42 Ibid, 14.10.1920
43 Ibid, 7.11.1921
44 Ibid, 12.7.1921, p152
45 SHDM, April 1922
46 SPG: CLR 118, Vol 7, 27.3.1922, p171
47 Ibid, 15.5.1922, p183a
48 Ibid, 8.11.1922, p211a
49 Ibid, 4.12.1922, p215a
50 Ibid, Dec 1922, p217a
51 Ibid, March 1923, p235a
52 Peck, R., *Social Philately*, p8
53 SPG: CLR 118, Vol 7, 23.7.1923, p259
54 Ibid, 28.1.1925, p292
55 SPG: CLR 119, 2.4.1925, p12
56 Ibid, 4.2.1925, p1a
57 Ibid, 17.4.1925, p12
58 Ibid, 6.2.1926, p42
59 SPG-LR: *Africa 1927*, April 1927
60 Ibid, 16.4.1927
61 Ibid, Aug 1927
62 Ibid, Feb 1928
63 Ibid, 28.2.1928
64 Ibid, 31.12.1928
65 Ibid, 23.2.1929
66 Ibid, 29.3.1929
67 Partridge Rev, *Daily Notes*
68 SPG-LR: op.cit., 15.5.1929
69 Ibid, 5.9.1929
70 Ibid, 6.8.1929
71 Ibid, 3.10.1930
72 Ibid, 6.3.1930
73 SPG-LR: *Africa 1930*, 3.5.1931
74 Crabb G., *The History and Postal History of TdaC*, p78
75 SPG-LR: *Africa 1941*, 5.11.1941

Chapter 12: 1942-1992

1 Jones, H., 'Tristan 20 Years On', *Sunday Times*, Nov 1981
2 Munch, P., op.cit, p160
3 Lawrence Rev, *Report to SPG*, 5.6.1943
4 Booy, D., *Rock of Exile*, p101
5 Ibid, p105
6 SPG: *Tristan da Cunha Newsletter*, May 1950
7 Flint, J., *Fortunate Island: The Story of Tristan da Cunha, 1961-1965*

(unpublished document, 1965)
8 Handley, Rev A., *Letter to SPG*, 1945
9 Handley, Rev A., *Report to SPG*, Feb/March 1946
10 Handley, Mrs, *Report to SPG*, 8.5.1946
11 Repetto, Lars, *Exercise Book*, October 1946 (held in Rhodes House, Oxford)
12 SPG: 'News from the Island', *Tristan da Cunha Newsletter*, August 1947
13 Gane, I., *Letter to SPG*, 10.9.1947
14 SPG: 'News from the Island', *Tristan da Cunha Newsletter*, December 1948
15 SPG: 'News from the Island', *Tristan da Cunha Newsletter*, May 1950
16 PersInt, Mrs M. Handley, May 1992
17 Mackay, M., *Angry Island*, p250
18 Ibid, p254
19 Munch, P., op.cit., p223
20 Keir, G., 'The Psychological Assessment of Children from the Island of Tristan da Cunha', in *Studies in Psychology, 1965*, by Banks, C. and Broadhurst, P. L., p142
21 Ibid, p134
22 Ibid, p136
23 Ibid, p161
24 Jones, H., op.cit.
25 *National Geographic Magazine*, January 1964, p73
26 Flint, J., op.cit.
27 St Mary's School pupils, *South Atlantic Island*, 1963
28 Flint, J., op.cit.
29 Flint, J, *Some Thoughts on the Future of Education on Tristan de Cunha*
30 PersInt, Jim Flint, 1992
31 Lewis, H. E., Roberts, D. F., Edwards, A. W. F., *Biological Problems, and Opportunities, of Isolation among the Islanders of Tristan da Cunha*, 1971
32 PersInt, Ken Schurch, 1992
33 PersInt, Nigel Humphries, May 1992
34 Swales, M. K., *The Tristan-Denstone Connection*, 1992
35 St Helena *Education Committee Minutes*, 31.1.1990
36 PersInt, John Bailey, September 1992

37 Swain, M., Personal Correspondence, Jan 1993

Part IV: The Falkland Islands

Chapter 13: 1843-1969

1 McWhan, F., *The Falkland Islands Today*
2 Brandon, L. E., *1902 Report*
3 CLEC: *Colonisation of the Falkland Islands*, 22.8.1840
4 Moody, Lt Gov R. C., Correspondence to Sec. of State, 14.4.1842
5 Smith, D. B., 'Church, State and Schooling in the Falkland Islands', in *Journal of Education Administration and History*, Vol XXII, No2, July 1990, p1
6 Ibid, p1
7 Cawkell, M. B. R., Maling, D. H. and Cawkell, E. M., *The Falkland Islands*, p142
8 Smith, D. B., op.cit., p1
9 Ibid, p2
10 Brandon, L. E., *1902 Report*
11 Cawkell, etc., op.cit., p143
12 Ibid, p136
13 Smith, D. B., 'Some Historical and Comparative Aspects of Schooling in Sparsely-Populated Areas of British Settlement in Australasia and the Falkland Islands', in *Compare*, Vol 19, No 1, 1989, p38
14 Cawkell, etc., op.cit., p135
15 Brown, G. L. R., *Colonial Report 1924*, No 1278
16 A Falkland Islander, Personal Correspondence, 19.2.1993
17 McPhee, O. and M., Personal Correspondence, 15.2.1993
18 PersInt, Joan Bound, July 1992
19 Cawkell, etc., op.cit., p145
20 HMSO to Col Office, *FI Report for 1960/61*
21 HMSO to Col Office, *FI Report for 1962/63*, pub 1965
22 Leonard, J., Personal Correspondence, September 1992

23 Leonard, J., 'Education in the Falkland Islands: A Fresh Start', in the *Guardian*, 1986
24 HMSO to Col Office, *FI Report for 1968/69*

Chapter 14: 1970-1992

1 F.I. Office: *Prospects for the Falkland Islands*, 1983
2 Stocks, B. S., *School Population Statistics, 1970-1975*, 16.5.1975
3 Leonard, J., 'Education in the Falkland Islands: A Fresh Start', *Guardian* 1986
4 HMSO to FCO, *Falkland Islands and Dependencies, 1974 and 1975*
5 Smith, D. B., 'Church, State and Schooling in the Falkland Islands', 1990
6 Actg. Superintendent: *Education Report* (Gov. Budget Address, May 1977)
7 Lamin, T. E., *Education Report*, (GBA, May 1978)
8 Summers, N., *Heritage Year, 1992*
9 Leonard, J., op.cit.
10 HMG (UK): *Report to the Sec Gen of UN, 1985-1986*
11 Leonard, J., op.cit.
12 Murphy, E., *Education Department Review* for HE Report to LegCo, 1987
13 Rendell, P., Personal Correspondence, 23.9.1992
14 Ibid, 23.9.1992
15 Cameron, J., *Education in the Falkland Islands*, 1990
16 Rendell, R., *Education Report*, 1991
17 Rendell, R., Personal Correspondence, 23.9.1992

Part V: The Future

Chapter 15: 1992

1 George, E. M., & O'Bey, S., Prince Andrew School Song, 1988
2 Twaddell, E., 1992, *The Islander*, 20.11.1992
3 Swain, M., 1984, *Tristan Times*, May 1984
4 Shackleton, Lord, Opening Speech, 17.8.1992

Appendix 1
Leading Educationalists

(a) St Helena: Superintendents, School Inspectors, Education Officers

Note: Until the early nineteenth century, the supervision of schools was the responsibility of the Company Chaplain or the appointed Schoolmaster of the Company school in Jamestown. Designated Inspectors are recorded as follows:

1808-1816	Rev Samuel Jones, Chaplain, Inspector of Schools
1816-1829	Rev Richard Boys, Senior Chaplain, Inspector of Schools

Following the transition to the Crown records of designated Inspectors of Schools are scarce until:

1851-1852	Rev J. Chambers, Inspector of Schools
1855	Rev G. Bennett, Chaplain, Inspector of Schools
1863	Mr Eden Baker, Official School Visitor
1865	Rev Grey, Inspector of Schools, Master of Head School
1868-1871	Mr Newenham Travers, Master of Head School
1871-1878	Mr Noel Janisch, Master of Head School

After the closure of the Head School in 1884, records of designated Supervisors of Schools resume several years later:

1900-1910	Canon Alfred Porter, Inspector of Schools
1910-1914	Mr Leslie Tucker, Supervisor of Govt Schools
1919-1921	Miss Eleanor Short, Acting Superintendent of Schools
1921-1939	Rev L. C. Walcott, Superintendent of Schools

From this time designated Education Officers were appointed:

1939-1943	Mr Davies Watkins
1943-1947	Mr Rawlings
1946-1950	(Woman Educ Officer/Head of Sec Sch) Miss P. Walker
1947-1953	Mr R. Colville Thompson
1953-1956	Mr Norman Kerr, BSc, DThPT
1956-1957	Mr Edgar Wagstaff (Acting EO)
1957-1960	Mr Charles G. Dixon
1958-1960	(Assistant EO) Mr Tony Cross
1960-1963	Mr Tony Cross
1962-1964	(AEO) Mr T. Lamin
1963-1968	Mr Alan Johns
1965-1968	(AEO) Mr Ralph Billing

1966, 1968-1972	(AEO) Mr Cliff Huxtable
1968-1972	Mr Ralph Billing, BAHons, DipEd
1969-1970	(AEO) Mr J. Cobbett
1970-1983	(AEO) Mr Basil George
1972-1983	Mr Cliff Huxtable, BA, DipEd
1973-1985	(AEO) Mr Arnold Flagg
1973-1985	(AEO) Mrs Edith Timm
1983-1985	Mr Basil George, BEdHons, DipEd
1984	(AEO) Mr T. Irons
1985-present	**Chief Education Officer: Mr Basil George**
1985-1989	(EO) Mr Arnold Flagg
1985-present	(EO) Mrs Edith Timm (1992 Head PAS)
1985-present	(AEO) Mrs J. (Patsy) Flagg
1985-present	(AEO) Mr Eric George
1986-1989	(EO) Mr John Birchall (Head PAS)
1985-1987	(AEO) Mrs Lilian Crowie
1988-present	(EO) Mrs Lilian Crowie
1989-present	(AEO) Mrs Betty Joshua
1990-1992	(EO) Mr Terry Ward (Head PAS)

(b) Ascension Island: School Teachers/Headteachers

1830	Lance Corporal Barber
1869	Sergeant Jowett
1900	A Sergeant Schoolmaster
1956-1960	(School Teacher) Mrs Lilian Greentree
1960-1962	(Schoolmaster) Mr Cyril Eyles
1962-1964	(Schoolmaster) Mr Kenneth Simmons
1964-1966	(Schoolmaster) Mr Cyril Eyles
1966-1973	(Schoolmaster) Mr Geoffrey Simpson
1973-1977	(Head Teacher) Mr Alun Thomas
1977-1982	(Head Teacher) Miss Margot Hutchinson
1982	(Acting Head) Mr McBride
1982-1984	(Head Teacher) Mr Alun Thomas
1984-1987	(Head Teacher) Miss Margot Hutchinson
1987-1990	(Head Teacher) Mr Keith Sedgwick
1990-date	(Head Teacher) Mr Bryan Grey

(c) Tristan da Cunha: School Teachers/ Headteachers/ Education Officers

1816	William Glass
1824	Augustus Earle
1830	Benjamin Pankhurst
1851-1857	Rev William F. Taylor

1870	Mrs Frances Cotton (for several years)
1881-1890	Rev E. H. Dodgson
1890	Peter Green
	Mrs Swain
	Mr G. H. Cartwright (ss *Allenshaw*)
1906-1909	Rev J. G. Barrow
1922-1925	Rev Martyn Rogers
1927-1929	Rev R. A. C. Pooley, with Philip Lindsay
1929-1933	Rev A. G. Partridge
1933	William Repetto
1934-1940	Rev H. Wilde
1940	Mrs Repetto
1943-1946	Rev C. P. Lawrence, with Station personnel
1946-1949	(Teacher) Mrs Handley
1949-1950	(Teacher) Miss E. Harvey
1950-1952	(Teacher) Mrs Handley
1952-1957	(Head Teacher) Mr R. J. Harding
1957	(i/c School) Rev P. H. Bell
1957-1961	(Head Teacher) Miss R. M. Downer
1961	(Head Teacher) Miss E. Bennett
1961-1963	(*Evacuation*)
1963-1965	(Head Teacher) Mr J. H. Flint
1966	(Acting Head) Mrs J. Hemming
1966-1968	(Head Teacher/Education Officer) Mr H. Burton
1968	(Head Teacher) Mr J. M. Lewis/ Mr R. Dodd
1968-1969	(Head Teacher) Mr Ian Fleming
1970-1971	(i/c School) Local Teachers
1971-1973	(Education Officer) Mr K. Schurch
1973-1974	(Education Officer) Mrs M. E. (Loretta) Richardson
1974-1978	(Education Officer) Mr Nigel Humphries
1978-1981	(Education Officer) Mr J. Whittington
1981-1982	(Acting EO) Mrs Marlene Swain
1982-1985	(Education Officer) Mr J. H. Cooper
1985-1988	(Education Officer) Mr S. V. Townsend
1988-1991	(Education Officer) Mr J. Kerr
1990	(EO-Designate) Mrs Marlene Swain
1992 to date	(Education Officer) Mrs Marlene Swain

(d) Falkland Islands: Inspector of Schools/Head Teachers/Education Officers/Director of Education

1859-1877	(Inspector of Schools) Rev Charles Bull
1877-1907	(Inspector of Schools) Dean Lowther Brandon
1916-1939	(Superintendent/Head) Mr A. Hoare

1939-1941	(Director of Education) Mr A. Hoare
	(Head Teacher) Mr T. D. Evans
1941-1944	(Superintendent/Head) Mr T. D. Evans
1944-1949	(Superintendent(Mr H. L. Baker
1949–1951	(Superintendent) Mr D. M. Honeyman
1952-1956	(Superintendent) Edward M. Cawkell
1957	(Superintendent) Rev E. Turner
1958-1960	(Supervisor) Mr J. B. Swann
1961-1965	(Supervisor) Mr D. J. Draycott
1966	(Supervisor) Mr S. A. Booth
1967-1974	(Supervisor) Mr D. J. Draycott
1975-1976	(Officer i/c) Mr B. S. Stocks
1977	(Vacant)
1978-1980	(Supervisor) Mr T. E. Lamin
1981-1984	(Supervisor) Mr J. T. Fowler
1985–1987	(Superintendent) Mr David Smith
1987-1988	(Education Officer) Mrs E. Murphy
1988-to date	(Director of Education) Mrs Phyllis Rendell

Appendix 2
A: Schools in Jamestown

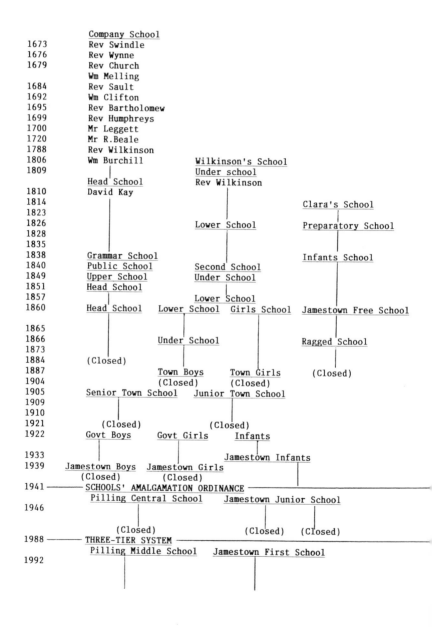

```
           Company School
1673       Rev Swindle
1676       Rev Wynne
1679       Rev Church
           Wm Melling
1684       Rev Sault
1692       Wm Clifton
1695       Rev Bartholomew
1699       Rev Humphreys
1700       Mr Leggett
1720       Mr R.Beale
1788       Rev Wilkinson
1806       Wm Burchill          Wilkinson's School
1809                            Under school
           Head School          Rev Wilkinson
1810       David Kay
1814                                                Clara's School
1823
1826                            Lower School        Preparatory School
1828
1835
1838       Grammar School                           Infants School
1840       Public School        Second School
1849       Upper School         Under School
1851       Head School
1857                            Lower School
1860       Head School  Lower School  Girls School  Jamestown Free School

1865
1866                     Under School               Ragged School
1873
1884       (Closed)
1887                 Town Boys      Town Girls    (Closed)
1904                 (Closed)       (Closed)
1905       Senior Town School   Junior Town School
1909
1910
1921       (Closed)                  (Closed)
1922       Govt Boys     Govt Girls      Infants

1933                                Jamestown Infants
1939   Jamestown Boys  Jamestown Girls
           (Closed)        (Closed)
1941 ————— SCHOOLS' AMALGAMATION ORDINANCE —————
           Pilling Central School    Jamestown Junior School
1946

           (Closed)              (Closed)    (Closed)
1988 ————— THREE-TIER SYSTEM —————
           Pilling Middle School   Jamestown First School
1992
```

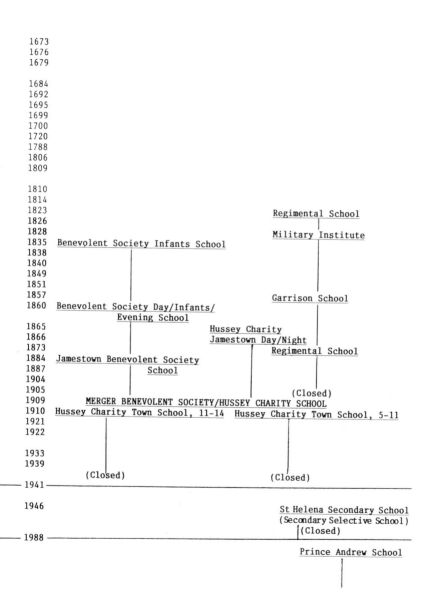

1673
1676
1679

1684
1692
1695
1699
1700
1720
1788
1806
1809

1810
1814
1823   Regimental School
1826
1828   Military Institute
1835 Benevolent Society Infants School
1838
1840
1849
1851
1857   Garrison School
1860 Benevolent Society Day/Infants/
               Evening School
1865   Hussey Charity
1866   Jamestown Day/Night
1873   Regimental School
1884 Jamestown Benevolent Society
1887   School
1904
1905   (Closed)
1909   **MERGER BENEVOLENT SOCIETY/HUSSEY CHARITY SCHOOL**
1910 Hussey Charity Town School, 11-14 Hussey Charity Town School, 5-11
1921
1922

1933
1939
        (Closed)   (Closed)
—— 1941 —————————————————————————————————

1946   St Helena Secondary School
                          (Secondary Selective School)
                            (Closed)
—— 1988 —————————————————————————————————

                       Prince Andrew School

B: Schools across St Helena

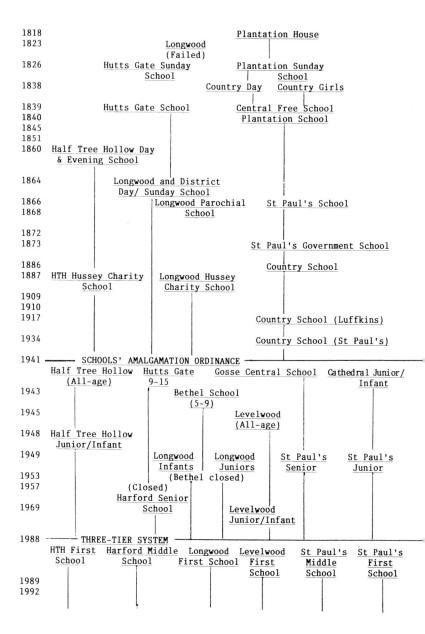

1818				Plantation House		
1823			Longwood (Failed)			
1826		Hutts Gate Sunday School		Plantation Sunday School		
1838				Country Day	Country Girls	
1839		Hutts Gate School		Central Free School		
1840				Plantation School		
1845						
1851						
1860	Half Tree Hollow Day & Evening School					
1864			Longwood and District Day/ Sunday School			
1866			Longwood Parochial School	St Paul's School		
1868						
1872						
1873				St Paul's Government School		
1886				Country School		
1887	HTH Hussey Charity School		Longwood Hussey Charity School			
1909						
1910						
1917				Country School (Luffkins)		
1934				Country School (St Paul's)		
1941	SCHOOLS' AMALGAMATION ORDINANCE					
	Half Tree Hollow (All-age)	Hutts Gate 9-15	Gosse Central School		Cathedral Junior/ Infant	
1943			Bethel School (5-9)			
1945				Levelwood (All-age)		
1948	Half Tree Hollow Junior/Infant					
1949			Longwood Infants	Longwood Juniors	St Paul's Senior	St Paul's Junior
1953			(Bethel closed)			
1957		(Closed) Harford Senior School				
1969				Levelwood Junior/Infant		
1988	THREE-TIER SYSTEM					
	HTH First School	Harford Middle School	Longwood First School	Levelwood First School	St Paul's Middle School	St Paul's First School
1989						
1992						

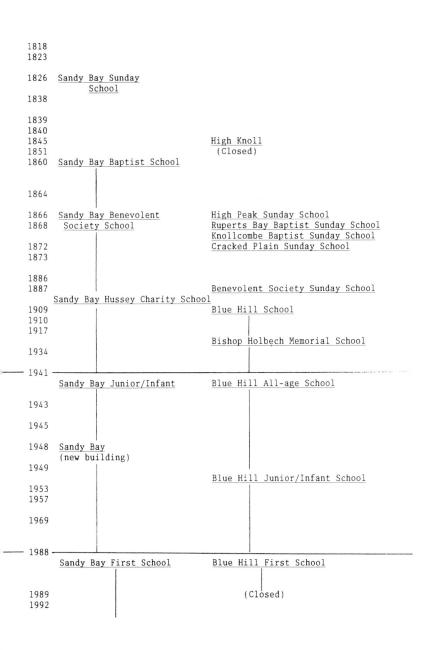

```
1818
1823

1826    Sandy Bay Sunday
            School
1838

1839
1840
1845                                    High Knoll
1851                                    (Closed)
1860    Sandy Bay Baptist School


1864

1866    Sandy Bay Benevolent            High Peak Sunday School
1868      Society School                Ruperts Bay Baptist Sunday School
                                        Knollcombe Baptist Sunday School
1872                                    Cracked Plain Sunday School
1873

1886
1887                                    Benevolent Society Sunday School
        Sandy Bay Hussey Charity School
1909                                    Blue Hill School
1910
1917
                                        Bishop Holbech Memorial School
1934

1941 ─────────────────────────────────────────────────────────────
        Sandy Bay Junior/Infant         Blue Hill All-age School

1943

1945

1948    Sandy Bay
        (new building)
1949
                                        Blue Hill Junior/Infant School
1953
1957

1969


1988 ─────────────────────────────────────────────────────────────
        Sandy Bay First School          Blue Hill First School

1989                                         (Closed)
1992
```

Appendix 3
Individual Schools and Head Teachers
on St Helena, 1788-1992

Leading Teachers as recorded in official texts
Note: Every effort has been made to provide continuity and accuracy in these lists by piecing together the available records. The author will welcome further information to complete these lists.

Key: The lists are arranged according to the area served, as far as possible in chronological order. Where a school name is included in brackets, records have indicated a change of name for the school.

Jamestown

JAMESTOWN COMPANY SCHOOL
1788   Rev Wilkinson
1806   William Burchell
1810   David Kay (Jun)
(Hon Co Head School)
1818   Mr Firmin/David Kay
1826   Rev Vernon/Mr Firmin
1832   Rev Vernon
(Col Grammar School)
1838   Mr Firmin/Henry Kay
(Public School)
1840   Henry Kay/W. P. Thompson
(Upper School)
1849   Henry Kay/W. P. Thompson
(Head School)
1851   Rev Chambers/Brown
1857   Rev Bennett/Brown
1860   Rev Bennett/Lambert
1865   Rev Grey
1868   Newenham Travers
1871   Noel Janisch
1878   Rev Lambert
1884   (Head School closed)

WILKINSON'S SCHOOL
1806   Rev Wilkinson

JAMESTOWN UNDER SCHOOL
1809   Rev Samuel Jones
1811   Mr McDaniel
(1826   Lower School)
1832   Mr Firmin
1838   Mr J. Thompson
(Second School)
1840   Mr and Mrs Jones
(1849   Under School)
1851   W. P. Thompson
(1860   Lower School (for Boys))
1860   W. P. Thompson
(1866   Under School)
1866   W. P. Thompson
1884   Mr A. S. Brady
1887   (Lower School closed)

TOWN BOYS' SCHOOL
1887   Mr A. S. Brady
1904   Mr Leslie Tucker/
        Mr A. S. Brady
1904   (Town Boys' School closed)

GIRLS' SCHOOL
1860   Miss E. Denton
1867   Miss E. Welch
1880   A. E. Harris
1884   Miss E. Welch/A. E. Harris

1886   E. Welch, Miss E. L. Warren
(1887   Town Girls' School)
1887   E. L. Warren
1889   Miss Eleanor Short
1904   (Town Girls' School closed)

SENIOR TOWN SCHOOL (MIXED)
1905   Leslie Tucker/A. S. Brady
1913   Leslie Tucker
1921   (Senior Town School closed)

JUNIOR TOWN SCHOOL (MIXED)
1905   Miss Eleanor Short
1910   Miss Ruby Smith
1921   (Junior Town School closed)

GOVERNMENT BOYS' SCHOOL
1922   William Corker
(1939   Jamestown Boys School)
1941   (Jamestown Boys School closed)

GOVERNMENT GIRLS' SCHOOL
1922   Miss Eliza Smith
(1939   Jamestown Girls School)
1941   (Jamestown Girls School closed)

GOVERNMENT INFANTS' SCHOOL
1922   Miss Mildred Smith
(1933   Jamestown Infants School)
1933   Miss Queenie Gunnell
1941   (Jamestown Infants School closed)

CLARA GEORGE'S SCHOOL
1816   Mrs Clara George
(1826   Preparatory School)
1839   Miss Leah Rich
(1860   Jamestown Free School)
(1866   Ragged School)
1866   Miss Leah Rich
1877   (Ragged School closed)

BENEVOLENT SOCIETY INFANT SCHOOL
1835   Miss Jane Preston
1839   Mrs Rich
(1850   Jamestown School for Infants and
Elder Girls)
1850   Miss Caroline Grant (to 1852)
1852

(1860   Jamestown Day and Infant School)
1860   T. Goodwin
(1873   Jamestown Benevolent School)
1873   Mr and Mrs Brady
1884   Miss Georgina Burchell
(1887   Benevolent Society Town School)
1887   Miss Mary Burchill
1909   (Benevolent Society Merger with
Hussey Charity)

HUSSEY CHARITY DAY AND NIGHT
SCHOOL
1865   Mr Hocking
1871   Mr Marriott
1902   Rev Gibbons
1909   (Benevolent Society Merger with
Hussey Charity)

HUSSEY CHARITY LOWER TOWN
SCHOOL (11-14)
1910
1932   Kate Joshua
1941   (Hussey Charity Lower Town
School closed)

HUSSEY CHARITY UPPER TOWN
SCHOOL (5-11)
1910
1932   Hilda (Cissie) Stevens
1941   (Hussey Charity Upper Town
School closed)

PILLING CENTRAL SCHOOL
1941   William Corker
1950   Jack LeBreton
1961   Eric Benjamin
1967   Mrs Hilda Stevens
1968   Mrs Martha George
1974   Mrs Gwen Yon
1976   Mrs Rita Nicholls
1988   (Pilling Central School closed)

PILLING MIDDLE SCHOOL
1988   Mrs Rita Nicholls

JAMESTOWN JUNIOR SCHOOL
1941   Miss Eliza Smith

1963   Mrs Martha George
1969   Mrs Betty Joshua (Acting)
1970   Stedson George
1981   Miss Joyce Harris
1986   Mrs Betty Joshua
1987   Mrs Gwen Yon
1988   (Jamestown Junior School closed)

JAMESTOWN INFANTS SCHOOL
1941   Miss Mildred Smith
1954   Mrs Martha George
1958   Mrs Una Thomas
1978   Mrs Muriel Leo (Acting)
1980   Mrs Muriel Leo
1988   (Jamestown Infants School closed)

JAMESTOWN FIRST SCHOOL
1988   Mrs Muriel Leo

Half Tree Hollow

HALF TREE HOLLOW ALL-AGE SCHOOL
1860   Mr Davids
        Mr Buxton (Evening School)
        (Under Hussey Charity
        Control)
1874   Mr Edward Short
1903   Mr James R. Sim
(1941   Under Government Control)
1941   Miss M. Hartvig
1943   Miss F. P. (Teeny)
        Constantine
(1948   HTH Junior/Infants School)
1963   Mrs Ivy Williams
1980   Miss Joyce Harris
*1988   (HTH Junior/Infants School
        closed)*

HALF TREE HOLLOW FIRST SCHOOL
1988   Miss Joyce Harris

Western Country Districts

COUNTRY SCHOOL
(1818   Plantation House School)
(1838   Country Day and Girls School)
1838   Mr Weston/Mr Hays

(1839   Central Free School)
1839   Mr and Mrs Weston
(1840   Plantation School)
1840   Mr Frey
(1866   St Paul's School)
1866   Mr Frey
(1873   St Paul's Government School)
1873   Mr and Mrs Storer (to 1903)
(1904   Country School)
1907   Mrs Evelyn Brady
1910   Miss Vida Evans
1941   (Country School closed)

GOSSE CENTRAL SCHOOL
1941   Miss Vida Evans
1943   Algernon Broadway
(1947   Country Senior School)
1959   Mr A. Evans
1964   Mr Eric M. George (Acting
        Head)
1967   Mrs Lilian Crowie
1968   Mr Eric George
1970   Mrs Rita Nicholls
1976   Mrs Gwen Yon
1979   Mrs Lilian Greentree (Acting)
1980   Mrs Gwen Yon
1984   Mr Stedson George
1988   (Country Senior School closed)

ST PAUL'S MIDDLE SCHOOL
1988   Mr Stedson George

CATHEDRAL JUNIOR/INFANT SCHOOL
1941   Mrs Lilian Samuel (to 1942)
1943
(1947   Country Junior/Infant School)
1949   Mrs Iris Clingham
1972   Mrs Betty Joshua
1974   Miss Joyce Harris
1981   Mrs Ivy Williams
1982   Mrs Muriel Leo
*1988   (Country Junior/Infants School
        closed)*

ST PAUL'S FIRST SCHOOL
1988   Mrs Maisie Thomas

SANDY BAY FREE SCHOOL
(Under Benevolent Society Control)
1839   Louisa Isaake
(1860   Sandy Bay School)
1860   Mr Edmunds
(1866   Sandy Bay Benevolent Society
         School)
1873   Miss E. Barker
1904   Mr Edward Constantine
(1941   Under Government Control)
1961   Mr Arnold Flagg
1962   Mrs Iva Henry (Acting)
1963   Mrs Iva Henry
(1969   Sandy Bay Junior/Infants School)
1988   (Sandy Bay Junior/Infants School
         closed)

SANDY BAY FIRST SCHOOL
1988   Mrs Iva Henry
1988   Mrs Hazel Thomas (Acting)
1990   Mrs Liz Young

BLUE HILL HUSSEY CHARITY SCHOOL
1907   Mr Caleb John
(1930   Bishop Holbech Memorial School)
(1941   Under Government Control)
(1941   Blue Hill All-Age School)
1941   Miss E. Bagley/Miss
         H. Williams
1943   Mr Algernon Broadway
1945   Mr Edward Benjamin
1946   Mr George Lawrence
(1951   Blue Hill Junior/Infants School)
1951   Miss Evelyn Bagley
1984   Mrs Liz Young
1988   (Blue Hill Junior/Infants School
         closed)

BLUE HILL FIRST SCHOOL
1988   Mrs Liz Young
1990   (Blue Hill First School closed)

Eastern (Longwood) District

HUTTS GATE SCHOOL
(Under Benevolent Society Control)

1839   Miss Flavilia Burnham
1849   Miss Fanny Dickson
(1864   Longwood & District Day/
         Evening School
1864   Mr Harper
(1866   Longwood Parochial School)
(Under Hussey Charity Control)
1874   Rev J. C. Hands
(1887   Hussey Charity School, Longwood)
1887   Miss Broadway (to 1902)
(1902-4   School closed)
1909   Mr L. Francis (student
         teacher)
1917   Mr Maurice Young
         (2 periods to 1941)
(1941   Under Government Control)
1941   Mrs Lily Corker
1949   Canon Hall
1956   Mr Maurice Young (Acting)
1957   (Hutts Gate School closed)

HARFORD SENIOR SCHOOL
1957   Mr Maurice Young
1965   Mrs Elvina Mercury
1988   (Harford Senior School closed)

HARFORD MIDDLE SCHOOL
1988   Mrs Elvina Mercury
1989   Miss Heather George

BETHEL (LONGWOOD) SCHOOL
1943   Mrs Noreen Evans
1950   Mrs V. Simon
1954   (Bethel School closed)

LONGWOOD JUNIOR/INFANT SCHOOL
1949   Mrs Lily Corker
1950   Mrs Mary (Betty) George
1953   Mrs Joan Thomas (Teacher
         i/c)
1958   Mrs Joan Thomas
1988   (Longwood Junior/Infants School
         closed)

LONGWOOD FIRST SCHOOL
1988   Mrs Joan Thomas

LEVELWOOD ALL-AGE SCHOOL
1945 Mr Louis Timm
1954 Mr A. Evans
1959 Mrs Ivy George
1964/5 Mrs Lily Crowie
1966/7 Mrs Lily Crowie
1967 Mrs Pat Thomas
(1969 Levelwood Junior/Infants School)
1976 Mrs Maisie Thomas
1988 (Levelwood Junior/Infants School closed)

LEVELWOOD FIRST SCHOOL
1988 Mrs Muriel Williams

Secondary Schooling

ST HELENA SECONDARY SCHOOL
(Secondary Selective School)
1946 Miss Penelope Walker
1950 Miss Jessie Cardwell
1951 Warren Harrison
(with Mr R. Chester)

1952 (Vacant)
1953 Norman Kerr
1956 Edgar Wagstaff (Acting)
1957 Charles Dixon
1958 R. Exley
1959 Algernon Broadway
1962 T. E. Lamin
1965 D. E. Streatfield
1966 Cliff Huxtable
1966 Ralph Billing
1968 Cliff Huxtable
1968 J. Cobbett
1970 Basil George
1977 (Acting) Dan Yon
1980 Basil George
1983 Tony Irons
1985 Eric M. George
1988 (Secondary Selective School closed)

THE PRINCE ANDREW SCHOOL
1986 John Birchall
1989 Terry Ward
1992 Mrs Edith Timm

Appendix 4
Bibliography and Sources

(a) St Helena

Abbott, G., *Second Report on the Education of Deaf Children on the Island of St Helena*, April 1986

Baptist Church: *Record Book*, 1845-1992

Bell, Dr A., *An Experiment in Education made at the Male Asylum at Egremont near Madras*, 1797

Benevolent Society: *Schools 1835-1852*

Benevolent Society: *Minute Book*, 1898-1949, 1972-1991

Bennett, G., *Reminiscences of George Brooks Bennett, 1816-1886*

Blakeston, O., *Isle of St Helena*, Sidgwick & Jackson, London, 1957

Board of Education: *Minute Book*, 1875-1878

Board of Education: *Minute Book*, 1907-1919

Braine, Sir B., *Report on St Helena*, Visit 1980

Brooke, T. E., *History of St Helena*, 1824

Burchell, W., *Journal, 1806-1809*

Cannan, E., *The Churches of the South Atlantic Islands, 1502-1991*, Anthony Nelson, Oswestry, 1992

Chaplin, A., *A St Helena Who's Who*, 1815-1821, Humphreys, London, 1919

Chippendale, H. A., *Sails and Whales*, Melrose, London, 1953

Codrington, J., *Report*, 1980

Colonial Office: *Annual Reports on the Blue Books*, 1838-1939

— *Blue Books*, 1838-1942

— *Col Secretary's In-Letters*, 1839-1908, 1885-1910

— *Colonial Secretary's Out-Letters*, 1839-1899

— *Governors' Despatches to SoS*, 1839-1909, 1927-1963

— *Lists*, 1862-1948

— Sec of State: *Despatches*, 1839-1942

Constantine, E., *Personal Writings, 1904-1960* (unpublished) (By kind permission of Mrs Phyllis John)

Cross, T., *St Helena, including Ascension Island and Tristan da Cunha*, David and Charles, Newton Abbot & London, 1980

Curtis S. J., Boultwood, M. E. A., *An Introductory History of the English Education System Since 1800*, 1970

Denbow, G., et al, *History of St Helena Secondary School*, 1957 (unpublished)

Dorrell, E., *Education Report*, 1974

East India Company:

— *Company Minute Book*, 1673

— *St Helena Letters from England*, 1673-1834
— *St Helena Records of Consultations*, 1678-1836, Vols 1-132
— *EIC Out Letters*, 1706-1834
— *EIC Register and Directory*, 1816-1831
Edmunds, Rev W., *An Isolated Family*, SA Baptist Press
Education Department: *Education Officers' Annual/Triennial Reports*
— *School Policy Documents*, 1991-1992
Education Committee: *Minutes of Meetings, 1983-1990*
Education Department: *Staff Lists*, 1947-1988
Education Ordinances, 1874-1990
Emmanuel, A., *Report on Education*, 1959
Evans, K., *The English Educational System*, ULP, 1975
Geen, M. S., *The Aims of Education on St Helena*, 1964
George, B., and SSS Pupils: *Gravestones and Memorials on St Helena, 1686-1975*, 1975
George, B., *378 Days Along the Road*, 1987
George, E. M., *Education in St Helena*, 1951-1991
George, E. M., *Report on Music in Schools*, 1981
George, E. M., *A Report on Training in England (Broadcasting)*, 1968
Gilles, H., Bequest: *Trustees Minute Book*, 1972-1991
Gosse, P., *St Helena, 1502-1938*, Cassell & Co, London, 1938
Greater Britain, Journal, 1892
Green, L., *Islands Time Forgot*, London 1962
Green, L., *There's A Secret Hid Away*
Hatfield, *St Helena*, 1853
HMSO: *British Islands in the Southern Hemisphere*, 1945-1951
HMSO: *Educational Systems of the British Empire*, Vol 12, 1905
HMSO: *Educational Systems of Chief Crown Colonies*, 1908
Hughes, Cledwyn: *Conditions on the Island of St Helena*, 1958
Hussey Charity Trustees: *Minute Book*, 1912-1991
Huxtable, C., *The Expansion of Third Level Opportunities*, 1977
Island Newspapers & Journals:
— *St Helena Advocate*, 1851 (also named *St Helena Weekly News*)
— *St Helena Chronicle*, 1852
— *St Helena Herald*, 1853
— *St Helena Record*, 1860
— *St Helena Guardian*, 1861-1923
— *St Helena Advertiser*, 1865
— *The Spectator*, 1866
— *St Helena Star*, 1866
— *St Helena Church News*, 1888-1889
— *The Mosquito*, 1888
— *The Bug*, 1888
— *St Helena Times*, 1889

— *Monthly Critic and Flashlight*, 1891-1892
— *St Helenian*, 1895-1896
— *St Helena Parish Magazine*, 1899-1907
— *St Helena Diocesan Magazine*, 1908-1936
— *De Krijgsgevangene* (Boer Newspaper), 1901
— *The Jamestown Monthly*, 1912
— *St Helena Observer*, 1917-1919
— *St Helena Magazine*, 1937-1947
— *The Wirebird*, 1955-1966
— *St Helena News Review*, 1958-1986
— *St Helena News*, 1986-1992
Jackson, E. L., *St Helena: The Historic Island*, Ward, Lock and Co, New York, 1903
Janisch, H. R., *Notes and Memoranda from Records of Council, June 1678 to April 1836, Volumes 1 to 132*
Johns, Alan, *Recommendations for Educational Policy*, 1965
Joy, Gov: *Information on St Helena Colony*, 1947
Kitching, G. C., *A Handbook and Gazetteer of the Island of St Helena, including a Short History of the Island under the Crown, 1834-1902*
Kitching, G. C., *English Historical Review*, July 1948 (article)
McCullogh, N., *The Status and Ecology of St Helena*, 1992
Martin, B., *Gravestones and Memorials on St Helena, 1975-1989*, 1989
Melliss, J. C., *St Helena*, Reeve and Co, London, 1875
Military Education Director-General, *Third Report on Army Schools and Libraries*, Eyre and Spottiswoode, London, 1877
Nicholls, R., *The Development of Secondary Education in St Helena*, 1968
ODA: *St Helena's National Development Plan, 1990-1995*
ODA: *National Development Plan, 1989*
Pitcairn, L., *Play Schools, 1973*
Pitcairn, L., *Report on a Ten-Week Visit to St Helena, August 1972*
Robson, T., *St Helena Memoirs*, c.1830
St Helena: *Calendar and Directory, 1830, 1833-1856*
St Helena *Constitution Order*, 1988, Statutory Instruments, SA Territories
St Helena Government: *Broadcasting (Sound) on the Island of St Helena*, 1976
St Helena Government: *Proceedings of the Legislative Council*, 13 March 1980
St Helena: *Government Gazette, 1845-1992*
St Helena: *Annual Register, 1874*
St Helena: *Almanack and Annual Register, 1872, 1913*
St Helena: *Annual Reports*, 1936-1973 (some missing)
St Helena Baptist Church: *Record Book, 1845-1918*
St Helena Baptist Church: *Membership and Record Book, 1989*
St Helena: *Govt Lace School, Day Book, 1908-1910*
St Helena: *Minutes of Legislative Council*, 1980
St Helena: *Literary Society Minute Book, 1825*

St Helena: *Literary Society Prospectus*, 1826
St Helena: *School Log Books* (various), 1943-1992
St Helena: *Staff Lists*, 1947-1988
Sidebotham, J. B., *Reports on Schools*, 1939 and 1955
SPG, *Capetown Letters Received*, 1876-1925
Sterndale, R. A., *Report to Both Houses of Parliament*, 1898
Sterndale, R. A., *St Helena in Ye Olden Tyme & St Helena in the Present Time*, 1901
Sterndale, R. A., *Sancta Helena: An Island in Extremis*, 1894
Teale, P. L., *Saint Helena: A History of the Development of the Island*, Volume II, 1972
Teale, P. L., *St Helena Records, compiled by the late H. R. Janisch*, 1980
Thomas, Joan, *Two Great Educationalists in the Early 1900s* (unpublished book written by a St Helenian teacher), 1969
Yon, Gwen, *Education in St Helena*, 1972 (unpublished dissertation)

(b) Ascension Island
Admiralty Letters, PRO London, 1867-1921
Ascension Island Newspaper: *The Islander*
Ascension Island Services: *Head Teachers' and Education Officers' Reports*
Bartlett, L. S., *Ascension Island, 1934-1936* (reproduced 1968)
Brandreth Report, PRO London, 1835
Cable and Wireless, *The Zodiac*, Journal, 1930s to date
Cross, T., *St Helena including Ascension Island and Tristan da Cunha*, David and Charles, London, 1980
Dominion Office & Colonial Office Lists, 1931-1964
Eastern Telegraph Company, *The Zodiac*, Journal, 1899-1930s
Gill, Mrs David, *Six Months on Ascension*, 1877
Hart-Davis, Duff, *Ascension: The Story of a South Atlantic Island*, London, 1972
HMSO: *British Islands in the Southern Hemisphere, 1945-1951*
HMSO: *Education Systems of the British Empire*, 1905, Vol 12
HMSO: *Education Systems of Chief Crown Colonies*, 1908
St Helena Annual Reports, 1966-1973
St Helena Diocesan Magazine, 1900 onwards
St Helena: *Education Committee Minutes*
St Helena Magazine, 1950 onwards
St Helena News Review
St Helena: *The Wirebird*, 1955-1957
Twaddell, E., 'South Atlantic Adventure', BBC Northern Ireland Staff Magazine *Air Waves*, reproduced in *The Islander*, 20.11.1992; 13.11.1992
Watts, Rev C. C., *Mid-Atlantic*, 1934

(c) Tristan da Cunha
Alexander, Joan, *Voices and Echoes*, Quartet Books, London, 1983
Baily, Leslie (Ed), *Travellers' Tales*. Allen and Unwin, London, 1945

Barrow, K. M., *Three Years in Tristan da Cunha*, Skeffington, London, 1910

Bazin, Hervé, *Tristan*, Hodder and Stoughton, London, 1970

Booy, D. M., *Rock of Exile*, Dent, London, 1957

Brander, J., *Tristan da Cunha 1506-1902*, Allen and Unwin, London, 1940

Cannan, Rt Rev Edward, *Churches of the South Atlantic Islands, 1502-1991*, Anthony Nelson, Oswestry, 1992

Colonial Office, *Dominion Office and Colonial Office List*, Downing Street, London, from 1939

Colonial Office, *Instrument of Management for Tristan School*, 1959

Crabb, George, *The History and Postal History of Tristan da Cunha*, Crabb, Surrey, 1980

Crawford, Allan B., *Tristan da Cunha and The Roaring Forties*, Edinburgh and London, 1982

Crawford, Allan B. (Ed), *Tristan Times, 1943*

Cross, Tony, *St Helena including Ascension Island and Tristan da Cunha.* David and Charles, London, 1980

Dodgson, Rev E. H., *Eight Years at Tristan da Cunha, 1881-1890*

Education Committee, St Helena: *Minutes*

Elliott, Elizabeth, *Personal Diary*, 1951-1952

Elliott, Hugh, *Personal Diary*, 1950-1952

Flint, J., *Tristan 1963-1965* (unpublished document)

Flint, J., *Some Thoughts on the Future of Education on Tristan da Cunha*, 1965 (unpublished document)

Gane, Douglas M., *Tristan da Cunha*, Unwin, London, 1932

Green, Lawrence G., *There's a Secret Hid Away*

Green, Lawrence G., *Where Men Still Dream*, Timmins, Cape Town, 1945

HMSO, *British Islands in the Southern Hemisphere*, 1945-1951

HMSO, *Educational Systems of the British Empire*, Vol 12, 1905

HMSO, *Further Correspondence related to the Island of Tristan da Cunha* (CD 3098), London, 1906 and 1907

HMSO, *St Helena Annual Reports*

Hosegood, Nancy, *The Glass Island.* Hodder and Stoughton, London, 1974

Humphries, N., *So This Is Tristan Da Cunha*, N. & G. Humphries, 1982

Jones, H., 'Tristan 20 Years On', *Sunday Times*, 8 November 1981

Keir, G., 'The Psychological Assessment of the Children from the Island of Tristan da Cunha', *Studies in Psychology*, Banks, C. and Broadhurst, P. L. (eds), 1965

Lewis, H. E., Roberts, D. F., Edwards A. W. F., *Biological Problems and Opportunities of Isolation among the Islanders of Tristan da Cunha*, 1971

Mackay, Margaret, *The Angry Island: The Story of Tristan da Cunha 1506-1963*, Barker, London, 1963

Mayer, P. (ed), *Socialization*, Tavistock Publications, London, 1974

Munch, Peter, *Crisis in Utopia: The Story of Tristan da Cunha*, Longman, London, 1971

National Geographic Society, *National Geographic Magazine*, November 1937
  (London), January 1950 (Washington), January 1964 (London)
Officers, HMS *Carlisle, Tristan da Cunha in 1937*, Stanford, London
Peck, Richard, *Social Philately*, Australia, 1991
Rogers, Rose A., *The Lonely Island*, Allen and Unwin, London, 1926
St Helena Diocesan Magazine, 1908-1936
St Helena Magazine
St Helena News Review, 1937-1947
St Helena: *Wirebird*, 1955-57
St Mary's School: Examples of Children's Work
SPG, *Africa II, Letters Received*, 1927-1938, London
SPG, Africa Sub-Committee *Minutes*, 1963
SPG, *Capetown Letters Received, Vols 1-8*, London
Swales, M. K., *The Tristan-Denstone Connection*, 1992
Tristan da Cunha: *Annual Reports on Education*
Tristan da Cunha Association, UK *Tristan da Cunha Newsletter*
Tristan Times, Island Publication

(d) The Falkland Islands
Boyson, V. F., *The Falkland Islands*, 1924
Brandon, Lowther E., *Education Reports, 1901, 1902*
Cameron, J., *Education in the Falkland Islands*, 1990 (2nd paper)
Cawkell, M. B. R., Maling, D. H. and Cawkell, E. M., *The Falkland Islands*,
  Macmillan, London, 1960
Cawkell, M. B. R., *The Falklands Story, 1592-1982*, Anthony Nelson, Oswestry,
  1983
Colonial Office, *Falkland Islands Reports*, 1960-1963, 1968/1969
Colonial Office, *Report on Education, Falkland Islands 1930, 1931*
Falkland Islands Education Dept: *Annual Summary Report, Dec 1970*
— *Annual Summary Report, Dec 1971*
— *Annual Reports, 1989 and 1990*
Falkland Islands Education Dept: *Superintendent's Reports to HE* for Budget
  Address to Legislative Council: May 1976; May 1977; May 1978; 1978/1979;
  1979/1980
Falkland Islands *Gazette*, 1951
Falkland Islands Office: *Prospects for the Falkland Islands*, 1983
FCO, *Falkland Islands and Dependencies, 1970 and 1971, 1976 and 1977*
Green, L. G., *Islands Time Forgot*, 1962
Green, L. G., *The Drums of Time*
HMGovt: *Report to Secretary General of the UN for the Falkland Islands, 1985/86*, in
  accordance with provision of Article 73e of the Charter for the UN for the
  Falkland Islands
HMSO: Colonial Office, *Annual reports in the Blue Books*, 1841, 1887-1938, 1941,
  1943, 1954, 1959-1966

HMSO: Colonial Office, *British Islands in the Southern Hemisphere, 1945-1951*
HMSO: Colonial Office, *Educational Systems of the Chief Crown Colonies*, 1908, 1968
HMSO: *Education Ordinance 1949*
HMSO: *Falkland Islands and Dependencies*, 1970 & 1971, 1974 & 1975
HMSO, *School Attendance Ordinance, 1895*
Island Publication: *The Falkland Islands Journal*, from 1969
Leonard, John, 'Education in the Falkland Islands: A Fresh Start', in the *Guardian*, 1986
McWhan, F., *The Falkland Islands Today*, Stirling Tract Enterprise, Scotland, 1952
Media Trust, *Penguin News*, Stanley, Falkland Islands
Moody, R. C., *The Colonisation of the Falkland Islands*, 1842
Rendell, P. and Cameron, J., *Education in the Falkland Islands, 1990* (Paper 2)
Rendell, P., *Education in the Falkland Islands, 1990*
Rhodes House Library, Oxford: Miscellaneous Official Letters, Reports and Documents, 1842 onwards.
Smith, D. B., *Church, State and Schooling in the Falkland Islands*, 1990
Smith, D. B., 'Some Historical and Comparative Aspects of Schooling in Sparsely-Populated Areas of British Settlement in Australasia and the Falkland Islands', in *Compare*, Vol 19, No 1, 1989
Summers, N., *Heritage Year 1992*

Index